In this wide-ranging and richly detailed book Alan Richardson addresses many issues in literary and educational history never before examined together. The result is an unprecedented study of how transformations in schooling and literacy in Britain between 1780 and 1832 helped shape the provision of literature as we now know it. In chapters focused on such topics as definitions of childhood, educational methods and institutions, children's literature, female education, and publishing ventures aimed at working-class adults, Richardson demonstrates how literary genres, from fairy tales to epic poems, were enlisted in an ambitious program for transforming social relations through reading and education.

Themes include literary developments such as the domestic novel, a sanitized and age-stratified literature for children, the invention of "popular" literature, and the constitution of "Literature" itself in the modern sense. Romantic texts – by Wordsworth, Shelley, Blake, Yearsley, among others – are reinterpreted in the light of the complex historical and social issues which inform them, and which they in turn critically address.

CAMBRIDGE STUDIES IN ROMANTICISM 8

LITERATURE, EDUCATION, AND
ROMANTICISM

CAMBRIDGE STUDIES IN ROMANTICISM

This series aims to foster the best new work in one of the most challenging fields within English literary studies. From the early 1780s to the early 1830s a formidable array of talented men and women took to literary composition, not just in poetry, which some of them famously transformed, but in many modes of writing. The expansion of publishing created new opportunities for writers, and the political stakes of what they wrote were raised again and again by what Wordsworth called those "great national events" that were "almost daily taking place": the French Revolution, the Napoleonic and American wars, urbanization industrialization, religious revival, an expanded empire abroad and the reform movement at home. This was an enormous ambition, even when it pretended otherwise. The relations between science, philosophy, religion and literature were reworked in texts such as *Frankenstein* and *Biographia Literaria*; gender relations in *A Vindication of the Rights of Woman* and *Don Juan*; journalism by Cobbett and Hazlitt; poetic form, content and style by the Lake School and the Cockney School. Outside Shakespeare studies, probably no body of writing has produced such a wealth of response or done so much to shape the responses of modern criticism. This indeed is the period that saw the emergence of those notions of "literature" and of literary history, especially national literary history, on which modern scholarship in English has been founded.

The categories produced by Romanticism have also been challenged by recent historicist arguments. The task of the series is to engage both with a challenging corpus of Romantic writings and with the changing field of criticism they have helped to shape. As with other literary series published by Cambridge, this one will represent the work of both younger and more established scholars, on either side of the Atlantic and elsewhere.

TITLES PUBLISHED

John Augustus Atkinson (1775–1831/33), *Going to School*. Pen and water color. (Reproduced by courtesy of the Yale Center for British Art, Paul Mellon Collection.)

LITERATURE, EDUCATION, AND ROMANTICISM

Reading as Social Practice, 1780–1832

ALAN RICHARDSON

Boston College

CAMBRIDGE
UNIVERSITY PRESS

PUBLISHED BY THE PRESS SYNDICATE OF THE UNIVERSITY OF CAMBRIDGE
The Pitt Building, Trumpington Street, Cambridge, United Kingdom

CAMBRIDGE UNIVERSITY PRESS
The Edinburgh Building, Cambridge CB2 2RU, UK
40 West 20th Street, New York NY 10011–4211, USA
477 Williamstown Road, Port Melbourne, VIC 3207, Australia
Ruiz de Alarcón 13, 28014 Madrid, Spain
Dock House, The Waterfront, Cape Town 8001, South Africa

http://www.cambridge.org

First published 1994
First paperback edition 2004

This publication was assisted by a grant from the Trustees of Boston College.

A catalogue record for this book is available from the British Library

Library of Congress cataloguing in publication data

Richardson, Alan, 1955–
Literature, education, and romanticism : reading as social
practice, 1780–1832 / Alan Richardson.
p.   cm. – (Cambridge studies in Romanticism)
Includes bibliographical references (p.   ) and index.
ISBN 0 521 46276 2 (hardback)
1. English literature – 19th century – History and criticism.
2. Literature and society – Great Britain – History – 19th century.
3. Literature and society – Great Britain – History – 18th century.
4. Books and reading – Social aspects – Great Britain – History.
5. English literature – 18th century – History and criticism.
6. Education – Great Britain – History.   7. Romanticism – Great
Britain. I. Title. II. Series.
PR457.R456 1994
820.9'145'09034 – dc20   93–49343 CIP

ISBN 0 521 46276 2 hardback
ISBN 0 521 60709 4 paperback

Transferred to digital printing 2004

To Brian

Contents

Preface

Commenting on his generation's unique experience of social change and dislocation, De Quincey considered that "fifty years of mighty revolutions amongst the kingdoms of the earth" only began to account for the "agitation" of British life from the 1790s to 1845. Other epochal shifts included the rapid spread of industrialization (epitomized by the rise of steam power), a host of new technologies, developments in artillery evoking "powers from hell," and, as though in response, "powers from heaven descending upon education and accelerations of the press." It is this last area – the transformation of education and, with it, of literature in all its forms – that makes the subject of this book. Although little has been written on the consequences for both literary practice and everyday life of the changes in schooling, in the spread of literacy, and in the publishing industry which so marked what we call the Romantic era, a list of notions now taken for granted which were first widely aired, if not codified, during the years 1780–1832 should suggest the force and extent of what amounts to a cultural revolution. That literacy should be universal, even considered a right; that schooling should be state-supported and available to all; that imaginative experience is important if not essential to proper development; that schools should divide children into classes by age and measure their progress and proficiency with tests; that fantasy is the proper literature for young children; that education does not end with adolescence, but should inform an entire life span; that childhood constitutes the "magic years," a period crucial for psychic development, an Edenic time to be treasured and, later, nostalgically regretted: these are ideas which were still considered rarefied and avant-garde if not patently absurd toward the end of the eighteenth century, and yet had become respectable, widespread, and destined to prevail by the middle of the nineteenth.

This book began life as a period study, an attempt to help clarify the increasingly central role of imaginative reading within late eighteenth- and early nineteenth-century British culture by specifying how changes in the definition and status of literature were implicated in and informed by changes in educational methods, institutions, and ideologies. But as I discovered how much of what now constitutes, at least within Anglo-American culture, "common sense" regarding childhood, schooling, and reading habits found its modern form in the writing and practice of the Romantic era, what began as a work of literary and cultural history also became a genealogy. I hope to have exposed some of the underlying assumptions behind and constraints on current educational thinking by reopening such issues as the conflicting motivations behind early calls for national education, or the array of complex, sometimes contradictory positions on female education that tend now to be collapsed into a simple opposition between reformers and reactionaries. The rise of the children's and "popular" literature industries in this period has similarly been re-evaluated through a critical look at the discursive and social matrix out of which they grew; one which tended to equate child and laborer with "rustic" and "savage" and to articulate educational and colonial policies in markedly similar terms. I have also tried to dislodge once and for all the simple dichotomy of "imagination" and "reason" that informs so much writing on Romantic approaches to education, children's reading, and early development in order to identify those assumptions that the Romantic group of writers and their contemporaries held in common, assumptions which we have – largely unconsciously and therefore uncritically – absorbed in turn.

Literature plays a central role in this study not only because so many Romantic-era writers – a number of whom could not meaningfully be considered "Romantics" – witnessed and registered the newly significant (and significantly new) role of education in their fictions, in their polemical writings, and in their self-representations. Literature also, from "high" to "low," from epic poems to Sunday-school prize books, played a key role in shaping and effecting transformations in schooling and in the social function of reading. I have therefore taken special account of those genres which might be grouped together as didactic: conduct books, "moral" and religious children's fiction, school texts, self-instruction manuals, and fictionalized primers on political economy for the "industrious" classes. But

I have also tried to suggest how pervasively literary genres not usually thought of as didactic were enlisted in the schooling of traditionally and newly literate groups alike: the reworking of the domestic novel by Maria Edgeworth and others as preferred reading for adolescent girls and young women; the development of poetry anthologies aimed explicitly at subaltern populations in the colonies and, concurrently, at young people in England; the popular dissemination of fictional and biographical narratives of "rising" intended to give lower-class readers a sense of belonging in the new capitalist order; the emergence by the end of the period of a modern conception of vernacular "Literature" and its transforming effect on the schools, the universities, and on the bookshelves of the middle-class home. In addition, I have paid close attention to those literary works explicitly critical of new educational methods and institutions, a common impulse throughout Romantic-era writing that ties together such disparate texts as Blake's "Holy Thursday" poems, Wollstonecraft's *Vindication of the Rights of Woman*, Wordsworth's "Anecdote for Fathers," Austen's *Mansfield Park*, Shelley's *Frankenstein*, and Cobbett's *Rural Rides*. It is significant that the most frequently cited authority in nineteenth-century writings on education and in Victorian children's literature alike – apart perhaps from the Bible – is not Locke's *Some Thoughts* or Rousseau's *Emile*, but Wordsworth's "Intimations" ode.

A character in Peacock's *Gryll Grange* (1860) remarks: "If all the nonsense which, in the last quarter of a century, has been talked on all subjects, were thrown into one scale, and all that has been talked on the subject of education alone were thrown into another, I think the latter would preponderate." He might have said, in the last three quarters of a century, so much did education occupy the journals, the Parliamentary debates, literary and discursive writings of all kinds, and (one must assume) casual conversation from the last decade of the eighteenth century to the middle of the nineteenth. We are again in a period of intensive and widespread educational debate, a good deal of it nonsense, some of it, if not precisely charged with powers from heaven, at least promising a means for effecting needed social change on earth. A genealogy of modern attitudes regarding schooling and literacy – toward which this is an exploratory, provisional contribution – may eventually help those promoting educational reform and universal literacy in the present avoid, or at least better perceive, some of the problems that have dogged such efforts from the beginning.

Several sections of this book have been published in preliminary versions: a section of chapter two in *ELH* (1989), sections of chapter three in *Romanticism and Children's Literature in Nineteenth-Century England*, edited by James Holt McGavran (1991), and in *Papers on Language and Literature* (1990), and a section of chapter four in *European Romantic Review* (1991).

I am grateful to the National Endowment for the Humanities for its support of this project both through a Summer Seminar grant in 1986, which helped me to get started, and through a Fellowship for University Professors in 1989–90, which enabled me to do much of the writing. I also thank Boston College and its Trustees for providing aid in numerous forms, including a summer grant in 1989 and, not least, a grant toward keeping the production costs of this volume within bounds. In taking on a project of this scope I found myself relying on the help and guidance of many friends and colleagues. I wish particularly to thank those who generously commented on parts of the manuscript in various stages: Uli Knoepflmacher, Vernon Shetley, Jim McGavran, Ash Nichols, Michael Harrawood, Andy Von Hendy, Jeff Decker, Paul Doherty, and, especially, David Perkins, Beth Kowaleski-Wallace, and Rosemarie Bodenheimer. I also wish to thank my editors at Cambridge University Press, Kevin Taylor and Josie Dixon, for their encouragement and patience, and I am lastingly grateful to Jon Klancher and Mary Poovey for providing exceptionally thoughtful and incisive readings of the manuscript. My brother, Brian Richardson, has inspired, challenged, and shared an education with me for as long as I can remember, and I dedicate this book to him. Finally, I thank those nearest to me: Deborah Blacker for her criticism, counsel, and support beyond reckoning, and Nathan Blacker Richardson, who has brought me to think about childhood and education with a different intensity and a renewed humility.

Abbreviations

CBL   Samuel Taylor Coleridge, *Biographia Literaria or Biographical Sketches of My Literary Life and Opinions*, ed. James Engell and W. Jackson Bate, 2 vols. (Princeton University Press, 1983).

CCL   *Collected Letters of Samuel Taylor Coleridge*, ed. Earl Leslie Griggs, 6 vols. (Oxford: Clarendon Press, 1956–71).

CLL   Coleridge, *Lectures 1808–1819 On Literature*, ed. R. A. Foakes, 2 vols. (Princeton University Press, 1987).

CLS   Coleridge, *Lay Sermons*, ed. R. J. White (Princeton University Press, 1972).

DQW   *The Collected Writings of Thomas De Quincey*, ed. David Masson, 14 vols. (London: A. & C. Black, 1896–97).

GE   William Godwin, *The Enquirer: Reflections on Education, Manners and Literature* (1797; New York: Augustus M. Kelley, 1965).

JCL   *The Letters of John Clare*, ed. Mark Storey (Oxford: Clarendon Press, 1985).

KL   *The Letters of John Keats 1814–1821*, ed. Hyder Edward Rollins, 2 vols. (Cambridge: Harvard University Press, 1958).

LW   *The Works of Charles and Mary Lamb*, ed. E. V. Lucas, 7 vols. (London: Methuen, 1903–5) (quotations from Charles Lamb's poetry silently follow this edition).

MLC   William Roberts, *Memoirs of the Life and Correspondence of Mrs. Hannah More*, 2 vols. (New York: Harper, 1835).

RMW   Jean-Jacques Rousseau, *The Minor Educational Writings of Jean Jacques Rousseau*, ed. and trans. William Boyd (1910; New York: Teachers College, Columbia University, 1962).

SP   *Shelley's Prose, Or the Trumpet of a Prophecy*, ed. David Lee Clark (Albuquerque: University of New Mexico Press, 1954).

VRW Mary Wollstonecraft, *A Vindication of the Rights of Woman*, ed. Carol H. Poston, 2nd edn. (New York: Norton, 1988).

WLE *The Letters of William and Dorothy Wordsworth: The Early Years*, ed. Ernest de Selincourt, rev. Chester Shaver (Oxford: Clarendon Press, 1967).

WLL *The Letters of William and Dorothy Wordsworth: The Later Years*, ed. Ernest de Selincourt, rev. Alan G. Hill, 4 vols. (Oxford: Clarendon Press, 1978–88).

WLM *The Letters of William and Dorothy Wordsworth: The Middle Years*, Part I, 1806–1811, ed. Ernest de Selincourt, rev. Mary Moorman; Part II, 1812–1820, ed. de Selincourt, rev. Moorman and Alan G. Hill (Oxford: Clarendon Press, 1969–70).

WP *The Prose Works of William Wordsworth*, ed. W. J. B. Owen and Jane Worthington Smyser, 3 vols. (Oxford: Clarendon Press, 1974).

Quotations from poems by Blake, Coleridge, Crabbe, Hemans, and Wordsworth, unless otherwise noted, follow these editions: *The Complete Poetry and Prose of William Blake*, ed. David Erdman, rev. edn. (Garden City: Anchor Press, 1982) (Blake's prose is cited in the text by page number). *The Poems of Samuel Taylor Coleridge*, ed. Ernest Hartley Coleridge (London: Oxford University Press, 1912). *The Poetical Works of George Crabbe*, ed. A. J. Carlyle and R. M. Carlyle (London: Oxford University Press, 1914). *Poems of Felicia Hemans*, 2nd edn. (Edinburgh: William Blackwood and Sons, 1849). *William Wordsworth: The Poems*, ed. John O. Hayden, 2 vols. (Harmondsworth: Penguin, 1977) excluding *The Prelude*, which follows *The Prelude 1799, 1805, 1850*, ed. Jonathan Wordsworth, M. H. Abrams, and Stephen Gill (New York: Norton, 1979); quotations are from the 1805 version unless specified as "1799" or "1850." Line numbers are given for quotations from longer poems only.

CHAPTER I

Childhood, education, and power

In *My Lady Ludlow*, a novella set in the first decade of the nineteenth century, Elizabeth Gaskell portrays the effect on a small English village of the education schemes then so much in vogue. The plot hinges on the opposition of Lady Ludlow, a dowager countess and virtual tyrant of the neighborhood, to the Sunday school which the new clergyman, Mr. Gray, wishes to establish for the poor children of the parish. Lady Ludlow, who "always said a good despotism was the best form of government," holds fast to the conservatism of her youth in the face of Mr. Gray's fashionable cause: "The cry for education was beginning to come up: Mr. Raikes had set up his Sunday schools; and some clergymen were all for teaching writing and arithmetic, as well as reading. My lady would have none of this; it was levelling and revolution, she said."[1] Indeed, Lady Ludlow maintains a policy of hiring none but illiterate serving maids, although she herself is not entirely immune to the "new hobby of education" (21) – she keeps an elitist charity school of her own, imparting the mysteries of baking, needlework, and general deportment to young women "of condition, though out of means" (11).

Mr. Gray, earnest and consumptive, holds that Bible reading and a sounder grasp of Church catechism will help prepare his humbler parishioners for the world to come. (Lady Ludlow's steward, Mr. Horner, takes a still more "new-fangled" approach, secretly envisioning a day-school to "train up intelligent labourers for working on the estate" [52–53]). The clergyman's energetic sermons on the need for "Sabbath-schools" seem calculated to ruin the peace of his patroness, who thinks of reading and writing as sinister "edge-tools" for undermining the class system: "If our lower orders have these edge-tools given to them, we shall have the terrible scenes of the French Revolution acted over again in England. When I was a girl, one never heard of the rights of men, only their duties. Now, here was

Mr. Gray, only last night, telling of the right every child had to instruction" (59). A good third of the novella is taken up by Lady Ludlow's narration of an incident from the chillingly recent upheavals in France, intended to prove beyond a doubt "how unfit the lower orders are for being trusted indiscriminately with the dangerous powers of education" (84), a Rousseauistic policy that leads inexorably to the guillotine. Nevertheless, Mr. Gray eventually prevails after nearly martyring himself to his cause, and the countess allows a "kind of rough schoolhouse to be built on the green," where the children can most readily be lured from their unruly sports. The boys are to learn only reading, writing, and the "first four rules of arithmetic," and the girls only "to read, add up in their heads, and the rest of the time to work at mending their own clothes, knitting stockings, and spinning" (199).

Gaskell's fictional account of an early nineteenth-century village brings out a central aspect of the period that most accounts of British Romanticism ignore or merely touch upon. The world represented in this all but forgotten novella is one in which education – as a topic for debate, as a vehicle for social change, as a locus for political fears – is ubiquitous. It forms the topic for sermons as a sure way to salvation, it appeals to practical men as the best means for guaranteeing a competent work force, it inspires visions of class warfare and evokes the terrors of the French Revolution. In *My Lady Ludlow*, education becomes a locus not only for tensions between classes, threatening to "unfit the lower orders for their duties" (149), but also divides the ruling interests among themselves. It is tied inextricably to issues of religion, of economics, of politics; it brings out inequalities between the genders no less than those between the classes. As a thematic site for rethinking Romantic-era culture apart from conventional disciplinary boundaries, education is particularly promising: it forms a conceptual space where politics, social history, ideology, and literary representations of all kinds meet, interpenetrate, and collide.

EDUCATION AND LITERARY CULTURE IN THE ROMANTIC ERA

The frankly ideological character of the educational debates in *My Lady Ludlow* holds true to the period in which the novella is set. Education was one of the most hotly contested and frequently discussed topics of what is often called the Romantic age, which will be considered here as extending roughly from the 1780s through the early 1830s. There are reasons, of course, beyond those of rough correspondence with an established academic field for centering a study of education, literature, and social change on these decades, although one could as easily begin much earlier (say, with the publication of Locke's *Some Thoughts Concerning Education* toward the end of the seventeenth century) or conclude much later, perhaps with the long deferred passing of an Education Act in 1870. The 1780s, however, have often served as a starting point in studies of British education because so much begins to change so quickly in the last two decades of the eighteenth century. These years saw the effective beginning of mass education with: the Sunday Schools movement, the first attempt to legislate schooling for lower-class children, the rise of a children's literature geared for instructional use at home and in the schools, the first experiments in didactic "popular" fiction, the practical working out of Locke's educational methods for use in the middle-class home, the popularization in England of Rousseau's educational theories, the publication of the first major feminist critiques of education, and the adumbration of a Romantic response to a number of these developments in poems by Blake and Wordsworth. By the early 1830s, the trajectories of cultural change I am most interested in exploring had already been well established, and following them through the nineteenth century would in any case require a second volume.

My use of the embattled term "Romantic" may need some initial clarification. We have recently been reminded, once again, of the dubious provenance of this term and of the distortions which it and the period concept it harbors may inflict upon literary and cultural studies. The notion of a "Romantic period" artificially abstracts a certain number of years from the historical record, lending them a factitious unity (a "spirit of the age") in the process; it encourages critics to extrapolate "characteristic" features from the textual record and then, in circular fashion, to concentrate upon those writers and texts which seem most fully to embody them; it tends to marginalize writers who do not obviously fit into the "period" thus abstracted and described – Godwin, Crabbe, Barbauld, Austen, Scott, Cobbett; and the term "Romantic" is itself anachronistic, not having been widely applied to late eighteenth- and early nineteenth-century writing until some fifty or sixty years after the "period" is held to have ended.[2] Granted. Nevertheless, I have found it useful to retain the term "Romantic" to describe the period covered in this study, in part simply because "late eighteenth and early nineteenth century" becomes, after a very few repetitions, such an unwieldy phrase. More substantively, I agree with Jerome McGann that one can productively employ the term "Romantic" to characterize the canonical group of male writers most often associated with it (Wordsworth, Coleridge, Lamb, De Quincey, Byron, Shelley, Keats) without either ignoring the differences among them (particularly the generational differences) or losing sight of those contemporaries who cannot be considered "Romantic" even in this cautious sense. As McGann points out, it was the esthetic ideologies of the writers we now call "Romantics" – distinct to be sure but overlapping signifi- cantly – which became culturally ascendant, so that speaking of a Romantic period may be more appropriate than is sometimes supposed.[3]

An intense concern with education finds its way into Romantic-era writings of all kinds – poems, familiar essays, novels, autobiographies, children's fiction, popular tracts, polemical pamphlets, and reviews, by canonical "Romantics" and many others – often with the abruptness of a cultural obsession. Wordsworth devotes a stanza of the "Immortality" ode to satirizing the new rational approach to education, with its emphasis on method and factual knowledge; a similar critique is developed in *The Prelude*, where rationalist educators are scorned for creating a "dwarf man" of the child who, in the words of the Ode, is born a "Mighty Prophet." In *The Excursion* the Wanderer, Wordsworth's principal spokesman, breaks off a discourse on truth and equality to express, in the words of the "Argument" to Book ix, the "Earnest wish ... for a System of National Education established universally by Government," and the poet adds a footnote specifically recommending the "Madras system" of Andrew Bell, a "simple engine" for bringing industrial organization into the schools. Coleridge begins the *Biographia Literaria* with a sketch of his education under the "very severe" Reverend Boyer (in Charles Lamb's blunter phrase, a "rabid pedant" [*LW* 2: 19]), and goes on to attack the "improved pedagogy" of the day, with its emphasis on facts, independent judgment, and "all the dirty passion and impudence, of anonymous criticism" (*CBL* 1: 8, 13). Lamb describes his own education at Christ's Hospital (a Charity School which had been largely taken over by the "middling" classes) not once, but twice: first under his own signature in "Recollections of Christ's Hospital," a nostalgic tribute to its "antiquity" and tradition (and a defense of its diversion from its original mission to the poor); then, as "Elia," Lamb takes issue with his earlier account to portray instead the rigors, the careless administration, and the sheer terrors (especially under Boyer) of the same institution (*LW* 1: 140, 2: 12–22). In "The Old and the New Schoolmaster," Lamb develops his own critique of the "didactive hypocrisy" (*LW* 2: 54) of rationalist educators along Wordsworthian lines. Southey, like his fellow "Lake Poets," was a polemicist for Bell's Madras system (an epithet that alerts us in advance to how issues of colonialism are implicated in those of education), and cautions against the excesses of rationalist education in *The Doctor*: "Oh! What blockheads are those wise persons who think it necessary that a child should understand every thing it reads."[4]

The Lakers were not, of course, the only poets caught up in the educational debates of their age. Crabbe devotes the final Letter of *The Borough* to "Schools" (it follows one on "Prisons"), critically surveying the "various seminaries" of modern education from "that of the poor widow, who pronounces the alphabet for infants, to seats whence the light of learning is shed abroad in the world." Blake, from his deliberately eccentric position on the periphery of the cultural establishment, both satirized rationalist education schemes (in *An Island in the Moon*) and attacked the new technologies for educating the "labouring poor" which the Lake Poets fitfully supported. In *Songs of Innocence* especially, a work which formally addresses the new children's literature industry, Blake criticizes educational institutions and methods in poems like "Holy Thursday" (aimed at the Charity Schools) and "The Lamb" (parodying the "catechistic" approach to instruction); the volume originally included "The School Boy," an attack on the schools' promotion of docility and "moral defeatism."[5]

> But to go to school in a summer morn,
> O! it drives all joy away;
> Under a cruel eye outworn,
> The little ones spend the day,
> In sighing and dismay.

An early exemplar of the self-taught artist or artisan so characteristic of the period (Crabbe was also self-taught), Blake could declare, "Thank God I never was sent to school." It is a sentiment shared by

Blake's fellow radical William Cobbett, who attacks "the '*education*' canters" for diverting attention from more fundamental social problems (underemployment, low wages), and describes the scene of his own "education" in *Rural Rides* as a "sand-hill" he would gleefully roll down with his two brothers, laughing till his mouth filled with sand and, thankfully, avoiding the fate of "those frivolous idiots that are turned out of Winchester or Westminster School."[6]

The second-generation Romantic poets tend to be less overtly concerned with educational institutions as such, although Byron compares Donna Inez in *Don Juan* to Sarah Trimmer and Hannah More, conservative (and influential) proponents of religious education for the lower orders; after failing to destroy Juan's "natural spirit," Inez sets up "a Sunday school / For naughty children" (1.50, II.10).[7] More importantly, as *Don Juan* attests, the younger Romantics are deeply concerned with education in the wider sense of intellectual and moral development, concentrating more on the period of youth than on childhood. Juan's real education takes place not among his battery of tutors but in "Nature's good old college" (II.136) and through an uncommonly rich, lightly worn "experience" (XII.50). In contrast to Byron's commingling of comedy, epic, and satire, Shelley takes up the epic-romance mode as a vehicle for the "educational programs" of the *Revolt of Islam*, a poem designed to represent "the growth and progress of individual mind aspiring after excellence" (*SP*, 315).[8] These recastings of epic form as a medium for portraying education are anticipated, of course, by Wordsworth's fusion of epic and autobiography in *The Prelude* to exhibit the "Growth of a Poet's Mind," although this work would not appear until 1850. In its wider sense of mental growth, education might be taken as defining the Romantic ethos, what one student of childhood in canonical Romantic writing sympathetically calls the "development of the perfected, totalized individual."[9] This program of moral and intellectual development, however, does not arise independently of contemporary concerns with educational institutions and practices; rather, it grows out of them. It is revealing that Keats, in his celebrated letter on the "vale of Soul-making," takes schooling as his metaphor for "forming the *Soul* or *Intelligence*": "I will call the *world* a School instituted for the purpose of teaching little children to read – I will call the *human heart* the *horn Book* used in that School – and I will call the *Child able to read the Soul* made from the *School* of its *hornbook*" (*KL* 2: 102). Such a metaphor would have appeared unthinkably trivial to the generation preceding Wordsworth. It seems almost inevitable by the time of Keats.

The novel in this era is still more obviously permeated by the growing emphasis on childhood and education, which accompanies the emergence in England of the *Bildungsroman*, or novel of development. Whereas the earlier novel tended to dispose of childhood expeditiously (Tom Jones grows from two to fourteen in two paragraphs)[10] and to stress an inherited character or "disposition" over experience and training, the Romantic-era novel more often reflects the notion, stated with typical assurance by Godwin, that "the characters of men are determined in all their most essential circumstances by education."[11] For the "Jacobin" novelists of the 1790s – Thomas Holcroft, Robert Bage, and Godwin himself – education is fate, and the advantages and mistakes of the hero's education (which usually takes place outside of schools) are carefully delineated. For radical women novelists like Mary Hays and Mary Wollstonecraft, education underscores woman's debased status (since it is either limited to "accomplishments" or simply withheld), and yet this very neglect can constitute a negative advantage. In Wollstonecraft's *Mary, A Fiction* the heroine is left to herself when her brother is sent to school, and after a servant teaches her to read, she ranges through the library on her own: "left to the operations of her own mind, she considered every thing that came under her inspection, and learned to think."[12] Wollstonecraft's first published work was *Thoughts on the Education of Daughters*, followed shortly by a children's book, *Original Stories*, which outlines a model education for young girls; her *Vindication of the Rights of Woman* is an extended polemic on female education indebted to Catherine Macaulay's *Letters on Education*, one of the first major works of English feminism. Maria Edgeworth, who with her father produced *Practical Education*, the most influential manual of the rationalist approach, helped invent modern children's fiction, and develops throughout her novels and tales a "mother-daughter educational narrative" that displaces the romance plot formerly dominant in fiction by, for, and about women.[13] Jane Austen's *Mansfield Park*, though less overtly concerned with schooling, has been rightly called "as much a novel about education as any in the language";[14] Mary Shelley's *Frankenstein* explores in exaggerated form the dilemmas of the self-education to which Shelley, like so many other women in the period, was largely consigned. *Waverley* is both historical novel and novel of education, showing how the hero's desultory and unguided program of reading (modelled on Scott's own) leads to romantic excesses which can only be cured by harsh and near fatal experience. Add to all this the detailed concern with schooling that comes at this time to mark biography, autobiography, and the familiar essay, the debates on national education taking place in Parliament, in the pages of economic and political treatises, and in the journals, the sudden plethora of educational manuals, Sunday School tracts, and school stories for children, and one begins to get a sense of how omnipresent the concern with education must have seemed to the common reader of the Romantic era.

This pervasive concern, even obsession, with education stands in need of careful examination in terms of the social, political, and ideological factors that motivate and shape both educational discourse and literary representations of schooling (which increasingly color debates on education as the nineteenth century progresses). As educational practices and institutions presuppose a child to educate, it may be helpful to consider first the complex and changing conception, or rather conceptions, of childhood informing Romantic-era writing. Contrary to the common belief that Romantic authors work from a shared notion of childhood such as "original innocence,"[15] no single or simple conception of the child characterizes the writings of the canonical Romantics, let alone the still more diverse body of texts from which their work is usually abstracted. Nor is this an issue which can be cursorily treated; the manner in which childhood is conceived and represented helps shape the theory and practice of education no less than these in turn affect conceptions of the child.

SOME VERSIONS OF CHILDHOOD

The notion of childhood as a qualitatively distinct stage of life, which we share with the Romantics, is (as Phillipe Ariès argued some decades ago) historically determined. Although subsequent studies of childhood have modified some of Ariès's conclusions, his basic contention that childhood is as much a cultural construct as a biological category has been widely accepted, and indeed has changed the shape of social history.[16] The modern "discovery of childhood" can be traced back to the thirteenth century, but begins to grow significantly noticeable only by the late sixteenth and early seventeenth centuries; the eighteenth century in England sees what J. H. Plumb calls the "new world of children" in full flower, with games, toys, books, and apparel designed specifically for children becoming increasingly available, at least among the middle and upper classes.[17]

If most social historians after Ariès agree that childhood is a socially constituted category, there is almost as wide an agreement as to what principally brought about the modern conception of a unique, extended childhood: education. For Ariès, the "great event" is "the revival, at the beginning of modern times, of an interest in education"; for Lawrence Stone, the shift from family to school as the prime institution for socializing children isolates childhood and growth as a unique and "increasingly prolonged" period; for Ivy Pinchbeck and Margaret Hewitt the school, in providing the child with its own institution, "gives to childhood an independent and recognisable status."[18] But if the prolonged, developmental childhood characteristic of the modern period is defined by educational practices and institutions, childhood is also shaped by received traditions, changing religious and political ideologies, shifts in philosophical and scientific thought, and, quite notably in the Romantic era, by literary representation. The notion of the child, not simply as distinct, but as somehow unique, qualitatively different from (and in some senses superior to) the adult becomes prominent only with Rousseau's *Emile* (1762), and it is to a large extent through Romantic literature that childhood has gained the central position it continues to hold in the Western cultural tradition.[19]

There was, however, no one dominant "Romantic" image of the child: literary representations of children during this era range from Wordsworth's "best philosopher" and Lamb's dream children to the over-indulged Middleton brats in Austen's *Sense and Sensibility* and the barely sentient, drooling "varlet" of Joanna Baillie's "A Mother to her Waking Infant." Across a variety of representational conventions, however, the child took on a virtually unprecedented significance. What one historian of the child-figure in Western literature calls the "classical silence" on childhood is barely troubled until the Reformation; in the England of the fifteenth and sixteenth centuries childhood is more noticeable, but for the most part as "a state to be endured rather than enjoyed."[20] Even the brief revaluation of childhood which appears in the religious poetry of Vaughan and Traherne forms an exception to the "major literature" of the seventeenth century, which remains "strangely silent" on the topic of children.[21] For neo-classical writers childhood is a "period to be rapidly passed over"; as the eighteenth century advances, one finds an increasing number of incidental descriptions of childhood, for the most part in the sentimental register of Gray's "Eton" ode, but childhood becomes central as a literary preoccupation only in the last two decades of the century.[22]

In his influential social history of the English family, Lawrence Stone posits four views about the given nature of the child available to writers, educationalists, and parents in the period 1640–1800: a "traditional Christian view" (the most common) that the child is originally sinful and must be ruthlessly subordinated to authority; an "environmentalist" view associated with Locke that the child is born a "*tabula rasa*" and formed by experience; a "biological" view that the child's character is "genetically determined at conception"; and a "utopian" view, associated with Rousseau but dating back to Renaissance humanism, that the child is born innocent and is corrupted only through contact with society.[23] Stone's schematization is valuable both for introducing heterogeneity into a subject that has often been oversimplified and for the interpretive value of the analytical categories it develops. These categories can be usefully applied to Romantic-era writing, however, only with a good deal of modification – particularly in terms of emphasis – and only if one remains mindful that such paradigms can at best be retrospective constructs, based on a selective (if informed) reading of the archive. In terms of emphasis, Stone's "biological" view rarely appears in literary or other texts of the period (although Crabbe speaks in *The Borough* of "the native bias of the opening mind" [208]), and by the late eighteenth century, "environmentalist" approaches to childhood have become ascendant (at least in written texts), and the orthodox Christian view somewhat rare. Especially in relation to the shifting conventions of literary representation, anything as neat as Stone's table of "views" swiftly breaks down before the complexity of the texts at hand: what might seem rival notions will often be found inhabiting the same text, and the most interesting literary versions of what Stone describes as discrete paradigms are those that distort, augment, or combine them. Nevertheless, a provisional adaptation of Stone's schema should help uncover distinctions among authors and texts too often lumped together uncritically, as well as helping to establish a context for the discussions of children's education and literature to follow.

What is by far the most common paradigm that can be abstracted from representations of childhood in the Romantic era, Stone's "environmentalist view," is closely related to associationist psychology. It governs the developmental model we have seen already in Godwin, and which Godwin inherited from Locke and Hartley, with the child's mind considered as a blank slate to be inscribed by experience; the infant is often compared to a "white paper" to be written over or to a plastic substance (like wax) to be molded. Also common in Romantic-era writing is what might be termed an organic paradigm (related to but not identical with Stone's "Utopian" view), first fully articulated in Rousseau's *Emile*. For Rousseau, the child is not simply innocent but is invested with organic principles of growth that can either be fostered or distorted by socialization; the child may be compared to a member of a "primitive" society (such as an aboriginal American) or to a growing plant. The Augustinian (or "traditional Christian") view of childhood is revived in the Romantic era by some Methodist and Evangelical writers, according to whom the child is born in sin and is by nature willful and in mortal need of discipline. A fourth paradigm comparable to Stone's "views" but not included among them, which could be termed "transcendental," features in Romantic poetry, particularly in that of Wordsworth, and becomes immensely influential over the course of the nineteenth century: the transcendental child is informed by a divine or quasi-divine nature which renders it superior to adults, and the new-born child can be figured as a prophet or angel.

Several identifiable conventions for representing childhood which also recur throughout Romantic-era writing, but which do not harbor paradigms analogous to Stone's, might be termed the sentimental, the maternal, and the ethnographic. These conventions are concerned less with the child's nature than with the quality of its experience and with its relation to the social world. The sentimental convention for portraying childhood, already present in mid-eighteenth-century poetry, focuses on the precious but "short-lived" innocence of childhood "in an otherwise blighted world";[24] children seem, in the words of Gray's "Eton" ode, "little victims." The maternal convention is one which I have found only among women writers of the era, most notably in poems addressed by mothers to their infants, and which is marked by a unique attentiveness to the infant's body, the dangers involved in birthing it and the trouble in nurturing it, and the bond between child and mother. The ethnographic convention is found in representations of the sufferings of poor children, particularly (but not exclusively) those brought on by industrialization. The street urchin or child laborer is at once rendered an object of pity, and objectified as a social fact to be dealt with through individual charity or social policy.[25]

The associationist psychology of Locke, especially as developed by Hartley, did much to establish the importance of childhood experience. If the infant's mind is a *tabula rasa* or, as Locke put it in his popular treatise *Some Thoughts Concerning Education* (1693), a "white Paper"[26] (325), early experience and education become all-important in shaping the adult: the child is father of the man. Locke's contagious metaphor resembles only superficially John Earle's comparison of the child's soul to "a white paper unscribbled with observations of the world" in *Microcosmographie* (1628). Earle's figure stresses childhood innocence, which can only lapse as the child matures, "wherewith at length it becomes a blurr'd Notebooke";[27] Locke emphasizes instead the child's malleability, which can lend itself equally to corruption or improvement. And insofar as experience can be controlled, the child's nature can be engineered: "of all the Men we meet with, Nine Parts of Ten are what they are, Good or Evil, useful or not, by their Education. 'Tis that which makes the great Difference in Mankind" (114). The child is a blank text to be inscribed almost at will, or, as Godwin puts it, a "raw material put into our hands, a ductile and yielding substance, which, if we do not ultimately mould in conformity to our wishes, it is because we throw away the power committed to us, by the folly with which we are accustomed to exert it" (112). Working from associationist premises, social theorists as diverse as Godwin, Adam Smith, Wollstonecraft, Robert Owen, and James Mill saw early education as crucial in forming (or reforming) society.

Associationism equally affected literary representations of childhood and education in the Romantic period. Mary Hays is representative of the "Jacobin" novelists of the 1790s when she states in *Emma Courtney* that "We are all the creatures of education"; associationist premises give her depictions of her heroine's early experiences a decidedly anxious tenor:

But in that education, what we call chance, or accident, has so great a share, that the wisest preceptor, after all his cares, has reason to tremble: one strong affection, one ardent incitement, will turn, in an instant, the whole current of our thoughts, and introduce a new train of ideas and associations.[28]

Coleridge writes in "The Nightingale" of teaching his son (named after Hartley) to love the night through association – "his childhood shall grow up / Familiar with these songs, that with the night / He may associate joy" – and concludes "Frost at Midnight" with an associationist program, promising Hartley a Wordsworthian childhood of natural objects in contrast to Coleridge's own urban school days "pent 'mid cloisters dim."[29] Wordsworth himself, once labelled "the associationist poet,"[30] delineates throughout *The Prelude* the effect of early associations and experiences on the growth of a poet's mind, particularly how Nature's "beauteous forms" (II.51–2) and "awful forms" (VIII.485) together provide a "real solid world / Of images" for a mind progressively "thronged with impregnations" (VIII.605, 791). The child's "early intercourse / In presence of sublime and lovely forms" (XIII.145–47) leaves the mind stocked with "objects that endure," predisposing it to seek in humankind "something of kindred permanence" (XII.36, 42).

Whereas Locke describes the child as morally neutral "wax, to be moulded and fashioned as one pleases" (325), Rousseau envisions the child in *Emile* as a "young plant," virtuous by nature: "there is no original perversity in the human heart."[31] In the tension between these two metaphors, plastic and organic, resides much of the ambivalence characteristic of Romantic-era writing on childhood and education. Although Rousseau thought education crucial within modern societies – "Plants are shaped by cultivation, and men by education" (38) – his stress on original innocence and organic principles of development led him to recommend a "purely negative" early education (93). This organic, benevolist, and implicitly primitivist view of childhood finds frequent voice in Romantic writing, as when Wordsworth describes his "five years'" self in *The Prelude* as a "naked savage, in the thunder-shower" (I.304), or names his "favorite school" the "fields, the roads, and rural lanes" (*Excursion* II.28–29).[32] Rather than follow the painstaking "negative" method, supervised by a seemingly omnipresent tutor, described in *Emile*, British writers depict natural associations working on their own, virtually unhampered by formal education, as in Coleridge's "Foster Mother's Tale":

> And so the babe grew up a pretty boy,
> A pretty boy, but most unteachable –
> And never learnt a prayer, nor told a bead,
> But knew the names of birds, and mocked their notes,
> And whistled, as he were a bird himself.

Rural childhoods with minimal schooling are standard in the radical novel of the 1790s, such as Holcroft's *Adventures of Hugh Trevor* or Hays's *Emma Courtney*, both of which complicate an associationist approach to representing development with a measure of Rousseau-istic primitivism. Bage is more overtly primitivistic in having the hero of *Hermsprong; or, Man as He Is Not* brought up by his father "amongst the aborigines of America."[33] Childhood in the literature of this era is frequently portrayed as Edenic, natural, and asocial. The organic child, like Adam, remains unfallen only so long as it remains solitary.

In stark contrast to the originally innocent child of Rousseau, the Augustinian conviction of the child's innate depravity was revived in the later eighteenth century among Methodists and Evangelicals. John Wesley held that the "bias of nature is set the wrong way: education is designed to set it right" (10.152), and counsels parents (against the fashionable but "empty" advice of Rousseau [10.151]) to "conquer" the child's will: "Break their wills betimes; begin this great work before they can run alone, before they can speak plain, perhaps before they can speak at all" (6: 172–73).[34] Wesley's harsh attitude was shared by Evangelical writers like Hannah More, for whom children "bring into the world a corrupt nature and evil dispositions, which it should be the great end of education to rectify."[35] However, the religious hymns for children written during the same period by the Wesleys and by Isaac Watts vary their dour portrayals of the child's "rebellious heart," as in Watts's "The Danger of Delay," with celebrations of childhood innocence recalling the religious lyrics of Vaughan and Traherne, as in Watts's song "Against Quarrelling and Fighting" (or "Innocent Play").[36] The Wesleys could similarly write of children in one hymn, "Born they are, like us, in sin," while in another praising the Methodist saints who "childlike innocence regain." As Thomas Walter Laqueur has argued, this "profoundly ambivalent" religious view of childhood (often further complicated by a Lockean approach to pedagogy) helps prepare the ground for the "mighty prophet" of the "Immortality" ode.[37]

Wordsworth's "seer blest" also owes something to the sentimental depiction of childhood naivety typified by Gray's "Eton" ode ("Where ignorance is bliss, / 'Tis folly to be wise") and characteristic of much verse of the later eighteenth century.[38] Although within this sentimental convention the child is not so much innocent as ignorant, maturation is nevertheless presented as a kind of fall, and childhood as a period less to be despised than fondly regretted. The notion of childhood as in some respects preferable or even superior to maturity receives futher support from such formative works of German Romanticism as Schiller's *On Naive and Sentimental Poetry* (1795–96), where rather than being viewed as imperfect – literally unfinished – the child comes to exemplify instead the latent perfection of as yet undiminished potentialities: "a lively representation to us of the ideal, not indeed as it is fulfilled, but as it is enjoined" in all its "pure and free strength, its integrity, its eternality."[39] For Schiller (as for Goethe in the *Sorrows of Young Werther*) the child belongs, in its naive perfection, with the works of Homer and Ossian, with fairy tales, and with classical Greek sculpture. The transcendental child of Wordsworth's "Immortality" ode brings together the "eternality" eulogized by Schiller with Gray's sentimental conceit that maturation entails the child's expulsion from a naive "paradise."

Even a brief consideration of Romantic-era poems on infancy by women brings out the oddly disembodied character of most representations of early childhood by male Romantic poets. Unlike the slumbering babe known only by its "gentle breathings" in "Frost at Midnight," for example, the "varlet" of Baillie's "A Mother to her Waking Infant" is described in all its slobbering, wailing materiality. Baillie's poem celebrates the unequal character of maternal love, which cannot be returned (except in an imagined future) and which takes for its object a graceless, irritating, inarticulate creature of "small understanding," valued for its very dependence rather than for a construed innocence or imagined angelic quality. In Anna Laetitia Barbauld's "To a little Invisible Being who is expected soon to become visible," the infant is invisible not because immaterial – awaiting birth in some antemundane heaven – but because it is enclosed in the womb of its mother, who:

longs to fold to her maternal breast
Part of herself, yet to herself unknown;
To see and to salute the stranger guest,
Fed with her life through many a tedious moon.[40]

If women poets were uniquely willing to address the earthier aspects of early childhood, however, many made use of other representational conventions as well: Felicia Hemans, for example, develops a version of Wordsworth's transcendental infant in the "cherub-soul and form," recalled to heaven before its innocence can be "stain'd" by mundane experience, memorialized in her once popular "Dirge of a Child."

A distinct convention for representing the sufferings of lower-class children (often labelled by writers of the era as the "children of the poor") begins to appear as well in the later eighteenth century. Blake's "Chimney Sweeper" and "Little Vagabond" in *Songs of Experience* (1794) and Wordsworth's "Alice Fell" are only the best known of a number of portraits of poor or exploited children found throughout later eighteenth- and early nineteenth-century lyric verse, which highlight the suffering of lower-class children in this era but often in a distancing and patronizing manner.[41] It is important to keep in mind that what has been called the "instructive" conception of childhood arising in the seventeenth and eighteenth centuries (childhood as a stage defined by education) was initially an upper and especially middle-class phenomenon.[42] Throughout the early part of the Romantic period lower-class children – that is, by far the majority of children – continued to work in the fields, in home industry, in shops and, increasingly, in mines and factories. Pinchbeck and Hewitt, in their social history of English childhood, point out that at the beginning of this period children above seven years were still legally held responsible for crimes (even if led into them by adults) and could be hung or transported. In the early nineteenth century, rural children (beginning at age seven or even younger) still worked from dawn to dusk in the winter, from eight in the morning till six in the evening in spring, and from five to nine at harvest time; in Wordsworth's "Pastoral" poem *Michael*, Luke begins putting in a full day's work with his shepherd father at age ten. Children worked twelve to fifteen hour days in small scale and domestic industries, especially at hand-looms and at lace making, and put in similar hours (under particularly brutal conditions) in mines and collieries. Although factory work was frequently *less* arduous than other forms of "indoor labour," the long hours at awkward positions nevertheless left child workers as what one observer called a "mass of crooked alphabets." Even the landmark Factory Act of 1819 stipulated only that no child could work in cotton mills or factories under the age of *nine*. Working-class children too small for employment were often left unattended (as their mothers put in long hours of their own) or fitfully watched, lulled into docility by opiates sold under names like "Mrs. Wilkinson's Soothing Syrup."[43] Crabbe portrays in stark, heart numbing verses the fate of destitute orphans ("parish-children") sold into virtual slavery by unscrupulous asylum wardens to brutal (and parsimonious) masters in the "Peter Grimes" section of *The Borough*:

> He wish'd for one to trouble and control;
> He wanted some obedient boy to stand
> And bear the blow of his outrageous hand;
> And hoped to find in some propitious hour
> A feeling creature subject to his power.

What makes "Peter Grimes" so unsettling is less the master's extraordinary brutality than the ordinariness of the procedures by which he purchases, exploits, and kills three children in succession; its Gothic conclusion seems tame beside its realistic premise.

There were, then, a number of conventions for representing the child adapted or developed by Romantic-era writers, some closely associated with philosophical or religious conceptions of childhood and education, others reflecting adult attitudes toward children, whether parental solicitude, self-regarding regret, or condescension. Although some of these conventions were obviously in tension with one another, they could readily coalesce or at least co-exist in the work of a given writer, as an Augustinian conviction of infant depravity accompanies references to "childlike innocence" in the Wesleys' hymns, or as an associationist conception of the formative role of experience and education adheres to something approaching an organicist faith in the bent of nature in novels by Hays and Holcroft. The poetry of Wordsworth runs nearly the entire gamut of the conventions I have sketched out above, portraying children sometimes as natural innocents, sometimes as preternaturally wise or holy, and sometimes as foolish or innately sinful.[44] In early lyrics and the first two books of *The Prelude*, Wordsworth celebrates the spontaneous, unsocialized, egotistical child of nature.[45] The Boy of

Winander, in one of the first sections of *The Prelude* to be written, stands alone in woods or by the lake to blow "mimic hootings to the silent owls" (v.398), exemplifying a purely natural education which Wordsworth opposes to the rationalist educational schemes of his time. In "The Danish Boy" and "Lucy Gray," the child becomes incorporated into the natural landscape, something between a shade and a genius of the wood. The frequent association of death with childhood in Wordsworth helps point out the limitations of his idealized child of nature: the Danish Boy ("Like a dead boy he is serene") and Lucy Gray, the Boy of Winander and Lucy in "Three years she grew in sun and shower" all must die in order to retain their natural "eternality." Encountering a beautiful and inexplicably rural "cottage-child" in a London theater, Wordsworth typically imagines him "as if embalmed / By Nature – through some special privilege / Stopped at the growth he had" (*Prelude* vii.400–2).[46]

Wordsworth gives thanks for his early immersion in the natural world throughout *The Prelude*, yet he allows his represented self (somewhat reluctantly) to mature past the age of spontaneity and union with nature at which the ideal children characteristic of his early lyrics remain fixed. In portraying his own childhood in *The Prelude* and in "Tintern Abbey," Wordsworth often treats nature less as a ground that might reabsorb the child figured against it, than as a rich mine of associations and experiences that contribute to the growth of a "chosen spirit." Despite this insistence on continuity, however, at times childhood strikes Wordsworth as a radically different and discontinuous period of life, as though his own child-self were somehow "embalmed," like the London "cottage-child," in its innocent state:

> so wide appears
> The vacancy between me and those days,
> Which yet have such self-presence in my mind
> That sometimes when I think of them I seem
> Two consciousnesses – conscious of myself,
> And of some other being.   (*Prelude* ii.28–33)

This tension between a developmental faith in the self's continuity and a haunting sense of one's childhood self as distinctly and irrevocably other also characterizes the prose works of Lamb and De Quincey, and becomes almost standard in the autobiographies and *Bildungsromane* of the later nineteenth-century.[47]

"To H. C., Six Years Old" (1807), a poem on Hartley Coleridge, marks a shift towards the transcendentalized vision of childhood more familiar from the "Immortality" ode. Although "exquisitely wild," Hartley is as much heavenly as earthly, a "faery voyager" whose "fancies from afar are brought." The transcendentalized child of this and other lyrics shares the silence and something of the deathliness of the Wordsworthian child of nature, as in Wordsworth's sonnet "It is a beauteous evening," in which the poet's seemingly very young daughter (Caroline was ten at the time recorded in the sonnet) lies "in Abraham's bosom all the year," as though already effectively in heaven. In the "Address to My Infant Daughter, Dora," the month-old child, compared in an extended simile to the moon, is literally unearthly, "Moving, untouched in silver purity." "Characteristics of a Child Three Years Old," which celebrates the odd combination of "Innocence" and wildness in Wordsworth's daughter Catherine, portrays her as (again like the child of nature) still unsocialized:

> this happy Creature of herself
> Is all-sufficient; solitude to her
> Is blithe society, who fills the air
> With gladness and involuntary songs.

One is reminded of the "self-sufficing solitude" ascribed to the boy-Wordsworth in *The Prelude*, and yet this "happy Creature" seems almost entirely detached from the world of experience.

In the "Ode: Intimations of Immortality from Recollections of Early Childhood," Wordsworth transfers the source of the child's integrity from the spontaneous interaction with nature commemorated in the early books of *The Prelude* to its pre-existence in a heavenly realm:

> Not in entire forgetfulness
> And not in utter nakedness,
> But trailing clouds of glory do we come
> From God, who is our home:
> Heaven lies about us in our infancy!

Nature now becomes a "homely Nurse" who beguiles the growing child, socialization is seen as a "prison-house," and adulthood is redeemed by the "Blank misgivings of a Creature" who dimly recollects the radiance of his true home. The infant is apostrophized in paradoxical terms, its tininess concealing its "Soul's immensity," its lack of sensory development enabling it to read "the eternal deep,

/ Haunted for ever by the eternal mind," a "Mighty Prophet," a
"Seer blest." The idealization of childhood could hardly go further;
in the "Immortality" ode, which would become immensely influential within Victorian culture, the nineteenth century's "inordinate
worship of childhood" was firmly established.[48]

And yet Wordsworth himself would turn to a much bleaker notion
of childhood. In "The Longest Day," a later poem to Dora,
Wordsworth assumes a didactic tone ("Be thou wiser, youthful
Maiden!") and recommends "duty," the "strict preceptor," in
place of spontaneity and immersion in nature. In "Maternal Grief"
Wordsworth still, though with evident unease, attributes a celestial
atmosphere to the "confines" of infancy – "Reflected beams of that
celestial light / To all the Little-ones on sinful earth / Not
unvouchsafed" – but he adopts a more severe, Augustinian conception of the child in his later sonnet on "Baptism": "a timely
shower / Whose virtue changes to a Christian Flower / A Growth
from sinful Nature's bed of weeds!" In Book VIII of *The Excursion*, on
the other hand, Wordsworth underscores the "degradation" of
contemporary lower class children, whether the urban factory child
– the "senseless member of a vast machine" (160) – or the uneducated "rustic Boy," the "slave of ignorance, and oft of want, /
And miserable hunger" (162–64). His harsh depictions of the rural
beggar child reared by "savage Nature" (353) and of the ploughboy,
with his "ignorant, and strange" demeanor (401), underscore the
fragility of Wordsworth's earlier appeal to nature in the face of an
increasingly mechanized and commercialized society.

William Blake's vision of childhood has been described both as
resting on a belief in "original innocence" comparable to that of
Rousseau and as harboring on the contrary a Calvinistic conviction
of "the devil in man and nature" lurking behind the "very innocence
Wordsworth glorifies."[49] Neither characterization is adequate for
Blake's complex portrayal of childhood, which (especially in *Songs of
Innocence and of Experience*) reworks the ambivalence of eighteenth-
century religious poetry for children into something like a coherent
system. Innocence for Blake is neither preferable to nor cancelled out
by Experience; both represent "States of the Human Soul" rather
than ideals, and both must be subsumed into the comprehensive (and
dynamic) vision Blake would eventually describe as "organized
innocence." Blake's various representations of childhood might be
initially thought of in terms of a dialectical triad.[50] In certain poems

childhood appears Edenic, a time of bodily joys and spontaneous, unrepressed delight, as in songs of Innocence like "Laughing Song," and "Infant Joy," and in the striking passage on early childhood in *Visions of the Daughters of Albion* (1793): "Infancy! fearless, lustful, happy! nestling for delight / In laps of pleasure." The perspective of Innocence, however, proves ultimately untenable in a fallen social world. Behind the apparent simplicity of Innocence lurks the harsher perspective of Experience, embedded in certain lyrics almost like the traces in a palimpsest, so that particular songs of Innocence tend to be more complex and ambivalent texts than their counterparts in *Songs of Experience*.[51]

The "Holy Thursday" poem in *Songs of Experience*, for example, offers a fairly straightforward critique of a "cold and usurous" approach to the plight of poor children, as do "The Chimney Sweeper" and "The Little Vagabond" in the same collection.[52] The "Holy Thursday" in *Songs of Innocence*, however, only initially seems an uncomplicated celebration of the Charity School children trooping into St. Paul's with "innocent faces" like "flowers of London town." But as one registers the intentionally hollow piety of the last line ("Then cherish pity, lest you drive an angel from your door"), the forced metaphors (London flowers are cut flowers; the children flow "like Thames waters" *upward* into the "high dome of Pauls"), and attends to such telling details as the beadles' disciplinary "wands," Blake's critique of the class oppression built into the Charity School system emerges from behind the speaker's laudatory accents. To remain in Innocence is to remain content with surface pieties and blind to systemic social injustice. The perspective of Experience is itself incomplete and distorting, however, as it envisions no alternative to the bleak, Hobbesian world of rational adulthood. It is because we once enjoyed the Edenic vision of Innocence that we can imagine (and so build towards) an alternative to the limited world of rational empiricism. The charity children in "Holy Thursday" represent a vision potentially more powerful than that of the "wise guardians of the poor" who supervise them: "Now like a mighty wind they raise to heaven the voice of song / Or like harmonious thunderings the seats of heaven among." Although the child must pass out of Innocence or be condemned, like Blake's Thel, to barrenness, children are natural visionaries, and the child's naive perception of an innocent world provides the foundation for imaginative life: "Some children are Fools and so are some Old Men.

But There is a vast Majority on the side of Imagination or Spiritual Sensation" (703). The perspectives of Innocence and Experience are both limited, but both are necessary aspects of the comprehensive vision of Imagination.

It is important to add that, despite their ready access to "Imagination," children for Blake, as for Rousseau and most of the first-generation Romantic poets, should not be pushed beyond their capacities or expected to conform to adult modes of reason and behavior. "The Little Boy lost" cries out in the *Songs of Innocence*, "Father, father, where are you going / O do not walk so fast," a plea glossed in the lyric's counterpart ("A Little boy Lost") in *Songs of Experience*. This child speaks from the foreshortened (and very un-Blakean) perspective of a child of nature:

> Nought loves another as itself
> Nor venerates another so.
> Nor is it possible to Thought
> A greater than itself to know:
>
> And Father, how can I love you,
> Or any of my brothers more?
> I love you like the little bird
> That picks up crumbs around the door.

What Blake condemns in this poem is not the speaker's childish materialism but rather the refusal of the adult world to let him fight his own mental way out of it. A priest is on hand to seize the child and sacrifice him, as "One who sets reason up for judge / Of our most holy Mystery," to a more orthodox creed:

> The weeping child could not be heard
> The weeping parents wept in vain:
> They strip'd him to his little shirt.
> And bound him in an iron chain.
>
> And burn'd him in a holy place,
> Where many had been burn'd before:
> The weeping parents wept in vain.
> Are such things done on Albion's shore.

Such things were done, at the level of intellectual confinement and spiritual abasement, in disciplinary institutions like the Charity Schools, "schools of industry," and Sunday Schools throughout England. Blake is no less suspicious than the Lake poets of the new educational systems springing up throughout the Romantic era, but unlike them he remains consistently critical of the fundamentally coercive and predominately anti-intellectual institutions for social-izing lower-class children.

If the second-generation Romantic poets favor youth over early childhood, the prose of Charles Lamb and Thomas De Quincey forms a bridge between the early Romantic poets and the Victorian cult of the child. Lamb develops in his essays both an intense nostalgia for childhood recalled as a lost paradise, and a senti-mentalized and altogether ethereal version of Wordsworth's "heaven-born" child. "Recollections of Christ's Hospital" sets a new standard for the regret of childhood:

For me, I do not know whether a constitutional imbecility does not incline me too obstinately to cling to the remembrances of childhood; in an inverted ratio to the usual sentiments of mankind, nothing that I have been engaged in since seems of any value or importance, compared to the colours which imagination gave to everything then (1: 146).

In "Witches, and Other Night Fears" Lamb finds in children's fantasies reflections of "our ante-mundane condition, and a peep at least into the shadow-land of pre-existence" (2: 68). In "Dream Children: A Reverie," the narrator's preternaturally silent son and daughter become by the end a bachelor's dream-children, whose features, "without speech," strangely express the "effects of speech" (2: 102), prose counterparts to Lucy Gray and the Danish Boy. "The Child-Angel; A Dream" more mawkishly portrays a half-earthly, half-celestial child in "a kind of fairyland heaven," an angel whose mortal taint privileges him to remain "a child forever" (2: 244–45). Lamb brings together in these essays two motifs from Wordsworth's poetry: the "celestial" attributes of the "Immortality" ode and the eternal childhood lent through early death to the child of nature.

De Quincey shares Wordsworth's conception of childhood as somehow discontinuous despite its "necessary" continuity with the adult self: "An adult sympathizes with himself in childhood because he *is* the same, and because (being the same) yet he is *not* the same ... he feels the differences between his two selves as the main quickeners of his sympathy."[53] Citing the "Immortality" ode, De Quincey attributes to children a "far closer communion with God" than that available to adults and an innate capacity for apprehending "truth" which they lose as they grow older: "into all the *elementary* feelings of man, children look with more searching gaze than adults" (127). For

De Quincey, as for Schiller, the child is more perfect than the adult it will become because of its greater "apprehensiveness" and a fuller "natural inheritance" which can only contract with maturation; again citing Wordsworth (De Quincey was one of the few to read *The Prelude* before 1850), he credits the child with a more profound experience of nature as well (*DQW* 1: 122). De Quincey's prose, like Lamb's, is haunted by spectral children: his sister Elizabeth, who dies at the age of nine and preys on De Quincey's memories and dreams for the rest of his life; his childhood visions of dying children rising slowly into heaven; his adult obsession with Catherine Wordsworth who, dying at the age of three, appears to De Quincey in the fields of Grasmere after he has spent his nights, "for more than two months running," sleeping on her grave (*DQW* 2: 443). De Quincey's fascination with Wordsworth's young daughter looks forward to the eroticized child-worship of Ruskin and Carroll: "On the night when she slept with me in the winter, we lay awake all the middle of the night – and talked oh how tenderly together: When we fell asleep, she was lying in my arms ... she would lock her little arms with such passionateness round my neck – as if she had known that it was to be the last night we were ever to pass together."[54] De Quincey himself presents the attachment as pathological, comparing it to the "old Pagan superstition of a nympholepsy," a term he also uses to describe his sense of being haunted throughout childhood by his dead sister (*DQW* 2: 445, *Confessions*, 119). Yet like Elizabeth, Catherine also makes part of De Quincey's "pantheon" of dead children, an "untouched, pure, self-sufficient but passionately desired Innocent."[55]

In attempting to convey something of the variety and sheer number of representations of children found in late eighteenth- and early nineteenth-century British texts, I hope to have underscored the unprecedented cultural importance attributed to childhood at this time. I also hope to have provided an initial sense of the possibilities for and constraints on writing concerning childhood and early education during the period covered in this study. We need to move from description to theory, however, in asking *why* childhood, and with it education, became so crucial within the social and literary discourses of the Romantic era. The construction of childhood in an age of revolution and reform is neither a politically disinterested nor an ideologically neutral matter. In order to grasp the historical significance of the rise of a child-centered British culture, it is necessary to explore links between education, ideology, and power within a society that underwent a profound shift from traditional hierarchical structures of domination to more consensual forms of managing political and social relations. This shift was facilitated, to a great extent, by a newly elaborated set of discursive relations among various social groups, the establishment and dissemination of which demanded in turn novel approaches to literacy and schooling. We can begin to understand something of these changes, which helped shape the discursive world we ourselves inhabit, by considering the status of childhood and education in recent social theory, particularly theories of ideology and hegemony.

IDEOLOGY AND THE PRODUCTION OF CHILDHOOD

From the beginning of its use as a critical term, "ideology" is related both to revolution and to education. Clifford Geertz suggests that it is only when received opinions and traditional patterns of daily life are thrown into question, as in a period of economic, political, or cultural revolution, that the "search for systematic ideological formulations, either to reinforce them or to replace them, flourishes." Citing Burke's response to the French Revolution, Geertz concludes that it is "precisely at the point at which a political system begins to free itself" from received traditions, whether religious, philosophical, or the unconsciously adopted system of social mores, that ideologies as such begin to emerge and compete for allegiance.[56] Wordsworth attests to this new sense of both intellectual dislocation and possibility in the "French Revolution" section of *The Prelude*, describing how "A veil had been / Uplifted":

> Suffice it that a shock had then been given
> To old opinions, and the minds of all men
> Had felt it – that my mind was both let loose,
> Let loose and goaded.   (x.860–64)

David McLellan also holds that ideology as a distinct concept grows out of the "social, political, and intellectual upheavals" accompanying the "Industrial Revolution." As opposed to traditional beliefs or myths, which generally remain static, rest on a "restricted and hierarchically structured" authority, and serve primarily to promote social coherence and integration, ideologies are the "products of an increasingly pluralist society" associated with "rival groups whose sectional interests they served."[57] The term *ideologie* in fact first emerges, as is well known, in the decade following the French Revolution in the works of Destutt de Tracy and his group, later called the *ideologues* (first by Napoleon) or *ideologistes*; what is less familiar is that the French *ideologues* hoped that their "science of ideas" would lead to a program of institutional reforms, beginning with the systematization and reform of the secondary schools. This project itself grew out of the more ambitious schemes for universal education of Condorcet and the Committee on Public Instruction advanced during the most radical phase (1792–94) of the French Revolution; it is not without provocation that Gaskell's Lady Ludlow associates "Rousseau, and his writings" and the "Reign of Terror" with "this talk about education" (138).[58]

In our own period another French philosopher, Louis Althusser, has been the most influential theorist to explore the relations between ideology and education. Following Antonio Gramsci's distinction between the state (or "political society") and the "private" social organizations which enable it to function (or "civil society"), Althusser emphasizes the role of the latter, particularly schools, in the "reproduction of the conditions of production" in modern societies.[59] Addressing the question "what do children learn at school," Althusser replies that schooling plays an ideological as well as directly economic function in reproducing the social order: "the reproduction of labour power requires not only a reproduction of its skills, but also, at the same time, a reproduction of its submission to the rules of the established order" (132–33). In this latter function, the school in "mature capitalist social formations" takes over from the church as the dominant instance of what Althusser calls an "ideological state apparatus," which, as for Gramsci, can as well be a "private" as a public institution (152). What enables schooling to fulfill its dominant role in social reproduction is the "universally reigning ideology of the School" which, ironically, represents it as a "neutral environment purged of ideology" (156). Pierre Bourdieu makes a similar point in explaining the role of schooling in both social reproduction and what he calls "cultural reproduction" (that is, the transmission via the family and schooling of varying degrees of literacy and other forms of "cultural capital," which help determine the child's eventual class status).

Among all the solutions put forward throughout history to the problem of the transmission of power and privileges, there surely does not exist one that is better concealed ... than the solution which the educational system provides by contributing to the reproduction of the structure of class relations and by concealing, by an apparently neutral attitude, the fact that it fills this function.[60]

Reproduction theories of education help uncover the school's central role in the transmission of dominant ideology as well as its more pervasive implication in the transfer of social power from one generation to the next, while exposing the particular ideology of the modern schools system as precisely the denial of any ideological function. Bourdieu's work in particular is valuable for its demonstration of how much, in the way of cultural capital, is passed on through the family, shaping the "expectations," "inclinations," and "desire" which in turn help determine a given child's school career, and for detailing how modern educational systems allow for a carefully controlled degree of social mobility in a manner that affirms rather than threatens the "existing structure of class relations" while simultaneously serving to validate democratic ideals.[61] Important as they are for any analysis of how educational systems function in modern, democratic societies, however, reproduction theories cannot by themselves explain the development over time of such systems, how, for example, in Britain, numerous independent educational enterprises, with overt and often competing ideologies, and more likely to evince hostility toward democracy and class mobility than otherwise, came to cohere into the kind of system Althusser or Bourdieu describe. If they do not attempt to account for historical change, moreover, reproduction theories have been faulted for an inability to explain present changes or allow sufficiently for future ones, harboring an "iron-clad" view of a system of social domination so insidious that, precisely because ideological transmission is largely unconscious or structural, "there appears to be no escape."[62] Such theories are hard pressed to account for the possibilities of resistance to domination and of contradiction within the dominant ideological constellation, and remain vague about how ideologies are contested or transformed.[63]

A number of contemporary social theorists, some remaining nominally within the Marxist tradition and others explicitly attempting to move beyond it, have looked back to Gramsci in search of a more dynamic and complex conception of ideology, supplementing or replacing it with Gramsci's notion of "hegemony." Raymond Williams, for example, emphasizes that hegemony includes not only the "conscious system of ideas and beliefs" usually understood by

ideology but also "the whole lived social process" – embodied in
institutions like the school and family, in customs, in "common
sense" – as "practically organized by specific and dominant meanings and values."[64] Williams's reading of hegemony helps sub-
stantiate Althusser's contention that ideology has a "material
existence" (165) inhering in social institutions and practices: "From
castles and palaces and churches to prisons and workhouses and
schools ... any ruling class, in variable ways though always ma-
terially, produces a social and political order. These are never
superstructural activities."[65] There are obvious advantages for the
historical, social, or cultural analysis of education in a material
conception of ideology or hegemony. Schooling takes place not
simply through instruction and texts but in terms of specific
institutions, buildings, and practices such as drill and recitation,
often prescribing rules for dress and behavior and regulating even
those learned bodily movements through which relations of power
and privilege become "somaticized."[66] Indeed, it is first and foremost
through educational institutions that, for Williams, hegemony is
imposed and maintained.[67]

Moreover, the notion of hegemony as developed (for example) in
the work of Chantal Mouffe allows Althusser's conception of ideology
as a "practice producing subjects" to be reworked so as to take into
account the importance of other determinants besides economic class
(which, for Althusser himself, remains supreme). "Within every
society," as Mouffe writes, "each social agent is inscribed in a
multiplicity of social relations – not only social relations of production but also the social relations, among others, of sex, race,
nationality, and vicinity. All these social relations determine position-
alities or subject positions, and every social agent is in the locus of
many subject positions and cannot be reduced to one."[68] Although it
must be evident already that the significance of education in the
Romantic period cannot be understood apart from "social relations
of production," any such analysis would be considerably impoverished by ignoring either gender relations or (especially given the
important links between British schooling and colonialism in the
early nineteenth century) questions of race and ethnicity. A model
(such as Mouffe's) of subjectivity as multi-layered, overdetermined,
and "fissured" or fragmented also allows for the possibility of
resistance within a system, not of monolithic, overt repression but of
dynamic, shifting constellations of power and knowledge.[69]

Understanding subjectivity as a "product of social practice" helps in two ways to clarify the importance of childhood and education in the modern era: it both provides a basis for understanding the role of education in producing subjects, and it helps expose the characteristic modern form of subjectivity – the "lone individual" – as a historically specific rather than universal or natural phenomenon.[70] Frederic Jameson, among others, has related the historical emergence of the modern "centred subject" – the "lived experience of individual consciousness as a monadic and autonomous center of activity" – to the "bourgeois cultural revolution" (of which Romanticism represents a key if ambivalent phase): "that immense process of transformation whereby populations whose life habits were formed by other, now archaic, modes of production are effectively reprogrammed for life and work in the new world of market capitalism." The modern form of subjectivity in turn demanded the reconfiguration of the family as a "private space within the nascent public sphere of bourgeois society," a "specialization" by which childhood is "qualitatively differentiated from other biological experiences."[71] Women as well as children are targeted and set apart in this process of specialization, children as the primary objects of the new technologies of the self which enable the "bourgeois cultural revolution" and women as guardians of the new private sphere. As Valerie Walkerdine writes, "the mother and child are both caught in the play of practices for ensuring the possibility of self-regulated, rational and autonomous subjects." Relegated more strictly than ever before to the domestic sphere by the need for maintaining a nurturing and stable early environment, women constitute the "price paid for autonomy, its hidden and dispensable cost" (212).

Drawing on the work of Michel Foucault as well as on Marxist and psychoanalytic thought, Walkerdine sees the school and the family as principal sites for the regulation and production of the modern individual through their construction of the "rational independent, autonomous child as a quasi-natural phenomenon who progresses through a universalised developmental sequence towards the possibility of rational argument" (203). The school, as the primary apparatus of social regulation, comes in the modern period to define not only knowledge, but also both "what 'a child' is and how learning and teaching are to be considered" (207–8). The new educational methods of the eighteenth and early nineteenth centuries, based on a "child-centred pedagogy" stressing rationality, a "normalized sequence of child development," and a new disciplinary ethos replacing overt coercion with securing the child's consent, are often viewed unproblematically as "progressive" developments that look forward to current educational practice. But from the perspective represented by Walkerdine, these "advances" in the theory and practice of schooling also represent innovative techniques of social discipline, which facilitate and attempt to guarantee the subject's participation in an increasingly regulated society.[72]

The great social transformations outlined above neither begin nor end in the period – 1780 to 1832 – singled out for special attention in this study.[73] But what can be called, with due wariness, the "Romantic" period offers a particularly intriguing focus for considering the emergence of modern conceptions and practices concerning childhood and education in relation to literary, pedagogical, and theoretical texts. As both Williams and Jameson have remarked, Romanticism constitutes a significantly "ambiguous" phase in the bourgeois cultural revolution, as at once its extension and a movement of resistance, a "counter-culture" nevertheless "tied to the hegemonic."[74] The same period also witnesses the interesting paradox, noted by Walkerdine, that the new technologies of power based on engineering consent rather than on overt repression were often advocated by the more "progressive" elements of society, usually in the name of professionalization, utility, and secularization.[75] It would be counter-productive either to valorize Wordsworth and other Romantic poets for their "defense" of the child, and more particularly the child's "imagination," in opposition to an increasingly industrialized and "normalized" society or, on the contrary, to praise writers like Wollstonecraft and Edgeworth for their "progressive" and rational approach to education.[76] In either case, a certain (and by no means negligible) expression of resistance to new or traditional forms of social domination is accompanied by ideological positions and discursive strategies that implicitly support the hegemonic practices by which domination is asserted and maintained. Such is the complexity of the issues at hand that taking sides with one discursive tendency or another is less useful than identifying and analyzing the conflicting valences of each position in a period rife with ambiguity.

Literature – broadly conceived as including both "high" and "popular" literature, from epic poetry to throwaway tracts – plays a key role in the production of new educational discourses and practices in this period, and in any attempt to analyze their contemporary significance. Most simply, literary texts of many kinds were directly implicated in the new educational strategies of the period. A new literature for children stressing rationality, developmental stages, and independent judgment was fashioned to facilitate new rational pedagogies by writers like Wollstonecraft, Edgeworth, and Barbauld; such efforts inspired in turn a revaluation of fairy tales and other traditional "imaginative" forms for children on the part of Wordsworth, Coleridge, and other Romantic writers. The same period witnessed the development of what has been called "industrial works of fiction"[77] – a "popular" literature devised by the dominant groups to serve their own purposes – in such enterprises as Sarah Trimmer's *Family Magazine* (1788–89), Hannah More's *Cheap Repository Tracts* (1795–98), and Maria Edgeworth's *Popular Tales* (1804), works designed to displace the genuinely popular chapbooks and broadsheets disseminated by street-hawkers and itinerant peddlers. As Terry Eagleton remarks, the simplest and most effective form of censorship is "the perpetuation of mass illiteracy," which was largely the case in England until the eighteenth century. But with the unforseen emergence of a "reading public," eagerly devouring the radical literature exemplified by Paine's *Rights of Man* and Cobbett's *Political Register*, it increasingly became the role of educational institutions to monitor and facilitate the proper ideological functioning of literary texts. "From the infant school to the University faculty, literature is a vital instrument for the insertion of individuals into the perceptual and symbolic forms of the dominant ideological formation, able to accomplish this function with a 'naturalness,' spontaneity and experiential immediacy possible to no other ideological practice." In this way, the Romantic era sees not only the emergence of a regulated "popular" literature, but also of "Literature" as such, a cultural institution predicated on a canonical set of "imaginative" works, disseminated through schools and centralized publishing venues, and managed by a professional group of critics and interpreters.[78]

In addition to interrelations on the level of institutions and large-scale social ventures, there exists a whole range of inter-connections between educational practices and literary representation at what might be termed the rhetorical or discursive level, inhering in the manner in which educational and literary discourses are inflected in terms of diction, syntax, figuration, and speech acts. Here the works of Bakhtin and his group, with their attempt to broach a "sociological poetics," can be especially useful.[79] Discourse, defined by Bakhtin as "language in its concrete living totality," permeates social life, and is in turn permeated by the social: "The life of the word is contained in its transfer from one mouth to another, from one collective to another, from one generation to another generation. In this process the word does not forget its own path and cannot completely free itself from the power of these concrete contexts into which it has entered."[80] The words and verbal structures encountered in the literary works analyzed in this study often come "filled," in Bakhtin's sense, with the "other voice" of contemporary educational and related institutional discourses, and thus are by no means ideologically inert. It is in large part through new discursive formations that the educational and other apparatuses of social regulation developing throughout the period function; indeed, the multilayered "subject positions" which make up the individual social agent in a modern, institutionalized, literate society are themselves constituted through the various "discourses that can construct that position."[81]

The relation between literary discourse and the discourses of social regulation in this period can obviously not be conceived of as a passive or simply "reflective" one. Literary texts, because of their inherently self-conscious relation to language, are particularly suited to take up, comment on, parody, or otherwise distort the discursive strategies of a disciplinary society. In the Romantic era any number of literary texts engage the discourses of education and related apparatuses of social control in critical fashion, sometimes in unexpected or unlikely forms. Wordsworth, for example, addresses the "catechistic method" popularized by Trimmer and other conservative educational innovators in "We Are Seven," a "lyrical ballad"; Blake employs the conventions of the children's religious hymn to criticize the colonialist discourse informing anti-slavery writing and the new children's literature alike in "The Little Black Boy"; Mary Shelley takes up the Gothic mode in *Frankenstein* to interrogate an educational discourse, stemming from *Emile*, which grounds women's pedagogy in the perceived monstrosity of the female body.

As literary texts help constitute the educational discourses and practices of their time as well as critically addressing them, studying the interrelations of literature and education in the Romantic period is not simply a matter of setting a literary foreground against a social-historical background. Children's books, domestic novels, religious tracts, "popular" tales, and poetry anthologies all play a material role in education, even narrowly conceived; they give form to and help disseminate new pedagogical technologies and idioms, as well as being produced in reaction to them. Moreover, as Williams notes, the notion of a close or predictable correspondence between literary works and social experience within a given "period" is itself problematic, as artistic works can variously endorse dominant cultural practices and meanings, embody archaic or "residual" cultural values (as in the Romantic cult of feudalism), or express "emergent" values or significations which may either become hegemonized or instead anticipate a new social order.[82] The posing of any simple fit between social and literary history is especially to be guarded against in examining the fundamentally "ambiguous" phenomenon called Romanticism, which (particularly in England) features as much "contradiction," "fracture," and "mutation" as coherence.[83]

The complex relation in the Romantic era between dominant, residual, and emergent practices noted by Williams can be seen informing a specific literary problem which, in addition, engages a number of the theoretical issues discussed above. In his poetry of childhood, and most notably in *The Prelude*, Wordsworth brings together two terms which, up to then, had remained almost entirely separate: childhood and power. This key and nearly unprecedented juxtaposition offers a site for exploring both the historicity of Wordsworth's revisionist portrayal of childhood and the deep ambivalence that inheres within it.

CHILDHOOD AND POWER IN *THE PRELUDE*

Wordsworth's most remarkable contribution to educational discourse in the Western tradition is encapsulated in a memorable phrase from *The Prelude*: "Knowledge not purchased with the loss of power" (5.449). The phrase is so well known, in fact, that familiarity has probably diminished its striking and original oddness, not least its clean break with common sense. For if the "real children" Wordsworth invokes in *The Prelude* are to be guarded against losing power as they gain knowledge, they must be possessed of some initial stock of power which could be lost; and yet childhood, particularly infancy, has traditionally been represented as a condition of relative impotence, while education has been usually viewed as adding to, rather than diminishing, the child's stock of power. It is more than a little paradoxical for Wordsworth to portray socialization, and education in particular, as a threat to the child's power, rather than as a prime source of cultural and self-mastery leading the child towards adult autonomy.

Rousseau, who shares Wordsworth's suspicions regarding conventional methods of socialization, views the child as originally innocent but emphatically not as strong or powerful. "We are born weak, we need strength; we are born totally unprovided, we need aid; we are born stupid, we need judgment. Everything we do not have at our birth and which we need when we are grown up is given us by education" (38). The originally innocent child can be deformed by a faulty education, but only education can compensate for the infant's condition of weakness and dependence. Indeed, it is this initial state of powerlessness that renders Emile educable in the first place: "Let him know only that he is weak and you are strong, that by his condition and yours he is necessarily at your mercy" (91). For De Quincey, who compares childhood to the "literature of power" in its capacity to invigorate the mind, it is the child's *weakness* that enables it to perform this function: "By the pity, by the tenderness, and by the peculiar modes of admiration, which connect themselves with the helplessness, with the innocence, and with the simplicity of children, not only are the primal affections strengthened and continually renewed, but the qualities which are dearest in the sight of heaven ... are kept up in perpetual remembrance, and their ideals are continually refreshed" (*DQW* 11: 55). When Coleridge defines the "character and privilege of Genius" in *The Friend* as the ability to "carry on the feelings of childhood into the powers of Manhood," it is a keener sense of "wonder and novelty" that uniquely belongs to the child, while power must wait on maturity.[84]

Wordsworth's influential connection of childhood and power, then, contrasts markedly with the mutual exclusion of childhood and power found in Rousseau, De Quincey, and Coleridge. And yet the connection could hardly be posed in stronger terms:

> our childhood sits,
> Our simple childhood, sits upon a throne
> That hath more power than all the elements.   (v.531–33)

In what sense are we to understand that, as Wordsworth writes of the "spots of time," the "hiding places" of the adult's "power" are to be located in the "dawn almost / Of life" (XI.334–35)? A number of critics have turned at this point to Freudian theory, which similarly poses a connection between infantile experience, the child's urge to master the external world (what Wordsworth calls the "world of sense"), and a sensation of power that diminishes with development, as in Freud's notion of "infantile omnipotence," or his interpretation of the "fort-da" game described in *Beyond the Pleasure Principle* as the child's attempt to gain mastery over his mother and the object world she initially represents.[85] While psychoanalytic theory can help elucidate the character and workings of the child's feelings and exertions of power in *The Prelude*, it does not tell us why Wordsworth should come to associate childhood and power at this particular moment in history, specifically, in the period from 1799, when the "spots of time" are first adumbrated in the "Two-Part Prelude," to 1805, when *The Prelude* reaches the form we generally read it in today. I will conclude this chapter by arguing that what makes Wordsworth's conjunction of childhood and power possible is the revolutionary character of the decade 1789–99 that precedes and, in a number of ways, conditions the production of his verse autobiography.

Laurence Goldstein has contextualized Wordsworth's revaluation of childhood in the iconography of the revolutionary decade: "Wordsworth's child is, like Blake's, an infant of the French Revolution."[86] He points, for example, to a passage in *The Prelude* which implicitly compares the promise of the Revolution's early days to the regeneration of humanity: "France standing on the top of golden hours, / And human nature seeming born again" (VI.353–54). Ronald Paulson, building on this account, remarks on the relative youthfulness of some notable leaders of both the American and French revolutions, and quotes Tom Paine stating in *Common Sense* that "Youth is the seed-time of good habits, as well in nations as in individuals"; he refers us also to Blake, whose Orc seems to epitomize the youthful virility of revolution, and in whose *Songs of Experience* "the 'innocence' of the Biblical lambs and children Christ suffers to come unto Him is overdetermined by the growing sense of 'innocence' in the newborn, unfettered, unexperienced, and so (to his parents) dangerous child of the newborn American and French Revolutions."[87]

These readings rely, however, on an over-literal connection between the figuration of childhood and that of revolution in Romantic poetry. For one thing, youth and childhood (especially infancy) are usually quite distinct both as construed in eighteenth-century thought and as represented in the literary tradition which Blake and Wordsworth (in their quite different manners) worked from. Some of the child-speakers of *Songs of Experience* may indeed resemble less the docile children of contemporary sentimental verse than the "little rebels of Freud and Melanie Klein,"[88] but the "Little Vagabond" is hardly the revolutionary as virile youth; Orc does not break his chains and assert his subversive energies until he reaches sexual maturity. The comparison of the dawning of a new age to a new birth belongs less with Romantic representations of childhood than with an allegorical convention going back at least to Virgil's fourth Eclogue and best known in the English tradition from Milton's "Nativity" ode, which celebrates a new world order but not revolutionary change in the modern sense. The only explicit comparison in *The Prelude* of the Revolution to childhood (rather than to youth or to rebirth) – where France under the Reign of Terror is portrayed as a child running heedlessly into the "blast" with a toy windmill (x.336–45) – seems incidental, and a comparable image is employed later in the same book to describe the conservative English *reaction* to the events in France under Pitt and his ministry, who "childlike longed / To imitate" the excesses of Robespierre (x.650–51).

If the allegorical connection between childhood in *The Prelude* and revolution seems, on closer examination, somewhat forced, there is nevertheless a strong metonymic link between Wordsworth's portrayal of childhood and the revolutionary character of the age in which he wrote. When Gaskell's Lady Ludlow associates the new talk of the "right every child had to instruction" with the "rights of men" and the French Revolution, she is metonymically connecting the new manner of thinking about childhood with the political and social upheavals of her era. Hannah More makes a comparable association in her *Strictures on the Modern System of Female Education* (1799). "The *rights of man* have been discussed," she complains, "till we are somewhat wearied with the discussion. To these have been opposed, with more presumption than prudence, *the rights of woman*. It follows, according to the natural progression of human things, that the next stage of that irradiation which our enlighteners are pouring in upon us will illuminate the world with grave descants on the *rights of children.*" Although this passage reads in part as an attempted *reductio ad absurdum* of the democratic principles advanced by radicals like Paine and Wollstonecraft, More also expresses a real fear that "not only sons but daughters" have "adopted something of that spirit of independence, and disdain of control, which characterise the times."[89] Relating the "increased insubordination of children" to the "new school of philosophy and politics" a decade later in *Coelebs in Search of a Wife* (1809), More connects changing parent–child relations and revolutionary politics still more explicitly: "There certainly prevails a spirit of independence, a revolutionary spirit, a separation from the parent state. IT IS THE CHILDREN'S WORLD."[90] A similar rhetorical gesture – and the same underlying anxiety – operates in Richard Graves's satirical lyric, "Maternal Despotism, or, The Rights of Infants" (1801):

> Though now an infant, when I can,
> I'll rise and seize "The Rights of Man";
> Nor make my haughty nurse alone,
> But monarchs tremble on their throne;
> And boys and kings henceforth you'll see
> Enjoy complete equality.

Graves, like More, attempts to reduce the "rights" upheld by contemporary apologists for the French Revolution to absurdity, but the "Rights of Infants" also bears witness to the widespread association between reforms in childrearing and schooling and revolutionary changes in government: Graves's infant begins by protesting against swaddling – "Thus, head and foot, in swathes to bind, / 'Spite of the 'Rights of human kind'" – an implicit reference to Rousseau's *Emile*, intimately connected in the British mind of the 1790s with Rousseau's political theory and held by many to be equally subversive.[91]

James Chandler has argued persuasively that Wordsworth's critique of contemporary educational reforms in *The Prelude* is grounded in just such an association between the revisionary approach to childhood developed in *Emile* and the revolutionary social experiments taking place in France in the 1790s, a period during which the long-standing links between political and educational theory became particularly evident. Chandler goes so far as to suggest that *The Prelude*, in its transitional "five-book" form, "comprised a polemic against the programs for systematic education that were perceived in the 1790s, both by Burke in England and by leading legislators in France, to stem from the writings of Rousseau."[92] Although his argument is made unnecessarily sketchy by ignoring such British adaptations of Rousseau as Thomas Day's *Sandford and Merton* (1783–89) and the Edgeworths' *Practical Education* (1798), Chandler's unique attentiveness to the "politics of education" in the age of Rousseau has shed a great deal of light on the contemporaneity of *The Prelude*. It helps us to see, for example, that the Wordsworthian "child of nature" is less a Rousseauvian construct designed to set off the corruptions of modern civilization, than a "natural foil" to the rational child satirized in *The Prelude* and the "Immortality" ode. It is the "dwarf man," the "monster birth / Engendered by these too industrious times" (v.291–92), that (for Chandler) embodies the principles of *Emile* and the educational reforms of the Committee on Public Instruction under the Directorate.[93]

Wordsworth's attribution of power to "simple childhood" is conventionally read, when analyzed at all, as evincing his faith in the child's "creative imagination" or in its transcendental apprehension of the "life of things." (The latter reading, incidentally, begins with Coleridge in the *Biographia*, who rather harshly dismissed this motif in Wordsworth's poetry as a prime instance of "*mental* bombast" [*CBL* 2: 138].) But this is to defer the problem rather than to resolve it. We are not told *why* the imagination (unlike other faculties) would be strongest in infancy, or whether a transcendental approach to the child's psyche makes sense within the larger system of Wordsworth's poetic thought (as Coleridge held it did not).[94] And, more importantly, we do not learn why, however he conceived of the child's imagination or transcendent intuitions, Wordsworth should express the child's unique capacity in terms of *power*, a word which, in contemporary discourse, would ordinarily evoke social relations of domination, as Wordsworth's own usage (in the *Letter to the Bishop of Llandaff*) suggests: "The end of government can not be attained without authorising some members of the society to command, and, of course, without imposing on the rest the necessity of obedience. Here then is an inevitable inequality which may be denominated that of power" (*WP* 1: 42). Wordsworth's linking of childhood and power in *The Prelude* can most productively be understood, I would argue, as both a response and a reaction to the contemporary politicization of childhood typified by (but by no means limited to) the new educational programs developed in revolutionary France. When Wordsworth speaks in the "dwarf man" passage of "these too industrious times," his frame of reference can be taken to include the increasing mechanization of industrial production, the rationalization and "improvement" of agriculture, and the growing commercialization of social relations generally in addition to the contemporary political upheavals ranging from revolution on the Continent, to attempted reform and successful reaction in Britain. Behind Wordsworth's association of childhood, knowledge, and power lie the pervasive social transformations which Jameson characterizes as the "bourgeois cultural revolution" and Foucault as the "disciplining" of society. Wordsworth seems acutely aware that, especially in light of the widening scope and greater systematization of education, the school is beginning to displace the church and other traditional communal institutions as the principal site for regulating social relations of power and domination. With the rise of the school as primary locus for producing and maintaining the "inevitable inequality" seemingly inherent in modern societies comes a more crucial role for (as well as sharper definition of) childhood than ever before. Wordsworth's awareness of this shift and of its importance, registered in once startling phrases like "knowledge not purchased with the loss of power," attests to the "prophetic" force that Wordsworth sometimes claimed for his poetry and which any number of apostles have claimed for it since.

Given that this shift from the church to the school as the dominant ideological apparatus begins to take place noticeably within the period of Wordsworth's own childhood and youth, it is significant that, before *The Prelude*, one can find power associated with early childhood only in the "hell-fire" strain of religious writing for and about children. James Janeway's *A Token for Children* (1672), for example, gives a series of portraits of "eminent" child-saints, whose "Conversion, Holy and Exemplary Lives, and Joyful Deaths" are presented as models for fellow-children and parents alike. Janeway's preliminary address to parents and teachers makes clear that, if within the Calvinist tradition children were known for their wilfulness and innate depravity – "they are not too little to go to Hell" – this attitude was somewhat counter-balanced by the redeemed child's Christ-like innocence when placed among the elect: "they are not too little to serve their great Master, too little to go to Heaven; *For of such is the Kingdom of God.*"[95] Although Janeway's religious prodigies (who find Christ as early as age two or three) confine their evangelical efforts mainly to other children, particularly their more worldly siblings, their infantile wisdom empowers them occasionally to challenge adults as well – this at a time when absolute parental authority was largely unquestioned. Mary A., who finds Christ before she is quite five, remonstrates with her mother whenever she finds her too "solicitous about any worldly thing" (1: 32); Anne Lane, who "no sooner able to speak plain ... but she began to act as if she was sanctified from the very womb" (2: 14), converts her father while yet "a very Babe and suckling" (15) and hastens to berate her parents "if she saw anything in them that she judged would not be for the honour of Religion, or suitable to that condition which the providence of God had set them, in the world" (2: 17).[96] Servants are special targets for these child evangelists. The precocious John Harvy, who learns to read at two, teaches his mother's maids the catechism and follows them about their work "with some good question or other" (2: 71–72), and even tries to convert a hapless Turk cast away on a nearby seacoast.

Despite Janeway's emphasis on docility and catechism, his portraits of "eminent" infants gave eighteenth-century readers a rare instance of children empowered by divine authority to scold their elders and even argue theological points with the local cleric. Godwin wrote of his own childhood reading of Janeway, "Their premature eminence, suited to my own age and situation, strongly excited my emulation. I felt as if I were willing to die with them, if I could with equal success engage the admiration of my friends and mankind."[97] The widespread and continuing popularity of *A Token* (reprinted well into the nineteenth century) inspired a number of tracts featuring spiritually precocious children, especially among Evangelical and Methodist writers. Laqueur has connected the "anti-rationalism" of this tradition with the "high culture of Romanticism": "just as Blake in the *Songs of Innocence*, or Wordsworth in *Intimations of Immortality*, proclaimed a unique vision of the world available only to children, so one strand of evangelical thought regarded the child as especially capable of receiving God's grace and therefore able to teach and convert adults whose spiritual vision had become clouded."[98] Wordsworth's empowerment of childhood in *The Prelude* – "how awful is the might of souls, / And what they do within themselves while yet / The yoke of earth is new to them"

(III.178–80) – secularizes this tradition at a time when the institutional dissemination and regulation of power and knowledge is itself in the process of becoming a predominately secular enterprise. Wordsworth's frequent use of the language of election in *The Prelude* – " I was a chosen son " (III.82) – underscores the connection between his vision of childhood and that of the Janeway tradition.

But to suggest that the linking of power and childhood in *The Prelude* is a simple matter of secularization would be to lose much of the complexity both of Wordsworth's representation of childhood and of the actual changes in the distribution of social power taking place in his time. With revolutionary France providing the nearest model of a secularized and overtly ideological educational enterprise, there was widespread ambivalence in England regarding the severing of schools from their traditional religious affiliations and, more generally, towards plans for giving the mass of lower-class children any learning beyond catechism and Bible reading. A kindred and profound ambivalence emerges also in Wordsworth's poetry, particularly as he revises the portrayal of his own childhood in the period from 1798–99, when the *Lyrical Ballads* were published and the "Two-Part Prelude" composed, and 1804–5, when the "Immortality" ode was completed and *The Prelude* extended to its thirteen-book form.

In the "Two-Part Prelude," the child's power is rooted not in some transcendental source but in bodily energies, libidinal desires, much as in Blake's celebration of infancy in *Visions* as "fearless, lustful, happy." The child at play in the 1799 *Prelude* feels a "grandeur in the beatings of the heart" (1.141); his blood, at "thoughtless hours," seems "to flow / With its own pleasure" (II.226–27); he is impelled by an intense "eagerness of infantine desire" (II.24) which the adult, in retrospect, can only envy. Looking back to the heightened experience of childhood for strength – "Reproaches from my former years, whose power / May spur me on, in manhood now mature" (II.45–52) – the adult poet finds this power as much in "fits of vulgar joy" (1.413) – akin to the "glad animal movements" of childhood experience remembered in "Tintern Abbey" – as in the "joys of subtler origin" which, belonging to "those first-born affinities that fit / Our new existence to existing things" (1.380–81, 387–88), anticipate the transcendentalized child of the "Immortality" ode. In the 1805 *Prelude* Wordsworth, while retaining something of his earlier emphasis on the body, especially in the depictions of "boyish sports" in the first two books, begins to shift his focus to "earliest" infancy, gesturing towards a pre-natal rather than bodily source for the power of "our simple childhood":

> I guess not what this tells of being past,
> Nor what it augurs of the life to come,
> But so it is. (v.534–36)

Infancy becomes a "long probation" in which power is already diminished – "The time of trial ere we learn to live / In reconcilement with our stinted powers" (v.540–41). The greater power of a dubiously remembered past existence reduces even the growing child to a state of "meagre vassalage" (v.543), much as the "Mighty" child of the "Immortality" ode is ultimately subjected to the imperial light of "heaven-born" transcendence:

> Thou, over whom thy Immortality
> Broods like the Day, a Master o'er a Slave,
> A Presence which is not to be put by.

In the ode, the child's power is desecularized, and resacralized; childhood becomes, as in Janeway, a period of trial, and its special intensity belongs to ante-natal experience rather than to the lived experience of childhood.[99]

In displacing the "eagerness of infantine desire" with a transcendental infant "trailing clouds of glory," the "Immortality" ode harks back to seventeenth-century depictions of childhood like Vaughan's "Retreate" not only in its imagery of "angel infancy" but in its implicit politics as well. The "little Child" apostrophized in the ode becomes for Wordsworth, as for the seventeenth-century Anglican poet, a vehicle for evading cultural anxiety, figuring at once an idealized genetic past and a similarly innocent, similarly imaginary historical past, both in stark contrast to the "disorientation and cultural fragmentation" of the present.[100] Wordsworth's earlier poetry, in registering the new secular associations between power and childhood, takes up the emergent significance of childhood as a primary locus for establishing and adjusting relations of social domination; the terms in which it does so, however, mark as well a certain resistance to the increasing regulation of childhood, by attributing power directly to the child rather than simply locating the child (as do Graves and More) in a network of ominously shifting social and political valences. In the years 1804–5, Wordsworth asserts instead a nostalgic (or residual) image of childhood – the angelic infant of Vaughan and Traherne – in an implicit return to the officially dominant, but ever more fragile and defensive, alliance of church and state for managing childhood along traditional religious lines.

During these same years, Wordsworth in his letters and public statements begins to abandon his advocacy of a natural or "negative" education in favor of the Madras system of Andrew Bell, the chief virtue of which was its promise of retaining the Established Church's hegemony over primary education, in opposition to the secularizing tendency of its rival (but otherwise quite similar) Lancasterian system. The metonymic connection between power and childhood posed by Wordsworth is ultimately enmeshed in the complicated and thorny area of changing educational institutions and methods, debates on the virtues and implementation of a national educational system, and the struggle between proponents of religious and secular approaches to schooling. These debates, particularly as taken up by Wordsworth and his contemporaries in both literary and polemical works, are what we turn to next.

CHAPTER 2

School time

It is no accident that the authors of the eighteenth century's two most important educational treatises – Locke's *Some Thoughts Concerning Education* and Rousseau's *Emile* – were also the major political theorists of their age. The interrelation between political and educational discourses – the constitution of the state and the construction of its citizens – runs back at least to Plato's *Republic*, which Rousseau called "the most beautiful educational treatise ever written" (40). But during the modern era in Europe, with formal schooling less and less confined to an elite and with the informal spread of literacy among an increasingly mobile population, education and indeed childhood itself were politicized as never before.[1] The ongoing debate on the uses and dangers of literacy and popular (if not yet mass) education became, during the later eighteenth century, what Raymond Williams has called the "central" issue in the "history of our culture."[2] With the notion of childhood increasingly defined in relation to schooling, theoretical and literary representations of childhood, including Romantic idealizations of the child, came inevitably to reflect and participate in the politics of literacy. As the educational base broadened, educational theory and practice became at once more "progressive" and more coercive, deeply implicated in what Jameson has termed the "collective re-education of a whole population whose mentalities and habits were formed in the previous mode of production, feudalism or the *ancien régime.*"[3]

Jameson's formulation cannot be adapted here without some qualification. One must stress that the "bourgeois cultural revolution" was neither the headlong process that "revolution" implies, nor was it limited either in its direction or its effects to the middle classes. Indeed, it could be argued that, since Parliament did not pass an act for national education until 1870, the term as applied to

Romantic-era England is premature. However, there is no doubt that both literacy rates and educational provisions for the "labouring poor" grew significantly throughout the period 1780–1832, and that education for the middle and, to a lesser extent, the upper classes changed extensively in its aims and methods as well. If education and literacy were far from universal, we can nevertheless note a number of trends that suggest how widespread and rapid some of these changes were. Between 1753 and 1792, for example, the circulation of newspapers (based on stamp duty statistics) more than doubled, from 7,411,757 to 15,005,760; the first part of Paine's *Rights of Man* (1791) sold as many as 50,000 copies and the inexpensive second part (1792) from 200,000 to 500,000, while some two million of Hannah More's *Cheap Repository Tracts* (written in part to counteract Paine's influence among the lower classes) were distributed in the late 1790s; the British and Foreign Bible Society issued two and a half million copies of the Bible between 1804 and 1819.[4]

These publication figures help flesh out Lawrence Stone's contention (based mainly on studying changing percentages of those able to sign their own names in marriage registers) that literacy rates rose gradually but significantly during the period 1780 to 1840, from 40 to 60 percent among the "labouring poor," from 75 to 95 percent among the rural middle classes (yeomen and husbandmen), and from 85 to 95 percent among the urban middle classes (artisans and shopkeepers). A similar study by R. S. Schofield suggests that the percentage of women able to sign their names rose from 35 to 40 percent in 1750 to better than 50 percent in 1840, with a marked rise in the mid-1780s; the percentage of men overall rose (with some variation) from 60 percent in 1795 to about 75 percent by 1840, with noticeable improvement occurring in the decade 1805–15. Moreover, the number of those able to read at some level was probably significantly higher than the number of those able to sign.[5] While schooling became by no means universal during this period, it expanded significantly: by 1819, according to a Parliamentary survey, there were 4,167 "endowed" schools in England, including about 700 traditional grammar schools, with 165,433 pupils; 14,282 unendowed schools, from "dame schools" to Dissenting Academies, with 478,849 pupils; and for the children of the poor, 5,162 Sunday Schools with 452,817 pupils.[6] Taken in themselves, these figures are not overwhelming; assuming a considerable overlap between Sunday School and day school instruction, they account for somewhat more than half of the eligible population (aged seven to thirteen).[7] But school statistics ignore the fact that many (if not most) children continued to receive basic literary instruction outside of school, while they represent an immense growth in educational institutions that continued throughout the period: by 1833 the number attending unendowed schools had doubled to well over a million.[8]

The rise in literacy among the poor was significant enough to strike contemporary observers with emotions ranging from pleasing wonder to something like terror. The self-educated bookseller, James Lackington, delighted to remark in the 1790s that "all ranks and degrees now READ," while a writer in the *Anti-Jacobin Review* noted more nervously in 1800 that "Those taught to read, to write, to reason, we now see grasping with curiosity every pernicious treatise within reach."[9] The latter attitude became common enough for Peacock to satirize in *Nightmare Abbey* (1818), in which Mr. Flosky (based partly on Coleridge) asks "How can we be cheerful when we are surrounded by a *reading public*, that is growing too wise for its betters?"[10] But radical writers also voiced suspicion concerning the education and reading of the poor, such as Cobbett's remark concerning Sunday Schools that "Society is in a *queer* state when the rich think, that they must *educate* the poor in order to insure their *own safety*: for this, at bottom, is the great motive now at work in pushing on the education scheme," or his condemnation of "'*religious Tracts*,' which would, if they could, make the labourer content with half starvation."[11]

If the new schemes for educating the poor sometimes amounted to what E. P. Thompson calls "direct indoctrination," however, they should not be seen as evidence of a concerted bourgeois conspiracy.[12] The middle classes might constitute the economically and culturally ascendant group during the period, but they could do very little in the way of setting public policy without the collaboration of the wealthy and politically powerful, to whom their proposals for Sunday Schools and tract societies were usually addressed.[13] Nor were the lower classes as readily containable as their sponsors might have wished: literacy proved indeed instrumental in the growth of class consciousness among the "labouring poor," and the Sunday School itself became, as the nineteenth century progressed, a predominately democratic working class institution.[14] The upper classes were affected in their own way by the "bourgeois cultural revolution": calls for reform in the two universities, Oxford and Cambridge, became steadily harder to resist, and the "great" public schools became increasingly aristocratic, in an effort to "hold back the flood-waters of democracy."[15] But it was indeed the middle classes that were most responsible for advancing the new educational theories and methods which eventually transformed schooling into something like its present form; and it is in the educational treatises which the "middling sort" so eagerly took up that one can begin to explore the ambivalences of a new approach to schooling which can be characterized as both disciplinary and progressive.

Two memorable images of childhood (both well known) may help establish a sense of the social climate at once produced by and hospitable toward the revisionist approach to educational theory in the later eighteenth century. One features the aristocrat Charles James Fox (born in 1749), the leader of the Whig opposition in Parliament during the earlier Romantic period; the other is from the autobiography of the middle-class evangelical children's writer Mary Martha Sherwood (born in 1775), author of the immensely popular *History of the Fairchild Family*. Fox was brought up by his father, Lord Holland, on "a system of the most unlimited indulgence of every passion, whim or caprice"; one evening when as a child Charles was brought into a state dinner, he noticed a "large bowl of cream in the middle of the table" and expressed an eager desire to climb into it, which was duly indulged (despite Lady Holland's remonstrations).[16] Sherwood describes in her memoirs the quite different system adopted by her own parents: "It was the fashion then for children to wear iron collars round the neck, with a backboard strapped over the shoulders: to one of these I was subjected from my sixth to my thirteenth year. It was put on in the morning, and seldom taken off till late in the evening; and I generally did all my lessons standing in stocks, with this stiff collar round my neck."[17] Fox's childhood seems to represent the utmost imaginable liberality and permissiveness, while Sherwood's constitutes an equally extreme example of coercion and restraint; yet both reflect the experimental attitude towards child-rearing and education characteristic of the times. What is most striking in the two upbringings taken together is the absence of a traditional or "common sense" approach, and how willing both fathers were to adopt systems so far removed from the practices of their own parents. In the practice as well as theory of child-rearing and early education, time-honored experience yielded increasingly to experiment. As Rousseau states at the end of his *Memoir on the*

Education of the Prince of Wirtemberg's Infant Daughter: "In a new road it is quite useless to look for beaten paths" (*RMW*, 87).

EXPERIMENTAL EDUCATION

The educational writings of Locke and Rousseau often tend to be viewed as primarily liberal and reformist in character, particularly as they anticipate current educational practice in many ways. Indeed *Some Thoughts on Education* and *Emile* are important both for their advocacy of freeing the child from physical restraint and punishment, and for setting out educational agendas which emphasize reasoning and judgment over rote learning. Locke's *Some Thoughts* was a best-seller of sorts throughout the eighteenth century: by 1800 it had gone through twenty-five editions.[18] In it Locke develops a double argument for treating the child both more and less like an adult: the child's growing reasoning powers should be respected ("children are to be treated as rational creatures") while its tendencies toward "Folly, Playing, and *Childish Actions*" should be indulged (152, 156). Locke advocates a number of reforms which have since been widely adopted throughout the industrialized West: abolishing the "strait-lacing" of infants (123); using the "Rod" only sparingly so as not to have children's "*Spirits*... abased or *broken* much" (148); granting children a "free liberty... in their *Recreations*" (212), with learning itself made as much "a play and recreation" as possible (255); training pupils in the "improvement of their own Language" instead of devoting the bulk of their time to Greek and Latin (300).

Within this reformist agenda, however, Locke develops a program of discipline, surveillance, and the insinuation of a self-regulating moral conscience. A prime reason to spare the rod is that its effects are only temporary: "For the Time must come, when they will be past the Rod, and Correction; and then, if the Love of you make them not obedient and dutiful ... What Hold will you have upon them, to turn them to it?" (146). Coercion gives place to an affectionate relation between parent and child precisely because the latter is seen as a more effective and durable form of discipline. Similarly, while the development of the child's powers of reasoning and judgment are stressed throughout, this process must be supervised and adjusted with great care, so that discipline can become properly internalized as "Habits woven into the very Principles of his Nature" (146). Private tuition under the direction of the father and a carefully chosen tutor is recommended over public education because a schoolmaster cannot possibly keep "50. or 100. Scholars under his Eye" (168); his vigilance is spread out over too many pupils, and can cover only a few hours out of each day. The "Eye" occurs throughout *Some Thoughts* as a figure for the parent or tutor's unceasing surveillance: the privately educated "young Gentleman" remains at home "in his Father's sight" (170); lessons are learned not by rote but through "repeated Practice... under the Eye and Direction of the Tutor" (159); children should be guarded from the "infection" of servants, and kept instead whenever possible "in their Parent's or Governor's Sight" (164). Observation should remain at once relentless and unobtrusive: "But though you have your Eyes upon him, to watch what he does with the time which he has at his own disposal, yet you must not let him perceive, that you, or any body else do so." The parent must play the double role of friend and spymaster; a secret agent ("somebody you can trust") is to follow or accompany the child even on his apparent "Seasons of perfect Freedom" (234).

Rousseau's system of education as outlined in *Emile* is at once more radical in its ends and still more overtly authoritarian in its means. Locke's treatise, while implicitly setting forth a bourgeois agenda, is explicitly concerned with the education of a "young Gentleman"; as a result, its "scientific" approach to developing the child's understanding and its emphasis on utility remain uneasily juxtaposed with traditional humanist notions of conduct, manners, and gentlemanly "accomplishments."[19] For Rousseau, on the contrary, "Everything is only folly and contradiction in human institutions" (81). In place of raising up a pupil who can conform to them, his speculative educational program would produce a new sort of activist citizen: "Rather than conform to the existing state, he wants his pupils to reconstruct it."[20] In *Emile*, the child is formed so as to become his own master, yet his habits and moral and intellectual bent are carefully instilled under the eye of a tutor even more vigilant and seemingly omnipresent than that of Locke.

Early in *Emile* Rousseau sets forth an impassioned and deservedly famous defense of the child's freedom from overt constraint and from cramming with early instruction: "Love childhood; promote its games, its pleasures, its amiable instinct... Why do you want to deprive these little innocents of the enjoyment of a time so short which escapes them and of a good so precious which they do not know how to abuse?" (79). At the same time, so crucial is childhood for the

formation of lasting habits and tendencies that even parents cannot
be entrusted with it. Although Rousseau declares that the "true
preceptor is the father" (48), he makes Emile a conceptual
"orphan," leaving his care entirely in the hands of his enlightened
tutor: "It makes no difference whether he has his father and mother.
Charged with their duties, I inherit all their rights. He ought to honor
his parents, but he ought to obey only me. That is my first, or, rather,
my sole condition" (52–53).

Emile is given the freedom to roam about his rural surroundings,
but his environment is carefully arranged in advance by the tutor,
who takes the additional precaution of befriending the household
retainers and neighboring villagers and enlisting them in his
educational schemes: "You will not be the child's master if you are
not the master of all that surrounds him" (95). Seemingly chance
incidents and meetings are carefully orchestrated by the tutor, who
(as in Locke) must be "wholly involved with the child – observing
him, spying on him without letup and without appearing to do so,"
keeping a step ahead through his knowledge of child development:
"sensing ahead of time all his sentiments and forestalling those he
ought not to have" (189). Again as in Locke, perfect mastery of the
child is sought not through overt discipline but through engaging
Emile's affections: "Spare nothing to become his confidant. It is only
by this title that you will truly be his master" (325). As Rousseau
writes elsewhere, children, "like lions," must be "tamed by
kindness": "The essential thing is to get them to love you. After that,
you may make them walk on red-hot irons" (*RMW*, 91). By playing
on the child's affections, by giving him the appearance but not the
reality of freedom, discipline can become all but perfectly internalized: "Let him always believe he is the master, and let it always be
you who are. There is no subjection so perfect as that which keeps the
appearance of freedom. Thus the will itself is made captive" (120).

The stratagems by which a rational education is carried out in
Emile put off many British educational theorists otherwise amenable
to Rousseau's suggestions; Godwin, for example, describes Rousseau's system as one of "incessant hypocrisy and lying" (*GE*, 120) in
his own educational treatise, *The Enquirer* (1797). Thomas Day,
however, includes a number of such tricks and deceptions in his
popular *Sandford and Merton* (1783–89), a combined educational
treatise and children's book which helped disseminate Rousseau's
educational theories among the British reading public.[21] Day's

Rousseauvian premise is that a sturdy yeoman's son like Harry Sandford will prove the intellectual, moral, and physical superior of a spoiled young gentleman like Tommy Merton, who must learn such truths as "the rich do nothing and produce nothing, and the poor every thing that is truly useful."[22] Tommy's first object lesson, however, is a work of cunning worthy of *Emile*, which reveals the tutor's coerciveness at the outset. Intending to teach Tommy the value of laboring for one's sustenance, Mr. Barlow and Harry ostentatiously devour a dish of cherries which the indolent Tommy is forbidden; an act which must grate against Harry's nature, for he is generally guileless and has been praised earlier for his unchildlike readiness in sharing his food (37, 4). The lesson seems more calculated to undermine Harry's openness and generosity than to remedy Tommy's laziness.

If the educational systems of both Locke and Rousseau harbor a pervasive "authoritarianism" at odds with the progressive tenor of many of their calls to reform, it is precisely this emphasis on relentless "direction and control" that most often inspires the critiques of "rational" education among the first-generation Romantics.[23] Lamb could be describing Emile's tutor or Day's Mr. Barlow in satirizing the almost mechanical vigilance of the "new schoolmaster," who must look out for edifying occasions not only in set lessons ("which he may charge in the bill") but "at school intervals, as he walks the streets, or saunters through the green fields." "He must seize every occasion – the season of the year – the time of the day – a passing cloud – a rainbow – a waggon of hay – a regiment of soldiers going by – to inculcate something useful ... The Universe – that Great Book, as it has been called – is to him, indeed, to all intents and purposes, a book, out of which he is doomed to read tedious homilies to distasting schoolboys" (2: 52–53). Wordsworth's satire on the rationally educated child in Book v of *The Prelude* cuts more deeply:

> Nay, if a thought of purer birth should rise
> To carry him towards a better clime,
> Some busy helper still is on the watch
> To drive him back, and pound him like a stray
> Within the pinfold of his own conceit.   (358–62)

But while such writers as Lamb, Wordsworth, Coleridge, and Southey deplore the methods of the new approach to education – particularly the dual emphasis on relentless edification and constant, often hidden, surveillance – their own writings on childhood are complicit with some of its more subtly disciplinary aspects. The ambivalences of the Romantic response to rationalist educational theory may become more evident in an examination of a more contemporary work, the Edgeworths' *Practical Education*, particularly in relation to Book v of *The Prelude*.

It is more than probable and less than certain that Wordsworth's critique of the new pedagogy was catalyzed by the appearance of the Edgeworths' treatise in 1798. The first chapter, on toys, was outlined by Thomas Beddoes, a mutual friend of Coleridge and the Edgeworths. Coleridge read the work shortly after its publication and recommended it (though with telling ambivalence) to his wife Sara in a letter he wrote while travelling with William and Dorothy Wordsworth in Germany:

> I pray you, my Love! read Edgeworth's Essay on Education – read it heart & soul – & if you approve of the mode, teach Hartley his Letters ... J. Wedgewood informed me that the Edgeworths were most miserable when Children, & yet the Father, *in his book*, is ever vapouring about their *Happiness*! – ! – However there are very good things in the work – & some nonsense! (*CCL* 1: 418)

In any case, *Practical Education* can be taken as exemplary of the progressive educational thought of its day; it assimilates many of the suggestions not only of Locke and Rousseau, but of the liberal-radical group of educational writers inspired by them as well – Day (a close friend of the Edgeworths), Godwin, Joseph Priestley, and Catherine Macaulay, among others. Like all of these writers, the Edgeworths begin from associationist premises which render early experience and education all important: "The temper acquires habits much earlier than is usually apprehended; the first impressions which infants receive, and the first habits which they learn from their nurses, influence the temper and disposition long after the slight causes which produced them are forgotten."[24] These basic premises, shared by most educational writers of the period, are not far removed from those informing the model of psychic development in Wordsworth's *Prelude*, but they could be developed (as David Erdman has pointed out) along remarkably different directions, as different as a lonely crag in the Lake district and a proto-Skinnerian cubicle.[25]

An initial look at the Edgeworths' opening chapter on "Toys" might make the differences between their approach to childhood and Wordsworth's seem minimal. The chapter begins not with stating abstract principles but with a represented dialogue between mother and child ("Why don't you play with your playthings, my dear?"), and goes on to praise the child for smashing his expensive toys (including a lacquered, detailed replica of a fashionable carriage) out of a "love of knowledge and spirit of activity": "as long as a child has sense and courage to destroy his toys, there is no great harm done" (1: 1–3). Here, it seems, is a member of the "race of real children" that Wordsworth evokes in *The Prelude*, not the cautious, cogitative "dwarf man" he lambastes. The differences soon begin to emerge, however, for the child's deconstructive energies are to be harnessed to the pursuit of experimental knowledge. "We were once present at the dissection of a wooden cuckoo, which was attended with extreme pleasure by a large family of children; it was not one of the children who broke the precious toy, but it was the father who took it to pieces" (20–21). Even in play, this rational family murders to dissect. Soon the reader is given details for the furnishings of a "rational toy shop" (29), and in place of the love of nature leading to the love of mankind, the Edgeworths outline a "love of play" leading to the "love of science" (24). Building on Locke and on Priestley's recommendation that "a taste for experimental philosophy be acquired pretty early,"[26] the Edgeworths pack their work with records of and recipes for practical experiments that children can perform, including an ingenious series early on by which an enterprising pupil breaks down the mystery of the rainbow into its component principles (70–71). We soon encounter the "telescopes, and crucibles, and maps" (330) of Wordsworth's "monster birth":

> He sifts, he weighs,
> Takes nothing upon trust. His teachers stare,
> The country people pray for God's good grace,
> And tremble at his deep experiments. (338–40)

Although critical of Rousseau's system of "contrivance and deceit" in *Emile* (1: 242), the Edgeworths propose an environment for the developing child which is no less scrupulously arranged and controlled. Their sparely furnished nursery, with its "pieces of wood of various shapes and sizes," which the children "may build up and pull down" (1: 14), is a humanized analogue to the "nursery of genius" which Thomas Wedgwood suggested that Godwin and Beddoes work out in theory, proposing Coleridge and Wordsworth as "superintendents of the practical part": "Should not the nursery, then, have plain grey walls with one or two vivid objects for sight & touch ... Let hard bodies be hung about them so as continually to irritate their palms as they happen to come in contact ... the child must never go out of doors or leave his own apartment."[27] In place of this abstract enclosure, the Edgeworths suggest a sanitized, carefully superintended version of the upper-class home, with every detail carefully arranged: "In the hands of a judicious instructor no means are too small to be useful" (45).

The controlled nature of the child's surroundings becomes particularly evident in the Edgeworth's chapter on servants, which had to be considerably revised after the first edition to accommodate those middle-class parents who could not easily afford the time or expense needed to effect the "total separation" between children and lower domestics they originally insisted upon.[28] "If children," they wrote at first, "pass one hour in a day with servants, it will be in vain to attempt their education"; even the half an hour spent being dressed by servants should be carefully superintended by "a mother, or a governess" (1798, 126). This advice was cut in the second edition of 1801 but the call to maternal vigilance remained: "Where the mistress of a family is obliged to mix with her servants, the evil which we point out may be prevented by her presence" (126). The Edgeworths' dour attitude towards servants could be traced back to Locke's humanist concern with the "Folly and Perverseness of Servants," who frighten children to "keep them in subjection" (154, 242), or even to Rousseau's more radical distancing of Emile "far from the rabble of valets – who are, after their masters, the lowest of men" (95). But their anxiety regarding servants and their emphasis on parental surveillance evokes the more disciplinary aspects of Locke's discourse, with its recurring imagery of the paternal or tutorial gaze. In *Practical Education* the family is at once nest and fortress, enclosed and guarded by parental watchfulness, a vision shared by such roughly contemporaneous works as Lord Kames's *Loose Hints Upon Education* (1781) – "keep children as much as possible under the eye of their parents" – and Catherine Macaulay's *Letters on Education* (1790): "Never suffer your offspring to be from under the eye of the tutor, or the governess; never let them converse with servants."[29] In these works servants represent the threat of incursions from an unregulated outside world, the controlled environment's messily human corner which, as it cannot be rearranged, must be cordoned off.

Another mark of the relentless character of parental surveillance in
Practical Education, and one that contrasts particularly starkly with
The Prelude, is the Edgeworths' attitude toward vacations and
recreational time. As does Locke, the Edgeworths prefer "domestic"
education to boarding school because the public schoolmaster cannot
sufficiently attend to the "formation of the moral character" of his
many pupils, and recommend private tuition guided by the father or
tutor as the most effective system (147, 168–69). But as children are
not ordinarily sent to school until the age of eight or nine, their
temper and their habits can be sufficiently molded at home in the
early years that public education might be hazarded. Parents in the
"middle ranks of life" are particularly advised to consider the "large
public schools" as a way of effacing their (male) children's
"rusticity" and "provincial" dialects, faults which local schools will
only confirm (148–49). In this case, parents should carefully manage
school holidays, which must not be given over to the "dissipation and
idleness" (159) that Wordsworth celebrates to such powerful effect in
The Prelude ("we lived / A round of tumult"; "We ran a boisterous
race" [II.8–9, 48]). Parents should take advantage of their companionate relations with their sons to reinforce their "school
acquisitions," which can be "drawn out in conversation" at home
(160). Again Book v of *The Prelude* leaps to mind:

> they who have the art
> To manage books, and things, and make them work
> Gently on infant minds as does the sun
> Upon a flower – the tutors of our youth,
> The guides, the wardens of our faculties
> And stewards of our labour, watchful men
> And skilful in the usury of time,
> Sages, who in their prescience would controul
> All accidents, and to the very road
> Which they have fashioned would confine us down
> Like engines. (373–83)

Wordsworth's lines bring out the mechanical character of the
Edgeworths' conception of psychic development, and their desire
to produce a child whose further progress can be predicted
with something approaching mathematical rigor. It is significant
that Richard Edgeworth's colleagues in the Birmingham "Lunar
Society," something between a club for liberal eccentrics and an
early industrial think-tank, included not only scientific speculators

like Priestley, Beddoes, and Erasmus Darwin, but also a group of pioneer industrialists including Josiah Wedgwood, Matthew Boulton, and James Watt, inventor of the modern steam engine.[30]

A final area of contrast between the rationalist tradition as codified in *Practical Education* and the Romantic reaction as set forth in *The Prelude* concerns the relation of things, words, and ideas in early education. Here again the Edgeworths draw on both Locke and Rousseau. Locke emphasizes the value of concrete example over abstract language throughout *Some Thoughts*, proposing that children be reasoned with "always *in very few and plain Words*": "The *Reasons* that move them must be *obvious*, and level to their Thoughts, and such as may (if I may so say) be felt, and touched" (181). Rousseau's suspicion of abstract language runs still deeper. He finds Locke's "great maxim" of reasoning with children "stupid" because it assumes a linguistic competence beyond their pre-rational understandings, and advocates instead a direct intercourse with an object world unmediated as far as possible by words: "Arrange it so that as long as he is struck only by objects of sense, all his ideas stop at sensations; arrange it so that on all sides he perceive around him only the physical world" (89). The Edgeworths stake out a middle ground. Although Rousseau rightly declaims against a mere "knowledge of words," words "which really represent ideas" are essential for developing the understanding; a proper care of children's physical and verbal environment (including rigorous supervision of their reading and conversation) will insure that their "simple ideas be accurate," and "their language will then be as accurate as their ideas are distinct" (1: 80–81, 92).

The Edgeworths' principle that words be rigorously paired with "uniformly distinct ideas" (2: 412) leads them into several of their more controversial positions, including their distrust of imaginative literature (most infamously, fairy tales, but also poetry) and their disinclination to discuss "metaphysical" matters with children, including (although this is carefully left implicit) religion. Their recommendation that children be guarded from the sublime, with its connotations of "obscurity and terror" (2: 284), is typical. Burke may have argued in his *Enquiry* on the sublime that a clear idea is "another name for a little idea," but little ideas were precisely what the Edgeworths found appropriate for little minds.[31] One thinks again of Wordsworth's rationalist "dwarf":

He is fenced round, nay armed, for ought we know
In panoply complete; and fear itself,
Natural or supernatural alike,
Unless it leap upon him in a dream,
Touches him not.   (314-18)

Whereas Burke values the obscurity and confusion of imaginative literature for its power to disrupt self-consciousness – the "mind is hurried out of itself" – the Edgeworth's child is never to lose its sense of self-possession, never to suspend its carefully inculcated habits of rational thought for a moment of pleasing (or frightful) wonder.[32] In contrast, the child who reads romances and fairy tales in *The Prelude* "at least doth reap / One precious gain – that he forgets himself" (368-69). Criticizing the new children's literature in "Miss Edgeworth's style" in a lecture of 1808, Coleridge similarly endorses chapbooks and fairy tales, "for at least they make the child forget himself" (*CLL* 1: 107-8). One of the most compelling features of the Romantic critique of rationalist education is this defense of ruptures in the child's ordinary sense of self. Rather than seeking to infiltrate the child's mind, Wordsworth and Coleridge propose that the child be left by itself to confront gaps and limitations in its habitual thinking process; the child's psychic growth will be stimulated by its own dissatisfaction with, or puzzled sense of something missing in, its conscious identity, rather than remorselessly guided through a graded and normatized developmental schema.

The Edgeworths' requirement that words represent age-appropriate, distinct and, wherever possible, concrete ideas leads them also to oppose the common practice of having children memorize and recite poetry. Most poetry is too replete with "vague expressions, and of exaggerated description," to be properly integrated into early education; scrupulous parents or tutors can scarcely afford the time needed to gloss so many unfamiliar words and explain such apparently arbitrary associations (1: 467). Their detailed examples of just how difficult and painstaking the proper explication of a few well-known passages can become, later expanded into two pamphlets illustrating the proper method of teaching poetry, curiously anticipate the "close analysis" methods taught in college classrooms today.[33] Defending the child's study of the classics in *The Round Table* (1817), Hazlitt questioned such attempts "to set up a distinction between the education *of words* and the education *of things*," citing Wordsworth in his support and turning associationist psychology back on the rationalist tradition. "We owe many of our more amiable delusions, and some of our superiority, to the grossness of mere physical existence, to the strength of our associations with words. Language, if it throws a veil over our ideas, adds a softness and a refinement to them, like that which the atmosphere gives to naked objects."[34] For Wordsworth himself, it is in the very indistinctness and unfamiliarity of poetic language that its most salutary effect on the child's mind resides:

> Visionary power
> Attends upon the motions of the winds
> Embodied in the mystery of words;
> There darkness makes abode, and all the host
> Of shadowy things do work their changes there
> As in a mansion like their proper home.
> Even forms and substances are circumfused
> By that transparent veil with light divine,
> And through the turnings intricate of verse,
> Present themselves as objects recognised
> In flashes, and with a glory scarce their own.   (619–29)

The passage is deliberately, and polemically, difficult. Indeed, much of the strength of Wordsworth's critique of rationalist education inheres in its being developed in verse rather than in prose; the "turnings intricate" of his argument ("My drift hath scarcely I fear been obvious" [290–91]) are all the more persuasive insofar as they resist the sort of reductive analysis the Edgeworths call for.

In the "Advertisement" to the 1801 edition of their treatise, the Edgeworths responded to two principal charges made against the first edition: one concerning their treatment of the servant question, and the other their alleged "design of laying down a system of Education, founded upon morality exclusive of Religion" (1 : xii). It was in response to the latter charge that they changed the title to *Essays on Practical Education*, hoping to forestall further objections that their "system" was meant to be complete in itself: "Children usually learn the Religion of their parents ... Can any thing material be added to what has already been published upon this subject?" (1 : xi).[35] Earlier educational theorists in the liberal tradition had followed Locke's recommendation that the child be taught "a Love and Reverence" of the "Supreme Being" without further explanation, lest "his Head be either fill'd with false, or perplexed with unintelligible Notions" (241). Priestley, noting that "there is hardly anything that a child does not believe before he is acquainted with the proper grounds on which his belief ought to rest," countenanced early Bible reading, and Macaulay argued that although children's minds resist "abstracted ideas," religious associations should be built up through simple prayers and hymns: "Let us give much of habit and principle, but very little of doctrine."[36] Given this climate, the Edgeworths' failure to even mention the question of religious education, coupled with their distaste for abstract or vague ideas in general and "metaphysical questions" in particular (1:92), left them open to the charge of irreligion, and may have helped fuel the Romantic defense of fairy tales and other forms of "imaginative" writing. In 1808 Wordsworth wrote to Francis Wrangham asserting that children should be given "chiefly religious" books to read, but in conjunction with the "indirect nourishment and discipline" of works like *Paradise Lost* and *Robinson Crusoe*: "if the books be all good, they would mutually assist each other" (*WLM* 1:249). The questions of children's imaginative reading and their religious training were more closely related in the early nineteenth-century than is generally remarked. As Geoffrey Summerfield points out, the "most coherent and radical" Romantic-era critique of the rationalist approach to children's reading, outside of Wordsworth's unpublished *The Prelude*, could be found in the preface to William Scolfield's *Bible Stories* (1804): "These modern improvers have left out of their system that most essential branch of human nature the imagination."[37] In their opposition to a critical rationalism too reminiscent of the French Enlightenment (and, by association, the French Revolution), Christian moralists and Romantic poets could find common ground.

To leave, however, the rationalist approach to education and that of the Romantic poets opposed simply as a choice of values between "reason" and "imagination" would be to remain uncritically within the terms set by the Romantics themselves. Despite their significant differences over the nature of the child's early environment, its relative freedom, and its reading of imaginative texts, there is a good deal that the two groups held in common. It is misleading, for example, to oppose the key Romantic distinction between "tuition" and "education" to the rationalist tradition as exemplified by *Practical Education*.[38] Most rationalist theorists would readily assent to Coleridge's remark that education consists not so much in mere instruction as in "*educing* the faculties, and forming the habits" (*CLS*,

40). They were, as a result, in the forefront of opposing "cramming" and rote learning – this made a good part of their critique of early instruction in classical languages. Rather than attempt to teach his pupil "all that is knowable,' Locke advised the aspiring tutor instead "to put him in the right way of knowing and improving himself, when he has a mind to it" (307). Rousseau declares that at fifteen, Emile "has little knowledge, but what he has is truly his own... Emile has a mind that is universal not by its learning but by its faculty to acquire learning; a mind that is open, intelligent, ready for anything" (207). The Edgeworths too were no Gradgrinds; they oppose the piling up of "facts" independent of their use and condemn rote learning as diminishing the child's "powers both of reasoning and of invention" (1 : 444, 2 : 22). In this the writers in the rationalist tradition and their Romantic critics are joined in a new consensus on education, one stressing not traditional skills, "accomplishments," and factual knowledge but rather, intellectual preparedness and the ability to quickly assimilate new information and learn new tasks, more responsive (as Rousseau argues in *Emile*) to increasing social "mobility" and generational change (42). With its emphasis on "habit," "association," and internalized discipline, this new mode of thinking (perhaps one should say, this new set of conditions for educational thought) reflects a shift in educational practice from the instilling of formal precepts to the imposition of "living rules," making part of a more general cultural shift which saw social power take less coercive and more consensual, individualistic forms.[39]

Wordsworth also agrees with rationalist theorists regarding the primacy of the object world in early education; he begins Book v of *The Prelude* by describing himself as one whose "mind hath looked / Upon the speaking face of earth and heaven, / As her prime teacher" (11–13).[40] It is rather the rationalist emphasis on the child's comprehension of its lessons and their constant integration into a progressive developmental scheme that most exercises Wordsworth and Coleridge in their critiques of contemporary educational theory. The modern child "takes nothing upon trust" (338):

> All things are put to question: he must live
> Knowing that he grows wiser every day,
> Or else not live at all, and seeing too
> Each little drop of wisdom as it falls
> Into the dimpling cistern of his heart.   (341–45)

There is no room for faith in such an education, no place for the supernatural. "It is true," Coleridge concedes in his letter on children's reading of fairy tales, "that the mind *may* become credulous & prone to superstition by the former method – but are not the Experimentalists credulous even to madness in believing any absurdity, rather than believe the grandest truths, if they have not the testimony of their own senses in their favor?" Cramming might represent a common abuse of education, but it was not perceived as dangerous. Insisting that children learn to reason exclusively from sense experience, however, threatened to upset the structure of authority on which education was traditionally based. Coleridge interjected a revealing aside into his 1808 lecture on education: "And yet what nobler judgement is there than that a child should listen with faith, the principle of all good things, to his father or preceptor?" (*CLL* 1: 106).

The term "Experimentalists" in Coleridge's letter to Poole is one the Edgeworths applied to themselves; it refers not to the plethora of guided experiments in their educational scheme but rather to the principle of child study on which it is based. Richard Edgeworth credited his wife Honora with first putting this principle into effect: "She thought if proper Experiments were made upon different Children from their earliest years, if these Experiments were registered, if the answers & questions of different children at different ages, Capacities and Educations were preserved and compared ... the success or failure of different Experiments might lead to some certainty upon a Subject of such extensive importance."[41] The Edgeworths put this scheme into practice in their own family; the results are recorded throughout *Practical Education* and account for its novelistic side, the "Conversations and Anecdotes of Children" which dot the text and overflow into an appendix (2: 437–71). The scheme as outlined by Richard Edgeworth demonstrates how greater attention to the individual child's development could support greater expectations of normalization, for once childhood is divided into discrete stages, a maturational pattern can be abstracted against which each child's progress is graphed.[42] This was noted (and objected to) early on by John Wilson Croker in the *Quarterly Review*, in what might be taken as a "Romantic" critique of the Edgeworths. "The varieties of the human mind and temper are innate and indefinite – they admit of no uniform law – all bodies gravitate, and gravitate by the same rules, but the qualities of the mind and temper

are nearly as numerous as the individuals of our species, and we
hardly can imagine a wilder scheme than the attempt to educate one
child by a system of observations made upon another."[43]

But the *literary* portrayal of an individualized, developing, psychologized self, supported by revealing anecdotes or epiphanic moments,
became a key aspect of the Romantic project. In works like *The
Prelude* – which Wordsworth calls a "history" of "intellectual power
from stage to stage / Advancing" (XI.42–3) – or the novels of Jane
Austen, writers of the period produced representative models for
psychic development founded on (in Clifford Siskin's phrase) "the
Romantic redefinition of the self as a mind that grows."[44] What was
objected to in educational theory was valorized in fictional practice,
as can be seen in the *Quarterly Review*'s praise for Maria Edgeworth's
departure from the "formed and finished" characterizations of the
eighteenth-century novel: "Miss Edgeworth loves to represent it
[character] even in its first elements, to trace the progress of its
formation, to mark the effect produced upon it by influences, which,
however real, have no connection whatever with the striking or the
romantic."[45] Although the reviewer goes out of his way to attack the
Edgeworths' secularism, he does not draw the connection between
their innovative child study and Edgeworth's novelistic portrayal of
a developing self, a connection which has led more recent critics to
relate the realistic fictional techniques pioneered by Edgeworth to
the period's "deep interest in the early growth of consciousness" as
exemplified by the Wedgwood circle – Barbauld, Priestley, Beddoes,
Day, Richard Edgeworth and, by extension, Coleridge and Wordsworth.[46]

Finally, it would be a mistake to view the theorists in the rationalist
tradition as soulless reasoners with no appreciation for what
Wordsworth in *The Prelude* calls "the discipline of love" (2.251). In
the educational writings of both Locke and Rousseau, the establishment of affectionate relations between the parent or tutor and
the child grounds the workings of a consensual rather than coercive
disciplinary system. Lord Kames based his own educational treatise,
Loose Hints Upon Education (1782), on the principle that the "culture
of the heart during childhood, is the chief branch of education" (6).
From this premise, Kames deduces a number of propositions which
are in turn adapted by the Edgeworths: that parents, especially
mothers, are essential to early education as natural adepts in the "art
of cultivating the heart" (8); that "a habit of submission to self-

authority" grows "naturally' from the "habit of submission to parental authority" (51–52); that, since "man is a creature from whom everything may be obtained by love, nothing by fear," punishment is less effective in imposing habits of obedience than affection (149–50); and that the associationist emphasis on early experience applies to feelings as well as to sensations and ideas. "First feelings are critical; by them the character is often decided" (231). The Edgeworths in turn include chapters not only "On Attention" and "On Obedience" but also "On Temper" and "On Sympathy and Sensibility"; for education to be effective and lasting, "the understanding and the *heart*" must be "cultivated together" (360). Coleridge is in fact rehearsing a truism of the rationalist tradition in beginning his 1808 lecture on education by stating that "little is taught or communicated by contest or dispute, but everything by sympathy and love" (1: 106). The principle that instruction and discipline must be rooted in the child's affections is shared by nearly every Romantic-era writer on education, including so conservative a moralist as Hannah More: "I have never tried the system of terror, because I have found that kindness produces a better end by better means" (*MLC* 2: 82).

The main grounds of contention between rationalists like the Edgeworths and their Romantic critics might be encapsulated, not in the terms "emotion" or "freedom" or even "imagination," but in the notion of "faith." The child requires faith in authority and in the existence of things beyond its comprehension, and the wise educator will trust in a providential design by which the object world is *already* arranged to best facilitate the "educing" of the child's faculties:

> when will they be taught
> That in the unreasoning progress of the world
> A wiser spirit is at work for us,
> A better eye than theirs, most prodigal
> Of blessings, and most studious of our good,
> Even in what seem our most unfruitful hours? (383–88)

It may be troubling to note that Wordsworth here retains Locke's disciplinary "eye," only shifting from a tutorial to a transcendental gaze; but even so his appeal to a "wiser" nature, underwriting the child's freedom from direction and constraint in playing, reading, and passing the bulk of its time, constitutes the most potentially radical element of Wordsworth's critique of contemporary educational thought. Yet the Utopian force of Wordsworth's idealized vision of childhood is significantly undercut by this same reliance on an uncritical or mystified notion of nature and natural experience. Both the promise and the limitations of Wordsworth's "child of Nature" (*Prelude* x.753) may become more clear as we turn from reformist theory aimed at the middle- or upper-class child, to more widespread changes in educational practice which affected children of all classes, but most particularly the "children of the poor." These changes were significant enough to have inspired two of Wordsworth's best known lyrics, "We Are Seven" and "Anecdote for Fathers," as well as Blake's song of Innocence, "The Lamb."

WORDSWORTH, BLAKE, AND CATECHISTIC METHOD

As formal education broadened in the later eighteenth and early nineteenth centuries to address more middle- and lower-class children, its methods and function shifted significantly. The Renaissance emphasis on dialectical argument, which Stephen Greenblatt has persuasively related to the rise of a small entrepreneurial class requiring intellectual (and ideological) flexibility, gave place in educational theory to an emphasis on the formation of proper intellectual and moral "habits," the development of independent reasoning, and the internalization of authority.[47] In actual practice, however, dialectic tended to yield to the mechanical production of set answers, obedient behavior within the educational setting, and (for the lower classes) passive literacy. Catechism displaced dialectic as an exemplary disciplinary mode, as the school (like the prison and the factory) became a site for functions of regulating and observation.[48] In the relative absence of the kinds of reform called for by Locke and other theorists in the rationalist tradition (which were long confined mainly to "domestic" applications), this shift affected even schooling for the elite. Grammar schools of the period, for example, emphasized "formal training by drill and repetition"; the better private academies relied on catechistic primers such as *Mangnall's Questions* (1800); and the oral examinations at Oxford University had degenerated into a routinized exchange of set questions and answers.[49] But the catechistic style of instruction played a more fundamental role in the re-education of the lower classes for an increasingly industrialized society, and found its way as well into the new children's literature designed for a largely middle-class readership.

We tend now to think of literacy in terms of democratization or even "empowerment," but, as Lawrence Stone has pointed out, this is a fairly recent conception.[50] Lévi-Strauss argues on the contrary that literacy as a social institution has generally "favoured the exploitation of human beings rather than their enlightenment," as yet another tool for maintaining hierarchical relations of power.[51] Stone qualifies Lévi-Strauss, however, in stressing the possibility that, if not strictly controlled, education may indeed move beyond its traditional function of "reinforcing class distinctions" to help facilitate the enfranchisement of the newly educated group.[52] The ruling interests felt threatened by just such a possibility in the late eighteenth century, during what Altick has called the literacy "crisis" of the 1790s in England, when a large group of new, informally educated middle- and lower-class readers established a vogue for the radical pamphlet literature exemplified by Paine's *Rights of Man*.[53] Many in positions of power advocated the curtailment of popular education, like the Bishop of Rochester who excoriated Charity Schools and Sunday Schools alike as "schools of Jacobinical rebellion."[54] Others, however, saw a remedy for popular discontent in these same institutions.

For the latter, the catechistic method came to be viewed as a prime means of containing the new literacy. Sarah Trimmer, for example, laments in the first number of *The Guardian of Education* (1802) the passing of an education dominated by (if not limited to) catechism, and identifies a "*conspiracy against* CHRISTIANITY *and all* SOCIAL ORDER," led by Rousseau and his English adapters, "endeavoring to infect the minds of the rising generation, through the medium of *Books of Education* and *Children's Books*." Her answer is both to police the distribution of reading matter for "the *lower orders of people*, and for *children*" and to reassert the role of catechism in education, a project she had begun in the mid 1780s with her involvement in the Sunday School movement.[55] Trimmer's *Sunday-School Catechist* (1788) makes her ideological purpose quite clear: The upper-class "visitor" is to begin her first lecture with the warning, "It is no uncommon thing to see persons who can read setting themselves up *above the station in life it hath pleased* GOD *to place them* ... I hope this will not be the case with any of *you*." An early question in the following catechism reinforces this message: "Should people who can read grow *proud*, and be above going to *cart* and to *plough* and to *common services?*"[56] If literacy gave the "lower orders" some measure of power, Trimmer's "catechetical method" was designed to teach them not to use it.

Trimmer's approach is representative of a broad pedagogical tendency which went well beyond the Sunday School movement. The Charity Schools supported by the Society for Promoting Christian Knowledge were founded as "Catecheticall schools," and remained largely limited to teaching Bible-reading and rehearsing the catechism throughout the eighteenth century.[57] The Charity School movement, like the Sunday School movement, held a mandate to buttress class distinctions rather than facilitate social mobility: An 1801 *Account* of the SPCK happily noted that as early as 1712 the Society had declared, "That however these Children are disposed of, it will be very necessary before-hand to teach them that great Lesson of *true Humility* ... lest the Advantages they receive from a pious Education, should incline them to put too great a Value upon themselves," and had mandated that the Masters "instruct them very carefully in the Duties of Servants, and Submission to Superiors."[58] Robert Raikes, the guiding spirit of the Sunday School movement, described his purpose as taking "little heathens" off the street to be instructed in "reading, and in the Church catechism"; writing, however, was often banned from the Sunday School curriculum.[59] Early in the nineteenth century the new monitorial schools combined the catechistic method with the organization and discipline of the factory; Sydney Smith in the *Edinburgh Review* defended the Lancasterian system (which Trimmer had attacked on account of Lancaster's nonconformity) with the argument that "a child is not very likely to put any questions at all to a catechizing master, and still less likely to lead him into subtle and profound disquisition."[60]

The catechistic method was also adapted in books for children, both secular and religious, and in grammar books addressed to the "ignorant"; nor was the distinction between religious and secular always clear, as "even the simplest hornbook alphabets and primers" usually included a catechism; the primer's catechistic elements would be retained in educational writings for children "well into the nineteenth century."[61] Barbauld's *Hymns in Prose for Children* (1781), a fairly progressive example of the newly emergent literature for small children, features such passages as:

But who is the shepherd's shepherd? who taketh care for him? who guideth him in the path he should go? and if he wander, who shall bring him back?

God is the shepherd's shepherd. He is the Shepherd over all; he taketh care for all; the whole world is his fold.[62]

The secularization of the catechistic method made part of a widespread program of popular re-education which held a double mandate. It was aimed primarily at supplanting traditional "plebeian forms of entertainment and belief" with a mechanical, regularized, and directly supervised program of moral "improvement," while simultaneously countering the incipient "intellectual vernacular" form of political discourse inaugurated by Paine with indoctrination in political and religious orthodoxy.[63] These two objectives could be pursued by means of a single method. To adapt Bakhtin's terms, catechistic instruction aimed at replacing the "joyful relativity" of an oral carnival-folkloric culture with "that one-sided and gloomy official seriousness ... which seeks to absolutize a given condition of existence or a given social order," and imposing a monologic, hegemonizing master discourse as the price of literacy.[64] Ironically, the strength of the catechistic method lay precisely in its mimicry of an authentic dialogic process; as Isaac Watts wrote earlier in the eighteenth century in his *Catechisms* (1730): "This way of teaching hath something familiar and delightful in it, because it looks more like Conversation and Dialogue."[65]

For Rousseau, who in *Emile* imagined a pedagogy founded on establishing the child's autonomous judgment before all else, catechism represented the antithesis to genuine education: "If I had to depict sorry stupidity, I would depict a pedant teaching the catechism to children. If I wanted to make a child go mad, I would oblige him to explain what he says in saying his catechism" (257). Rousseau's critique of catechism was taken up in England by Romantic poets who were equally suspicious of rote learning, and who (much more than Rousseau) tended to resist the politicization of childhood. Byron, for example, depicts Don Juan "shut ... up to learn his catechism alone" with Donna Inez, herself a walking abstract of "Mrs. Trimmer's books on education" (Canto 1, stanzas 16, 52). Shelley, in his bitter lines "To the Lord Chancellor," curses Lord Eldon (who had deprived him of custody of two of his children) "By those unpractised accents of young speech" which will be trained to orthodoxy "under a hireling's care":

> By the false cant, which on their innocent lips,
>   Must hang like poison on an opening bloom,
> By the dark creeds which cover with eclipse
>   Their pathway from the cradle to the tomb.[66]

Blake and Wordsworth, writing contemporaneously with Trimmer, more directly engage the irony behind Watts' praise of catechism: the attempt to impose a monologic discourse through a travesty of dialogue. But their poetic distortions of catechism in "Anecdote for Fathers," "We Are Seven," and "The Lamb" differ significantly, in ways which bring out the limitations as well as the critical force of an idealized representation of childhood.

"We Are Seven" was originally published immediately following "Anecdote for Fathers" in *Lyrical Ballads* (1798).[67] Both lyrics portray an adult doggedly, earnestly attempting to catechize a child, and the child resisting, in the first poem through lying, in the second through an obstinate "will" equal to if not greater than the adult's. "Anecdote for Fathers, Shewing How the Art of Lying May Be Taught," underscores the automatic quality of the adult's catechistic approach to the child, in a period when methods of social discipline enter increasingly into familial relations.[68] In a moment of "idleness," without quite knowing the answer himself, the adult insists on grilling his child on an apparently meaningless issue:

> "My little boy, which like you more,"
> I said and took him by the arm –
> "Our home by Kilve's delightful shore,
> "Or here at Liswyn farm?"

When the child guesses and dutifully produces the desired answer (Kilve), the father, still questioning his own regret for Kilve, presses the child "five times" (in later versions softened to "three times") for a reason. The father has unintentionally but, given their radically unequal discursive relation, inevitably trapped the child in a painfully ambiguous rhetorical position. His demand for a reason – "'Why? Edward, tell me why?'" – implies a cognitive response, but the coercive form of the question – "I said and took him by the arm" – seems to demand instead the performative response of catechism: rehearsing the answer which the adult expects. Although Edward can initially read his father's cues well enough to answer "Kilve," at this point there is no answer for him to intuit (let alone repeat), as the father has none in mind.

Edward's dilemma in "Anecdote for Fathers" can be taken as an extreme version of that of Mrs. Trimmer's catechist. For Trimmer, who inherits the rationalist suspicion of "rote" learning, it is crucial that the child's responses in catechism do not take the form of set, mechanical answers, but manifest a degree of thoughtfulness and understanding: "When I question you, do not answer *hastily* and *carelessly* 'YES,' or 'NO,' as you are apt to do, but *think* before you speak."[69] While the child's answers should seem to reflect thinking, they must simultaneously fit within the narrow parameters of official doctrine and demonstrate as well, in their tone and physical performance, the child's docility. The adult "Visitor" prefaces her injunction to the child to "think" by underscoring her monopoly on a "truth" guaranteed by revelation: "We shall tell you nothing but the truth, as revealed in the Scriptures, for we have your happiness sincerely at heart; therefore I beg of you to give your earnest attention."[70] The child's rhetorical stance is ultimately an untenable one, which can be met only by hypocritically reproducing the instructor's "truth" with the *appearance* of thinking. As Rousseau had argued in *Emile*, the catechistic relation can only produce hypocrisy or lying: "All the answers of the catechism are misconceived ... In the mouths of children these answers are really lies, since the children expound what they do not understand and affirm what they are not in a position to believe" (378).[71] Edward, in Wordsworth's "Anecdote for Fathers," can similarly be released from a speech situation which "looks more like Conversation and Dialogue" but is decidedly coercive and one-sided only by lying, as he catches sight of a weather-vane and improvises, "At Kilve there was no weather-cock, / And that's the reason why." As a representation of the catechistic relation of adult and child, "Anecdote for Fathers" is doubly ironic. Not only does a monologic discourse disguised as dialogue teach primarily the "art of lying," but in this case it is the adult rather than the child who is portrayed as mindlessly repeating himself, in his effort to produce a "truth" which does not exist.

Although "Anecdote for Fathers" and "We Are Seven" have been grouped together as "dialogic" works, Wordsworth's "Anecdote for Fathers" is more attuned to the contemporary politics of education in its demonstration of how formally dialogical exchanges between adults and children inexorably take on the monologic, disciplinary character of catechism.[72] Much the same process occurs throughout the adult-child "dialogues" frequently represented in children's books of the period. In Ellenor Fenn's *Cobwebs to Catch Flies; Or, Dialogues in Short Sentences, Adapted to Children From the Age of Three to Eight Years* (1783), for example, what purports to be a conversational exchange between "Mr Steady" and a boy playing hooky from school, abruptly grinds to a halt when the child thinks to ask why he should go to school at all: "Good children ask for no reasons – a wise child knows that his parents can best judge what is proper; and unless they choose to explain the reasons of their orders, he trusts that they have a good one; and he obeys without inquiry." "Little Steady," who acts in this dialogue as a kind of chorus to his father, chimes in with the superfluous remark, "I will not say Why, again, when I am told what to do; but I will always do as I am bid directly. – Pray, sir, tell us the story of Miss Wilful."[73] The main point of this dialogue has less to do with attending or not attending school (as though that could really be in question) as with establishing the child's and adult's unequal positions in the "dialogue" itself, teaching the child that its place is to obey, echo, and request further instruction rather than to question. Bakhtin's description of the degeneration of the Socratic dialogue from a discursive method for apprehending truth as "born *between people* ... in the process of their dialogic interaction" to yet another vehicle for "*official* monologism, which pretends to possess *a ready-made truth*" provides a historical parallel to the fate of the pedagogical dialogue in the later eighteenth century. "When the genre of the Socratic dialogue entered the service of the established, dogmatic worldviews of various philosophical schools and religious doctrines, it lost all connection with a carnival sense of the world and was transformed into a simple form for expounding already found, ready-made irrefutable truth; ultimately, it degenerated completely into a question-and-answer form for training neophytes (catechism)."[74]

In "We Are Seven" catechism is addressed more directly and in terms of a more familiar moral purpose, although here too the catechistic method is exposed as a fundamentally closed travesty of discursive exchange. Wordsworth began the poem with the last stanza, which stresses the adult's repetitive questioning (here also he has rephrased his question five times) and the child's countervailing will:[75]

> "But they are dead; those two are dead!
> "Their spirits are in heaven!"
> 'Twas throwing words away; for still

> The little Maid would have her will,
> And said, "Nay, we are seven!"

Although the child has duly received some measure of religious instruction ("Till God released her of her pain"), she fails to give her questioner the doctrinal response his question regarding death anticipates. Her refusal to distinguish between dead and living siblings strikes the adult as paganistic; his repeated questions attempt to elicit a more orthodox Christian recognition of mortality. To his insistence that "two are in the church-yard laid" she counters with what Bakhtin would term a typically "ambivalent" carnival image,[76] emphasizing yard over church – "Their graves are green, they may be seen" – and portraying her siblings as both dead *and* living:

> "My stockings there I often knit,
> "My 'kerchief there I hem;
> "And there upon the ground I sit –
> "I sit and sing to them."

These lyrics have been read by Mary Jacobus as confronting the adult's "misplaced didacticism" with the child's "inspired obstinacy at odds with adult preconceptions" and similarly by Heather Glen as the "irritating insistence of the rationalizing adult ... defeated by the child's refusal to accept his categories."[77] But in a more subtle manner adult preconceptions and categories are affirmed in these poems. Rather than more fundamentally addressing the question of authority in the relation of adult and child these lyrics instead displace that authority, ultimately reversing the roles of adult and child while maintaining the hierarchical structure of their relation:

> O dearest, dearest boy! my heart
> For better lore would seldom yearn,
> Could I but teach the hundredth part
> Of what from thee I learn.

Similarly in "We Are Seven" the child is mother to the man, her "utter inability to admit" the notion of death validating the poet's own childhood intimations of immortality.[78] Significantly, in these anti-didactic lyrics as in the "Immortality" ode, the child's authority rests on an idealized notion of childhood. Both the boy (who is five) and the girl (who is eight) are presented as naturals, primitives: Edward "graceful in his rustic dress" and the "little cottage girl" "wildly clad" with a "rustic, woodland air." These noble savages are naturally resistant to the adult attempts to form (or deform) them; their mentalities are rooted in a transcendentalized nature rather than being culturally produced. Wordsworth protests against the ideological construction of childhood by envisioning an ideology-proof, organic sensibility, a move which tends to leave the child unsocialized and frozen in a state of eternal innocence. Wordsworth's idealized representations of childhood tend to close in upon themselves, rather than opening into a critique of the child's dilemma at a time when a "natural" education such as the one Wordsworth himself claimed to have enjoyed was less and less available, and the increasing politicization of childhood invited a more complex response than an imagined transcendence, however powerfully expressed.

Blake's "The Lamb" also portrays a scene of thwarted instruction, but in this case it is the child who plays catechist, with a lamb as his unresponsive though docile pupil. It begins innocently enough:

> Little lamb who made thee
> Dost thou know who made thee
> Gave thee life & bid thee feed,
> By the stream & o'er the mead;
> Gave thee clothing of delight,
> Softest clothing wooly bright;
> Gave thee such a tender voice,
> Making all the vales rejoice!
> Little Lamb who made thee
> Dost thou know who made thee.

The song has been read by critics like E. D. Hirsch and Zachary Leader as a "joyous and mild" portrayal of religious instruction, the child mimicking the "gentle" and "affecting sincerity and simplicity" of his parents; other readers (like Harold Bloom) have emphasized instead its "profound" emphasis on creation and the parallels with Blake's "Tyger" in *Songs of Experience*.[79] What has gone unnoticed, however, is that the question concerning creation and the representation of catechism are crucially related.

The child's catechism typically began with just this question. John Cotton's *Milk for Babes* (1646), for example, begins: "*What hath God done for you?*" with the answer, "God hath made me, He keepeth me, and He can save me."[80] Isaac Watts begins his popular *Young Child's Catechism* (1730), recommended by Trimmer, "Can you tell me, Child, who made you?"[81] In Cotton and Watts, this line of questioning is not particularly "mild" or "gentle"; rather, it leads the child to a confession of moral depravity and of having deserved "the Wrath and Curse of the Almighty God who made me."[82] In Trimmer's *The Teacher's Assistant: Consisting of Lectures in the Catechetical Form* (2nd edn. 1800), the same question begins the first (secularized) catechism: "Who made all things that are? [*Ans.* GOD THE FATHER ALMIGHTY]"; and soon is extended to the lamb's "clothing of delight": "Where does wool come from? [*Ans.* Sheep.] Who made the sheep, and caused so much wool to grow upon them? [*Ans.* God.]" Trimmer leads the "Children of the Poor" towards a confession of social abasement which secularizes the Calvinism of Cotton and Watts:

Have working people time to make themselves quite clean on working days? [*Ans.* No.] Is not a day of rest very comfortable after six working days? [*Ans.* Yes.] What should you return to God for appointing the Sabbath day? [*Ans.* Thanks.] How should you spend it? [*Ans.* In learning your duty.][83]

That the "duty" of the poor begins in a passive acceptance of the class system, ordained by the same God that created them, is clear in Trimmer's *Sunday School Catechist*: "Who made all mankind? Who made some rich and some poor?"; "We should consider that it is the wish of GOD that there should be different ranks among mankind, *high* and *low*, *rich* and *poor*, and that all the good things in this world are dealt out by His providence as He sees best for His creatures" (207, 202). For Trimmer, the Sunday Schools and Charity Schools with their secularized catechisms were institutions not only for fighting apostasy but equally for controlling the lower classes from *within* literacy, from within a reconstructed subjectivity. Encouraging "The Ladies" to act as visitors for their local schools in her aptly entitled *The Oeconomy of Charity* (1787), she begins: "God only knows what the lower orders of people will become if Sunday-schools are suffered to drop"; and once more moves to ground class distinctions in an appeal to God's creation: "In appointing different ranks among mankind, our all-wise and beneficent CREATOR undoubtedly intended the good of the whole." Young ladies in particular would be well-advised, Trimmer argued, to support an institution that would lead to better servants and a more docile underclass: "The rising generation of poor is instructed by us, that our children may be better served than their parents have been … and travel the road free from the painful apprehension of being molested by the daring highwayman."[84]

It is against this background that Blake's portrayal of catechism in "The Lamb" takes on a new significance. Its child speaker can be seen as an ordinarily passive victim of the catechistic method who here attempts to reassert some measure of power through playfully, even parodically catechizing a figure still more naive and helpless than himself. That the lamb cannot possibly answer is both pathetic (as a comment on the child's own passive position) and comic (as a reflection of the child's retaliatory urge to satirize his masters). While the child's repetitive questioning brings out the mechanistic quality of catechism addressed by Wordsworth in "Anecdote for Fathers," Blake goes beyond Wordsworth's hint at a compensatory creative response (Edward's "lying") by having the child articulate a counter-statement that directly addresses the "one-sided and gloomy official seriousness" of the adult world. His answer to his own question is subversive rather than doctrinal, implicitly confronting the authority claimed by his pastors, masters, and parents with an image of the creator not as the Almighty Father but as himself childlike:

> He is called by thy name,
> For he calls himself a Lamb:
> He is meek & he is mild,
> He became a little child:
> I a child & thou a lamb,
> We are called by his name.

In the catechisms of Blake's time this would hardly have been an acceptable answer, for all its meek and mild tone. Rather than confessing his own abasement and accepting his place, however humble, in God's benevolent scheme (a lamb to the slaughter?), the child has creatively supplemented the catechism with his knowledge of the Christmas story and the Psalms to subvert the structure of authority on which the catechism is based. In naming his creator as God the Child rather than God the Father, the speaker of "The Lamb" disrupts at its source the traditional associative chain of authority which leads, as in Trimmer's *Sunday-School Catechist*, from "The Duty of Loving God" to "Honouring the King" ("to love him as the father of his country, and to submit peaceably to the laws of the land, not to suffer ourselves to be persuaded to join in any riots or cabals") and finally to "Submitting to Teachers, Spiritual Pastors, and Masters" ("It is part of your duty to your neighbor to order yourselves lowly and reverently to all your betters ... your parents, governors, teachers, spiritual pastors and masters ... All rich and great people are also to be considered your betters on this account" [137, 147]). In revising the catechism, the child both frees himself from a coercive discourse and simultaneously throws the terms of that discourse into question.

Although Blake's *Songs of Innocence* has been read against the background of contemporary education theory and the tradition of religious children's poetry represented by Watts and Barbauld, it is usually considered not as a children's book proper but rather as a "children's book for adults."[85] Those who, on the other hand, do read the *Songs* as a children's text tend to deny its satirical force, sometimes quite harshly: "To read the book thus [as satire] and classify it as children's literature removes Blake himself from decency of manners ... Blake did not address *children* in veiled and sardonic satire."[86] Either the child reader is dismissed in order, as Bloom puts it, to rescue the "perilous ambiguity" of a text like "The Lamb" from "namby-pamby," or an "innocent" child reader is posited along with a text uncomplicated by ambiguity, as in Martha Winburn England's assertion that Blake "meant every namby-pamby word."[87] Recent work in the narrative theory of children's literature suggests, however, the option of approaching Blake's *Songs* as an "ambivalent text," addressed not to one but "two ... implied readers," child *and* adult.[88] "The Lamb" offers the adult reader a satirical portrayal of the catechistic method rather along the lines of "We Are Seven," and Glen in fact reads it as such: "His answer to the lamb is not a series of dogmatic assertions; rather, it innocently emphasizes the extraneousness of such assertions, their distance from the reality they purport to define."[89] Along with such related lyrics as "The Chimney Sweeper" and "The Little Black Boy," which also feature a child resisting indoctrination through imitatively instructing a still more naive figure ("little Tom Dacre," the "little English boy"), "The Lamb" offers its child reader a model for evading adult coercion by means of parody.

For Bakhtin, parody subverts monologic discourse by representing it and implicating an antithetical voice within that representation: "The second voice, once having made its home in the other's discourse, clashes hostilely with its primordial host and forces him to serve directly opposing aims."[90] In Blake's *Songs of Innocence*, "official" adult discourse is regularly invaded by the child's comically distorting voice, giving the child reader an opportunity for less than innocent laughter at the disciplinary strategies of the adult world. Although the humor may elude us now, a child who had been catechized weekly if not daily beginning with "Child, who made you?" could hardly fail to be amused by a child speaker addressing this very adult question to a lamb, and then inventing an answer that would shock most eighteenth-century parents and Sunday School "visitors." Not only are two readers, child and adult, implied in the *Songs*, but Blake's child-narrators speak in a double register, at once innocent and experienced, putting the subject positions of child and adult into a dialogical relation that critically undermines the catechistic relation prescribed by Trimmer and not so much subverted as inverted by Wordsworth.

David Erdman has argued that in reading the *Songs of Innocence* as satire we miss Blake's "larger" social purpose: "To construct one of the foundations of an imaginatively organized and truly happy prosperity."[91] The Utopian element of Blake's songs, however, need not be sought in their pastoral imagery and evocations. In his reading of Blake's "A Poison Tree," John Brenkman argues on the contrary that the utopian "does not... reside in the semantic storehouse of images of happiness and freedom," but rather in "a poetic speaking which manifests the struggle between the social conditions of the poet's speech and the latent possibilities of speech."[92] My reading here of *The Songs of Innocence* follows Brenkman in locating its social purpose not in its pastoral elements, but by looking instead towards what he terms the "*promise* of uncoerced mutual understanding and mutual recognition" in an "ideal speech situation" not yet realizable.[93] Reading "The Lamb" against contemporary educational practice also enables us to see that Blake's implicit critique of the catechistic method addresses "social conditions of... speech" much more directly and more locally than Brenkman's account suggests, and helps us trace in greater detail the differences between Blake's attitudes toward childhood and education and those of a more idealizing, nostalgic poet like Wordsworth, or of a conservative and unabashedly didactic writer like Trimmer. In several of the *Songs*, moreover, the devices of parody and satire not only facilitate social criticism, but become, in the mouths of Blake's child speakers, means in themselves for pursuing a less coercive and one-sided social discourse this side of utopia. Blake's songs for and of children most directly engage the politics of the age less in imaging forth a visionary or Utopian alternative than when they parody, dismantle, and subvert a hegemonic discourse designed to impart a knowledge always purchased with the loss of power.

If Blake responded more radically to the increasingly disciplinary methods for "educating" the lower classes than did the Lake poets, the same can be said for his response to such institutions for socializing the "children of the poor" as the Charity Schools. The limitations of the Lake group's response to institutional education becomes particularly clear in an examination of their support – for a time quite unqualified – for the "monitorial" or "Madras" system of Andrew Bell. But before turning to the thorny "monitorial" controversy, it will be necessary to examine somewhat more systematically the existing provisions for education when Bell's system arrived on the scene, as well as the quite different ideological motivations behind the various arguments for a national educational system articulated during the Romantic period.

TOWARDS NATIONAL EDUCATION

An account of eighteenth-century English schools might best begin with a list of negatives, so different was the educational prospect from what is now taken for granted. England not only had no national system of education until 1870, but there was for a long time nothing resembling a system whatsoever. Rather, schooling was carried out through a patchwork of dissimilar institutions, endowed (or "public") and private-venture, some offering advanced and thorough educations and some providing little beyond basic reading (if that). Entrance requirements for what would now be called "secondary" schools (there was as yet no clear distinction between primary and secondary education) were minimal, usually depending more on the parents' connections and finances than on the student's proficiency. Examinations were infrequent and casual when given at all, and graduation requirements were similarly nominal. Classes (or "forms") were not yet keyed to age-groups – pupils in a higher form might range from twelve to eighteen – and in the private schools, there were often no separate classes at all; students of all ages and levels of proficiency would share the same room and books, depending on individual tuition from the master, usher, or a sympathetic classmate to move forward in their studies. This general lack of standardization was often aggravated by the indiscriminate shuttling of children among a number of different institutions, as the fortunes of their families (and of the schools) rose and fell. Southey, for example, began at a dame school, attended three different private schools in and around Bristol, and spent a year studying privately with a former usher before entering Westminster at the age of fourteen, from which he was eventually expelled for publishing a diatribe against flogging in a student periodical entitled (ironically enough) *The Flagellant*. Nevertheless, he had little trouble in entering college at Oxford.[94]

It is important to remember that much education went on outside of schools altogether. Private education at home with a tutor, perhaps followed by a tour of Europe, provided the wealthy with an alternative to grammar school; if children were too much underfoot at home, they could be sent to board and study with a neighboring clergyman. Domestic education superintended by the parents themselves was, as we have seen, enjoined on the middle classes by Priestley, Macaulay, Kames, the Edgeworths, and others. It is hard to know how many parents of the "middling" sort followed this advice, but on the basis of anecdotal evidence it seems to have been common for girls and for the first years of boys' educations as well. In her survey of eighteenth and early nineteenth-century diaries, Linda Pollack notes that many parents, "particularly mothers," taught their children the three R's at home. M. M. Sherwood gives a typically engaging example in her autobiography: "I remember my mother teaching me to read with my brother, in a book where was a picture of a white horse feeding by star-light." Later her mother studied Latin in order to teach it to both children, as Sherwood's father lacked his wife's "regularity."[95] Mary Shelley's early instruction is still more memorable than Sherwood's: her father, Godwin, first taught her to read and spell by tracing the letters on the gravestone of her mother, Mary Wollstonecraft.[96] For the "labouring poor," rudimentary home instruction was often all that was available. Thomas Holcroft, for example, was taught to read by his father, an itinerant cobbler; his formal education (aside from some training in psalmody) amounted to three months of daily arithmetic lessons with a journeyman breechmaker "between stable hours," and three days at a Newmarket school kept by a master who took Holcroft in gratis, but shamed him by appearing drunk in the streets each afternoon.[97]

Private schools ranged from "dame" schools charging a weekly fee of fourpence or less to the great Dissenting Academies, where non-conformists could receive scientific and technical training more advanced than that available at Oxford or Cambridge. Dame schools were informal establishments, often kept by widows, which took children off their parents' hands and (sometimes) provided basic instruction in reading, writing, and perhaps needle-work or other skills. Teaching might alternate with other employment, as with Shenstone's "School-Mistress," who "eyes her fairy throng, and turns her wheel around," or Crabbe's dame in *The Borough* who "awes some thirty infants as she knits."[98] "Another matron of superior kind" kept what Crabbe calls a "*preparatory*" school, "The step first made to colleges and halls." This higher class of dame school is probably the sort attended by Southey, Coleridge, and Wordsworth, who warmly remembered his school at Penrith: "The old dame did not affect to make theologians and logicians; but she taught to read; and she practised the memory" (*WLY* 1: 686).[99] Dame schools and other humble institutions – evening classes taught by artisans, day schools for laborers' children, obscure village schools – were frequently attacked for the low quality of their instruction and the dubious qualifications of the teachers, who were widely seen as having failed in other callings, and as themselves being poorly educated. Although many historians of education have accepted this dim view of the private-venture schools, some recent studies have defended them as community-based institutions, more responsive to parents' needs and views than systems imposed from above, "one of those indigenous working-class institutions against which mass schooling was defined and which it was intended to replace."[100] Contemporary criticisms of the private schools, however, must often have been justified; Samuel Bamford, for example, went through a "free school" conducted by the parish clerk, a Sunday School, a local private school, and still another school kept by a Methodist preacher before he finally "learned to read well" at the Manchester Free Grammar School.[101]

There were also more ambitious private schools, arranged in an unofficial hierarchy according to parents' status; to quote again from *The Borough*: "To every class we have a school assign'd, / Rules for all ranks and food for every mind." Crabbe begins his survey of private boarding-schools with academies for "young ladies" – virtually the only educational provision for girls, outside of home study with a governess or parent – where they could learn penmanship, French (and sometimes Italian), drawing, music, and "curious works" with the needle. Even the best girls' schools were limited to such "accomplishments" along with a sound education in English. Boys' schools covered a considerable range in terms of quality. At the lowest end were obscure academies of the sort later encountered in Victorian novels, where an unwanted child could be deposited for a modest fee and where he would find little in the way of education or such basic comforts as edible food. The better private academies, however, led the way in instituting some of the reforms (such as greater emphasis on the vernacular) called for by Locke and other rationalists, not being limited by charter (as were the endowed schools) to instruction in the classical languages. A few schools, like the Rousseauvian David Williams's Laurence Academy and the Hazelwood School, founded by Priestley's friend Thomas Wright Hill, were quite progressive.[102] Nearly all (unlike the bulk of the grammar schools) gave instruction in English, and the better schools offered arithmetic, drawing, history and geography, navigation, and modern languages. They were widely seen as offering the best preparation for a career in business or manufacturing.

Some of the best private academies were those which catered to the sons of non-conformists, who were effectively shut out both from the grammar schools and the two universities. The dissenting academies prepared their students for commercial life and for the professions – law, medicine, and the non-conformist ministry. They taught modern as well as classical languages, and some were at the cutting edge of scientific education as well. During his years at Warrington Academy, Priestley – the model Dissenting intellectual – gave classes in chemistry, anatomy, history, geography, languages, and *belles lettres*.[103] As a group, however, the dissenting academies declined towards the end of the eighteenth century, some undone by sectarianism, some by the widespread sympathy on the part of masters and students with the French Revolution. The famous New College at Hackney, for example, which Hazlitt attended, fell apart in the mid 1790s after a "Republican supper" honoring Thomas Paine led to inquiries and arrests.[104]

The grammar schools were institutions endowed (mostly in the sixteenth and seventeenth centuries) for the explicit purpose of providing instruction in the classical languages. But as the market value of a strictly classical education dropped, many of the grammar schools lost pupils and became virtual sinecures: the Lord Chief Justice Kenyon described them in 1795 as "empty walls without scholars and everything neglected except the receipt of the salaries and emoluments. "[105] Some endowed schools, however, changed with the times, adding instruction in English and arithmetic, like Hawkeshead Grammar School, which provided Wordsworth with an excellent background in mathematics as well as in the classics.[106] Most grammar schools had been endowed as local institutions with a mandate for educating poor students, but (partly in order to remain solvent) had become increasingly middle- and upper-class institutions by the later eighteenth century. Christ's Hospital, chartered in 1552 to care for and educate orphans and neglected children of the poor, had followed just this path, as Leigh Hunt charged in *The Examiner* (1808): "That hundreds of unfortunate objects have applied in vain for admission is sufficiently notorious; and that many persons with abundant means of educating and providing for their children and relatives have obtained their admission into the school is equally well known" (*LW* 1: 436.)[107] Lamb's "Recollections of Christ's Hospital," originally published in the *Gentleman's Magazine* (1813), was intended to counteract such criticism. "For the Christ's Hospital boy feels," Lamb wrote, "that he is no Charity-boy; he feels it in the antiquity and regality of the foundation to which he belongs ... he feels it ... in that measure of classical attainments ... which it would be worse than folly to put it in the reach of the labouring classes to acquire" (*LW* 1: 140).

This process of bourgeoisification was particularly evident in the so-called "public" or "great" schools – Eton, Winchester, Harrow, Rugby, Westminster, Shrewsbury, and a few others – which had stagnated along with other grammar schools earlier in the eighteenth century but had become fashionable, elitist institutions by its end. Before this period, Eton and Winchester were alone among this group in taking boarders exclusively; but they were now joined by schools which, like Harrow and Rugby, lost their local character and took fewer and fewer boys "on the foundation." Some were forced to fight their charters in court: the governors of Harrow argued in the Rolls Court in 1810 that "the school is a school for classical learning; that however wise the intentions of the founder might have been, the school is not now adapted generally for persons of low condition, but better suited to those of a higher class."[108]

The "public schools" retained their traditional emphasis on classics and, as virtual "schoolboy republics" outside of class hours, became associated with moral depravity and brutality in the popular mind.[109] In boarding schools generally, Mary Wollstonecraft wrote in 1792, "the relaxation of the junior boys is mischief; and of the senior, vice"; moreover, the "great schools" foster a "system of tyranny and abject slavery" through such institutions as "fagging," regulated by the boys themselves (*VRW*, 159). Southey, in his autobiography, similarly warns against the "pollution" characteristic of boarding schools generally, and singles out the public schools as "nurseries" of "tyranny and brutality."[110] This brutality owed less to the masters than to the students; although there were a few noted sadists like Boyer at Christ's Hospital, who knocked out one of Leigh Hunt's teeth "with the back of a Homer," and John Keate, Shelley's headmaster at Eton, who once flogged eighty boys on a single day, corporal punishment had fallen off in general over the course of the eighteenth century, as Samuel Johnson dourly noted: "There is now less flogging in our great schools than formerly, but then less is learned there; so that what the boys get at one end, they lose at the other."[111] But the boys themselves were often quite remorseless, as Edgeworth remembered from his own grammar school days. "A full grown boy, just ready for college, makes it his favorite amusement, to harass the minds, and torment the bodies, of his younger schoolfellows."[112] At times the boys would go so far as to rise against the masters. In 1793 the Winchester boys held the college buildings for two days and "set up the red cap of liberty," and at Rugby in 1797 they mined the door of the headmaster's study with gunpowder. Similar mutinies took place at Eton, Westminster, and Harrow, and in a few cases the militia was called in.[113] Defenders of the public school tended to extol what De Quincey calls the "bracing intercourse of a great English classical school" (*DQW* 1: 151), the give and take among peers best suited to give the boy a sense of himself and of the world. Many writers came to advocate day schools as a compromise between parental control and the "jostlings of equality" experienced at a public school (*VRW*, 173), combining (as Sydney Smith wrote in 1810) "the emulation which results from the society of other boys, together with the affectionate vigilance which he must experience in the house of his parents."[114]

The nearest approach to a school system in eighteenth-century England could be found in the network of Charity Schools and Sunday Schools sponsored by the SPCK. Both the Charity Schools and the Sunday Schools were exemplary "catechistic" institutions, founded less with a regard to the instruction of their lower-class pupils than to their religious orthodoxy and social complacence. Nevertheless, both institutions became subject to polemical attacks, some motivated by fears of burgeoning lower-class literacy, some by more subtle anxieties. The most famous (or infamous) such attack was the "Essay on Charity and Charity-Schools," which Bernard Mandeville added to the "second" (1723) edition of *The Fable of the Bees*. Mandeville summarizes the popular argument for Charity Schools (made by writers like Addison and Steele) as follows: "Children that are taught the Principles of Religion and can read the Word of God, have a greater Opportunity to improve in Virtue and good Morality, and must certainly be more civiliz'd than others, that are suffer'd to run at random and have no body to look after them."[115] The view of literacy as a means to inculcating religion and morality, and the project of "civilizing" the English poor (through a sort of internalized colonialism), are conceptions which would continue to dominate discourse on popular education through to the end of the century. But Mandeville is left unimpressed by these considerations. He argues instead, first, that "Ignorance is, to a Proverb, counted to be the Mother of Devotion"; second, that children follow the "Precept and Example of Parents," not schoolmasters (anticipating the importance that rationalist and Romantic writers alike would come to place on the child's extra-scholastic environment); and finally (and most importantly) that early training consists more in the inculcation of habits than in the dissemination of precepts. "Charity-schools, and every thing else that promotes Idleness, and keeps the Poor from working, are more Accessary to the Growth of Villany, than the want of Reading and Writing, or even the grossest Ignorance and Stupidity" (1: 268–71). Child labor is both a cheaper and a more appropriate and effective education for the children of laborers than any form of indoctrination that removes them from the workplace: "Going to School in comparison to Working is Idleness, and the longer Boys continue in this easy sort of Life, the more unfit they'll be when grown up for downright Labour, both as to Strength and Inclination" (1: 288).[116]

This last argument was not so much refuted by later advocates for Charity and Sunday Schools as defensively integrated into their proposals. Isaac Watts, in his *Essay Towards the Encouragement of Charity Schools* (1728), published shortly after Mandeville's attack, states as the first of his "*Propositions* by way of *Concession*" that "among Mankind there should be some Rich and some Poor ... nor is it possible ... to alter this Constitution of Things, nor is it our Design to attempt any Thing so unreasonable. "[117] Still more significant is the sixth and last of these propositions: "Children of the Poor" in Charity Schools "might be employed in some Work and Labour, generally one Half of the Day; that it might have partly the Nature of a *Work- House*, as well as of a *School*, for all those who are to live by their hard Labour, rather than by their Learning" (15). By means of its "joyning of Labour and Learning together in the Education of the poorer Parts of Mankind" (28), the Charity School is brought into line with the new, post-Lockean discourse of instruction, with its emphasis on habit and the inculcation of certain modes of thinking rather than linguistic skills and academic knowledge.

Significantly, Locke himself was among the first to advocate Schools of Industry. In his 1697 "Report to the Board of Trade," Locke proposed that "working schools" be established in every parish for children ("not otherwise employed") of "labouring people"; mothers would be "at the more liberty to work," children "kept in much better order ... and from infancy inured to work, which is of no small consequence to the making of them sober and industrious all their lives." Moreover, the schools could quickly become self-supporting, particularly as the children would live on "bread and water" with "a little warm water-gruel" in cold weather.[118] Schools of Industry found an enthusiastic advocate in Sarah Trimmer, who proposed in *The Oeconomy of Charity* that "manufactories" be introduced wherever possible, to employ "industriously inclined" women and "train up children from their early years, so that they should become habitually industrious" (62). If women and children were particularly desirable as factory workers for their manual dexterity and tractability, such labor would, in Trimmer's view, make the children more tractable still.[119] This happy marriage of the needs of factory owners and the social agenda of Christian reformers would be facilitated by "Schools of Industry for poor girls" set up in each parish. Trimmer's proposals were further elaborated by the novelist Clara Reeve in her *Plans of Education* (1792), perhaps the most reactionary educational treatise of the eighteenth century. Moved by the moral depravity of poor urban children, Reeve responds with a Mandevillean prescription: "I would have these children brought up to hard labours and qualified to get an honest livelihood."[120] Much more effectively than the Charity or Sunday School, the School of Industry forms an "industrious" character while secondarily inculcating "duties," with reading (let alone writing) seen as unnecessary. Reeve's proposal reflects the climate of reaction and suspicion among the established interests in the wake of revolution in France and radical agitation in England: "As to Sunday Schools, I have no great expectations from them ... It is Schools of *Industry* that are wanted, to reform the manners of the common people; where they are taught their duties *every day*, and *all the day long*" (99).

Sunday Schools could not, by definition, integrate working into their curricula, as keeping the sabbath day holy (by keeping children off the streets and village greens) was their stated mission; moreover, basic literacy geared towards enabling all children to read the Bible remained a principal goal. Nevertheless, the discursive emphasis on habit and discipline found in writers like Watts, Trimmer, and Reeve came to mark the language of the Sunday School movement as well. In his *Essay on the Depravity of the Nation, With a View to the Promotion of Sunday Schools* (1788), Joseph Berington developed an associationist defense of the Sunday School movement. "For if children be taken early to the schools, where it cannot be but good impressions must be made, they will grow up with the happy bias. The subordination in which their exercises must be performed, will habituate them to discipline." Although Berington includes reading in the Sunday School curriculum, writing and arithmetic are deemed superfluous.[121] Hannah More, who with her sister Martha had set up a group of Sunday and work schools in the Mendip Hills, was forced to respond to charges of Methodism and Jacobinism simply as a result of teaching the poor to read. "That the knowledge of the Bible," she explained to the bishop of Bath and Wells in 1801, "should lay men more open to the delusions of fanaticism on the one hand, or of jacobinism on the other, appears so unlikely, that I should have thought the probability lay all on the other side" (*MLC* 2: 74–75). More limited instruction to reading, and kept her pupils busy during the week: "My plan of instruction is extremely simple and limited. They learn, on week days, such coarse works as may fit them for servants. I allow of no writing for the poor. My object is not to make fanatics, but to train up the lower classes in habits of industry and piety" (*MLC* 2: 72). As the Charity Schools and Sunday Schools helped lay the groundwork for the "voluntary system" of popular education that was to be characteristic of the earlier nineteenth century, they also helped set the agenda for that system, which stressed "subordination" and "discipline" in an instructional setting – "habits of industry and piety" – as more important goals than the sort of "liberal" education reserved for the elite.

Although the official ideology of the compulsory, state-directed school system eventually became one of ideological neutrality and equal access, this is by no means the case with early calls for and debates on national education; the nationalistic ideological agenda and class-specific instructional hierarchies which are for the most part kept latent in the modern schools system become patent in a study of its genealogy. The implication of nationalist ideology in the tentative establishment of a national system can be seen in Rousseau's "Considerations on the Government of Poland" (1773): "It is education that must give the souls of the people a national form, and so shape their opinions and their tastes that they become patriots as well by inclinations and passion as by necessity" (*RMW*, 97). "To make men citizens," Rousseau writes elsewhere, "you must train them up from infancy" (*RMW*, 40). Rousseau's argument that citizenship must be rooted in childhood experience as organized by the state became a key element of various Revolutionary platforms later in the century, although (in the general disorganization characteristic of the Revolutionary period) such plans for educational reform were never put extensively into practice. Moreover, only one such plan (that of Lepeletier) was "radically democratic," specifying the same education for all.[122] Calls for state-directed education were not, however, limited in France to revolutionaries and "ideologues." Under the *ancien régime* the anti-Jesuit de la Chalotais had produced his "famous" *Essai d'Education Nationale où Plan d'Etudes pour la Jeunesse* in 1763, claiming "for the Nation an education dependent on the State alone ... because in short the children of the State should be brought up by those who are members of the State."[123] In the first years of the nineteenth century, Napoleon would support his own program for educational reform in similarly hegemonic terms: "So long as one does not learn from childhood whether to be republican or monarchist, catholic or non-religious, the State cannot form a Nation."[124]

Advocates for national education in England could easily produce grounds for systematic reform. The private schools were disorganized and often ephemeral in character, rising and falling with the careers of their underpaid, over-worked, and (if contemporary accounts are to be credited) frequently drunken masters; the grammar schools were, as a group, moribund and out of touch with the educational needs of most of their clients; the "great" schools (and the two universities) were seen as "hotbeds of vice and folly" where instruction was only incidental (*VRW*, 58). But early calls for a national system were in general less concerned with pedagogic reform than with broadly social aims. Thomas Sheridan argued in *British Education* (1756) that "In every state ... the education of youth should be particularly formed and adapted to the nature and end of its government" and that the political "principle by which the whole community is supported ought to be most strongly inculcated on the minds of every individual." Absent such ideological training, Sheridan warned, "no state can flourish or even subsist for any length of time."[125] In his *Thoughts on Civil Liberty, On Licentiousness, and Faction* (1765), John Brown reworked this nationalistic agenda in line with a post-Lockean emphasis on internalized discipline and early training. For Brown a *"permanent foundation"* for civil liberty requires the "Power of such a System of *Manners* and *Principles* effectually impressed on the human Mind, as may be an *inward Curb* to every inordinate Desire; or rather, such as may so frame and model the human Heart, that its ruling Desires may correspond, coincide, or coalesce, with all the great and essential Appointments of public Law."[126] Rather than leaving the "Culture of the Heart" (156) in the private hands of parents, Brown proposes a national "prescribed Code of Education, to which all the Members of the Community should legally submit," and in the absence of which "the Manners and Principles on which alone the State can rest, are ineffectually instilled, are vague, fluctuating, and self-contradictory" (157).

The frankly hegemonic character of these proposals helps explain why many English radicals, despite their interest in educational reform, resisted schemes for a national system. Joseph Priestley responded directly to Brown in *An Essay on the First Principles of Government* (1768), arguing that any national education scheme would hinder intellectual and scientific progress, replace England's fund of "original" characters with a dull "uniformity" of mind, invade the sanctity of the domestic sphere and, most important, facilitate "despotism" by allowing government ideological control over children's minds.[127] Paine, in the second part of the *Rights of Man* (1792), declared (with arguments of the Mandevillean sort in mind) that only "monarchical and aristocratical government ... requires ignorance for its support"; but although the nation should leave none uninstructed, it should democratize education by enabling parents "to pay the expenses themselves" rather than through mandatory schooling, funded (and directed) by the state.[128] Godwin makes a strong case against national education in *Political Justice*, writing that public education has always supported prejudice: "even in the petty institution of Sunday schools, the chief lessons that are taught are a superstitious veneration for the church of England, and to bow to every man in a handsome coat" (614–15). Following Priestley, Godwin warns that national education will tend to enshrine error and "form all minds upon one model," as well as enabling government to "strengthen its hands, and perpetuate its institutions" (616–17). As is often noted, Priestley, Paine, and Godwin all came from Dissenting backgrounds and thus had first-hand experience of the Anglican hegemony that would undoubtedly accompany any national schools scheme instituted by the state. Among English radicals of the period, Mary Wollstonecraft was virtually alone in advocating state-controlled education (based on a system of day-schools) as a means to "make good citizens" and facilitate social and political equality between the sexes, who would be educated together (*VRW* 162, 165).

National education found considerable support, however, among economists, most notably Adam Smith and Thomas Malthus. It should be borne in mind that the interest of economists in educational reform was not principally motivated by concerns for a better educated, more highly-skilled work force. In fact, as Smith's important discussion of education in *The Wealth of Nations* (1776) makes clear, industrialized labor was seen as requiring fewer and more easily mastered skills than traditional artisanal work or even the multiple tasks characteristic of small-scale agriculture. If the "education of the common people" had come to require "the attention of the publick," it is because labor had become less skilled, more repetitive and mind-numbing: "The man whose life is spent in performing a few simple operations ... has no occasion to exert his understanding"; "as stupid and ignorant as it is possible for a human creature to become," he is unfitted for civic life or military service.[129] The debasement of English laborers attendant upon industrialization can be mitigated by public universal instruction in reading, writing, and simple accounting, perhaps also (and here the need for the occasional skilled worker does come into play) in the "elementary parts of geometry and mechanics" (785). But the main social benefit of universal education will consist in a more ideologically stable populace, "less apt to be milled into any wanton or unnecessary opposition to government," more disciplined in their domestic and work habits as well: "An instructed and intelligent people besides are always more decent and orderly than an ignorant and stupid one" (788). Malthus adopts Smith's proposal for a system of "parochial education" (modelled on that of Smith's native Scotland) in the second edition of the *Essay on the Principle of Population* (1803), in which he offers hope for population control through enlightened self-interest. In order for the "lower classes of society" to voluntarily postpone marriage and limit the size of their families, the state must "endeavor to infuse into them a portion of that knowledge and foresight which so much facilitates the attainment of this object in the educated part of the community."[130] This can be accomplished through adding to the elementary instruction proposed by Smith training in the "simplest principles of political economy" and the "principles of population." In advocating an elementary education designed to bring the perceived self-interest of laborers into line with the interests of the middle classes, Malthus looks forward to the social strategy of the utilitarian-Radical group and praises, in a footnote added in 1825, their exemplary institutions, the "projected University in the Metropolis" and "above all the Mechanics Institution" (212). But early training will help bring the lower classes under the sway of the disciplined *habits*, as well as the economic interests, of their betters:

Besides explaining the real situation of the lower classes of society ... the parochial schools would, by early instruction and the judicious distribution of rewards, have the fairest chance of training up the rising generation in habits of sobriety, industry, independence, and prudence, and in a proper discharge of their religious duties; which would raise them from their present degraded state and approximate them, in some degree, to the middle classes of Society, whose habits, generally speaking, are certainly superior (214).

Malthus's discussion of national education both looks forward to the Philosophical Radicals' institutions for extending middle-class hegemony – typified by the Mechanics' Institutes and the Society for the Diffusion of Useful Knowledge – and at the same time participates in the discourse of industrious habits, religious "duty," and temperance characteristic of conservative Christian reformers like Trimmer and More.

There were, of course, conservative arguments against as well as for the extension of educational provisions for the lower classes. The well-known exchange between Samuel Whitbread and Davies Giddy in the House of Commons over Whitbread's Parochial Schools Bill in 1807 is representative of the climate of debate at least until the 1820s. Davies Giddy opposed Whitbread's motion on familiar conservative grounds: "it would teach them to despise their lot in life, instead of making them good servants in agriculture, and other laborious employments to which their rank in society had destined them; instead of teaching them subordination, it would render them factious and refractory ... it would enable them to read seditious pamphlets, vicious books, and publications against Christianity; it would render them insolent to their superiors."[131] In addition, parochial schools would help drain the public purse; Davies Giddy, like Mandeville, would "abolish the Poor-Laws altogether" (9: 798–99). Whitbread replied with equally characteristic liberal arguments: "All the lower orders had an education of some sort, good or bad ... At St. Giles's there was an education; children were taught to pick pockets," and most of those who finally came to the gallows were illiterate. Among Quakers, "crime was almost unknown, and this was accounted for by their being educated in their earliest years." The people, "if generally educated," would not refuse to plough, but rather become better tillers of the earth. Nor would they be corrupted by political pamphlets: "When a riotous mob was assembled, it was called an illiterate mob. If one man had knowledge, he would have a much better chance of leading a thousand ignorant creatures to mischief, than if they were all so far informed as to read what might appear on both sides of the question" (9: 802–3). The debate in the House of Lords took a different form, the speakers all conceding the utility of educating the "lower orders of the community," but with several Lords objecting to the Bill's lack of reference to the "religious establishment"; "it tended to a departure from the great principle of instruction in this country, by taking it in a great measure out of the superintendence and controul of the clergy" (9: 1175–76). The Archbishop of Canterbury himself rose to uphold the "controul and auspices of the establishment" over English education, and to hope that "their Lordships' prudence would ... guard against innovations that might shake the foundations of our religion" (9: 1177). Such resistance to the widespread secularization of English schools provided, along with manufacturers' continued demand for child labor, the meat of the opposition to a national system which, if under Anglican control, would prove unacceptable to "catholics, presbyterians, quakers, and all the other innumerable sects of dissenters" (1177), and, if secularized, would be anathema to the "religious establishment." This split along religious lines would, at least on a superficial level, also dominate the debates on the rival monitorial systems, debates which drew in Southey, Coleridge, and Wordsworth along with a variety of political and literary figures including Trimmer, Henry Brougham, Jeremy Bentham, and James Mill.

A SIMPLE ENGINE: THE LAKE POETS AND THE MADRAS SYSTEM

In first outlining his scheme for a national education system in Parliament, Whitbread remarked on the recent and timely invention of "a plan for the instruction of youth, which is now brought to a state of great perfection; happily combining rules, by which the object of learning must be infallibly attained with expedition and cheapness" (8: 884). This was the "Madras" system – also known as the "monitorial" or "mutual improvement" system – the discovery of which Whitbread diplomatically credited jointly to Andrew Bell and Joseph Lancaster, who indeed seem to have hit independently upon the notion of instructing children through the use of student assistants or "monitors," and who later borrowed from one another freely. Bell's version of the system, which was pushed forward by the Archbishop of Canterbury and others as an Establishment countercheck to that of the Quaker Lancaster, found some of its most vocal and influential supporters in the Lake poets. Coleridge added an extra lecture on education to his 1808 series on poetry at the Royal Institution, attacking Lancaster and linking Bell with Thomas Clarkson (the anti-slavery agitator) as the two contemporaries "who had done most for humanity" (1: 109). Eight years later in *The Statesman's Manual* (1816) he described Bell's system – "this incomparable machine, this vast moral steam-engine" – as an "especial gift of Providence" (41). Southey, who added a pamphlet to the Bell-Lancaster controversy and eventually became Bell's biographer, compared "Dr. Bell's discovery" in the *Quarterly Review* (1812) to the "invention of printing."[132] Wordsworth, echoing Southey, wrote to Thomas Poole in 1815, "If you have read my Poem, the 'Excursion,' you will there see what importance I attach to the Madras system. Next to the art of Printing it is the noblest invention for the improvement of the human species" (*WLM* 2: 210). In a note to Book IX of *The Excursion* Wordsworth had publicly praised the "discovery of Dr Bell": "it is impossible to over-rate the benefit which might accrue to humanity from the universal application of this simple engine under an enlightened and conscientious government."[133]

As Whitbread stressed, the "cheapness" of the monitorial system removed one of the principle objections to the institution of a national education scheme in England. Lancaster boasted in *Improvements in Education* (1803) that a single master could teach "a thousand children, or more" by means of the monitorial method.[134] But economy was the least of the system's virtues. By using students to teach other students, it capitalized on a practice which (in the crowded, unstructured classrooms of the period) was often tacitly relied upon in any case, and which, if properly organized, could ensure that while teaching his fellows, the "assistant" or "monitor" would be reinforcing lessons he himself had learned a few weeks (or even days) before. As Lancaster pointed out in *Improvements*, the monitor "cannot possibly teach the class without improving *himself* at the same time" (47). More important, the system was organized in such a manner as to maximize discipline as well as instruction, by giving the students themselves a stake in the rigidly hierarchized but constantly fluid "order" of the school. "The very moment you have nominated a boy a Tutor," Bell wrote in his *Analysis of the Experiment in Education, Made at Egmore, Near Madras* (1797), "you have exalted him in his own eyes, and given him a character to support, the effect of which is well known."[135] Lancaster made the same point in *Improvements*: "the surest way to cure a *mischievous boy* was to *make him a monitor*" (32).

In both its versions, the monitorial system brought the practice of instruction into line with the post-Lockean consensus on the means and ends of education. By making boys teachers or monitors, it helped internalize authority; by keeping the hierarchy fluid – any boy could, by mastering his lessons, become a monitor himself or, by forgetting them, sink back to pupil status or to a lower form – it maximized competition or, in Lancaster's phrase, "constant emulation" (42); and it freed the master to concern himself with enforcing discipline and supervising the entire school. The monitorial school has been aptly described by Foucault as "a machine for learning, in which each pupil, each level and each moment, if correctly combined, were permanently utilized in the general process of teaching."[136] This remarkable degree of pedagogical economy was accomplished primarily by the frank adaptation of factory methods to instruction. Bell states in his handbook *The Madras School, or Elements of Tuition* (1808): "It is the division of labour, which leaves to the master the simple and easy charge of directing, regulating, and controlling his intellectual and moral machine."[137] And by making "every boy," as Sydney Smith wrote in the *Edinburgh Review* (1806), "the cog of a wheel – the whole school a perfect machine," the monitorial system could ensure that moral and work habits would be properly internalized rather than merely imprinted in a manner that might or might not "take."[138] Coleridge stressed this virtue in a second lecture on the "New System of Education" in 1813: "in former systems children might, to be sure, acquire virtuous habits from instruction; but now they were imposed upon them, in the *mode* of giving that instruction" (2: 587–88).

The monitorial school adopted not only the basic principle of factory production – the division of labor – but also a contemporary vision of the factory as exemplary disciplinary institution, characterized by clockwork regularity and subject to constant surveillance.[139] Locke and other rationalist theorists had complained that the schoolmaster, unlike the parent or tutor, could not keep an entire classroom "under his Eye," but this objection was obviated by the monitorial system. By means of constant examinations and the "continual eye" of the monitor, students could never remain idle or unobserved; "every thing they do," wrote Lancaster in *Improvements*, "is brought to account, or rendered visible in some conspicuous way and manner" (85, 55). Bell's Madras system includes the responsibility of all students to report on the lapses of those immediately below them in the hierarchy, or be reported for negligence in their turn; faults are recorded in that "most powerful operator," the "black book," which is regularly inspected by the master (11). The spatial organization of the classroom and its division into an appropriate number of forms ensures that each student assistant "sees, at every instant, how every boy in his class is employed, and hears every word uttered" (7); the system of mutual informing gives the master, who in any case "overlooks the whole School" from his desk at the front, "the hundred eyes of Argus" (9, 14). And the black book remains open to a centralizing authority, the "Superintendent, or Trustee, or Visitor, whose scrutinizing eye must pervade the whole machine" (2). The Madras system's more elaborate mechanism of surveillance helps explain why the secularist Bentham, who planned an ambitious day school adapting the monotorial method for the "Use of the Middling and Higher Ranks in Life," drew more on Bell than on Lancaster, despite Bell's Establishment ties; Bentham wanted his own school designed on "the *Panopticon* principle," "by which every human object in the whole building is kept throughout within the reach of the *Head-master's* eye."[140]

"It is in a School as in an army," Bell wrote in the *Analysis*, "discipline is the first, second, and third essential" (27). Students were to be kept continually at work, disciplinary problems were to be immediately reported, and proper punishment (based more on public contrition and demotion than on the rod, a last resort) would be meted out upon an open examination of the black book. Lancaster went further, inventing a rather baroque array of punishments based on humiliation rather than pain, and prescribing rules for the bodily movements of the pupils, which were to become as mechanized as the system of instruction itself. Lancaster's handbook *The British System of Education* (1810) includes the following "paper of commands" for the use of monitors:

Out. Front. Look (to the right or left, by a motion made with the hand by the commanding monitor.) Take up slates. *Show slates.* (Here the monitor inspects.) Left hand slates. Right hand slates. Single. (In a line.) *Double.* Step forward. Step backward. Go. Show slates, to the master, or inspecting monitor.
On returning to the class.
Look. Go. Show slates. Lay down slates. In.
On going home.
Out. Unsling hats. Put on hats. Go.[141]

By applying the principles and discipline of factory production to instruction and classroom behavior, the monitorial school was able to combine into a unified system the inculcation of moral behavior and the instilling of "industrious" habits which were merely juxtaposed in the combined Charity School and School of Industry characteristic of the previous century. Schooling for the poor could no longer be considered a period of "idleness" if conducted with the same orderliness and productive of the same work-discipline as the factory, "forcing them," Bell stressed, "to habits of diligence, industry, veracity, and honesty" (49). The all but perfect fit between the school and the factory would help facilitate, as Bell's title-page promised, "converting schools for the lower orders of youth into Schools of Industry"; Lancaster similarly outlines a plan for "employing 50,000 Children, so that they may earn their Livelihood and obtain useful Learning at the same Time" (102–20).

Why did the Lake poets, usually seen as defenders of the child's freedom and imagination, give such vocal and, for a time, unqualified support to a system which has been described as marking "perhaps the most coercive and negative moment in the whole history of schooling"?[142] This question, when asked at all, has too often been shrugged off; it is argued that the monitorial system, whatever its faults, was at least preferable to unrelieved child labor, and (most recently) that the Lake poets were not "consciously aware of the ideological significance of the new system of education."[143] In fact, Southey, Coleridge, and Wordsworth in *The Excursion* were quite active in framing and disseminating the ideology of the monitorial system. It represented for them a radical cure for England's social ills and political unrest, a means for facilitating and justifying colonial expansion, and (in Bell's version) a prop for that great edifice of stability, the Established Church.

Coleridge had been among the first to recognize the social utility of a system by means of which "virtuous habits" could be "imposed" in the very process of providing basic instruction. His enthusiasm, along with the perceived threat to the Establishment represented by Lancaster's vigorous efforts in promoting a non-denominational version of the system, helped inspire Southey to write two articles on education and the poor for the *Quarterly Review* in 1811–12, a period of social and political crisis. The first article (1811) is mainly concerned with establishing the alleged priority of Bell's system, attacking Lancaster's scheme of punishments, and underscoring his system's tendency to undermine the marriage of church and state, the "two pillars of the temple of our prosperity"; it ends, however, with a broader social agenda. "Of all important measures of domestic policy, that of establishing parochial schools would be the most important and the most beneficial, for the ignorance of the poor is the root of all those evils for which our poor laws are but an inadequate alleviation."[144] Southey's claims for the social utility of the Madras system were restated at greater length a year later in an article ostensibly on the Poor Laws. There is "something rotten in our internal policy," the article begins; not only are one in nine English residents dependent on the parish, but the "great mass of the manufacturing populace" is "utterly improvident, because their moral and religious education has been utterly neglected."[145] Writing in the wake of the Luddite riots and the assassination of the prime minister, Spencer Perceval, Southey feared that if revolution was not itself at hand, the "preparatory work of revolution" might be well under way. With the manufacturing poor ripe for sedition, the "mob," no longer a "headless multitude," "are now an organized association, with their sections, their secret committees, and their treasury" (345); jacobinism, once the amusement of middle-class philosophers, is now spreading among an uneducated populace; and the unchecked "licentiousness" of the radical press can be counted on to fan the flames (350). Poor relief and public works programs are recommended as temporary "palliatives", but it is only "Dr. Bell's discovery to vaccinate the next generation against the pestilence which has infected this" that promises lasting remedy (353). Although he goes out of his way to attack the *laissez-faire* economics of Smith and Malthus, Southey ends with an argument for national education not very different from theirs: "Lay but this foundation, poverty will be diminished, and want will disappear in proportion as the lower classes are instructed in their duties, for only then will they understand their true interests" (354). What surplus vaccinated poor cannot be accommodated in England will help spread British institutions and the English language to its colonial possessions and beyond. "The seas are ours, and to every part of the uninhabited or uncivilized world our laws, our language, our institutions, and our Bible may be communicated" (356). Southey's roles as social critic and epic poet converge in an image of heroic colonization borrowed from the *Aeneid*: "Britain should become the hive of nations, and cast her swarms; and here are lands to receive them" (355).

Southey's dovetailing of two pressing social questions – the moral training of the poor and the management of British colonies – brings out a coincidence in the origins of the monitorial system the significance of which has been obscured by the question of priority. Bell's "Madras" system was initially designed to facilitate the socialization of the "half-cast children" of British soldiers in India, who, if left to their uncivilized mothers, would become a "degenerate race" (50). Lancaster's "monitorial" system arose when he began a school "for the instruction of poor children" (1) in George's Fields in Southwark, a poor section of London. The "mutual" approach, then, was concerned from the beginning with the disciplining of England's colonial subjects and the internal colonization of its unruly "industrious classes," and these twin problems inspired a single method of approach. Lancaster's version of the system, founded to redeem the urban poor, was spread by means of the British and Foreign School Society (as the Royal Lancasterian Society was reorganized in 1810) to Asia, Africa, and the West Indies; Bell's "Madras" version was retooled in England for the cheap training of the "lower orders of youth." Both educationalists wished to see their systems become universal. "It is inconceivable what a nation this might become," wrote Lancaster, "if a proper system of education was universally adopted; combining moral and religious instruction with habits of subordination" (140). Bell wished for the "consolidation" of Charity Schools and Schools of Industry under his system in England (91), and the National Society for the Education of the Poor in Accordance with the Principles of the Established Church (which Wordsworth's brother Christopher helped establish in 1811) duly took over the administration of Charity Schools from the SPCK.[146] Bell looked forward in *The Madras School* to seeing his "successful mode of propagating Christian knowledge, and industrious habits, with the elements of letters... spread, like any mechanical improvement, over the civilized world; and, in the course of ages, be the happy means of civilizing those regions, which are now barbarous and savage" (114).

Coleridge, in *The Statesman's Manual*, seconded Bell's wish to see "this vast moral steam-engine... adopted and in free motion throughout the Empire" (*CLS* 41). He also shared Bell's uneasiness regarding an insufficiently disciplined "READING PUBLIC": "For our Readers have, in good truth, multiplied exceedingly, and have waxed proud" (*CLS* 36–38). In the *Analysis*, Bell contrasts his own system to those "Utopian schemes, for the universal diffusion of general knowledge" which might "confound that distinction of ranks and classes of society, on which the general welfare hinges," and presumes to avoid the "risque of elevating, by an indiscriminate education, the minds of those doomed to the drudgery of daily labour, above their condition" by limiting the education of the "generality" to Bible reading and catechistic instruction in Anglican doctrine (90). These statements caused considerable embarrassment to Southey, who explained Bell's caution as a reflex of the "frightful circumstances" of the French Revolution; Henry Brougham commented more bluntly in the *Edinburgh Review* (1810): "We lament to find Dr. Bell among the followers of Mandeville."[147] Coleridge, however, himself defended the "sufficiency of the Scriptures" for the education of the "great majority" in *The Statesman's Manual*: "Of the labouring classes ... more than this is not demanded, more than this is not perhaps generally desireable" (7). There is less irony than is sometimes supposed in Coleridge's praise, in his 1808 lecture on Bell, for Sarah Trimmer, who had similarly recommended in her anti-Lancasterian pamphlet, *A Comparative View* (1805), that the instruction of the poor remain carefully limited to Bible reading and catechism: "but this indulgence is certainly carried too far when a taste is excited in them for studies which might tend to render them discontented in their proper station, and to alienate their minds from those employments which must be performed by the bulk of the people in every nation."[148] For Coleridge, even Bell's system might "become confluent with the evils, it was intended to preclude" (42), if not carefully managed by a properly educated "clerisy" drawn from the middle and upper classes.

Wordsworth's lines on national education and the dilemma of the laboring poor in *The Excursion* read in places almost like a versification of Southey's 1812 article on the Poor Laws in the *Quarterly Review*. Wordsworth had read Bell's treatise in 1808, "a most interesting work and entitles him to the fervent gratitude of all good men"; by 1811 he was active in setting up a school on the Madras plan at Grasmere which Bell visited, "he kindly taking it upon him to teach the Boys, and also the Master and myself" (*WLM* 1: 269, 514–15). The discussion of national education in Book IX of *The Excursion* grows out of an interrupted exchange between the Wanderer and the Solitary in Book VIII on the lamentable state of the English poor, particularly children. Although praising the technological wonders of an "inventive Age" (87), the Wanderer expresses great concern for the "old domestic morals of the land" (236), fast being undermined by the massing of laborers in urban areas and the blighting effects of an effectively unregulated factory system. In contrast to the former "short holiday of childhood" (281), supervised by a watchful father – "Idlers perchance they were, – but in *his* sight" (279) – the factory system both separates children from their parents and pens them in a physical and mental prison, "shuts up / The infant Being in itself, and makes / Its very spring a season of decay" (289–91). One recalls the "mind-forg'd manacles" of Blake's

"London" as the Wanderer cries out against the psychic and moral effects of child factory-labor:

> "Oh, banish far such wisdom as condemns
> A native Briton to these inward chains,
> Fixed in his soul, so early and so deep;
> Without his own consent, or knowledge, fixed!"
>
> (297–300)

The child becomes insensitive to the ministrations of nature, dead to physical sensation and dull of spirit; "liberty of mind / Is gone forever" (321–22). Not to be outdone by the Wanderer's critique of industrialization, the Solitary adds that the commercialized agricultural system produces children as ignorant and debased as any in the manufacturing districts.

> "Two eyes – not dim, but of a healthy stare –
> Wide, sluggish, blank, and ignorant, and strange –
> Proclaiming boldly that they never drew
> A look or motion of intelligence
> From infant-conning of the Christ-cross-row
> Or puzzling through a primer." (409–14)

"This Boy the fields produce" (425), the Recluse insists, adding rhetorically, "what liberty of *mind* is here?"

In Book IX, the discussion is continued, with the Wanderer now proposing a solution to the dilemma of both the factory child – "The senseless member of a vast machine" (159) – and the "rustic Boy, who walks the fields untaught," the "slave of ignorance" (162–63). Assuming an "impassioned majesty" (292), the Wanderer begins a speech which deserves quotation at some length:

> "O for the coming of that glorious time
> When, prizing knowledge as her noblest wealth
> And best protection, this imperial Realm,
> While she exacts allegiance, shall admit
> An obligation, on her part, to *teach*
> Them who are born to serve her and obey;
> Binding herself by statute to secure
> For all the children whom her soil maintains
> The rudiments of letters, and inform
> The mind with moral and religious truth,
> Both understood and practiced, – so that none,
> However destitute, be left to droop
> By timely culture unsustained; or run
> Into a wild disorder; or be forced

> To drudge through a weary life without the help
> Of intellectual implements and tools;
> A savage horde among the civilized,
> A servile band among the lordly free!" (292–310)

In developing his cure for a system which commodifies people (makes "man ... a tool / Or implement, a passive thing" [114–16]) and robs children of their "liberty of mind," the Wanderer adopts a distinctly reactionary and hegemonic language. Underlying his desire for the spread of knowledge and culture are the sorts of fears which animate Southey's *Quarterly Review* articles: that those who are "born to serve" will "run / Into a wild disorder"; that the colonial ambitions of "this imperial Realm" will be undermined by a "savage horde" *within* England, its uncivilized and restive lower orders. The answer is not simply a national education system, but one which combines the "rudiments of letters" (more than this is not demanded) with the inculcation of "moral and religious truth." It is a vision at once reformist and reactionary, as is so much of the educational discourse of the period. Like Coleridge and Southey, Wordsworth seems blinded by fears of "disorder" to the contradiction involved in criticizing the factory system for rendering children (and adults) parts of a "machine" and then recommending an educational system which he himself characterizes, in his note to line 299, as a "simple engine," one explicitly based on the application of factory methods to elementary instruction.

These fears become more evident as the Wanderer continues. Adverting to the social and political upheavals on the Continent caused by two decades of the Revolutionary and Napoleonic Wars – "Long-reverenced titles cast away as weeds; / Laws overturned; and territory split" (338–39) – the philosophic peddler rejoices at the thought that British "sovreignity" remains "entire and indivisible" (344–45). And Britain stands well to "preserve" her "beautiful repose," so long as "that ignorance were removed, which breeds ... Dark discontent, or loud commotion" (346–49), the revolutionary ferment and mob actions which Southey similarly decries in the *Quarterly Review*. Wordsworth's influential advocacy of the "Madras" system in *The Excursion* is directed not only at counteracting the dehumanizing effects of industrialization, but also at containing the political threat posed by laborers massed together in factory towns and displaced agricultural workers, primed for concerted action by organized radical movements and the unstamped press. "Prudent caution," no less than duty, requires that "the whole people should be taught and trained" (358). The Wanderer sounds almost Mandevillean in declaring that, as the "discipline of slavery is unknown" in Britain, the "more do we require / The discipline of virtue" (351–53); but such discipline is to be maintained by carefully removing rather than fostering ignorance among those "born to serve."[149] It is "unambitious schools / Instructing simple childhood's ready ear" (395–96) that can best guarantee social and political stability. As we move from Book VIII of *The Excursion* to Book IX, we find that Wordsworth's defense of childhood is equally a defense of the realm.

Like Southey, Wordsworth dismisses Malthus ("avaunt the fear / Of numbers crowded on their native soil" [363–64]) both by adopting an educational program not far different from Malthus's own and by advocating increased colonialist activity. Borrowing his epic imagery as well as his argument from Southey, Wordsworth (still in the voice of the Wanderer) envisions "industrious bees" leaving the "thronged hive" for "fresh abodes" in England's colonial empire:

> "So the wide waters, open to the power,
> The will, the instincts, and appointed needs,
> Of Britain, do invite her to cast off
> Her swarms, and in succession send them forth."   (375–78)

Still following Southey, Wordsworth foresees an instructed surplus population carrying British "civil arts" across the globe, "Even till the smallest habitable rock ... hear the songs / Of humanized society" (387–89). The Wanderer ends by rousing "British Lawgivers" to carry on the colonization of England's "savage" poor and, ultimately, the habitable world by swiftly enacting legislation for national education: "Your Country must complete / Her glorious destiny" (407–8). Invented for the training of "half-cast" children in India, organized for the large-scale instruction of the lower orders in England, and exported to the colonies and beyond, the "Madras" system will have come full circle.

The Lake poets' public advocacy of Bell must also be seen in terms of their resistance to the ongoing secularization of education and of English social life generally. The monitorial systems of both Bell and Lancaster retained a central catechistic element, while going beyond the catechistic method to render all aspects of elementary instruction equally disciplinary. Bell suggests a method for breaking the catechism into short questions in *The Madras School* (85) and Lancaster similarly includes a section on teaching catechisms in *Improvements* (128–34); both recommend the use of Trimmer's *Teacher's Assistant*. But only Bell enjoins (as he writes in the *Analysis*) the "strictest conformity with the doctrines and disciplines of the Church" (79). In line with Trimmer's attack on Lancaster in her *Comparative View*, both Southey and Coleridge vehemently opposed what the latter calls Lancaster's "plan of poisoning the children of the poor with a sort of *potential* infidelity" by imparting a non-denominational version of Christian teachings (*CLS* 40). Bell's National Society, on the other hand, was designed to support the Established Church. In a sermon for the benefit of the National Society preached in 1823, William Lisle Bowles (whose sonnets had meant so much to the young Coleridge) could attribute the success of parochial schools for the poor to "that excellent formulary of belief and Duties which has been constantly and earnestly impressed on the Childrens minds; I mean our short but comprehensive Church catechism."[150]

Wordsworth resists the secularization of education both directly (through his public support of Bell) and, as we have seen, indirectly in his representations of childhood. The social implications of Wordsworth's transcendental portrayal of childhood can be examined from a different angle if we contrast his child "trailing clouds of glory," to the one described by James Mill in his contribution to the monitorial controversy, *Schools for All, in preference to Schools for Churchmen Only* (1812). For Mill, writing in support of Lancaster, it is immaterial whether children learn an Anglican creed or a syncretic one at the age at which they begin to read. "If it be said that at the tender age when children learn to speak, they cannot understand the principles of religion; we believe it may with equal certainty be affirmed, that at the age when it is proposed to teach them reading, they are equally incapable of understanding the principles of religion." As a result, no great harm or great good either can be done by early religious instruction: "A child at four, five, six, and seven years of age is just as incapable of annexing any rational ideas to the terms God, Salvation, Trinity, &c. as a child at two or three; and a child at two or three is just as capable of being made to repeat a few words by rote as at six or seven."[151] If childhood is not, however, the blank slate presupposed by the associationist Mill but rather, as the

Wanderer puts it in *The Excursion*, the site of the Soul's "native vigour," pregnant with "reverberations" of the heavenly "choral song" it so recently made part of (IX. 40–41), then early religious instruction will critically foster or deform the child's inborn sense of divinity. The child is father of the Churchman.

The intensity of the Bell–Lancaster controversy should not obscure the fact, however, that writers on both sides of the debate were most often on ideological common ground, as evidenced not only by the congruence of their principal arguments in favor of educating the poor, but also by their adoption of the same discursive conventions. Richard Johnson aptly describes the monitorial literature in terms of a "common language" marked by the use of such key terms as "restraint," "habit," and "order"; by mechanical and military analogies; and by medical metaphors, such as inoculation; to this could be added "supervision" as another pervasive term and the predominance of colonialist metaphors.[152] This set of discursive conventions is operative in the treatises of both Lancaster and Bell, and marks the monitorial writings of Mill, Bentham, and Brougham no less than those of Trimmer, Southey, and Coleridge. Once its traces have been noted in Wordsworth's writings on education, it becomes much harder simply to ignore the divergence between his libertarian critique of rationalist upbringing (relevant mainly for middle- and upper-class children) in *The Prelude*, and the disciplinary, nationalistic approach to educating those born to serve and obey in *The Excursion*.

CODA: NATURE, EDUCATION, AND THE CHILD'S FREEDOM

Wordsworth's eventual disenchantment with the Madras system was motivated by the same complex of libertarian ideals and reactionary fears that led him to support it in the first place. Like Coleridge, Wordsworth came to feel that even Bell's system, "from not understanding the constitution of our nature and the composition of society," might aggravate the social ills it set out to remedy. Writing to Hugh James Rose in 1828 regarding a projected Madras school for girls in Ambleside, Wordsworth doubts if "Dr Bell's sour-looking teachers in petticoats" will impart anything of real value. "What are you to do with these girls? ... Will they not be indisposed to bend to any kind of hard labour or drudgery?" Wordsworth prescribes instead more labor and less instruction: "A hand full of employment, and a head not above it, with such principles as may be acquired without the Madras machinery, are the best security for the chastity of the wives of the lower rank." But Wordsworth also criticizes the "Madras machinery" for its undue emphasis on instruction over imaginative development. "The Bellites overlook the difference; they talk about moral discipline; but wherein does it encourage the imaginative feelings, without which the practical understanding is of little avail?" (*WLL* 1: 685–86).

A year later Wordsworth criticizes the Infant Schools movement in similar terms: "Natural history is taught in infant schools by pictures stuck up against walls, and such mummery. A moment's notice of a red-breast pecking by a winter's hearth is worth it all" (*WLL* 2: 20). By 1845, Wordsworth had returned to the position articulated in *The Prelude*, faulting modern schools for neglecting the importance of "intercourse with nature" and "books of imagination." Active experience of a nature providentially stocked with "Knowledge… infused thro' the constitution of things" is central for the education of all social classes (*WLL* 4: 733). Coleridge, even in praising Bell's "machine," also upholds the value of unstructured natural experience: "Never, however, imagine that a child is idle who is gazing on the stream, or laying upon the earth; the basis of all moral character may then be forming; all the healthy processes of nature may then be ripening" (*CLL* 1: 586). In the unpublished *Logic* Coleridge departs decisively from the rigid order and constant drill of the Madras system, stating that education begins in the "happy delirium" which is "Nature's kind and providential gift to childhood," when she "promiscuously" fills the mind with a "chaos of facts, and forms, and thousandfold experiences": "by this seeming confusion alone could Nature… have effected her wise purposes, without encroachment on the native freedom of the soul."[153]

In the Romantic poet's appeal to nature lay the basis for a potentially radical critique of the disciplinary forms of contemporary educational theory and practice. A trust in nature provided a ground for valuing unstructured childhood experience and opened a space for the role of free play in psychic development, the "freedom of the soul." Nature had been used to ground the critique of contemporary schooling in the Jacobin novel of the 1790s. Whereas Scott and Austen would portray unguided learning as a dangerous thing, practitioners of the radical novel represent a sporadic, largely self-motivated education, set in the country and freely intermixed with play and other forms of "idleness," as a saving alternative to the tyranny and forced socialization characteristic of eighteenth-century schooling. In Holcroft's *Hugh Trevor* (1794–97), the hero's creative genius and mental independence are fostered by his father's eccentric and spontaneous approach to child-rearing. "He played with me as a cat does with her kitten, and taught me all the tricks of which he was master." Hugh's education is rooted in boisterous "bodily" lessons, "such as holding me over his head erect on the palm of his hand; putting me into various postures; making me tumble in as many ways as he could devise... with abundance of other antics, at which he found me apt; yet, being accompanied with laughter and shouts, and now and then a hard knock, they tended, or I am mistaken, not only to give bodily activity, but to awaken some of the powers of mind." This schooling by hard knocks is supplemented by his mother's initiating Hugh in "the mysteries and pleasures of the alphabet," which opens up a period of undirected (or rather self-directed) reading: the Bible, broadside ballads, popular chapbooks.[154] The heroine of Mary Hays's *Memoirs of Emma Courtney* spends her first twelve years at her aunt's, where she mostly "ran, bounded, sported, romped" with her cousins; she learns to read after hearing her aunt recite tales from the *Arabian Nights*, and is thereafter left to "wander unrestrained in the fairy fields of fiction" (1: 16, 31). Hays makes her opinion of contemporary girls' schools clear when Emma briefly endures a private academy: "my body was tortured into forms, my mind coerced, and tasks imposed upon me, grammar and French, mere words, that conveyed to me no ideas" (1: 20). Hugh Trevor's benevolent uncle similarly condemns "boarding-schools, where every thing is taught and nothing understood" (11).

The Jacobin novel – with its valorization of unsupervised play, bodily enjoyment, fairy tales, and its related critique of contemporary schooling – established a set of conventions for representing childhood which Wordsworth may well have drawn on in the early books of *The Prelude*, recording as they do the development and "natural" education of a youthful radical. A quasi-Rousseauvian, "negative" approach to early education also underlies the "system" for bringing up the young Basil Montagu, which Dorothy Wordsworth describes in a letter of 1797:

We teach him nothing at present but what he learns from the evidence of his senses. He has an insatiable curiosity which we are always careful to satisfy to the best of our ability. It is directed to everything he sees, the sky, the fields, trees, shrubs, corn, the making of tools, carts, &c. &c. &c. He knows his letters, but we have not attempted any further step in the path of *book learning*. Our grand study has been to make him *happy* (*WLE*, 180).

The ideal of wise passiveness in deference to a providentially arranged and animate nature characterizes both Wordsworth's early and late approaches to childhood and education, and is kept sight of even in *The Excursion*, in which the Wanderer's call for moral discipline through national education co-exists uneasily with his enjoyment at the spectacle of two boys "let loose" from school to "breathe and to be happy, run and shout, / Idle" (ix.261–64). There is a significant difference, however, between the radical novelists' appeal to nature as a basis for social critique and Wordsworth's apprehension of "Nature" as itself a numinous, educative force. In Wordsworth's poetry, the appeal to nature tends to slide into a sort of primitivism, which closes off the prospect for intellectual development; many of his represented children are left stranded in an eternal childhood, like Lucy Gray, the Danish Boy, Johnny Foy (the "Idiot Boy"), the Lucy of "Three years she grew," and, most famously, the Boy of Winander.

The Winander boy is presented in Book v of *The Prelude* as a counter-example to the "monster" produced by rationalist tuition. The passage (389–422) is among the earliest written for *The Prelude*, and was originally autobiographical; included as "There was a boy" in the 1800 edition of *Lyrical Ballads*, it is also one of the few sections of *The Prelude* published during Wordsworth's lifetime. This boy's negative education takes place in natural settings – "Beneath the trees or by the glimmering lake" – where he skillfully cups his hands to blow "mimic hootings to the silent owls," who are tricked into answering and revealing their presence. The passage celebrates not only the fostering aspect of nature but also those suspensions of habitual consciousness which, for both Wordsworth and Coleridge, are actively prevented by rationalist tuition. Such spontaneous moments of self abandonment allow nature to enter directly and unconsciously into the heart of the child's being:

> And when it chanced
> That pauses of deep silence mocked his skill,
> Then sometimes in that silence, while he hung
> Listening, a gentle shock of mild surprize
> Has carried far into his heart the voice
> Of mountain torrents; or the visible scene
> Would enter unawares into his mind

> With all its solemn imagery, its rocks,
> Its woods, and that uncertain heaven, received
> Into the bosom of the steady lake.

These lines have been celebrated at least since De Quincey as an exemplary instance of the Wordsworthian sublime; they have also become notorious for the manner in which they complicate issues of language, subject-object relations, and self-representation in *The Prelude*. I want here, however, to comment only briefly on the passage as it represents childhood and education, a perspective which generates a problematic of its own. The uncanny silence of this passage, its strong sense of closure and the mind's peculiarly wakeful passiveness here in relation to natural experience, all contribute to its sense of sublimity; but silence, closure, and passivity also carry over into our sense of the boy himself. His relation to the owls appears strangely monotonous and circular – one might even say catechistic – constituted by an exact, repetitive mimicry. His development is similarly closed off: "This boy was taken from his mates, and died / In childhood ere he was full ten years old." The boy appears uncannily detached from a human environment, isolated from his fellows and prevented from growing into the greater degree of socialization that comes with sexual maturity ("taken from his mates" in a double sense), seemingly alien to language itself. His early death can be read as a sign of the contradiction underlying Wordsworth's ideal of a "natural" education, for education can only distance us from an imagined natural existence, and remaining one with nature means, in Wordsworth's poetry, never to grow out of childhood. If the "dwarf man" is forced to become a premature adult, the Winander boy is preserved as an eternal child.

That the child's free development could be defended without either appealing to a transcendentalized nature or idealizing childhood experience, is clear from Godwin's forceful and undervalued writings on education in *The Enquirer*. Beginning from the rubric that "all education is despotism," Godwin advocates public over private education for precisely the reason that others in the rationalist tradition oppose it: because it grants the child a greater degree of "comparative liberty," freedom from constraint and observation (*GE*, 60).[155] He outlines a form of schooling which would maximize the initiative and control of the child, who "proceeds upon a plan of his own invention ... three fourth's of the slavery and restraint that are now imposed upon young persons would be annihilated at a stroke" (*GE*, 80). Punishment would be banished altogether from education, its place taken by the pupil's "desire" to master the physical and cultural environment (*GE*, 123, 79).

Godwin advances an explicitly anti-transcendental conception of childhood which contrasts starkly with that of Wordsworth. "I do not say that a child is the image of God. But I do affirm that he is an individual being, with powers of reasoning" (*GE*, 87). Although advocating an education designed to develop the child's powers of independent thinking, Godwin is no less critical than Wordsworth of the precociously adult child, who lacks the "chief blessing of youth ... a thoughtless, bounding gaiety," and who is marked by "forced and artificial behavior" and a "frigid" temper. Godwin does not, however, wish to seal off childhood in an equally artificial perpetual innocence: "But, if hilarity be a valuable thing, good sense is perhaps still better ... The world in which we are engaged, is after all a serious scene" (*GE*, 111–114). Despite (or perhaps in reaction to) his early identification with the infant prodigies of Janeway's *Token*, Godwin stays clear of a representational model of childhood which leads to early death, however sublime or beatific. "Let us never forget that our child is a being of the same nature with ourselves; born to have passions and thoughts and sentiments of his own; born to fill a station, and act a part; with difficulties that he ought to surmount, and duties that he is bound to discharge" (142). This strong sense of continuity between the child and the adult it must eventually (and, in most cases, impatiently desires to) become is what the first-generation Romantics, with their child-angels, and best Philosophers, and spectral children of the woods, habitually repress. Their defense of the child's freedom has made a lasting, perhaps crucial contribution to our cultural history; but to read the Romantics on childhood uncritically is to forget (as Godwin does not) that the child is a "being of the same nature as ourselves."

CHAPTER 3

Children's literature and the work of culture

The beginning of the children's book industry in England is conventionally dated from the publication of John Newbery's *A Little Pretty Pocket-Book* in 1744. Books had, of course, been produced for children well before this period – courtesy books, children's bibles, hornbooks and primers, religious works, and fable collections.[1] Nor was Newbery alone in perceiving, around the middle of the eighteenth century, the potential for a lucrative new market among the growing number of middle-class parents anxious to provide their offspring with a modern education and competitive literacy skills. Children had become, as J. H. Plumb writes, "luxury objects upon which their mothers and fathers were willing to spend larger and larger sums of money," while initiating them indirectly, through a growing proliferation of children's books, toys, games, and clothing, into their eventual role as consumers in a commercial society.[2] More directly, children's books were required for use in the "domestic" instruction of children (recommended by Locke and his followers) and as supplemental reading for children in schools. Though Locke somewhat distrusted the printed word as a didactic medium, the children's book became a principal vehicle through which his educational theories were disseminated, and Lockean pedagogy was textualized by a host of writers providing instructive, entertaining books for parents eager to increase their children's stock of cultural capital.[3] Thomas Boreman and Mary Cooper were notable among the publishers successfully working this new field. But Newbery dominated and largely set the tone for the early children's book trade through a happy coincidence of personal qualities and ideological allegiances, including his considerable energy and entrepreneurial skills, his Lockean conception of childhood and of books that would beguile while instructing his juvenile readers, and his identification (particularly as a self-made man) with the bourgeois values held by their parents.[4]

In his essay on education for *The Bee* (1759) Oliver Goldsmith called for a new children's literature that would impart such values as "frugality" and hard work through featuring a hero "who might be praised for having resisted allurements when young" and who "at last became Lord Mayor"; in short, Dick Whittington without the cat.[5] That this plot outline describes the typical Newbery scenario – the achievement of worldly success through deferred gratification and habits of industry – is hardly coincidental; Goldsmith himself contributed several titles to the Newbery catalogue, including perhaps *The History of Little Goody Two-Shoes* (1765), the most celebrated of the lot.[6] This formula proved extremely successful, and Newbery's attractively produced books were valued by child readers as well as by adult purchasers. Robert Southey was given a set of Newbery titles as soon as he could read, and associated with them "that love of books, and that decided determination to literature" which marked him for life; Richard Edgeworth also traced his "early taste for reading" to the Newbery books he pored over as a young child.[7] Others in the period were less generous. Catherine Macaulay, in *Letters on Education*, considers fairy tales "mere negatives" in their effect on the growing mind but books of the Newbery sort, which attempt to "bribe" children into virtuous habits, positively pernicious (53). Looking back on his own childhood reading Leigh Hunt laments the "sordid and merely plodding morals" of children's books in which "every good boy was to ride in his coach, and be a lord mayor; and every bad boy was to be hung, or eaten by lions"; he scorns books of the Newbery sort for the "mercenary and time-serving ethics" which were "necessary perhaps for a certain stage in the progress of commerce ... but which thwarted healthy and large views of society for the time being."[8]

Hunt's analysis of the early children's book trade has recently been restated by Isaac Kramnick, who similarly relates the "Trade and Plumb-Cake" ethic of the Newbery tradition to a certain stage in the development of bourgeois capitalism.[9] For Kramnick, children's fiction in the later eighteenth century is informed by a "radical and progressive" middle-class ideology, which made part of the "political assault on aristocratic England" by calling for the liberation of the "self-reliant, hardworking, independent individual" from traditional constraints.[10] While Kramnick's linking of early children's fiction with bourgeois ideology, like Plumb's relation of the children's book trade to the rise of consumerism, helps account for its sudden growth in the mid-eighteenth century among a predominately middle-class group, there are several important limitations to his approach. To begin with, a single "ideology" is made to embrace so ideologically diverse a group of writers as the radical William Godwin, the liberal Maria Edgeworth, and the arch-conservative Sarah Trimmer. In contrast, for Hunt the "mercenary" ethic of the Newbery era was "first blown over by the fresh country breeze" of Day's Rousseauvian *Sandford and Merton*, a work which for Kramnick is ideologically cognate with *Goody Two-Shoes*; more recently, Mary Jackson has contrasted Newbery's "lower-middle-class vision," which allows for a certain amount of playfulness and celebrates upward mobility, with the more aridly didactic children's books of the period 1780–1800, exemplified by Trimmer's works, which enjoin upon the child reader sobriety, moral seriousness, and contentment with one's God-given lot.[11]

A second limitation to Kramnick's approach has been found in its concern with the "manifest content" of children's texts to the virtual exclusion of intertextual (especially generic) and formal aspects, its reduction of literary discourse to plot outlines and dominant thematic motifs.[12] The notion that the children's text is particularly transparent, and can be taken at face value as a "kind of cultural barometer," is a common one, in part because children's texts are frequently designed to *seem* transparent, and in part because what Jackson calls their "propagandistic" character tends to announce itself more overtly than in most literary texts aimed at adults.[13] Such a conception of children's literature tends, however, to reduce discussions of "ideology" to the mechanical application of formulas drawn uncritically from other fields like social history, and remains largely blind to the more subtle ideological functions of non-didactic works for children such as fairy tales. However accomplished their illusion of transparency, children's books are (like other literary forms) complexly encoded texts whose formal strategies may reveal as much or more about their ideological import than can their thematic content alone, and whose silences may be as meaningful as the stories they manifestly tell. In addition, approaches which dwell on the "radical" and "progressive" elements of early children's literature tend to minimize or ignore altogether the disciplinary function of the children's book, which has traditionally served as a "tool or engine constructed to direct and control the development of the child," but which does not always perform this function in a simple or obvious fashion.[14]

The discussion that follows will offer regrettably little in the way of extended readings of particular children's texts, attempting instead to identify larger trends. Nevertheless, by attending more closely to issues of genre and to formal and other discursive strategies than have most existing accounts of early children's literature, a different and perhaps more productive understanding of the role of the children's book in late eighteenth- and early nineteenth-century culture may emerge, beginning with a reconsideration of the two realms into which early children's literature is conventionally divided: the "fairy tale" and "moral tale." In addition, two areas which have only recently come into critical focus ask for special consideration: the eclipse of children's satire in a period of expanding literacy and social unrest, and the discursive links between children's reading and colonialism at a time of hegemonic educational initiatives in England and imperial expansion abroad.

FAIRY TALES AND THE POLITICS OF LITERACY

In his *Miscellanies* (1696) John Aubrey records a late sighting of an English fairy: "Anno 1670, not far from Cyrencester, was an Apparition: Being demanded, whether a good Spirit, or a bad? returned no answer, but disappeared with a curious Perfume and a melodious Twang. Mr. W. Lily believes it was a Fairie." With this memorable exit, the fairies seem to have left England both in person and, largely, by reputation, thanks in part (as Aubrey elsewhere records) to the growth of literacy among the lower classes: "Before Printing, Old-wives tales were ingeniose: and since Printing came in fashion, till a little before the civil-Warres, the ordinary sort of People were not taught to reade: now-a-dayes Bookes are common, and most of the poor people understand letters... and the divine art of Printing, and Gunpowder have frighted away Robin-good-fellow and the Fayries."[15] By the time antiquarians like Percy and Scott began collecting oral traditions in earnest, the "authentic" folk tale, in contrast to the popular ballad, was relatively scarce in England. In its place, however, and among a sophisticated, upper class and mostly adult audience, a vogue had developed for imported, modernized, and often moralized fairy tales translated from French collections – d'Aulnoy in 1699, Perrault in 1729, le Prince de Beaumont in 1761 – and from Galland's French version of the Arabic *Thousand and One Nights*, first translated into English in 1706.[16] If a newly literate "ordinary folk" had banished Robin Goodfellow and his like from their hearths, Cinderella and Scheherazade had found a place in the libraries of their betters.

The traditional fairy tale did not readily find a place, however, in the new literature for children which emerged in the latter half of the eighteenth century. Instead, fairy tales and fantasy in general came under attack from two sides: the rationalist school of education drawing on Locke and Rousseau, and (although with notably less consistency) the Christian moralist critique of children's fiction which found exponents in writers like Sarah Trimmer and M. M. Sherwood.[17] Locke's *Some Thoughts* set the tone for over a century in its harsh dismissal of supernatural fictions: "I would not have children troubled whilst young with Notions of *Spirits* ... I think it inconvenient, that their yet tender Minds should receive early impressions of *Goblins*, *Spectres*, and *Apparitions*, wherewith their Maids, and those about them, are apt to fright them into compliance with their orders" (302–3). For Locke, Aesop's *Fables* (a work tailored for children's reading well before the development of a children's literature proper) is virtually the only existing book fit for children (298).

Rousseau, on the contrary, does not consider fables, not even La Fontaine's, fit for Emile's education (112); on the contrary, "reading is the plague of childhood" and fables "contain nothing intelligible or useful for children" (116, 113). Rationalist educationalists and children's authors such as the Edgeworths, John and Lucy Aikin, Barbauld, and Wollstonecraft followed Locke and Rousseau in rejecting any form of fantastic or supernatural reading (often including too early an exposure to Christian notions of the soul and afterlife). In his preface to his daughter's *The Parent's Assistant* (1796) Richard Edgeworth, for example, takes Samuel Johnson to task for condescending to children's fairy tales: "Why should the mind be filled with fantastic visions, instead of useful knowledge? ... It is to be hoped that the magic of Dr. Johnson's name will not have power to restore the reign of fairies."[18]

The objections posed by Christian moralists were on the whole gentler, but only somewhat less dismissive. Although Sarah Trimmer, writing in *The Guardian of Education*, initially considered her own

childhood reading of Perrault relatively "harmless" (1 : 63), she soon
came to reject fairy tales as "only fit to fill the heads of children with
confused notions of wonderful and supernatural events, brought
about by the agency of imaginary beings" (2 : 185). While Trimmer
dismissed Sarah Fielding's *The Governess* (1749) for its inclusion of
fairy tales, M. M. Sherwood (who had happily "enacted" fairy tales
as a child) revised such "fanciful productions" out of it in the
interests of "juvenile edification"; still, she inserted one of her own
invention to give her version of *The Governess* (1820) a period flavor.[19]

Edgeworth's emphasis on "useful knowledge" over the "fantastic," or Sherwood's on "edification" over the "fanciful" suggests
the dualistic model – didacticism and imagination, instruction and
delight, reason and fantasy – underlying most accounts of the
development of children's literature. The latter term in each
opposition is, of course, invariably privileged at the expense of the
former. F. J. Harvey Darton, for whom children's literature forms a
perpetual field of conflict between "instruction and amusement,"
nevertheless finds in the "return" of the fairy tale with such
collections as Benjamin Tabart's *Popular Fairy Tales* (1818) and
Edgar Taylor's translations of Grimm (1823–6) the transition to a
more humane children's library dominated by delight.[20] Samuel
Pickering, who provides a detailed and unusually sympathetic
account of the rationalist tradition, still looks forward to the wiser
Victorian age when "fairy tales would be welcomed with a more
open imagination."[21] The triumph of the fairy tale over a didactic
tradition largely perpetrated by a "monstrous regiment" of women
writers plays a similarly pivotal role in the progressive narrative
informing most accounts of English children's literature.[22]

The official role of the Romantics within this pervasive schema is
their defense, in the name of the imagination, of the popular fairy
tale, although this "defense" admittedly took place more in private
– through letters and unpublished manuscripts – than in public.[23]
Charles Lamb, who wrote with his sister Mary a didactic children's
book – *Mrs. Leicester's School* (1809) – in the Fielding vein, is often
cited for his 1802 attack on Barbauld and Trimmer in a letter to
Coleridge: "Is there no possibility of averting this sore evil? Think
what you would have been now, if instead of being fed with Tales and
old wives fables in childhood, you had been crammed with
Geography & Natural History? *Damn them.* I mean the cursed
Barbauld crew" (*LW* 2: 82). Coleridge had already written to

Thomas Poole (in 1797) of his own "early reading of Faery Tales" in the same vein: "Should children be permitted to read Romances, & Relations of Giants & Magicians & Genii? – I know all that has been said against it; but I have formed my faith in the affirmative. – I know no other way of giving the mind a love of 'the Great,' & 'the Whole'" (*CCL* 1: 354). For Geoffrey Summerfield, whose study *Fantasy and Reason* constitutes the most recent refinement of the dichotomized, progressive history of children's literature codified by Darton, both Lamb and Coleridge pale beside Wordsworth's "uniquely powerful defence of freedom and of fantasy in the lives of children" in Book v of *The Prelude*, the period's "most coherent and radical critique of 'moral' literature" and the standard against which Summerfield measures all other treatments of the subject.[24]

Such accounts, although they have begun to seem inevitable, still remain attractive, appealing as they do to contemporary notions of the importance of fantasy in the lives and books of children. When placed in its historical context, however – a period when the rapid and unforeseen growth of popular literacy, the mass distribution of radical political pamphlets, and the reaction of established interests in the form of censorship and mass propaganda of their own produced the literacy "crisis" of the 1790s – Wordsworth's patronage of fairy tales may be interpreted as something other than disinterested libertarianism.[25] Moreover, when read critically, Wordsworth's valorization of the fairy tale can be seen as relying on a conservative, traditionalist conception of "oral literature" which, despite its presence behind most current studies of the fairy tale as children's literature, has long been discredited. Before addressing either of these problems, however, the stock opposition of fantasy and reason, imaginative and didactic literature should itself be called into question. Especially in regard to the fairy tale, it is not always clear where the moral tale leaves off and the fantasy begins.

If one concentrates on children's books themselves rather than the ongoing polemic in reviews and prefaces, the relation of didactic writers to the fairy tale might better be described as one of appropriation than of censorship. Fairy tales were regularly appropriated for didactic purposes in at least four ways. Children's familiarity with fairy tale personages and trappings could be exploited most simply by borrowing them for the titles, prefatory matter, and packaging of otherwise didactic works, a fairy coating over the moral pill. Eleanor Fenn, author of *The Rational Dame*, entitled one of her thoroughly didactic works *The Fairy Spectator* (1789); John Newbery's playful but decidedly Lockean *A Little Pretty Pocket-Book* draws in its child readers with two letters ("to little Master Tommy" and "to Pretty Miss Polly") written by Jack the Giant-Killer, returned from fairyland as an enlightened moralist. Even the "Purple Jar" of Maria Edgeworth's most celebrated moral tale has been described as "a property from a stage fairy-land."[26]

More elaborately, the didactic writer could borrow fairy tale motifs, types and settings to construct moral fairy tales of her or his own. Both Rousseau and Samuel Johnson produced didactic fairy tales, and many of the "Oriental tales" in *The Idler* and *The Rambler* moralize the conventions of *The Arabian Nights*.[27] Some of the most popular didactic story books included such moral fairy tales as: "The Story of the Cruel Giant Barbarico" and "The Princess Hebe: A Fairy Tale" (an Oriental tale after Johnson) in Sarah Fielding's *Governess*; "The Transmigrations of Indur" and "Order and Disorder, A Fairy Tale" in Aikin and Barbauld's *Evenings at Home* (1792–96); "The History of Princess Rosalinda" in Sherwood's revision of Fielding, a surprisingly energetic tale which is, if anything, more imaginative than the one it replaces. Maria Edgeworth included a rational fairy tale, "Rivuletta," in the second part of *Rosamond* in *Early Lessons* (1800), in order to show (as the tale's narrator puts it) that "even in the wildest flights of the imagination, reason can trace a moral."[28]

A didactic writer could also silently adapt fairy tale plots or patterns into the empirical world of the rational tale. The hero of Thomas Day's "The Good-natured Little Boy" in *The History of Sandford and Merton* helps out a dog, a horse, a blind man and a crippled sailor, who fortuitously reappear to save him from danger as night comes on; his pendant in "The Ill-Natured Little Boy" spurns a similar series of potential helpers and is later punished by them. The two tales together illustrate an extremely common fairy tale motif, the test which separates the kindly hero or heroine from unkindly (and usually older) siblings or other rivals; they evoke as well one of the most common fairy tale plots, the "Kind and Unkind Daughters" type familiar from such tales as Perrault's "Diamonds and Toads."[29] The Cinderella story was moralized as *The Renowned History of Primrose Prettyface, Who By Her Sweetness of Temper and Love of Learning, Was Raised from Being the Daughter of a Poor Cottager, to Great Riches and the Dignity of Lady of the Manor* (c. 1783); and Goody Two-Shoes, despite her own warning against "tales of *Ghosts, Witches* and *Fairies*" as "the Frolics of a distempered Brain," herself rises from poverty to a bourgeois establishment in Cinderella fashion.[30]

Finally, traditional fairy tales were themselves moralized by their redactors, translators, and editors. The early fairy tale collections designed for middle-class children were cleaned up and often given didactic applications. An early children's version of *The Thousand and One Nights* by the "Rev'd Mr Cooper" (a pseudonym for Richard Johnson) was entitled *The Oriental Moralist* (c. 1790); the author claimed in the preface to have "expunged everything which could give the least offence to the most delicate reader" and to have added moral reflections "wherever the story would admit of them."[31] Tabart's *Popular Fairy Tales*, the first important English collection for children, had a "decidedly moral slant" and was designed to meet the approval, in Tabart's words, of "every tender mother, and every intelligent tutor."[32] In the Tabart version of *Jack and the Beanstalk*, for example, which first appeared in 1807, the editor, Mary Jane Godwin, interpolates a long section in which a thoroughly respectable fairy assures Jack that the Giant's treasure was unlawfully seized from Jack's father, so that he may steal it back "with impunity" – and without violating the sanctity of private property.[33] Even the Brothers Grimm, despite their claims to unvarnished folk authenticity, censored some tales, selected the most acceptable version of others, and further refined the tales both in transcribing them and in revising them for later editions; Maria Tatar has recently argued that most of these revisions were made specifically with the burgeoning children's book market in mind.[34] Edgar Taylor's English translations of the Grimms' tales in the 1820s, which have been hailed as a "point of no return" in the victory of the fairies over didacticism, were marked by a still greater degree of the "bourgeoisification" of the folk tale.[35] Taylor assured his adult purchasers that a number of the Grimms' tales, despite their "great merit," had been passed over in deference to "the scrupulous fastidiousness of modern taste especially in works likely to attract the attention of youth."[36] Those Taylor selected were further sanitized in the interests of middle-class morality. In Basile's seventeenth-century Italian version, Cinderella is a determined young woman who murders her first stepmother by breaking her neck; in the Grimms' version, "Aschenputtel" is much more child-like and docile, although she does allow her attendant ravens to peck out her stepsisters' envious eyes at her wedding.[37] In

Taylor's translation, the stepsisters are spared, the better to support her character throughout as a pattern child, "always good and kind to all about her" (2: 34).

Contrary to what has been called the "Whiggish" version of the history of children's literature as "a progress toward pure amusement," the opposition between moral didacticism and the imaginative fairy tale is hardly absolute.[38] Although the fairy tales remembered by Coleridge, Lamb, and Wordsworth would more likely have been in chapbook versions than in the blatantly moralized collections characteristic of the early nineteenth century, the Romantic sponsorship of fairy tales can nevertheless be described as a special instance of fairy tale appropriation for moral ends. It may be less ironic than is usually supposed that Lamb begins his fulminations against the cursed Barbauld crew with a lament for the passing of *Goody Two-Shoes*, which if representing a more playful style than books of the Trimmer era, nevertheless constitutes "the very foundation of the Moral Tale."[39] And it seems relevant that, at a time when debates on children's literature were highly politicized, the Barbauld "crew" was dominated by liberal and radical figures like the Aikins, the Edgeworths, Wollstonecraft, and Godwin (who also ran a children's publishing firm with his second wife).[40] The Romantic advocates of fairyland, on the other hand, had already turned from Godwin and their youthful radicalism toward the conservative social and political stances that would mark their later careers.

Aubrey, writing in the late seventeenth century, felt that the rise of literacy among the "ordinary sort of People" had driven away the fairies, but some folktales and literary fairy tales did find their way into the chap-books that formed much of this group's reading.[41] Although its production and distribution were almost wholly uncontrolled, and its uncensored contents gave pause to moralists of Christian and rationalist persuasions alike, the chap-book did not represent a *direct* threat to the established interests. While chap-books could be populist in tone and critical of the upper classes, Olivia Smith has argued against overestimating the political significance of Robin Hood or Jack the Giant Killer: "While the [lower-class] audience read chap-books and ballads, it was considered to have a distinct and subordinate province. Although such material might express ideas about political events, it was not regarded as an attempt to participate in public life."[42] Not so the new political literature, written in a vernacular intellectual style and distributed in pamphlet form at low prices, that emerged in the late eighteenth century and found its apotheosis in Paine's vastly popular *Rights of Man* (1791–92). As T. J. Mathias lamented in the fourth part of *Pursuits of Literature* (1797), the mass distribution of Paine's two-part tract marked a revolution in English reading habits: "We are no longer in an age of ignorance, and information is not partially distributed according to the ranks, and orders, and functions, and dignities of social life ... We no longer look exclusively for learned authors in the usual places, in the retreats of academick erudition, and in the seats of religion. Our peasantry now read the *Rights of Man* on mountains, and moors, and by the way side."[43]

Although literacy rates seem to have risen only gradually throughout much of the eighteenth century, the spectacle of a mass readership in the 1790s, brought out so vividly by the unprecedented sales of *The Rights of Man*, caught many contemporary observers by surprise, and was perceived as a serious and immediate threat by the established political and religious interests.[44] As Lawrence Stone has pointed out, the "notion that literacy is somehow good in itself, one of the natural rights of man" dates back only a hundred years or so, and schooling in basic reading skills (like education generally) has for the most part served, "and indeed until very recently has been designed to serve – the purpose of reinforcing class distinctions and reducing social mobility."[45] But in order to facilitate social control literacy, and the distribution of literature, must be carefully managed by those in power. The mass readership of the 1790s had been formed, however, as if spontaneously through a highly unregulated, disorganized, private, and largely unprofessional patchwork of educational institutions: village schools, Sunday Schools, Charity Schools, "dame" schools, evening and Sunday classes held by clerks or artisans, not to mention home instruction and self-tuition.

The English establishment's answer to the literacy crisis was to call for increased systematization and superintendence of the schools, lest they remain, as the Bishop of Rochester characterized them in 1800, "schools of Jacobinical rebellion."[46] This position was outlined, with specific reference to children's reading, by Coleridge in *The Statesman's Manual*:

Books are in every hovel. The Infant's cries are hushed with *picture*-books – and the Cottager's child sheds his first bitter tears over pages, which render it impossible for the man to be treated or governed as a child. Here as in so many other cases, the inconveniences that have arisen from a thing's having become too general, are best removed by making it universal. (*CLS* 39–40)

In addition to systematizing education under establishment control, however, it was also necessary to hegemonize the writing and distribution of popular reading matter. Radical tracts were prohibited in 1795 and 1798, but something was needed to fill their place.[47] As Hazlitt pointed out from the perspective of 1817 (with a pointed allusion to Coleridge), "It is the fear of the progress of knowledge and a *Reading Public*, that has produced all the fuss and bustle and cant about Bell and Lancaster's plans, Bible and Missionary, and Auxiliary and Cheap Tract Societies, and that when it was impossible to prevent our reading something, made the Church and State so anxious to provide us with that sort of food for our stomachs, which they thought best."[48] Hannah More had earlier stated as much from the opposite end of the ideological spectrum: "To teach the poor to read without providing them with *safe* books, has always appeared to me an improper measure"; More's response was to take on the "laborious undertaking" of the Cheap Repository (*MLC* 2: 73).

In a period when reading designed for the working classes and for children was grouped together as "class-literature," which Charlotte Yonge (writing in 1869) defined as "books ... for children or the poor," children's literature was critically affected by the dominant group's program for hegemonizing popular reading through such institutions as More's Cheap Repository, the Religious Tract Society, the SPCK, and the Association for Preserving Liberty and Property against Republicans and Levellers.[49] This program included the deliberate appropriation by conservative writers of existing popular modes and styles. More, for example, who wrote fifty Cheap Repository Tracts and published one hundred between 1795 and 1797, two million copies of which had been distributed by 1796, had made her own chapbook library in order to pursue the "secret of their popularity."[50] More and other tract writers developed what Smith terms an "anti-intellectual" style meant to counteract not only the message of radical pamphlets but the popular engagement with political thought which they had fostered as well.[51] For such purposes an appropriation of the chapbook mode, turning its "characters and narrative devices ... to moral purposes," helped both to insure the tracts' popularity and to restore the simpler, apolitical discursive mode temporarily displaced by Paine's intellectual vernacular.[52]

Within this context it becomes evident that fairy tales, as the most "innocent" titles in the chapbook repertoire, could represent a harmless, pacifying alternative to radical intellectualism rather than a threat to moral seriousness, and in the early nineteenth century, fairy-land found unexpected allies in writers who found in fantasy a happy escape from more direct assaults on conventional morality and conservative politics. If not always edifying, the fairy tale was at least, when compared with the "master pamphlets of the day" (*Prelude* IX.97), innocuous. A reviewer for the *Christian Observer* (censuring, of all things, Dr. Bowdler's *Family Shakespeare*) commended fairy-land for its very distance from controversial issues: "Had the creative fancy of the poets merely summoned into being elves, fairies, and other denizens of their ideal world, not the most marble-hearted moralist would have interdicted the perusal of the drama."[53] *The London Magazine* in 1820 praised the "moral tendency" of Tabart's *Popular Fairy Tales*, while deploring the "corrupting" and "contaminating" "licentiousness" of the current vogue for social satire in children's poetry, a dangerous form undoubtedly produced by political hacks: "They are most probably the same who bring out the political caricatures, and personal lampoons of the day ... They are evidently done by men ready to do anything."[54]

The *London Magazine*'s reviewer was further exercised by the imposition of "modern criticism" on "the solemn traditions of a people": "The nursery songs and stories, to have their proper effects, should be permitted, like the common law, to depend solely on tradition" (482). Here the appeal to "solemn traditions," the privileging of oral over written discourse, and the analogy with English common law signal the reviewer's conceptual adherence to the Burkean conservatism which, as James Chandler has shown, had so decisive an influence on the development of Wordsworth's thought in the later 1790s.[55] Chandler traces the increasing emphasis in Wordsworth's writing on custom, on rural traditions, and on oral tales to Burke's valorization of habit and tradition, which together constitute what Chandler terms a "second nature" for both writers.[56] Wordsworth's Pedlar in *The Ruined Cottage* exemplifies an education guided by "second nature" rather than the suspect rational approach associated with Godwin and the Edgeworths:

> Small need had he of books; for many a tale
> Traditionary round the mountain hung,
> And many a legend peopling the dark woods
> Nourished Imagination in her growth.   (167–73)

Although Chandler does not consider the role of fairy tales in Wordsworth's attack on rational education in Book v of *The Prelude*, his discussion of Wordsworth's "tales traditionary" and of the "ideological purport of writing that aspires to the condition of speech" helps situate the early Romantics' defense of fairy tales in terms of the contemporary politics of literacy.[57]

Wordsworth argues in *The Prelude* for a kind of "natural" or "negative education" which might seem to ally him with Rousseau. Yet, as we have seen, his criticisms of innovatory educational schemes in Book v are in fact directed against the rational school of educators and writers for children in a direct line of descent from *Emile*. Wordsworth opposes the literature of this movement, with its emphasis on utilitarian knowledge and rational explanations, to the fairy tales and legends of his own childhood:

> Oh, give us once again the wishing-cap
> Of Fortunatus, and the invisible coat
> Of Jack the Giant-killer, Robin Hood,
> And Sabra in the forest with St. George.   (364–67)

In contrast to the Satanic architecture of the rationalists –

> the mighty workmen of our later age
> Who with a broad highway have overbridged
> The froward chaos of futurity (370–73) –

the traditional tales are presented as a literal "second nature," a landscape through which Wordsworth and Coleridge freely wandered as children:

> wandering as we did
> Through heights and hollows and bye-spots of tales
> Rich with indigenous produce, open ground
> Of fancy, happy pastures ranged at will.   (234–37)

The organic "produce" of the tales is further equated with the traditionary teachings of the poet's mother, "Fetching her goodness ...from times past" (267), a "parent hen amid her brood" (246) whose maxims are as natural as the "innocent milk" of "mothers' breasts" (272).[58] The popular ballads of children and peasants are no less natural: "Wren-like warblings made / For cottagers and spinners of the wheel ... Food for the hungry ears of little ones" (208–12). And his childhood "slender abstract of the *Arabian Tales*" (484) makes part of a textual landscape, "a block / Hewn from a mighty quarry" (487–88). Because of their rootedness in tradition, their oral perpetuation among the folk, the "tales that charm away the wakeful night / In Araby" (520–1) gain the permanence and inevitability of rocks, and stones, and trees: "These spread like day, and something of the shape / Of these will live till man should be no more" (528–29).

Although the organic text is a common trope throughout Words-worth's poetry and criticism, his particular insistence on naturalizing fairy tales through metaphor and his Burkean emphasis on an oral tradition equivalent in its permanence to nature suggest a subtly conservative impetus behind the Romantic "defense" of fantasy. Wordsworth in *The Prelude* is hardly advocating increases in undirected reading and political awareness among the rural laboring classes. By 1805, he had firmly rejected the "master pamphlets of the day" (presumably a reference to Paine and other radical pam-phleteers), maintaining that their effect upon him had been disastrous and barely reparable. Wordsworth's advocacy of fairy tales as "innocent" food for rural folk and children – readers of "class-literature" – can perhaps even be seen, like More's use of the chap-book, as yet another appropriation of the popular tale in the interests of returning the new mass readership to an apolitical, class-specific discourse.

Wordsworth's defense of fairy tales in *The Prelude* is usually viewed from a very different perspective, as growing out of his deep suspicion of new educational modes seeking to limit, indoctrinate, and trap the child in a "pinfold of his own conceit," constantly superintended by "some busy helper" (5.356–58). Here fairy tales might be seen as providing an ideologically neutral "open ground" between the radical pamphlet and the reactionary tract, both symptomatic of the politicization of education in "these too industrious times" (293). There is still much to be said for such a perspective, although it should be placed within a more fully developed account of con-temporary theories of education than one based on Wordsworth's simple opposition of rationalist jailers and undisturbed natural fosterage. Wordsworth's public sponsorship (along with Southey and

Coleridge) of Bell's Madras system starkly underscores the limitations of an approach to the Romantics' involvement in debates on children's education and reading based on terms set by the Romantics themselves. By 1829, Wordsworth would articulate a still more explicitly reactionary position, expressing his suspicion of new institutions designed to provide continuing education for English laborers like the London University and the Mechanics' Institutes, and characterizing the latter as "unnatural" schemes whose "means do not pay respect to the order of things," hotbeds of "discontented spirits and insubordinate and presumptuous workmen" (*WLL* 2: 23–24). In discussions of education and mass reading, the standard of "nature" could serve to ground repressive as well as libertarian arguments.

Wordsworth's depiction of the fairy tale as a natural, rather than cultural product – which parallels his natural, idealized vision of the child – demands critical scrutiny not simply for its contemporary ideological implications. In assigning the fairy tale an absolute origin, and thus lending it a transcendent status beyond criticism, the early Romantics set the tone for many of the literary studies of fairy tales to follow. The Romantic belief in the fairy tale's unproblematic traditional status and oral, folk origins continues to inform much recent work on the fairy tale and its relation to the history of children's literature, a view typified by W. H. Auden: "Most fairy tales and myths have come down to us from a prehistoric past, anonymous stories which cannot be attributed to the conscious invention of any individual author."[59] Appeals to an ahistorical, communal, and necessarily oral origin underwrite the claims of a number of more recent literary approaches to fairy tales as well, whether grounded in humanist, psychoanalytic, or even Marxist perspectives. There is no reason, however, to believe that many traditional fairy tales are particularly ancient, orally (or collectively) composed, or of a folk origin.[60] The Romantic approach obscures the problematic generic status of the fairy tale, a (sometimes quite sophisticated) literary form which depends on oral traditions (folktales) for much of its content. And it ignores as well the crucial role of context in the telling or writing of any tale, which cannot be accurately interpreted apart from its specific tellings, shaped by a complex interaction between teller, tale, audience, and social expectations.[61] However traditional oral tales originate, their reception tends to be communal in character; the storyteller, in direct communication with a tale's audience, remains aware of their responses and will vary a specific telling in response to their desires or needs. Children listening to a tale (in traditional societies, most often in the company of adults) can, as David Reisman points out, "criticize, question, and elaborate" on it, and it may in turn be "modulated" for them; whereas the growth of literacy takes the "process of socialization out of the communal chimney corner" and "into the private bedrooms and libraries of the rising middle class." The child reader who "forgets himself" in solitude is in a markedly different discursive position from the children who, as part of a group of listeners, actively respond to and help shape the particular telling of a tale: the reception situation is "no longer controlled and structured by the teller – or by their own participation."[62] This is not to say that the new situation is without its advantages – the privacy of reading can offer the child a kind of "refuge" from the family or immediate social group – but it retains little of the communal or "folk" character associated in the Romantic tradition with fairy tales.[63]

For the folklorist Rudolf Schenda, who dismisses the "orality of fairy tales" and their "folk or lower-class origins" as Romantic myths, the "idolatry" informing most literary approaches to fairy tales is not only ahistorical but politically misguided as well: "a denial of what the folk really recounted and what the actual psycho-social requirements of the members of the lower class were."[64] Folklorists and social historians tend to view the folk tale as a conservative rather than Utopian form, more concerned with inculcating community values than with encoding "subversive" wishes.[65]

Whether the fairy tale is read as a traditional and inherently conservative form, as politically neutral entertainment, or as a particularly subtle instrument of socialization, however, it would be naive to celebrate uncritically Wordsworth and his circle for liberating children's literature. When the Romantic brief for the fairy tale is set against contemporary debates on literacy and education, and when the traditionary, conservative discourse of Wordsworth's defense has been traced to its Burkean matrix, it becomes more difficult to distance the Romantics from the common practice of fairy tale appropriation. Unlike the Grimms or the English ballad collectors, the Romantics were not motivated by the rediscovery of a national folk culture or by local antiquarianism, since the tales they mention most often and most fondly derive from a Persian literary collection by way of an Arabic recension and French translation. The "revival" of the fairy tale does fit remarkably well, however, with the call for a harmless "food" for the new mass readership recalled by Hazlitt, with the conscious attempts of More and others to re-establish the apolitical discourse of the chap-books, and with Burke's influential valorization, in response to revolution in France and radicalism in England, of custom and tradition.

Wordsworth's conception of the fairy tale as "open ground" for the child's developing imagination, stands in the same problematic relation to contemporary educational debates and practices as does his transcendental vision of childhood. Taking up the fairy tale as a critical standard enables Wordsworth to expose the propagandistic and morally stunting aspects of "books about Good Boys and Girls, and bad Boys and Girls, and all that trumpery" (*WLM* 1: 287); books which Coleridge similarly dismisses as vehicles for "debtor and creditor principles of virtue," teaching not goodness but "goody-ness" (*CLL* 2: 193, 1: 108). Yet unlike Blake, whose *Songs of Innocence* expose and deconstruct the disciplinary strategies informing con-temporary children's literature, schooling, and religious instruction, Wordsworth responds to the politicization of childhood in the 1790s by idealizing the child and attributing to it an organic sensibility naturally resistant to radical and conservative indoctrination alike. In contrast to Blake's development in *Songs of Innocence* of a poetics of subversion, Wordsworth advocates an "innocent," traditionary children's reading that implicitly supports the reaction against an informed and politically engaged reading public – "discontented spirits" and "presumptuous workmen."

Godwin again provides a useful contrast. At a time when many (including Coleridge) urged that children be "wholly forbidden" to read novels (*CLL* 2: 193), Godwin defended the child's freedom to "wander in the wilds of literature" unrestrained; he was also, like Wordsworth, Coleridge, and Lamb, an early defender of fairy tales (*GE*, 144). Answering a friend's query on his young daughter's reading in 1802, Godwin recommends fairy tales as books "calculated to excite the imagination, and at the same time quicken the apprehensions of children"; among the specific titles he mentions are Perrault, de Beaumont's "Beauty and the Beast" (a tale Wordsworth considered "disgusting"), the *Arabian Nights*, and the popular chapbook romances *Valentine and Orson* and *The Seven Champions of*

Christendom.[66] But these popular tales are designed to complement, rather than supplant, the works of the Barbauld school; in promoting the nurture of the imagination, Godwin did not find it necessary to dismiss the claims of reason. Among those in the rationalist tradition, however, Godwin's libertarian approach to children's reading was virtually unique. In the context of providing a "progressive" alternative to fairy tales and chapbooks, eighteenth-century moralists developed a disciplinary approach to children's fiction which makes the Romantic nostalgia for "lawless tales" (*Prelude* v.548), whatever its implicit politics, seem a valuable, perhaps inevitable, counter-movement.

DISCIPLINE AND PUBLISH: THE CHILD AS TEXT

Whether or not one senses, with Leigh Hunt, a "fresh country breeze" in Day's *Sandford and Merton* (1783–89), there is no doubt that children's fiction changed considerably over the course of the 1780s. It was a decade of remarkable expansion for the children's book trade – John Marshall alone published seventy books for children between 1780 and 1790 – and one which saw a shift from a juvenile library shaped and to a large extent determined by publishers like Newbery and Marshall, to one in which authors played a much greater role.[67] Many of the children's authors who began publishing in the 1780s – Day, Barbauld, Maria Edgeworth, Trimmer, Wollstonecraft, Ellenor Fenn, John Aikin – were actively involved in education as theorists or teachers, and frequently as both. These author-educators brought to the children's book a concern with child development and a seriousness of purpose which make works like *A Little Pretty Pocket Book* and *Little Goody Two-Shoes* seem intellectually vapid and refreshingly crude by comparison. Improving on Newbery's trade and plum-cake morality, many authors in this group sought to instruct their child readers in such "progressive" issues as kindness to animals, the anti-slavery cause, charity toward beggars and other unfortunates, respect for hard-working laborers (particularly those content in their station), the Sunday School movement, and toleration of those who are physically different from oneself. There is less unanimity on these issues than is sometimes supposed: Barbauld condemns slavery in *Hymns in Prose*, whereas Maria Edgeworth temporizes in *Popular Tales*, and Woll-

stonecraft's portrayal of the ruthlessness of landlords in *Original Stories*
would hardly be endorsed by Trimmer, who felt that the depiction of
"oppressive 'squires and hard-hearted overseers" made even *Little
Goody Two-Shoes* a dangerous book (*Guardian* 1: 431).[68] But if not
united by a single "ideology," the writers who came to prominence
at the end of the eighteenth century did share a set of discursive
practices, codes, and constraints. Their concern with the child's
moral and intellectual development led them not only to introduce
children to progressive causes, but also to reinvent the children's
book along new discursive lines, creating a juvenile library no less
disciplinary in character and intended effect than were the educational technologies that the same group of authors helped
disseminate.

In 1778 Richard Edgeworth, searching for texts to use in educating
his own children, examined over forty children's books and found
only one, Barbauld's *Lessons for children, from two to three years old*
(1778), in which the "vocabulary was simple, the backgrounds
homely, and the lessons kept short." According to Marilyn Butler,
Edgeworth found a theoretical basis for Barbauld's unique success in
associationist psychology, as presented in Joseph Priestley's popular
abridgment of Hartley's *Observations.* "So long as the child responded
to what he met in his reading, he would himself, by the associative
process of the human mind, combine that experience with an
infinitely proliferating number of fresh impressions. He would relate
the significantly chosen single instance to analogous cases: intellectually and imaginatively, what he read would become part of
him."[69] Hartley's associationist psychology, as implemented in
developmentally appropriate texts like Barbauld's *Lessons*, enabled
not only a new approach to writing children's texts, but also a
reconceptualization of the child *as* a kind of text.

The notion of the child's mind as a text in process can be traced
back to Locke's conception of the young child in *Some Thoughts* as a
"white Paper" to be "fashioned as one pleases" (325). This
metaphor did not originate with Locke – it can be found still earlier
in Earle's *Microsomographie* and Bunyan's *Book for Boys and Girls* – but
towards the eighteenth century it loses its Protestant tenor (the child
as receptacle for God's written word) and begins to convey instead
the child's susceptibility to the forming influences of education.[70] As
Sir Roger L'Estrange writes (a year before Locke) in the preface to
his moralized *Fables*, "it is the Education, in short, which makes the

Man. To Speak All, in a Few Words, *Children* are but *Blank Paper*, ready Indifferently for any Impression, Good or Bad, for they take All upon Credit; and it is as much in the Power of the first Comer, to Write Saint, or Devil upon't, which of the Two He pleases."[71]

As popularized by Locke's *Some Thoughts*, the "white paper" metaphor became a commonplace in eighteenth- and early nineteenth-century writing. It comes up in educational treatises like Godwin's *Enquirer* (70), in novels of development like Hays's *Emma Courtney* (22), in primers like John Parson's *First Book for English Schools*, in children's books like Maria Edgeworth's *Parent's Assistant*: "Youth and white paper, as the proverb says, take all impressions" (3: 85).[72] Toward the close of the Romantic period the metaphor is sufficiently hackneyed for Lamb to satirize it in his "Letter to an Old Gentleman Whose Education Has Been Neglected" (1825): "Your mind as yet, give me leave to tell you, is in the state of a sheet of white paper. We must not blot or blur it over too hastily ... We may apply the characters; but are we sure the ink will sink?" (*LW* 1: 214–15). Lamb's playful tone belies a more serious argument: from his Romantic standpoint, the by now pervasive rationalist view of the mind as a text to be inscribed enables a vision of near absolute control over the child-pupil on the part of the parent-teacher. If the child's mind is a blank tablet to be filled in (as Lamb puts it) with "authentic characters or impresses" by the judicious "hand of science," then the adult can, beyond merely guiding the child's development, actually manufacture its subjective life. The child's "character" can be directly informed by the "characters" imprinted on the page it reads, which are impressed in turn on its ductile mind.[73] Many "moral" works of children's fiction produced in the Romantic era are animated by the desire to reconstruct the child through fictions which simultaneously mirror the child's mind and refashion it; ironically, *Mrs. Leicester's School* (by Charles and Mary Lamb) can be numbered among them.[74]

In order for the child's text to successfully penetrate and reform the child's mind (itself conceived of as a text in progress), it had to reflect the child's presumed developmental level in the relative simplicity of its style, the length of its individual chapters or lessons, and the familiarity of its examples and images. When Richard Edgeworth could find no books aside from Barbauld's *Lessons* which properly corresponded to his notion of the mental level of young children, he set about producing his own children's library in concert with his daughter Maria, who ended up doing most of the writing. The Edgeworths eventually produced a whole series of children's books geared to progressive developmental stages, the first such project of its kind (although Barbauld had pointed the way by adding three more volumes to *Lessons* taking the reader up to "from three to four years old"). Maria Edgeworth's *Parent's Assistant* was published in 1796, designed for children who had already mastered Barbauld's *Lessons* and *Hymns in Prose*; some of the stories and instances were taken from the same family "register" of educational experiments, begun by Honora Edgeworth, which provides the basis for *Practical Education* (1: vi). Richard issued *A Rational Primer* in 1799, with a child's first story by Maria, teaching the elements of reading through a rationalized alphabetical system (different vowel sounds indicated by diacritics, silent letters marked by a vertical bar, and so forth). In 1800 *The Parent's Assistant* was augmented and revised, with several stories transferred to a work for younger children, *Early Lessons* (1801), which was begun by Richard and Honora in 1778 and completed by Maria. *Early Lessons* introduced children to characters – Harry and Lucy, Rosamond, and Frank – whose ages corresponded to the presumed ages of the child readers, initially from four to ten years; further volumes entitled *Rosamond*, *Frank*, and *Harry and Lucy Concluded* were produced over the years to show the protagonists growing older along with their readers. Maria also published *Moral Tales* in 1801 for "young people" (adolescents). For every age its book; for every developmental stage its template.

The Edgeworths were the most systematic but by no means the only authors at work in this period inventing a new children's literature geared to specific age-groups. According to Maria Edgeworth, Day initially began *Sandford and Merton* as a section of "Harry and Lucy" (the first part of *Early Lessons*), but it soon grew into a much longer work for somewhat older children.[75] Barbauld, together with her brother John Aikin, wrote *Evenings at Home* for children of a similar age-group (around eight to twelve). Trimmer produced, in addition to her popular *Fabulous Histories* (1786), a small collection of books of the "easy introduction" variety for young children, beginning with her *Easy Introduction to the Knowledge of Nature* in 1780. For children in Sunday and Charity Schools, Trimmer employed the graded method in *The Charity School Spelling Book*, Parts I and II, progressing from "Words of One Syllable Only" to "Words Divided into Syllables," with short didactic stories geared to boy and girl readers (a separate version was produced for each gender).[76] John Parsons adapted the "new Method" for private schools in *The First Book for English Schools; or The Rational Schoolmaster's First Assistant*, leading children "from Syllables of two, and easy Words of three Letters, to Words of Eight, rising gradually by the addition of only one Single Letter at a time; and from Words of one Syllable to Words of Eight, increasing also in a gradual manner." Other notable writers in the new mode included Ellenor Fenn ("Mrs. Teachwell"), whose *Cobwebs to Catch Flies* is arranged progressively for readers from three to eight years of age, and Dorothy and Mary Ann Kilner. English translations of two French children's authors, both influenced by Rousseau, also helped establish the new climate for developmentally suitable books: Arnaud Berquin, whose *L'Ami des enfans* was translated as *The Children's Friend* in 1783, and the comtesse de Genlis, whose *Veillées du Château* appeared as *Tales of the Castle* in 1785. In the last two decades of the eighteenth century, the modern children's library – with its stratification by age-groups, its carefully screened and typically instructive content, its schematic tailoring of vocabulary, style, and narrative structure to adult perceptions of children's abilities and needs – was all but fully established; only the rehabilitation of fantasy under the rubric of "innocence" was lacking.

The English authors most directly influenced by Rousseau – Day, Aikin, and (to a lesser extent) the Edgeworths – had to confront a particularly vexing theoretical problem. Whereas Locke's objections to children's fiction were based in large part on the lack of suitably simple, rational, and instructive titles – a lack that would be remedied over the course of the century – Rousseau's objections were more essential: "reading is the plague of childhood" (116). This difference reflects in turn a more absolute opposition in Rousseau between words and things, and a different conception of how the child learns. For Rousseau, the child's mind is not like a text, in that it cannot be "inscribed" by words alone, no matter how clear and distinct the ideas they express: "The child retains the words; the ideas are reflected off of him" (107). The natural "suppleness" of the "child's brain" makes it susceptible not to imprinting, as in Locke, but to a direct "engraving" or "impressing" – like a three-dimensional seal or etching rather than a two-dimensional text – by means of active experience: objects alone "may be impressed on his brain at an early age," and therefore the object world, "all that surrounds him is the book in which, without thinking about it, he continually enriches his memory" (112). Even *Robinson Crusoe* is more of a how-to manual for the child to follow than a book to be read as fiction. Authors like Day and Aikin, who were swayed by Rousseau's arguments but nevertheless wished to help redeem the children's book, compromised by writing fictions *about* direct experience of the object world, featuring active child protagonists through whom the reader would vicariously live and learn. Richard Edgeworth reduces this practice to a maxim in an 1814 preface to *Early Lessons*: "Action should be introduced – Action! Action! Whether in morals or science, the thing to be taught should seem to arise from the circumstances, in which the little persons of the drama are placed. "[77] This compromise was not a particularly happy one, resulting in a "pale simulacrum" of the active experience called for by Rousseau; but the fictionalized "object lesson," however theoretically inconsistent, came to shape the moral tales of many children's authors of the period, including those who, like Trimmer and Sherwood, held Rousseau's writings in anathema.[78]

The pervasiveness of the object lesson, which frequently shapes the plot of the didactic or instructive children's tale, should not, however, lead one to overlook the equally widespread strategies practiced (with still more inconsistency) by the same group of authors for "inscribing" the child's mind more directly through the medium of language itself. The common use of the catechistic method, resolutely condemned in *Emile* (257), provided one obvious model for how "dialogue" could be used to impress lessons in the child's memory; carefully scripted dialogues (often between a mother and child) are frequently employed in this period to spell out the moral of an object lesson, or to graft a moral onto received material like the fables of Aesop and La Fontaine. Occasionally these "dialogues" take an explicitly catechistic form, as in Barbauld's *Hymns in Prose* (e.g. 13–14). In other works, the catechistic effect is produced by repeated oral performance on the part of the child reader and supervising parent, as Fenn suggests in the preface to the "Morals" section of her *Fables in Monosyllables*, worth quoting for its unabashed portrayal of parental and authorial manipulation:

Therefore, having written a few Fables, from whence unexceptionable Morals may be drawn, I chose to make the little folk themselves seem to discover them – indeed, I took care they should be sufficiently obvious for them to do it – and the frequent repetition appeared to me of use, as it would enable the child really to make the remarks which I put in his mouth, as well as inculcate more strongly the notions which I wished to infuse.[79]

But in addition to adapting oral methods of instruction, children's writers in this period developed fictional strategies which capitalized more directly on the presumed textual nature of the child's mind, bringing child and book into a peculiarly intimate and specular relation. These strategies include encouraging the child to take its place in a discursive universe through thematizing the act of reading; training the child to participate in its own textualization by writing about itself; and instilling a sense in the child of its own legibility, its status as a text open to the perusal of its parents and (ultimately) to the all-seeing eye of God.

Publishers are hardly less interested than authors and educators in bringing children together with books, and reading is made a common theme from the beginnings of the juvenile book trade. *Goody Two-Shoes*, for example, typically includes a chapter on "How Little Margery learned to read, and by Degrees taught others." With the growing sense of the child as itself a kind of text, and thus of the children's text as both analogous to and potentially contiguous with the child's mind, the thematization of reading in children's books takes on a new intensity. Some books, like Fenn's *Fables* or the Edgeworths' *Early Lessons*, open with a message congratulating the child for having a book and being able to read it: "YOU must have been good, else your mam-ma would not have bought a new book for you" (1 : xv); "Little children, who know the sounds of all the letters, can read words, and can understand what is told in this book" (1 : 1). Barbauld's *Lessons* teaches the child to base its superiority to animals (if not its right to existence) on its ability to read: "I never saw a little dog or cat learn to read. But little boys can learn. If you do not learn, Charles, you are not good for half so much as Puss. You had better be drowned."[80] Maria Edgeworth's "The way to my Grandmother's," appended to *A Rational Primer*, turns Perrault's "Little Red Riding Hood" into a fable about reading. Two sisters wish to take flowers to their grandmother, but succeed only because the elder can read the way sign at a dividing path, leading to the younger sister's (and the story's) conclusion: "it is very useful to know how to read; I wish that I could read."[81]

Children's books in this period frequently portray children reading or learning to read, and gaining both immediate pleasure and material or spiritual benefits from their literacy skills. When Harry Sandford teaches Tommy Merton to read, a delighted Mr. Barlow declares, "I know of scarcely any thing which from this moment will not be in his power" (1: 61). Some books open with a scene of reading, or are framed by such scenes. The Lambs' *Mrs. Leicester's School* begins with Elizabeth Villiers telling how she was taught her letters (oddly like Mary Shelley) by her father tracing them on her mother's gravestone; "the epitaph on my mother's tomb being my primmer [sic] and my spelling-book, I learned to read." In a manner recalling the daughter's nurturing and protection by her dead mother in most versions of "Cinderella," Elizabeth "had an idea that the words on the tombstone were somehow a part of mamma, and that she had taught me" (3: 276). Aikin and Barbauld's *Evenings at Home; Or, The Juvenile Budget Opened* features a large family whose ingenious visitors "would frequently produce a fable, a story, or dialogue, adapted to the age and understanding of the young people." These texts are kept in the famed "*Budget of Beachgrove Hall*," and are drawn out at random to be read aloud by the children during family soirées devoted to the practice of juvenile critique.[82]

The fictional portrayal of reading reaches its apotheosis in *Visits to the Juvenile Library; Or, Knowledge Proved to Be the Source of Happiness* (1805) by Eliza Fenwick, a member of the Godwin-Wollstonecraft circle. The book is designed as an elaborate advertisement for Tabart's Juvenile Library, a children's bookstore in London owned by Fenwick's publisher; but it goes beyond the self-puffery characteristic of the Newbery era in portraying the ability to read less as the key to worldly success than as the foundation of happiness and the underpinning of a moral character. *Visits* tells the story of five orphaned children taken in by the enlightened Mrs. Clifford, who also supports a school for the "children of the poor." Having been previously brought up in the West Indies by "an ignorant Negro woman," Nora, who (perhaps not surprisingly) "had never learned to read," the children are barely literate, and thus (according to the logic of the tale) fractious, ill-natured, and incredibly prone to boredom. Fortunately, they live "in an age when a great number of wise persons employ themselves in composing books which, while they shew young people how to amend their faults, give them the greatest amusement," and a course of Tabart's books soon makes new children of them. The moral is pointed out by none other than Nora, whom the children discover attempting to teach herself to read: "Since you come to England, you get books, you read books, you talk together, play together, read again, play again, be happy, be merry, fetch your own playthings, put them away ... Nora think you learn it all out of books, so Nora learn books too."[83] The overt equation here between a black West Indian adult and a group of English children, with literacy portrayed as the key to the moral development and true happiness of both, suggests how the moral tale is implicated in a project, analogous to colonialism, for disciplining the middle-class child, much as the literature surrounding the monitorial or Madras system reveals discursive links between the "civilizing" of British colonial subjects and that of the labouring classes in England.

In featuring such scenes of reading, the moral tale encourages children to define themselves in terms of their relation to texts; it makes the relation of child and text more intimate still by training children to make written works out of their own lives. This discursive strategy again predates the full flourishing of the moral tradition in the late eighteenth century, and can be seen at work as early as 1749 in Sarah Fielding's *The Governess or, Little Female Academy*, an early school-story (presided over by a "Mrs. Teachum") often described as the first novel written specifically for children. Fielding prefaces the book by asking her child audience to consider the "true Use of Reading": "and once you can fix this Truth in your Minds, namely, that the true Use of Books is to make you wiser and better, you will then have both Profit and Pleasure from what you read."[84] But as the book progresses, it becomes apparent that producing texts is no less important than reading them for the proper development of the "*Female Character*" (xi). Jenny Peace, Mrs. Teachum's favorite and the school's unofficial monitor, initiates a practice of assembling the girls for regular reading and discussion sessions, devoted mainly to each girl's narration of her life and principal errors, as "there is nothing more likely to amend the future Part of any One's Life, than the recollecting and confessing the Faults of the past" (12). (Other sessions are devoted to training the girls in proper reading methods, such as seeing through the "supernatural Assistances" of fairy tales and learning how to draw the "Moral" out of plays [34, 106]). Mrs. Teachum is extremely taken with the confessional aspect of Jenny's project; but as "she thought that being present at those Relations might be a balk to the Narration," she instructs Jenny to "get the Lives of her Companions in Writing, and bring them to her" (40).

The girls' acts of narration, duly recorded by Jenny, thus take on a two-fold disciplinary function, at once enabling their teacher to "know their different dispositions" and, more importantly, training the girls in self-criticism through narrating their "past Faults" (40). Jenny's full transcription of these confessions (with the sessions of reading and literary analysis interspersed among them) becomes the book which Fielding publishes in order to "cultivate ... the Minds of young Women" (xi), who presumably discover in turn both how to become moral readers and how to discipline themselves through turning their lives into confessional texts.

Both Wollstonecraft's *Original Stories* and the Lambs' *Mrs. Leicester's School* adapt the confessional project and the self-reflexive framing device developed by Fielding in *The Governess. Original Stories, From Real Life; With Conversations, Calculated to Regulate the Affections, and Form the Mind to Truth and Goodness* features two girls entrusted to a governess after having been earlier left to the devices of "servants, or people equally ignorant."[85] Mrs. Mason redeems the girls from their "vulgar" upbringing through a program of object lessons, instructive dialogues, and reading: "in reading, the heart is touched, till its feelings are examined by the understanding, and reason regulates the imagination" (xii, 106–7). As the girls' parting gift, designed to facilitate their internalization of her teachings, Mrs. Mason presents them with a book retailing their discussions: "recur frequently to it, the stories will illustrate the instruction it contains, and you will not feel the want of my personal advice" (172–73). This book, presumably, is *Original Stories*, and contains a record of the girls' errors and rehabilitation; in addition, they are to "write often" to their teacher, who adds, "and let me have the genuine sentiments of your hearts" (174). Taking *Original Stories* as a model, the girls (and the child reader as well) can learn to discipline their own hearts through constructing moral tales out of their lives. *Mrs. Leicester's School: Or, the History of Several Young Ladies, Related by Themselves* is presented as a teacher's "fair copy" of the confessional sessions or "biographical conversations" held one winter by the girls in a boarding school (3: 273). As in Fielding's *Governess*, this collection of autobiographical sketches both enables the girls' teacher to "form a just estimate of [their] dispositions," and functions for the girls themselves (and the intended reader) as a course of lessons in self-discipline through self-representation (3: 274).

Because Protestantism is, as Stone puts it, a "religion of the book,"

English religious writing aimed at children had long emphasized reading and textuality.[86] Janeway exhorts "all Parents" in his preface to *A Token* to let their children "Read this Book over an hundred times, and observe how they are *affected*... Put your children upon Learning their Catechism, and the Scriptures... let them Read" (iii–v). Bunyan encourages readers of his *Book for Boys and Girls* to envision themselves as sheets of "white Paper," "indited" by those they traffic with and legible to every "reading man": "Each blot, and blur, it also will expose / To thy next Readers, be they Friends, or Foes" (74–75). Watts, who combines the missionary zeal of a Calvinist divine with a Lockean approach to child development, was among the first to produce books deliberately attuned to the "feeble Capacities" of children.[87] His *Divine Songs Attempted in Easy Language for the Use of Children* includes a hymn of "Praise to God for learning to read" (Song VIII [11–13]); the speaker of Song XXVIII ("For Lord's Day Evening") prays, "O write upon my Memory, Lord, / The Texts and Doctrines of thy Word" (38); and the "Sluggard" ends with thanks to those "Who taught me betimes to love Working and Reading" (47). Trimmer's *Easy Introduction to the Knowledge of Nature, and Reading the Holy Scriptures, Adapted to the Capacities of Children* presents the "*Book of Nature*" as a text "preparatory" to children's bible reading: "But Here is still another Book in which the goodness of GOD to mankind is more fully developed, I mean the BIBLE; from which you may learn to worship your Creator, to please and obey him."[88]

This Protestant emphasis on reading and textuality is combined with the confessional mode of books like *The Governess* in Sherwood's immensely popular *The Fairchild Family* (1818), subtitled in some editions as *The Child's Manual*. The book starts out as a sort of novelization of the catechism: the children's first lesson is on the "Creation of All Things by the Sacred Three in One," the next two on the Fall and the "General Depravity of Mankind," including the "exceeding wickedness" of the children's own natural hearts.[89] In addition to oral practices like catechism, confession, and recitation – "May we say some verses, about mankind having bad hearts?" (25) – the children are also disciplined through particularly striking object lessons (such as being taken to see a murderer's rotting corpse on a gibbet) and through keeping journals. When Lucy, the eldest, repents after a day of misbehavior, Mrs. Fairchild opines that her "heart is the same": "it is only because I am with you, watching you

... that you seem to be better than you were that day" (77). So that Lucy can internalize the watchful parental presence, she is given a book "neatly bound in red leather" which literalizes (in a double sense) the metaphor of the child as text: "There was nothing written in the book; the leaves were all blank" (78). Lucy is instructed to "write in it every day the naughty things which pass in [her] heart"; it is less important that she show it to her mother than that she study it herself. The narrator (in a rare aside) addresses the child reader directly in order to recommend the same practice: "perhaps, when you are able to write, you will get your friends to give you a blank book and a pen and ink, that you may also keep an account of the sins of your heart"; a few extracts from Lucy's journal are given as an example (81).[90]

A related strategy for internalizing discipline in the child, again practiced by "moral" writers across a broad ideological spectrum, lies in convincing the child of its own legibility – its openness to inspection by parents and teachers and (still more effectively) to their moral conscience and to God. Mrs. Mason instructs her students that lying is an "affront" to God, who "reads" their "very thoughts ... nothing is hid from him" (36). The conscience or moral "monitor" as internalized guardian of behavior and representative of God's omniscience at the level of each individual child provides the governing conceit of Fenn's *The Fairy Spectator; or, The Invisible Monitor* (1789), in which Miss Sprightly, a pupil at Mrs. Teachwell's, dreams of an exceedingly moral fairy: "I am your guardian, to watch over your mind; although you never saw me before, yet I have always seen you. I have known every action, every word, nay, every thought." Mrs. Teachwell interprets the dream in Christian terms ("He, who sees all you do; who knows all you say, or think") in order to make sure her charges find the moral beneath the fairy machinery of Miss Sprightly's dream; the implied author (also "Mrs. Teachwell") expresses a wish, in dedicating *The Fairy Spectator* to a particular child, that she might have a fairy's power of invisibility, for the "friendly purpose" of observing her young reader unnoticed and unseen: "and I hope that I should have the pleasure to see you act always, as if you were in the presence of your dear Mamma; or, to speak in still higher terms, as if you remembered that *there is an Eye which sees us wherever we are.*"[91] The fairy "monitor" figures as an internalized and (thus) omniscient representative of the authority represented by parents ("Mamma"), teachers (the character "Mrs.

Teachwell"), God (whose all-seeing eye guarantees the internal monitor's functioning) and, significantly, the children's author as "friendly" disciplinarian (the "Mrs. Teachwell" of the dedication).

That Fenn's term "monitor" evokes the "monitorial method" is surely not a coincidence: where the "monitorial method" (primarily designed for lower-class children) consists of internalizing discipline in a classroom by making each student supervise the others, Fenn's monitor guarantees discipline and moral behavior by making the more highly literate middle-class child supervise itself. Edgeworth advances a secularized version of the same conceit in "The Bracelets," from *The Parent's Assistant*: "Let those who are tempted to do wrong by hopes of future gratification, or the prospect of certain concealment and impunity, remember, that unless they are totally depraved, they bear in their own hearts a monitor who will prevent their enjoying what they have ill obtained" (3: 53–54). A related figure, familiar from contemporary educational discourse, is that of the teacher's (or parent's, or God's) relentless "eye," which again must be internalized in order to become most effective. This metaphor can also be traced back as early as Fielding's *Governess*: Mrs. Teachum (who has read her Locke) takes "no more scholars that she could have an Eye to herself"; her "lively and commanding Eye" creates "an Awe in all her little Scholars" (2). In the interpolated moral fairy tale, "Princess Hebe," the heroine turns her face away from her mother, "wanting to Shun the piercing look of that Eye, which she imagined would see the Secret lurking in her Bosom" (83). Mrs. Mason's eye in *Original Stories* is equally piercing: "I cannot go to sleep," Mary confesses after a day of misbehaving: "I am afraid of Mrs. Mason's eyes" (51). Sherwood's children's story "The Father's Eye" (1830) explicitly equates the parental gaze with the omniscient eye of God, which facilitates the children's internalization of the father's moral authority: "But be it remembered by you, my children, that as the time will come when the eyes of your earthly father can no longer be upon you, and that, as even now, it must often happen that you are withdrawn from my sight, yet that you never can escape the searching eye of your heavenly Father."[92]

Sherwood's *The Fairchild Family* develops the same conceit in a manner which suggests that the child's proper internalization of the disciplinary gaze depends to a degree upon prior training in literacy. The section on "The All-Seeing God" tells how the younger daughter, Emily, learns that she is never unobserved, not even in the closet (which contains some tempting but forbidden plums) of a little-used storage room: "no eye was looking at her but the eye of God, who sees everything we do, and knows even the secret sins of the heart" (101). Emily ends up suffering from a fever, brought on indirectly by her attempts to cover up her theft, in which she dreams that "a dreadful eye was looking at her, from above, wherever she went" (104). Emily's sin in this case is an obvious one, and the lesson at first seems to be simply that there is no hiding our ill deeds from God's "dreadful" eye; but the phrase "the secret sins of the heart" relates her experience to the earlier section on Lucy's journal, entitled "Story of the Secret Sins of the Heart." The logic of this connection and of the order in which the two stories are presented is that Lucy is not aware of many of her "sins" until she begins keeping a diary and textualizing her "secret" thoughts; the internalized gaze of moral authority will detect only the most apparent faults unless the child learns first to construct a moralized narrative out of its most seemingly casual experiences. Lucy's journal, moreover, is presented by her mother as an extension of and substitute for the watchful parental presence which must sometimes be suspended. Sherwood is drawing in this section on "The All-seeing God," Song IX of the *Divine Songs*, in which Watts teaches his child reader that each sin is "writ" in God's "dreadful Book":

> O may I now forever fear
> T'indulge a sinful Thought,
> Since the Great God can see, and hear,
> And writes down every Fault!   (14)

But by making the child itself, rather than (or along with) God, the inditer of sinful thoughts, Sherwood intensifies the child's sense of implication in its own moral regulation.

The connection posited by Sherwood between internalized observation and self-representation suggests why the more highly literate middle-class child – the child addressed in the texts I have been discussing – can become its own "monitor," whereas lower-class children, learning to read but (often) not to write, must monitor one another. The child consumer of "moral" fiction learns, above and beyond any discrete ethical lesson, to conceive of its own life in terms of a succession of moral narratives based on those (typically concerning a child of its own age and class) presented in the tales it reads. The most apparently trivial experience – choosing a purchase, preparing a birthday present, swinging in a barn – can become a moral tale, a chapter in the child's ongoing spiritual or ethical autobiography, and thus subject to the internalized eye of moral authority figured externally by parent or teacher, with God, as a mediating figure at once internal and external, underwriting the process. Beyond any specific content, the "subject" of moral children's fiction is the child reader itself, whose subjective experience becomes refashioned by the narratives it reads. That is, in addition to representing a moralized world to the child, and beyond even providing the child with an idealized representation of itself, the "new" children's book sought to reconstruct the child's subjectivity as an ordered, legible, normative, and moralized text in its own right. By drawing the child reader into a fictional world, and then inscribing it (and teaching it to inscribe itself) with a series of moral narratives geared to developmental stages, the children's book was designed to have a material effect on the middle-class child it typically portrayed; it simultaneously represented and attempted to embody in its readers, the bourgeois vision of the child as innocent and manageable. The goal this genre set itself was one of reforming the child in every sense – capitalizing on the alleged textual quality of the child's mind to make word become flesh and flesh become word.

Attending to the fictional strategies at work in the moral tradition helps remind us that, in children's fiction as in educational theory, the more "progressive" authors were often at the forefront of establishing new disciplinary methods and discursive strategies. It also helps distinguish the more deep-seated Romantic critique of the moral tradition from the strictures of such writers as Trimmer, who endorses (and herself practices) the manipulative discourses of the "new" children's fiction while objecting only to the content of those "*Books of Education* and *Children's Books*" produced by radicals "endeavoring to corrupt the minds of the rising generation" (*Guardian* 1 : 3). For the Romantics, it is the disciplinary stance taken toward the child and the authoritarian poetics of the genre as a whole that render the moral tradition obnoxious. But the opposition between Romantics and moralists (rationalist, Christian, or both) is no more absolute in relation to children's reading than is the opposition of Romantic and rationalist in relation to new educational methods and institutions. Just as the Lake poets' advocacy of the child's freedom from constraint does not prevent them from endorsing the repressive Madras system, their critique of moral "trumpery" in children's fiction does not prevent Wordsworth from recommending "chiefly religious Books" for the children of the poor (*WLM* 1 : 247), or Coleridge from urging that novels be "wholly forbidden to children" (*CLL* 2 : 193), or Lamb from turning his own childhood experience of "Witches and Other Night Fears" into a fable about the dangers of unsupervised reading in the "Maria Howe" section of *Mrs. Leicester's School* (*LW* 3 : 318–23). In relation to children's reading, as with changing conceptions of education, a significant (and by now too familiar) area of disagreement between the first-generation Romantics and a collection of more overtly disciplinarian writers can be seen as bracketed within a wider region of consensus. However much they scorned the "goodyness" of contemporary children's fiction, the Romantics participated in the larger discursive project of redefining childhood in terms of "innocence," a project which entailed both the censorship of children's books and a new, more manipulative conception of the child reader.

A POETICS OF INNOCENCE

If the stock opposition of "fairy tale" and "moral tale" belies how readily an appeal to fantasy or the imagination could be reclaimed within a more entertaining, more subtly didactic children's library, the same dichotomy also obscures – or keeps from becoming articulated – certain latent assumptions underlying a good deal of children's fiction in the didactic and fantastic modes alike, amounting to a set of discursive constraints inseparable from the governing notion of childhood innocence which emerged in tandem with the juvenile book industry. In studying the resistance not to children's fairy tales but to children's satire, a resistance for the most part left out of the history of children's literature, we can call into question our own cultural assumptions regarding children and their books, which we inherit from eighteenth-century moralists and nineteenth-century fantasists alike.[93]

Both the moral tale and the children's fairy tale, for example, share an underlying assumption that the child reader is not to make moral evaluations on its own. In the moral tale, the child is taught to regulate its behavior according to an ethical code clearly established by the author; although the child *protagonist* may at times be called upon to make an "independent" judgment, it is always made clear to the child *reader* which choice is the correct one. Moral tales featuring such choices, whether practical (as in "The Purple Jar" in *Early Lessons*) or ethical (as in "Mademoiselle Panache" in *The Parent's Assistant*), almost invariably include a controlling adult figure who guides the child protagonist's choice and makes the moral reasoning behind it clear to the child reader. In the fairy tale, on the other hand, the fiction either conveys a similarly unambiguous moral lesson or alternatively takes place in a fundamentally amoral fantasy world. That is, in the cases in which literary fairy tales for children do not simply (like more frankly didactic literature) reflect the social morality of the day, they can be seen as essentially irrelevant to discussions of social morality altogether. This is the brunt of Coleridge's famous response to Barbauld's complaint that the *Rime of the Ancient Mariner* "had no moral": "It ought to have had no more moral than the Arabian Night's tale of the merchant's sitting down to eat dates by the side of a well, and throwing the shells aside, and lo! a genie starts up, and says he *must* kill the aforesaid merchant *because* one of the dates had, it seems, put out the eye of the genie's son."[94] Whether we view the world of fairy tales as a "morally-charged universe" or as a "moral no-man's-land" where questions of value become meaningless, the fairy tale exacts no more original an ethical response from the child reader than does the moral tale.[95] Satire, on the other hand, as the "literary genre most implicated in historical and social particulars," deals almost by definition with the revaluation of social values, and children's satire, unlike children's fantasy, found no early defenders among the Romantics or elsewhere.[96] In fact, advocates of imaginative literature for children could make common ground with didactic writers in attacking satirical works intended for or made available to children.

The tacit notion that children are too naive to perform complex moral evaluations makes part of the fundamentally new conception of childhood innocence that arose with and conditioned the development of the children's book industry in the latter half of the eighteenth century.[97] Children's fiction, as Jacqueline Rose has argued, "draws in the child, it secures, places, and frames the child," situating "the child who is outside the book" within the grasp of adult desires: "The child... is innocent and can restore that innocence to us."[98] This insistence on childhood innocence separates "official" children's literature since the later eighteenth century from the uncensored chapbooks which children and adults for a time continued to share, as well as from earlier books for children (such as the abridged "but not bowdlerised" editions of *Tom Jones* and similar novels produced for children before the 1780s) that did not as strictly differentiate between an adult sensibility and a pristine childhood realm.[99] It is precisely because of what Wilhelm Grimm termed their "simplicity, innocence, and artless purity" that fairy tales could become accepted into the new children's canon in a way that the more earthy or "coarse" segments of the chapbook repertory could not.[100] As Rose suggests, in the children's fairy tale an imagined "primitive" innocence ("nature or oral tradition") meets an equally imaginary "childhood innocence," the genetic counterpart to the "childhood" of culture, and the locus where the oral tradition is maintained.[101] From this perspective, the eventual recuperation of the fairy tale as an "innocent" children's form seems inevitable.

The social construction of childhood innocence initially entailed – in the relative absence of an appropriate juvenile library – a good deal of censorship on the part of parents and educators. Isaac Watts warned parents against filling the child's memory with such "rubbish" as cradle songs, nurses' "conundrums," and bed-time rhymes: "Something more innocent, more solid, and more profitable may be invented, instead of these fooleries."[102] Watts added "A Slight Specimen of Moral Songs" to his *Divine Songs* in the hope that "some happy and condescending genius" would adopt the mode and produce an innocent secular counterpart to Watts's hymns for children, as an antidote to "those Idle, Wanton or Profane Songs, which give so early an ill Taint to the Fancy and Memory" (46). The Edgeworths, in *Practical Education*, praise a mother who with some "necessary operations by her scissars" bowdlerized the home library, and warn that "few books can be safely given to children" without a good deal of crossing or snipping out: "We should preserve children from the knowledge of any vice, or any folly" (411–12).

The *Guardian of Education* was designed as a guide to the book-buying and scissors-wielding parent; for Trimmer, even *Goody Two-Shoes* (which, as Ronald Paulson has shown, borrows a great deal from the eighteenth-century tradition of "satiric fiction for adults") demanded a judicious use of the pen for its inclusion of anti-establishment satire.[103] As Jackson points out, the "new child" as codified by Trimmer, Fenn, Barbauld, and others in the 1780s and 1790s was to be held at a pristine distance both from the more boisterous humor of the Newbery era *and* from the moral evaluations implicit in satire: "This child lapped up lessons hungrily, was eagerly obedient or lavishly repentant, but most important, the new good child seldom made important, real decisions without parental approval."[104] In her preface to *The Adventures of a Pincushion* (c. 1783), Mary Ann Kilner explicitly rejects satire, despite the "zest" it might give her work, as improper for children: "To exhibit their superiors in a ridiculous light, is not the proper method to engage the youthful mind to respect."[105] But it was not simply the anti-authoritarian tendencies of satire that made it virtually incompatible with the "new child" of the later eighteenth century; it was also its implicit appeal to a child reader too sophisticated to be contained within a definition of childhood based on guilelessness and naivety.

The ruling notion of childhood innocence and simplicity affects the narrative poetics of children's texts no less than their manifest content. The requirement for simplicity and "artlessness" underwrites any number of formal constraints identified by recent theorists of children's narrative, from the "norm of closure" which has been called the "most strictly observed narrative convention in children's literature," to the preference in the "most popular" juvenile books for "strong, traditional story lines," to the "apparent sameness" in generic format and archetypal "evocations" found throughout the children's book, not to mention its pervasively "stereotyped" characterizations.[106] (These are all, of course, requirements which the traditional fairy tale is eminently suited to meet.) These formal limitations should not be seen simply as concessions to unpracticed readers; as Peter Hunt argues, children's books are in general "overcoded," reflecting the desire for "strong narrational control" on the part of adult authors and adult purchasers.[107] In the children's literature which developed during the final decades of the eighteenth century, and which in terms of narrative poetics set the tone for most children's books until quite recently, the child inside the text was to be as manageable as the child outside the text.

A key "overcoded" narrative feature concerns the implied child reader. Applying reader response theory to children's fiction, Aidan Chambers describes the "development of the implied reader into an implicated reader": although (or perhaps because) children are initially "unyielding readers," writers for children develop techniques designed to "draw the reader into the text in such a way that the reader accepts the role offered and enters into the demands of the book."[108] Or as Rose puts it, "Children's fiction sets up the child as outsider to its own process, and then aims, unashamedly, to take the child *in.* "[109] The role which children's narrative sets up for the reader is above all simple and circumscribed; the reader, like the text, is stable, stereotyped, linguistically naive, and contained. The child reader, like the children's text, is integral and innocent.

It is significant in this regard that Watts, in recommending that "nothing but what is chaste, pure, and innocent" be placed within the reach of children, makes particular reference not only to "immodest Stories" and "wanton songs" but also "riddles and puns with double meanings" (315). Ambiguity, puns, riddles – the very stuff of traditional nursery rhymes, which remained largely un-censored until well into the nineteenth century – must be avoided precisely because they subvert the notion of a stable and unitary child reader.[110] The adult desire to control and contain the implied (or implicated) child reader in relation to linguistic duplicity emerges quite starkly in Richard Edgeworth's remarks on irony in the *Rational Primer*: "Children, especially those who are well-educated, take every thing which they read, in its direct and obvious sense...To point out what is ironical, I prefix a mark of admiration with two dots underneath it (!.)" (14–15). Edgeworth's qualifying clause suggests that the "well-educated child" is one who, as Watts had recom-mended, has been kept carefully guarded from the "double mean-ings" of such oral material as puns, "conundrums," and nursery rhymes; irony can be introduced into the new children's literature only when carefully marked and deliberately controlled by the adult author. A similar program of strict narrative control operates at the level of plot throughout the children's tales of Maria Edgeworth, in which the apparent moral ambiguities encountered by her child heroes and heroines are invariably exposed to the reader as equivocal only from the limited perspective of the child protagonist, with an adult figure spelling out the correct moral choice.

Edgeworth's "The Birth-Day Present," included in *The Parent's Assistant*, provides a characteristic example of strategic narrative containment. It verges at several points toward satire, but the child reader is kept from making undirected judgments, being subjected instead to the monitory guidance of three parental figures – the mother, the father, and the narrator. This moral tale also illustrates a number of features characteristic of the genre: the appropriation of folktale types and motifs, the didactic use of parent-child dialogue, the fictionalized object lesson, and the father's overseeing gaze. At the same time, "The Birth-Day Present" is far from dry or mechanical.

Its heroine, Rosamond, is represented in a natural and engaging manner, and the reader is made to sympathize with her while simultaneously registering her faulty reasoning and wrong moves.

The tale opens with a mother-daughter exchange on the value of celebrating birthdays that, unlike the stilted dialogues found in Fenn or Barbauld, initially sounds like a conversation one could imagine overhearing. ("'Mamma,' said Rosamond, after a long silence, 'do you know, what I have been thinking of all this time?'") But the colloquial tonalities of the dialogue are offset by the mother's remorseless assertion of pedagogic and parental authority, pressing the child to define her terms ("'What do you mean by keeping your birthday?'") and clarify her arguments, and unilaterally setting limits to the dialogue's scope and duration ("'Nay, Rosamond, thank you, not just now; I have not time to listen to you'") (2: 3–6). Needless to say, this rational family chooses to ignore such accidental occasions as children's birthdays. A later exchange between Rosamond and her father on the value of the present she has made for her more broadly indulged cousin – a delicate and hence not very useful work basket – reads even more like a pale simulacrum of Socratic dialogue. When Rosamond asserts that her father wishes people to be generous, for example, he replies "So do I ... but we have not quite yet settled what it is to be generous" (2: 18). The parent-child conversations in this text are dialogic only in form; the adults remain as resolutely in control of the discursive relation as they would in a formally catechistic situation, and there is similarly no possibility that a truth might arise through dialogue that the parents did not already have in mind.

The tale's two-part plot places Rosamond in relation to three other children: her sister Laura, her spoiled cousin Bell, and a nameless lower-class girl. The first part constitutes a moralization of the "Kind and Unkind Daughters" folktale type, with Rosamond and Laura each given a golden coin (by their godmother, of course) to lay out as she pleases. Rosamond, here the unkind daughter, spends her half-guinea on filigree for Bell's work basket, an act of false generosity since it is motivated by a desire to *appear* generous. Laura, the "little miser" (2: 8), hoards her cash only long enough to use it to relieve the nameless girl, a child lace-maker whose fragile means of production (a weaving pillow and set of bobbins) have been casually destroyed by a vicious footman. The longer second part contrasts the sense and decorous behavior of both sisters with their cousin's foolishness and

ill-breeding, the first attributable to her mother's indulgence, the
second to her being left too much in the hands of servants. Bell throws
several tantrums, spoils the work basket, and colludes with a
housemaid in blaming its ruin on the nameless girl who, as the plots
converge, comes to the house to deliver lace and again to request
payment. Her second appearance allows her not only to expose Bell
and the maid but also to publicly thank Laura, whose kindness thus
meets with its reward as the tale-type demands.

The story verges toward satire in its depictions of Bell's folly and
the housemaid's deceptions, and the sisters are allowed to smile
demurely at the former. But the child reader is kept fully apprised of
which characters and actions to approve and which to condemn, in
part through the dialogues between Rosamond and her parents, in
part through narrative and editorial intrusions. Rosamond's father,
for example, has defined Bell as a "silly" girl, and the narrator has
confirmed his judgment, before the reader even encounters her (2:
17, 19). A different sort of confirmation takes place in the course of
the same exchange, when the father, displeased by the dubious utility
of Bell's present, tells Rosamond that she "better have given her the
purple jar" (2: 16), and a footnote directs the reader to *Early Lessons*.
More than just a bit of self-advertisement in the Newbery vein, the
allusion and footnote set both Rosamond and the reader against a
model developmental narrative. Rosamond is reminded of an object
lesson she learned at an earlier stage, and which the ideal reader has
also learned (through reading "The Purple Jar"); growing up with
Rosamond, the reader has progressed from a fictionalized object
lesson on utility in *Early Lessons* to a more advanced lesson on
generosity in *The Parent's Assistant*.

Another, implicit alliance between the father and the parental
narrative voice is formed at the tale's end, when Rosamond is shown
successfully internalizing her father's teachings under his watchful
gaze. "Rosamond, during this scene, especially at the moment when
her present was pushed away with such disdain, had been making
reflections upon the nature of true generosity. A smile from her
father, who stood by, a silent spectator of the catastrophe of the
filigree basket, gave rise to these reflections" (2: 41). The child reader
has ideally, by this point, been led to make identical reflections,
watched over by the narrator who intervenes at key moments to
"observe" the tale's progress (2: 19) and at one point to halt it. This
point marks an explicit narratorial intervention just as the tale most

closely approaches satire, with Bell brattily snatching at and breaking the basket and the maid coolly enlisting her in a lie. "We hope that both children and parents will pause for a moment and reflect. – The habits of tyranny, meanness, and falsehood, which children acquire from living with bad servants, are scarcely ever conquered in the whole course of their future lives" (2: 24–25). This intrusion plays a complex function: it displaces blame from parents to their servants, it reiterates the power of early experience in shaping character, and it implicitly calls for relentless parental supervision over children. But most important here, it deliberately anticipates the child reader's movement to pass judgment over Bell's and the maid's actions at this critical juncture in the narrative. The term "reflect" reveals more, perhaps, than Edgeworth intends, for the child reader's conclusions are meant to reflect back those of the narrative voice, just as Rosamond's "reflections" mirror the father's teachings.

The requirement that children's fiction be both innocent – free from indecency or lewdness as well as overt political content – and scrupulously contained helps explain the ambivalence expressed toward traditional forms of children's reading during this period in which the "new child" was codified. Because fairy tales, once purged of their occasional lewdness and ethical uncertainties, fit so well with the new model, opposition to them was less entrenched than is often supposed, particularly among Christian moralists, who were aware that the rationalist distrust of the supernatural often applied to religious teachings no less than to fantasy writing. Trimmer originally described fairy tales in *The Guardian of Education* as "harmless," dismissing them only in reaction to a letter from a concerned reader (1: 63, 2: 448); Sherwood had grown up on fairy tales and could not resist including a moral fairy tale in her revised *Governess*, despite her own qualms. Other Christian writers were less cautious. William Scolfield, in the preface to his *Bible Stories* (1804), held that the "old books" were superior in their appeal to the imagination, in their cultivation of the heart, and in their descriptions of "real tempers and passions of human beings" to "modern" children's books: "They would not for the world astonish the child's mind with a giant, a dragon, or a fairy, but their young people are so good, and their old people so sober, so demure, and so rational, that no genuine interest can be felt for their adventures."[111] Adam Clarke, a Methodist preacher, Bible scholar, and close associate of Wesley, read chapbook romances and fairy tales as a child and defended them in terms reminiscent of Coleridge's famous tribute to his own "early reading of Faery Tales." "Books of enchantments, &c., led me to believe in a spiritual world, and that if there were a *devil* to hurt, there was a *God* to help ... and when I came to read the Sacred Writings, I was confirmed by their authority in the belief I had received, and have reason to thank God, that I was not educated under the Sadducean system."[112] For Scolfield and Clarke, fairy tales and romances were easily preferable to children's fiction in the rationalist or "Sadducean" mode, which tended to proscribe the supernatural altogether.

The lewder forms of chapbook literature, however – the jestbooks, the collections of "wanton songs," and the adventures of such as *Long Meg of Westminster*, a servant who dresses in men's clothes and beats her "betters" whenever provoked – were universally dismissed as "mischievous trash," even by those who otherwise defended imaginative reading for children.[113] Wordsworth, in a letter of 1808, expressed his ambivalence toward the "half-penny Ballads, and penny and two-penny histories" circulated by chapmen: some, "though not very religious," he could approve; others were "objectionable, either for the superstition in them (such as prophecies, fortune-telling, etc.) or more frequently for indelicacy." Wordsworth goes on to align himself with the "happy and condescending genius" called for by Watts in *Divine Songs*: "I have so much felt the influence of these straggling papers, that I have many a time wished that I had talents to produce songs, poems, and little histories, that might circulate among other good things in this way, supplanting partly the bad" (*WLM* 1:248).

As Susan Pedersen has argued, enterprises like More's Cheap Repository were directed as much against the "ribald crudity" and satirical tendencies of the chapbooks as they were against the political pamphlets of Paine and other radicals. Although the chapbooks did not contain "conscious radicalism" – and thus posed much less of an immediate threat than did the radical pamphlets of the day – they were nevertheless frequently "anti-authoritarian" and "subversive" in tone, presenting a "fictional world where the sexual and social order was fluid and changeable."[114] In the "Plan" of the Cheap Repository More announced her intention to combat the "vulgar and licentious publications" and "profane and indecent songs and penny papers" of the day; Trimmer similarly described her *Family Magazine* as an effort "to counteract the pernicious Tendency of immoral Books, etc., which have circulated of late years among the inferior classes of People to the obstruction of their improvement in Religion and Morality."[115] Both children and the lower orders were to be weaned away from "licentious" and "immoral" books and returned to an innocent reading, which might well share in the "simplicity" and "artlessness" of the chapbook tradition – like the sanitized fairy tale or More's tracts themselves – so long as they avoided oppositional politics, sexual indecency, and linguistic or moral ambiguity.

It is instructive to consider in this context the publisher John Harris's attempt, in the first decade of the nineteenth century, to bring other segments of the chapbook tradition besides fairy tales into the children's book market.[116] In *Pug's Visit, Or the Disasters of Mr. Punch*, a children's book published by Harris in 1806, Punch, Pug (a monkey), and Dame Punch get excessively drunk together and sleep "all three in a bed"; the Dame then elopes with Pug, the two are eventually caught by Punch dancing a "minuet," and the story ends as Dame Punch is tossed in a blanket and Pug is put in the stocks "Till he promised he never would do it again." That such a children's story seems bizarre, if not unthinkable, today says less about the experience of children than about how entirely the notion of childhood innocence – textual as well as sexual – has become culturally axiomatic since its codification in the eighteenth century. Significantly, *Pug's Visit* has been all but forgotten in the history of children's literature, while several equally playful but decidedly innocent titles which Harris brought out during the same period – the *Old Mother Hubbard* series, William Roscoe's *The Butterfly's Ball* (1807), and Lady Dorset's *The Peacock "At Home"* (1807) – have been heralded as classics that helped establish the tradition of light verse for children.[117] These titles were immediately popular with children, parents, and reviewers alike, while the more satirical children's books were condemned. The same reviewer in *The London Magazine* (1820) who praised Tabart's collection of fairy tales also attacked the "poisonous" books being produced, in the chapbook vein, by Harris and Marshall. "When the scandals of the drawing-room become the sports of the nursery; when fathers and mothers present their children with caricatures of their own foibles and ridiculous pretentions," the myth of innocence is fatally threatened by satire: "Are such worldly ridicules fit to be put into the hands of innocent children – of mere infants?" (481).

Attitudes like the one expressed in *The London Magazine* helped assure that the genre of children's satire, despite its brief flowering in the early nineteenth century with books like *Pug's Visit* and Charles Lamb's *The King & Queen of Hearts* (published anonymously by the Godwins in 1805), which ends by affirming that "Great Kings & Queens indeed get tipsey", did not develop. Lamb's involvement with the children's book trade brings out more overtly the Romantic ambivalence toward children's reading informing the scattered remarks of Coleridge and Wordsworth. In *The King & Queen of Hearts*, Lamb elaborated upon a traditional nursery rhyme to stretch the limits of the new innocence: the King and Queen (obvious parental figures) are satirized, festive elements (such as a "merry dance / Round rustic maypoles") are included, and childhood sexuality is evoked by the illustrations showing a diminutive black page dressed only in a loin-cloth with a single heart over the crotch. Lamb also refused to make the cuts from his *Adventures of Ulysses* (1808) demanded in the name of propriety by Godwin, who confessed that he had begun to think more like a "bookseller" than an author; "It is children that read children's books, when they are read," Godwin argued, "but it is parent's that choose them," and "We live in squeamish days."[118] *Tales from Shakespear* (1807), however, written by Charles and Mary Lamb, has recently evoked comparison with Bowdler's *Family Shakespeare* (1818) for its consistent excision of low comedy and bawdy humor from Shakespeare's texts, and Charles's story "Maria Howe" in *Mrs. Leicester's School* describes its heroine's cure from a neurotic fear of her "Witch Aunt" as a course of reading supervised and censored by adults: "no books were allowed me but what were rational or sprightly; that give me mirth, or gave me instruction. I soon learned to laugh at witch stories" (3: 323).[119] By bracketing the rational and "sprightly" together as healthy reading for children, Lamb's tale suggests how an innocently humorous work such as *The Butterfly's Ball* could, like the (duly sanitized) traditional fairy tale, be made to fit the new conception of children's reading whereas satirical, horrific, overtly sexualized, or otherwise "anti-social" material could not; *The King & Queen of Hearts* hovers interestingly on the edge between the licit and the unconscionable.

The subversive energies of the popular chapbook would survive, however, in underground form and eventually resurface in "official" children's literature over the next two centuries. The chapbooks' fascination with horror, ghost stories, and criminals and other anti-social figures would be taken up by the Penny Dreadfuls, cheap

magazines (read by children and adults) which began appearing in
the 1830s; the chapbooks' "anti-authority" humor surfaced again in
the British comic books of the mid-twentieth century – which were
eventually censored in turn.[120] Satire returned more obliquely to
official children's literature in the critical parodies found in Carroll's
Alice in Wonderland, Thackeray's *The Rose and the Ring*, and a few other
works from the "golden age," which challenged the related notions
of an innocent text and a unitary child reader not by directly
assaulting the fiction of childhood innocence but (in positing a
sophisticated child reader who could operate on two discursive levels
at once) by subverting the innocence of children's fiction.[121] In this
the Victorian fantasists are anticipated by Blake, whose *Songs of
Innocence* demonstrate how several voices – and several levels of reader
response – could be implicated within a thematically "innocent"
text. Given the discursive interrelation of childhood, innocence, and
the construction of the "primitive" in an age of imperial expansion,
Blake's complication of an "innocent" reader is particularly worth
examining in "The Little Black Boy," a text which represents the
child as colonial subject, and which at once adopts and undermines
the conventions of religious children's verse.

BLAKE, CHILDREN'S LITERATURE, AND COLONIALISM

It seems odd that, despite its obvious relevance to such contemporary
issues as colonialism and the anti-slavery movement, Blake's "The
Little Black Boy" – one of his best known lyrics – is ignored or
mentioned only in passing in recent studies emphasizing the
ideological significance and social contexts of Blake's poetry.[122] This
critical reticence may stem from suspicions, articulated by S. Foster
Damon as early as 1924, that "The Little Black Boy" reflects the
racist assumptions underlying much anti-slavery writing, a charge
most recently (and most forcefully) stated by the Kenyan writer
Ngugi in his essay "Literature and Society."[123] In the course of his
critique of colonialist discourse and of the "racist structure" of
European languages, Ngugi cites "The Little Black Boy" as
manifesting a "negative" image of the African and, more insidiously,
as embodying the "white liberal's dream of a day when black and
white can love one another without going through the agony of
violent reckoning."[124] Ngugi's critique situates Blake's lyric as an
exemplary text of the anti-slavery movement, which character-

istically attacks slavery while supporting colonialism, rejects violent solutions, and maintains a condescending, if not explicitly racist attitude toward black Africans even in lamenting their plight.[125]

Most readings of "The Little Black Boy" tend either to group it uncritically with the tradition of anti-slavery writing or to present it in more complex terms but with questions of race and history in brackets, recognizing its "dramatic" character and multiple ironies but viewing them as expressing a "more universal meaning than anti-slavery propaganda," whether that meaning is sought in terms of a "Christian paradox" or a critique of "Christian dualism."[126] Read against the contemporary discourses of education and children's fiction, however, Blake's lyric can be seen as critically addressing the racist and colonialist attitudes informing both anti-slavery writing and children's literature alike during the Romantic era. The lyric's complex ironies arise from Blake's immanent critique of colonialist ideology; because the Christianizing of the colonial subject played a key role in that ideology, questions of race and of religion in the lyric must be examined together, not bracketed apart. Moreover, the form and genre of the poem – a children's hymn in the tradition running from Watts to Barbauld – also reflect Blake's concern with the colonialist subtext of anti-slavery literature, as issues of race and especially colonialism were tied both discursively and institutionally to the development of children's literature in the eighteenth and early nineteenth centuries.

Although the *Songs of Innocence* does not seem to have been marketed as a children's book, it clearly situates itself in the tradition of children's hymns and religious poetry represented by Watts, Smart, Wesley, and Barbauld. Blake was quite familiar with the newly emergent children's book market as an illustrator of volumes like Wollstonecraft's *Original Stories*, and had met a number of writers for children personally through his association with Joseph Johnson, the publisher of Barbauld and Maria Edgeworth.[127] Many writers of children's and "popular" literature – categories which significantly overlapped at the time – were active in the anti-slavery movement; the list includes Barbauld, Thomas Day, Hannah More, and William Roscoe, who wrote *The Wrongs of Africa* as well as *The Butterfly's Ball*. Works for "the *lower orders of people*, and for *children*" (typically grouped together by Trimmer in 1802) often featured anti-slavery themes: Day's *Sandford and Merton*, Barbauld's *Hymns in Prose*, Aikin and Barbauld's *Evenings at Home*, Ann and Jane Taylor's *Rhymes for the*

Nursery, Edgeworth's *Moral Tales* and *Popular Tales*; and such
"popular" tracts as *The Black Prince: A True Story* and *The Sorrows of
Yamba* in the Cheap Repository or Legh Richmond's *The Negro
Servant*, published by the Religious Tract Society.[128]

Besides its didactic character and tract-like format and distribution, anti-slavery literature held deeper affinities with popular and
children's literature. As the equation of English children and a West
Indian adult of African descent in Fenwick's *Visits* suggests, if the
anti-slavery movement had to deal, sometimes explicitly, always
implicitly, with issues of colonialism, children's and popular literature
were themselves conceived of as instruments in colonizing a newly
literate public; the key trope of "primitive" was applied to children,
"rural folk," and colonized peoples alike. Jacqueline Rose has
argued that the new conception of childhood innocence codified
toward the end of the eighteenth century held within it a central
justification for colonialism: "Childhood is seen as the place where
an older form of culture is preserved (nature or oral tradition), but
the effect of this in turn is that this same form of culture is *infantilised*.
At this level, children's fiction has a set of long-established links with
the colonialism which identified the new world with the infantile
state of man."[129] Or as Ariel Dorfman states from a post-colonial
perspective: "Since those communities, classes, races, continents,
and individuals who don't fit the official mold tend to be viewed as
'children,' as incomplete beings who haven't yet reached the age of
maturity, it is children's literature, or the infantilization of mass
market adult literature, which forms the basis for the entire process of
cultural domination."[130] The links theorized by Rose and Dorfman
manifest themselves in Rousseau's singling out of *Robinson Crusoe* as
the only book fit for children (184), and in the succession of children's
books, beginning with *Sandford and Merton*, which vary Defoe's
scenario of a stranded European colonizing an island or desert area
inhabited only by "savages" (a tradition extensive enough to
constitute its own sub-genre, the *Robinsonnade*).[131] Those tendencies
within later eighteenth-century and Romantic thought that led to
the idealization of childhood, of rural laborers, and of "primitive"
peoples also supported the view that all three groups were uncivilized
and needed to be properly trained or educated – disciplined – if they
were to fit into the industrialized and regulated world then in the
process of emerging.

Even in children's texts which explicitly condemn slavery, the

Crusoe scenario typically includes a justification of European colonialism based on superior technology and the moral qualities that presumably go with it, such as industriousness and intellectual curiosity. In the first volume of *Sandford and Merton*, a dialogue on slavery affirming natural rights (66–68) is offset by the tale of a European stranded among a "rude and savage kind of men" who gains ascendancy through his skill at basket weaving (47); in later volumes, a European defeats an entire African army with the aid of a telescope (2: 199–204) and a scientific Asian succeeds (like Crusoe himself) at defeating a barbarian horde by means of gunpowder (3: 242). Aikin and Barbauld's *Evenings at Home* includes an anti-slavery dialogue in which a recaptured slave convinces his master of his natural right to liberty (6: 81–88); another dialogue "On Man," however, distinguishes Europeans from "savages" like the Hottentots by their "*curiosity,*" or "superior ardour after knowledge," thanks to which they "have been enabled to command the rest of the world" (3: 10–12). These texts bring out a crucial ambivalence within the Rousseauvian celebration of the "innocent" or "primitive," which represents at once a kind of purity lost to European civilization and a weakness which justifies the management of "primitive" groups – whether colonial subjects or children – in the name of "improvement" or education. In criticizing the metaphoric conjunction of child and "savage" below, however, I wish to avoid inadvertently reasserting it by implying too close a correspondence between the experience of children and of colonized or otherwise subordinated adult groups. Unlike, that is, adult groups which were implicitly (and so often explicitly) infantilized within later eighteenth- and nineteenth-century social discourses – women, immigrants of non-European ethnic origin, and the lower classes as well as colonial subjects – children *are* lacking in judgment relative to adults, are in need of protection, guidance, and socialization, and are put at serious risk of exploitation if allowed, say, to make legal, employment, or sexual contracts on their own. Any comparison of children's subordinate status to the historical disenfranchisement and domination of adult groups in the name of "children's rights" remains suspect, given how deeply such metaphors remain implicated in disciplinary and colonialist social discourses which invariably worked these metaphors both ways.

The figurative equation of children (especially poor children) and "primitives" is all too common within the educational discourses of the eighteenth and early nineteenth centuries. Watts warns in his essay on Charity Schools against abandoning children "to the Wildness of their own nature," and allowing them to "run loose and savage in the streets" (12); Raikes similarly describes lower-class children as "a set of little heathens" in his letter on Sunday Schools in the *Gentleman's Magazine*.[132] Trimmer compares poor children to the "savages of America" in *The Oeconomy of Charity* (143), as does Clara Reeve – "so rude and uncivilized were these unhappy children" – in *Plans of Education* (97); More writes that, in terms of the inhabitants' ignorance, two of her Mendip parishes are "as dark as Africa" (*MLC* 1: 395). Many of the same educational institutions, using similar methods, took on the burden of civilizing children and "primitives" alike. The SPCK was concerned not only with supporting Charity Schools and Sunday Schools in England but also with missions in the colonies, and produced a great body of tract literature and educational material for both groups.[133] The Cheap Repository Tracts were distributed by the millions both among the poor in Britain and throughout the colonies; by 1797 Bishop Porteous could write to More: "The sublime and immortal publication of the 'Cheap Repository' I hear from every corner of the globe. To the West Indies I have sent ship-loads of them. They are read with avidity at Sierra Leone, and I hope our pious Scotch missionaries will introduce them into Asia" (*MLC* 2: 4). The Religious Tract Society and its offshoot, the British and Foreign Bible Society, were similarly concerned with reaching children and the "labouring poor" at home and subject populations abroad.[134] A program of minimal or passive literacy and simplistic tract literature inculcating basic religious principles and reinforcing docility was deemed suitable for the lower classes in England and non-white peoples throughout the British empire alike. It should be added that, as one historian of the Society for the Propagation of the Gospel points out, "identical arguments" were also used *against* educating lower-class whites in Great Britain and black slaves in the Americas: the former would become "presumptuous and unruly," and the latter "dissatisfied" with slavery and "unwilling to work."[135]

If the colonization of childhood in the later eighteenth century helps account for Blake's use of a children's literary form in critically addressing anti-slavery writing, the infantilization of the colonial subject helps elucidate the terms in which Blake poses his dual critique of children's and colonial discourses. For the anti-slavery literature of Blake's time, which peaked in terms of quantity and distribution in 1788, the year before *Songs of Innocence* was published,[136] relied extensively on two related tropes critically addressed in Blake's lyric, Africa (and Africans) as culturally "dark" or "benighted," and the "savage" as uncivilized or "untutored." Although the image of Africa as the "dark" continent, metonymically extending the blackness of the sub-Saharan African's skin to African culture and Africa itself, is sometimes said to be a Victorian invention, the trope of darkness or blackness (already present in children's poems by Bunyan and Watts) comes up throughout the anti-slavery literature of the eighteenth and early nineteenth centuries.[137] James Montgomery's *The West Indies* (1807), for example, metaphorically connects the darkness of the "untutor'd" African's "mind, where desolation reigns," to that of the African continent, "Fierce as his clime, uncultur'd as his plains."[138] Hannah More's *Slavery, A Poem*, one of five major anti-slavery poems published in 1788, qualifies its Christian acknowledgment of the "immortal principle" within black Africans by later characterizing them as "dark and savage, ignorant and blind."[139] Throughout most anti-slavery verse, even when allegedly non-racist, the African is depicted as first and foremost an uncivilized "savage," childlike and "unenlightened."

The same emphasis on the African's related darkness and ignorance can be found throughout the tradition of religious writing for children from which Blake works most directly in *Songs of Innocence*, as well as within popular and children's anti-slavery literature. Bunyan's *Book for Boys and Girls*, for example, which anticipates Blake's use of the emblem book as a children's form, includes an emblem on "Moses and his Wife," a "swarthy Ethiopian": "Nor did his Milk-white Bosom change her Skin; / She came out thence as black as she went in"; and the child who adores the Law rather than the Life "Shall yet by it be left a Black-a-more" (42–43). Watts's *Divine Songs* includes a hymn in "Praise for Birth and Education in a Christian Land" ("How do I pity those that dwell / Where Ignorance and Darkness reigns [sic]" [8]). In seeing his own blackness initially as an emblem of privation, Blake's "Little Black Boy" takes up the racist imagery inscribed in this tradition, and restated in the religious anti-slavery tracts of Blake's time. In *The Black Prince*, for example, one of the *Cheap Repository Tracts*, Naimbanna, a noble savage, is brought to England and "delivered ... from the state of darkness in which, in common with millions of his countrymen, he had been lately plunged"; "rude and ignorant, with no just ideas of religion," he embraces Christianity with a "child-like simplicity" which fosters missionary hopes that "those who now sit in darkness shall be brought, like Naimbanna, to know God and themselves."[140] The title character (never otherwise named) of Legh Richmond's *The Negro Servant* (1804), distributed by the Religious Tract Society, is similarly changed from "the once dark, perverse, and ignorant heathen" to a "now convinced, enlightened, humble and believing Christian"; exemplifying the "simplicity and sincerity of real Christianity," he testifies: "God let me be made slave by white men, to do me good ... He take me from the land of darkness, and bring me to the land of light."[141]

Underlying all of these texts is the system of discursive oppositions – white and black, civilization and savagery, good and evil, self and Other – which Abdul R. JanMohamed has termed, after Fanon, the "manichean allegory" of colonialist writing.[142] It is this system of dichotomies, to which one can add enlightenment and darkness, and Christian and heathen, which Blake critically manipulates in "The Little Black Boy," distancing his own treatment of the African subject from that of most anti-slavery writers. The lyric begins disarmingly by seeming to confirm the same hierarchical valuations – white and European over black and "southern" – which inform nearly all contemporary anti-slavery no less than pro-slavery writing:

> My mother bore me in the southern wild,
> And I am black, but O! my soul is white;
> White as an angel is the English child:
> But I am black, as if bereav'd of light.

Without (for the moment) considering where his notions come from, we can see here the black child's own speech conforming to the Manichean ideology pervading the anti-slavery discourse of Blake's time. Angels and souls are white; blackness is a purely negative ("bereav'd") condition. It is only in the second stanza that one begins to sense the distance between Blake's stance and that of Montgomery or of the tracts:

> My mother taught me underneath a tree
> And sitting down before the heat of day,
> She took me on her lap and kissed me,
> And pointing to the east began to say.

At a time when "untutored savage" is stock poetic diction, Blake's emphasis on the African mother's teaching (which forms the subject of the design for the first plate) is extremely significant.[143] It was essential to apologists for slavery and anti-slavery evangelists alike to view the African as untaught, uncivilized; Hume's infamous remark that Africans have "no ingenious manufactures among them, no arts, no sciences" or Chesterfield's that Africans are "the most ignorant and unpolished people in the world" are only particularly harsh statements of a view shared by nearly all Europeans in the eighteenth and early nineteenth centuries.[144] As a recent study of nineteenth-century exploration narratives shows, Africans were frequently portrayed during this period as lacking not only civilization and writing, but language itself; insofar as the "natives" made sounds to one another, theirs was "a language of demonstrated emotion rather than of ideas and communication."[145] The phantasmal Africans depicted in these narratives are quite literally infantilized in the etymological sense of being *infans*, without language. Again, in regard to Africans' alleged lack of civilization, law, traditions, and rationality, it makes little difference whether they are portrayed as "noble" or as "beastly" savages; as Dorfman remarks of the ideology of children's and popular literature: "All insubordination must be left by the wayside. If it has its origins in a plausible misunderstanding ... then we are in the presence of noble savages who will have no choice but to see the light of Rousseau and climb into the sheepfold of progress. If the savages are ornery, they will have to be exterminated or caged up."[146]

Although the eighteenth-century convention of the "noble savage" is sometimes presented as a progressive (if ethnocentric) ideal which lubricated Europeans' sympathies and helped pave the way for eventual equality, it should be clear that, as JanMohamed insists, the notion of savagery (noble or ignoble) supported the larger colonialist project independent of the more temporary slavery question: "If... the barbarism of the native is irrevocable, or at least very deeply ingrained, then the European's attempt to civilize him can continue indefinitely, the exploitation of his resources can proceed without hindrance, and the European can persist in enjoying a position of moral superiority."[147] Characterizations of "native" peoples as "barbaric," "savage," or "primitive" participate in what Johannes Fabian, in his critique of Western anthropological discourse, calls the "denial of coevalness," another infantilizing strategy which, in implicit support of colonialism and neo-colonialism, turns spatial relations into temporal ones, repressing the geo-political fact that the colonized "Other" is "ultimately, other people who are our contemporaries."[148] English perceptions of Africans as culturally backwards and "mentally defective," well established by Blake's time, remained dominant throughout the nineteenth century and were, if anything, intensified in support of the "colonization, Christianization, and commercialization" of the African peoples.[149]

Initially, it might seem that Blake's lyric, as it goes on to represent the mother's teaching in the "wild," conforms to rather than departs from the colonialist image of the African as noble but childlike, presenting her in the "pastoral" mode of anti-slavery writing, "a pseudo-African in a pseudo-Africa":[150]

> Look on the rising sun: there God does live
> And gives his light, and gives his heat away.
> And flowers and trees and men and beasts receive
> Comfort in morning joy in the noon day.
>
> And we are put on earth a little space,
> That we may learn to bear the beams of love,
> And these black bodies and this sun-burnt face
> Is but a cloud, and like a shady grove.

One could read these lines in terms of a "natural" theism, somewhere in between pagan sun-worship (a conventional attribute of the "noble savage") and Christian monotheism, and not unrelated in tone to the patronizing remark in Adanson's *Voyage to Senegal* cited in the notes to Day's *Dying Negro* (1773): "It is amazing that such a rude and illiterate people should reason so pertinently in regard to the Heavenly Bodies."[151] It is at this point, however, that one must consider not only the divergence between the mother's quoted statements and the quite different language of her son, but also what in the child's experience makes this divergence possible. Heather Glen has argued that what distinguishes Blake's poems about children like the chimney sweeper and the black boy from those of his contemporaries is that "the unprivileged ... have their own distinctive voices: they are not the objects of sympathetic or protesting comment – of any comment at all."[152] Part of what makes these voices distinctive is that they are not the children's "own" in any simple manner. Unlike such single-voiced lyrics in the same collection as "The Shepherd" and "The Blossom" – and in marked contrast to the containment of the child reader via the "innocent" poetics informing most contemporary children's fiction – "The Chimney Sweeper" and "The Little Black Boy" critically juxtapose several disparate discourses, each resonant with a different range of ideological meanings and commitments. These discourses conflict productively in a manner that Volosinov terms "lyric irony," the "encounter in one voice of two incarnate value judgments and their interference with one another."[153] There are in fact three competing discourses implicated in the "distinctive" voice of "The Little Black Boy": the mother's, as quoted by her child; his iteration of the Manichean allegory in the first stanza; and his articulation of the quite different perspective informing the last two stanzas.

Other readers have emphasized the disparity between the mother's African teaching (one calls it "the little heathen myth of the mother"), quoted in the middle three stanzas of the poem, and her son's Christian notions, developed in the framing stanzas, without considering how the black child might have received the latter.[154] It seems most likely that the boy has been in the hands of missionaries, or evangelizing masters, or a Sunday School, either in the West Indies – where some plantations sponsored mission schools – or in England, where the child might have come by way of previous enslavement in the West Indies or elsewhere in the Americas.[155] Displaced from the "southern wild" to a region where he has contact with or at least direct knowledge of an English child, the black child has retained his mother's "heathen" teaching while exposed, as the first stanza makes clear, to the Manichean discourse of contemporary missionary tracts: guaranteed his place in heaven, but taught to know his subordinate place on earth until then.

But the poem's two concluding stanzas represent a perspective distanced both from the missionary propaganda informing the first stanza and the child's quotation of his mother's teachings, which, rather than presenting blackness as negative or "bereav'd," instead celebrate it as a "shady grove." The stanzas in which the mother is quoted, while they invert the dichotomy established in the first stanza, remain caught within its discursive polarities, evoking the no less "Manichean" counter-perspective described by Fanon: "If I am black, it is not the result of a curse, but it is because, having offered my skin, I have been able to absorb all the cosmic *effluvia*."[156] The final two stanzas, however, represent an attempt to move beyond the binary oppositions governing the lyric up to this point by collapsing

blackness and whiteness together as parallel kinds of "cloud," and by
unsettling the hierarchical relation of the black child and his white
counterpart:

> Thus did my mother say and kissed me,
> And thus I say to little English boy.
> When I from black and he from white cloud free,
> And round the tent of God like lambs we joy:
> I'll shade him from the heat till he can bear,
> To lean in joy upon our fathers knee.
> And then I'll stand and stroke his silver hair,
> And be like him and he will then love me.

The notions expressed in these stanzas, sometimes compared to
those of Swedenborg, quite evidently were not received through
Sunday School or plantation missionary efforts.[157] Rather, the black
child has at this point managed to revise the Manichean gospel
taught him by his masters, and articulated in the poem's first stanza,
by mingling it with his memories of his mother's African teachings,
producing a self-affirming discourse of his own. His revisionist gesture
bears a striking resemblance, in the foreshortened space of the lyric,
to Eugene Genovese's account of how West Indian slave communities
transformed Christianity from an alienating, colonialist ideology into
an empowering, assertive one through Africanizing it. This is not, of
course, a matter of Blake's intuiting or "anticipating" the developments described by Genovese but rather of his adapting a similar
discursive strategy, most likely in reaction to what he saw as the
limitations and hypocrisy of the anti-slavery movement.[158] As
Jameson remarks, Genovese's approach to black religion "restores
the vitality of these utterances by reading them, not as the replication
of imposed beliefs, but rather as a process whereby the hegemonic
Christianity of the slave owners is appropriated, secretly emptied of
its content, and subverted to the transmission of quite different
oppositional and coded messages."[159] Through his use of lyric irony
in "The Little Black Boy," Blake constructs, from the imagined
position of a Christianized African child, a similarly counter-
hegemonic utterance. The mother's view of black skin as a "shady
grove," at once a sign of the African's closeness to God and a defense
from God's excessive light and heat, helps the "Little Black Boy"
throw the colonialist mentality imposed upon him – "But I am black
as if bereav'd of light" – back into question. Taught to feel inferior to
the "little English boy" – his master's child in Jamaica? his

persecutor in England? – the black child is able to counter, through his intermixture of Christian teachings and what Blake presents as an African religious doctrine, with a myth of his own devising that restores to him, if not a measure of real power, at least the potential for resistance. Although he continues to portray himself in the role of servant to the English boy, the black child is able by the end of the poem to see white and black skin as (in Erdman's words) "equally opaque," and his own, "southern" ability to bear the divine heat as bringing him closer to God, and placing him in the role of older brother or protector to the white child.[160]

It might be objected that the lyric enacts not ideological resistance but rather, as one critic has recently put it, "psychological escape," perhaps even broaching a Nietzschean critique of Christianity as a "slave religion" in its displacement of the black child's desire for social amelioration to heaven.[161] But Genovese's caution against applying such a critique too schematically to the religion of slave communities in the Americas is applicable to the representation of religious discourse in "The Little Black Boy" as well. Slave religion was inherently subversive because it "meant that the slaves had achieved a degree of psychological and cultural autonomy" and, if it looked to heaven, it helped set the needed preconditions for racial equality on earth: "The religious leaders first had to combat that sense of unworthiness and inferiority which the slaveholders constantly tried to infuse in the slaves. The doctrine of spiritual equality and a future without white supremacy therefore had great positive value despite its restricted and conservative political content." Particularly as shaped by black preachers, Christian teachings could dissolve the ideological ground on which the principle of absolute mastery rested.[162] Blake's "Little Black Boy" achieves a still greater degree of "cultural autonomy," more analogous to the slave religions of the West Indies, by supplementing Christian propaganda with (alleged) African religious beliefs to create a synthetic religious vision of his own, one that breaks down the Manichean oppositions of colonial discourse. Making use of his otherwise difficult position between cultures, the black child is able (however provisionally) to establish a critical perspective which temporarily reverses his relation to the English child, placing him in the role of instructor: "And thus I say to little English boy." In rehearsing and then collapsing together the teachings of his mother and his Christian masters, the Little Black Boy is able to take on something of their authority as well, a position reflected in the design for the second plate, which depicts him presenting the smaller white child to Christ as a catechist presenting his pupil.[163]

The inability of scholars to determine whether the *Songs of Innocence* is a children's book proper or a "children's book for adults" reflects the deliberate ambivalence of a text which addresses two implied readers (if not two actual readerships): the English child evoked by the language and conventions of contemporary children's religious poetry (and figured within the text by the "little English boy"), and an adult reader familiar (as the parent who selected, purchased, and often recited such poetry) with the discourse of children's literature and sophisticated enough to detect Blake's frequently ironic relationship to it.[164] "The Little Black Boy" addresses both readers in its marked departures from the conventions of children's poetry and in its more subtle assertion of links between the discursive position of the black child and that of his English counterpart; moreover, in provocatively juxtaposing several levels of discourse within the child speaker's narration, it encourages the child to supplement its "innocent" reading with the critical perspective of the more experienced adult. Through presenting the black speaker as a potential equal and, if anything, as closer to God than the "English boy," Blake offers the child reader of his time a powerful alternative to the lesson in condescension enacted in a poem like Ann Taylor's "The Little Negro":

> Ah! the poor little blackamoor, see there he goes
> And the blood gushes out from his half frozen toes,
> And his legs are so thin you may see the very bones,
> As he goes shiver, shiver, on the sharp cutting stones.
>
> He was once a negro boy, and a merry boy was he
> Playing outlandish plays, by the tall palm tree;
> Or bathing in the river, like a brisk water rat,
> And at night sleeping sound, on a little bit of mat.[165]

In displacing the bestial "outlandish plays" of the typical African of most children's and popular literature with a scene of maternal instruction, Blake not only counters the "untutored savage" convention, but also underscores the relation of the black child's experience to that of the English child. The children of Blake's time had become subject to a program of "civilizing" efforts unprecedented in British history, designed to contain the threat of a reading public through programs of minimal, mass education and a popular tract industry aimed at supplanting both the "intellectual vernacular" of radicals like Paine and the carnivalesque anti-authoritarianism of the popular chapbook.[166] In Blake's representation of a black child's attempt to challenge a crippling ideology through creative subversion, the English reader – child or adult – could find a discursive site for opposition and a rare lesson in radical dissent. "The Little Black Boy" both poses a critique of the colonialist discourse informing anti-slavery poems and tracts, and offers a paradigm for resisting the new forms of social discipline epitomized by industrial children's fiction and tracts for the lower orders, a "popular" literature imposed from above.

CHAPTER 4

Women, education, and the novel

As teachers, educational theorists, and writers for the young, British women had established a newly prominent social role by the beginning of the nineteenth century. But this decided gain in cultural authority was not without its costs. For the "Mrs. Teachwells" of the age had to work within, even more stringently than did women writers for the adult market, the domestic ideology which governed codes of literary no less than social propriety.[1] In fact, the heightened prestige of the woman writer for or about children can be seen as a direct outgrowth of domestic ideology. Despite its significant limitations, however, the advantages of this role were considerable. Mitzi Myers has argued that the refashioning of motherhood in the "stylish new mode of enlightened domesticity" both redefined women's traditional function (at least for the upper and middle classes) in terms of "maternal and pedagogical power" and helped women writers – of children's books, of the domestic novel, of popular literature, of calls to educational reform – establish a more authoritative public voice.[2] Myers's work provides a strong corrective to the once standard view of early women writers for children as a "monstrous" group of arid didacticists; she demonstrates instead how the growing importance of education, combined with women's seemingly natural role as mothers and domestic caretakers, could provide an opening for the exercise of "teacherly force" and "expressive power."[3] Such redefinitions of the maternal role also gave new weight to arguments for better, more substantial schooling for girls, who would require a more intellectually demanding, extensive education themselves if they were to later prove fit teachers of their children.

An emphasis on women's enhanced cultural role also complicates notions of "bourgeois ideology" in relation to the eighteenth-century reinvention of childhood. Whereas Kramnick, for example, sees the

new children's fiction industry as simply endorsing "sexual stereo-
types emergent in the new notion of the family" – as they did in part
– Myers emphasizes instead the importance of the mother-daughter
dyad in children's fiction and the cultural alternative of "enlightened
womanhood" that portrayals of educated, responsible mothers
guiding their children toward rational autonomy endorsed.[4] And yet
in its very generosity, Myers's recuperative delineation of a peculiarly
female "bourgeois progressivism" shares something of the over-
schematic quality which hampers Kramnick's definition of bourgeois
ideology.[5] Her grouping of reformist "sister authors for the young,"
for example, collapses together such ideologically disparate positions
as the outspoken radicalism of Wollstonecraft, the liberal com-
promises of Edgeworth and Barbauld, and the deep-seated conservatism of Trimmer and More. Barbauld, in fact, rejected a
proposal (Edgeworth's) to co-edit a "periodical paper" featuring the
work of "all the literary ladies of the present day" on the grounds of
political differences: "There is no bond of union among literary
women, any more than among literary men; different sentiments and
different connections separate them much more than the joint
interest of their sex would unite them. Mrs. Hannah More would not
write along with you or me, and we should probably hesitate at
joining Miss Hays, or if she were living, Mrs. Godwin."[6] The urgency
of these ideological differences – for us as well as for Barbauld –
becomes quite clear if issues of class and gender are considered
together and not, as in too much recent writing on the subject, held
apart.[7] Moreover, the writers in this same "group" advanced
significantly divergent views in relation to women's rights, including
the right to an equal, not simply better, education. More, Edgeworth,
and Barbauld, for example, all explicitly distanced themselves from
Wollstonecraft's defense of the rights of women, More in *Strictures* (1:
147), Edgeworth in a chapter of *Belinda* which associates women's
rights with a self-serving, "Amazonian" transvestite, Barbauld in a
poem entitled "The Rights of Woman" which argues, much as had
Rousseau, that woman's "empire" is inextricably related to her
subordinate position and culturally encoded weakness: "Soft melting
tones thy thundering cannon's roar, / Blushes and fears thy magazine
of war."[8]

Barbauld's lyric, which equates woman's rights with "sacred
mysteries" – "Felt, not defined, and if debated, lost" – underscores
how Romantic-era domestic ideology was as restrictive as it was

enabling in relation to women writers, excluding women from political debate even while granting them a certain authority within the confines of pedagogical and didactic discourse. Domestic ideology was rooted in an artificial separation of political and economic life on the one hand and domestic life on the other, a split between public and private spheres which left the former in the hands of men and relegated women to the narrowly circumscribed world of the latter.[9] If the revaluation over the course of the eighteenth century of traditionally designated "feminine" qualities like sympathy, sensibility, and empathy contributes toward, in Terry Eagleton's analysis, a "feminization of discourse" – amounting by the Romantic period to a virtual colonization of the feminine on the part of male writers – it also "prolongs the fetishization of women at the same time as it lends them a more authoritative voice." The "exaltation" of women, while representing a partial advance, also helps "shore up the very system which oppresses them."[10]

Moreover, as Mary Poovey has argued, the allegedly female trait most valorized by contemporary writers of conduct books and other "moral" genres – emotional responsiveness – was itself regarded in a deeply ambivalent fashion. Throughout these works – produced by male and female authors alike – women's allegedly livelier imagination and more acute sensibility could lead them into frivolity, luxuriousness, or excessive sexual desire.[11] The same ideology which entrusts mothers with the production of rational, autonomous individuals also attributes to women an irrationality, rooted in the body, which continually threatens to erupt unless carefully managed. In Valerie Walkerdine's formulation, the modern conception of the rational defines itself against an "irrational" which is "invested in and understood as the province of women, who must contain it at the same time as being responsible for its removal in their children." Women become, in relation to children and their own "hystericised" bodies, the "guardians of the irrational," while female desire is channeled into maternal love, sublimated into a controlled and controlling nurturance.[12]

If the ideology of the home and the "proper lady" simultaneously gave women a more credible public voice and excluded them from active participation in the public sphere, valorized women as guardians of education and devalued their bodies and desires as potentially dangerous strongholds of the irrational, however, these same contradictions also engender a productive and implicitly critical tension throughout women's writing of the period. Women's cultural role as teachers of and writers for children, for example, can be seen as embodying the ideal of the "perfect mother" within domestic ideology – a "woman who lives for and through her children and who finds fulfillment in the very act of forming her children into certain kinds of individuals"; yet what Myers calls the "feminization of socializing practices" during this period also facilitates the appropriation of reason on the part of women authors as a counterpoint to the male writer's appropriation of sensibility.[13] As the domestic novel, particularly in the hands of Edgeworth and Austen, becomes increasingly concerned with female education, it also develops "strategies of subversion and indirection" which facilitate the telling expression of social criticism from within an acceptable literary form.[14] Its specific mode of suppressing female desires which challenge the self-denial required by "perfect" motherhood simultaneously reveals the urgency of those desires, though their expression, like Marianne Dashwood's "silent agony" in *Sense and Sensibility*, is often tacit.[15]

THE EDUCATION OF DAUGHTERS AND MOTHERS

The rise of British feminism is closely tied to the question of female education, as the careers of such early feminists as Mary Astell, Catherine Macaulay, and Mary Wollstonecraft attest. But calls for educational reform were not invariably feminist in any meaningful sense. The continuities in the educational thought of women writers like Macaulay, Wollstonecraft, Edgeworth, and More have recently received a great deal more emphasis than have their equally important differences, which become particularly pressing in relation to questions of social and political change (including changes in women's legal and economic status).[16] While nearly all women writers of educational treatises and conduct books asserted the need for a more substantial education and condemned the emphasis on superficial "accomplishments" in girls' boarding schools, they did so with a variety of ideological motivations, ranging from Wollstonecraft's radical egalitarianism to the efforts of reactionaries like More and West to buttress the existing political and social order through selective reform.[17] Moreover, improvements in women's education were called for by most male writers of conduct books as well, including James Fordyce (relentlessly attacked by Wollstonecraft in the second *Vindication*) and the Evangelical writer Thomas Gisborne. That existing provisions for the education of daughters cried out for reform was in fact a commonplace demand by the time the *Rights of Woman* appeared in 1792, an issue which all of its early reviewers (however coolly they reacted to Wollstonecraft's feminism) could agree on.[18]

Wollstonecraft begins her extended critique of the female conduct book with an attack on Rousseau's *Emile*, which lays out in particularly clear terms the assumptions underlying most British writing on women's conduct and education as well. Rousseau's theory of female education in Book v of *Emile* ("Sophie, or the Woman") begins with an open avowal of the necessary inequality between the sexes, grounded in both "nature" and social custom. Woman, because of her relative physical weakness and her supposed need for protection while bearing and suckling infants, requires man's strength; from this "natural" relation of dependence follow divergent roles in the "moral relations" between the sexes: "One ought to be active and strong, the other passive and weak." Man's "merit" resides in his power; woman, on the other hand, is "made to please and to be subjugated" (358). Because woman's social role is an essentially subordinate one, the "whole education of women ought to relate to men": "To please men, to be useful to them, to make herself loved and honored by them, to raise them when young, to care for them when grown ... these are the duties of women at all times" (365). Woman's compensatory "empire" also inheres within her relation to man, specifically in the "law of nature which gives woman more facility to excite desires than man to satisfy them." Thus man, "whether he likes it or not," is dependent for sexual gratification on woman's "wish" and must "seek to please her in turn" (360).

Another consequence of the natural disparity between the genders concerns the special relation of women to social decorum (361). "It is up to the sex that nature has charged with the bearing of children to be responsible for them to the other sex." That is, women are responsible not only for bearing and nurturing children, but also for insuring their legitimacy, on which the integrity of the family unit (and the transmission of private property from father to son) depends. The "unfaithful" woman "dissolves the family and breaks all the bonds of nature." For this reason, the "strictness of the relative duties of the two sexes is not and cannot be the same"; a woman must not only *be* chaste but must *appear* to be so, to her husband, to those about her, to "everyone." From the relative importance of woman's "reputation" arises her unique social demeanor, "modest, attentive, reserved." The double standard for sexual behavior (and reputation) entails a second general rule for female education, that women, destined to be "enslaved" to propriety, be trained early in repression. "They must first be exercised in constraint, so that it never costs them anything to tame all their caprices in order to submit them to the wills of others" (369).

This same cultural logic – that woman's "natural" condition entails both a subordinate social role and an unequal responsibility for the legitimacy (as well as care) of offspring, and that female education should emphasize at once "pleasing" and "modest" behavior – runs throughout eighteenth-century British conduct books and educational treatises. Educational reform may be advocated in order to make women better companions to (and even civilizers of) men, and more adequate tutors of their children, but such "mental improvement" must never challenge woman's fundamentally subordinate role, or interfere with the cardinal virtue of modesty, or disrupt the sexual division of society into distinct spheres of activity. Fordyce, in his widely read *Sermons for Young Women* (1766), defines women's social "importance" in terms of their extensive (though indirect) "influence" over men's morals and behavior, their unique role in superintending the "gradual openings" of their children's minds and forming their "passions"; indeed, he condemns boarding schools for producing "accomplished" pupils who "think of nothing that is domestic or rational."[19] But women's importance also inheres in a sexual double standard: "The world, I know not how, overlooks, in our sex, a thousand irregularities, which it never forgives in yours"; the integrity of the family is "much more dependent on the conduct of daughters than of sons" (15). Female education must therefore elicit not active but "negative" virtues, including "sobriety," "filial piety," and the "unremitted exercise of prudence, vigilance, and severe circumspection" (62); women's negative "empire" has the "heart for its object, and is secured by meekness and modesty, by soft attraction, and virtuous love" (126). John Gregory, in *A Father's Legacy to His Daughters* (1774), similarly holds that women should be educated not as "domestic drudges" but as men's "companions and equals," yet from women's "natural character" and social position arises a "peculiar" propriety of conduct, centered on "modest reserve."[20] Even Hester Chapone, whose *Letters on the Improvement of the Mind* (1773) is the only conduct book Wollstonecraft can approve, emphasizes "passive" virtues, social behavior marked by compliance and a "due regard to reputation," and defines the female character as principally "private and domestic."[21] The double standard in sexual mores, and the female education in constraint that follows from it, also finds voice in Lord Kames's *Loose Thoughts Upon Education* (1781): man's conduct depends on the "approbation of his own conscience," woman's "greatly on the opinion of others." Therefore, "modesty and reserve are essential in young women; to acquire which, they ought to be taught early to suppress their desires, and to have a strict attention to decency and decorum" (162–63).

Kames, like Fordyce, notes that the "culture of the heart during childhood" is central to education, which becomes for this very reason the "mother's peculiar province" (6, 8). Drawing on the separation of spheres and the conventional designation of sympathy and sensibility as "feminine" qualities, a number of eighteenth-century moral writers, male as well as female, stress the mother's central role in education; the same point is made, for example, by Thomas Gisborne in 1797 and by William Wilberforce in 1798.[22] As Beth Kowaleski-Wallace has argued, the "maternal" cultural role of women in Romantic-era society, as educators of children and more pervasively as social reformers and civilizers of the men around them, can be seen, not simply in terms of "empowerment," but also as approximating the "designated function of any mother within patriarchy – namely the inculcation of values necessary for the perpetuation of the patriarchal structure." It is in their own interest for male writers to advocate rational (but affectionate) motherhood and celebrate woman's civilizing "influence." Moreover, as Kowaleski-Wallace points out (citing Wilberforce), women's role as maternal educators may be advocated "precisely because their situation most closely resembles that of the child; for example, the woman's mind is 'soft and ductile,'" more susceptible to impressions.[23] Thus women are (ironically) infantilized at the same time as their role as educators of children and socializers of men is celebrated. Gregory informs his daughters that their "natural softness and sensibility" fit them particularly for the "practice of those duties where the heart is chiefly concerned" (10); Fordyce, in *The Character and Conduct of the Female Sex* (1776), holds that women "polish" and "humanize ... mankind," while insisting that their "empire of the breast" "precludes the affectation of power, will rarely appear to exert it, and will generally prevail by submitting."[24] The exercise of female "power" is thus firmly tied to a conviction of female weakness and effected by submissive behavior. Women are also, like children in this period, associated with innocence and "simplicity": "I wish you to possess the most perfect simplicity of heart and manners," Fordyce writes (45); Chapone hopes that her niece might "retain the simplicity and innocence of childhood, with the sense and dignity of riper years" (135).[25]

Writing in advance of the full-blown English reaction to the French Revolution, and strongly sympathizing with its assertion of "equal rights" against a patriarchal regime, Macaulay and Wollstonecraft together develop a much more deeply critical response to the conduct book tradition than will the educational writers (male and female) who immediately follow them.[26] With the "absolute exclusion of every political right to the sex in general," Macaulay declares in *Letters on Education* (1790), "women ... have hardly a civil right to save them from the grossest injuries" (210). Reconceptualizing the relation of the sexes in terms of political rights rather than "natural" characters, Macaulay can break decisively with the theory of female "influence" propounded by writers like Gregory and Fordyce: "when the sex have been taught wisdom by education, they will be glad to give up indirect influence for rational privileges" (215). The first educational theorist to push associationist psychology to the extreme in relation to sexual difference, Macaulay asserts that, as there are no "innate ideas, and innate affections," the "difference that actually does subsist between the sexes" can be "imputed to accident" (203–4); education thus becomes critical in determining sexual character, in establishing and maintaining sexual difference, and in perpetuating male domination. Conceding (in an attack on *Emile*) that "some degree of inferiority, in point of corporal strength, seems always to have existed between the two sexes," Macaulay argues that in the "barbarous ages of mankind" this physical disparity was so abused "as to destroy all the natural rights of the female species." In modern Europe, female education has been similarly designed to "corrupt and debilitate both the powers of mind and body" (206–7), perpetuating male domination through systematically aggravating sexual differences in physical strength and engineering disparities in mental strength as well.

It is on the premise of "natural rights" rather than arguing from woman's traditional role as nurturer that Macaulay bases her argument for equal education. For Macaulay, there must be no separation of male and female – active and passive – behavior and virtue: "There is but one rule of right for the conduct of all rational beings" (201). Macaulay denounces the key term of female modesty – and with it the double standard that entails for girls an education in constraint – as implicated in a system of male domination: "the great differences in the external consequences which follow deviations from chastity in the two sexes, did in all probability arise from women having been considered as the mere property of the men"; it has been deliberately perpetuated by men who maintain their dominant position through "mutual support and general opinion" (220). The surest remedy for this oppressive state of affairs is to replace the "degrading difference in the culture of the understanding" characteristic of European societies with an equal education facilitated by raising and instructing children of both sexes together (49–50). Once the "same rules of education" are applied to female and male children alike (142), culturally produced sexual differences will diminish, and women will be in a position to replace indirect influence with the exercise of civil rights and duties.

Wollstonecraft restates and extends these arguments in the *Vindication of the Rights of Woman*, a work which is pervasively indebted to Macaulay's *Letters*, but elaborates its hints on the genealogy of women's presently "degrading" social position and socially produced character into a thoroughgoing critique of modern European culture. Moreover, Wollstonecraft expands Macaulay's appeal to "natural rights" into a radically democratic call for the enfranchisement of oppressed groups of men as well as women; she also constructs a line of argument turning the conduct book against itself by using its vision of women's socializing function to argue for equal (not separate) education. This last strategy, however, is the least radical aspect of the second *Vindication*; it is in arguing from women's rights rather than from their traditional function that Wollstonecraft most decisively breaks with the conduct book verities which Hannah More and Jane West will later reassert.

Arguing (as does Macaulay) from associationist principles (*VRW*, 115–21), Wollstonecraft holds that sexual differences in mind and character are largely if not wholly produced by education. There is some ambiguity on this point: noting that the "female in point of strength is, in general, inferior to the male," Wollstonecraft states (rather obscurely) that "from the constitution of their bodies, men seem to be designed by Providence to attain a greater degree of virtue"; virtue can not, however, be different in kind (*VRW*, 9, 26). Later, Wollstonecraft admits the "inferiority of woman" only "according to the present *appearance* of things"; still later, she contends that the "sexual distinction" insisted upon by male writers is "arbitrary" (*VRW*, 35 [my emphasis], 193). It is social practices that "enslave women by cramping their understanding and sharpening their senses." Such practices include those legislated by "all" writers on "female education and manners" from Rousseau to Gregory, who have together "contributed to render women more artificial, weak characters, than they would otherwise have been" (*VRW*, 22).

As her appeal to the companionate marriage and rational motherhood suggests, Wollstonecraft is willing to attack the conduct book tradition on its own grounds, asking, for example, whether women trained in "passive obedience" have "sufficient character to manage a family or educate children," and even concedes that most women "should not be taken out of their families," should remain, that is, within the private sphere (*VRW*, 35, 63). However, Wollstonecraft argues that careers in medicine, business, and politics should be opened to women and that women's "first duty is to themselves as rational creatures," defining the maternal role (next in importance) as a civic rather than natural duty (*VRW*, 145–8). Women would properly perform their "domestic duties," she argues, only "if political and moral subjects were opened to them" (*VRW*, 169); limiting women to a domestic sphere only unfits them for domestic life.

Moreover, Wollstonecraft (like Macaulay) directly attacks the stock emphasis on "sexual" virtues, particularly modesty and the double standard that underwrites it; she also criticizes the pervasive infantilization of women within the conduct book tradition. Citing Gregory as representative, Wollstonecraft describes the conduct book education as a "system of slavery," labelling "absurd and tyrannic" the "attempt to educate moral beings by any other rules than those deduced from pure reason, which apply to the whole species" (*VRW*, 33). She dismisses such passive virtues as gentleness, docility, and "spaniel-like affection" for their corrosive effect on the female character and on society in general. As for the double standard: "I here throw down my gauntlet, and deny the existence of sexual virtues, not excepting modesty" (*VRW*, 47). In a remarkably frank defense of the legitimacy of female desire, Wollstonecraft declares that "women as well as men ought to have the common appetites and passions of their nature ... the obligation to check them is the duty of mankind, not a sexual duty."[27] The advice on "reputation" in conduct books is a collection of "specious poisons," which eat away the substance of morality by emphasizing the appearance of it (*VRW*, 130–31). Innocence is roundly dismissed for its infantilizing effects: "Children, I grant, should be innocent; but when the epithet is applied to men, or women, it is but a civil term for weakness" (*VRW*, 20). If women continue to have "peculiar duties" within the domestic sphere, the "only method of leading women to fulfill them" is, not to stunt their physical, mental, and moral growth – keeping them "in a perpetual state of childhood" – but to "free them from all restraint by allowing them to participate in the inherent rights of mankind" (*VRW*, 9, 175).

As this appeal to "inherent rights" suggests, Wollstonecraft's defense of the rights of woman is intimately related to her earlier defense, in the first *Vindication*, of the "rights of man," constituting what Elissa Guralnick calls a "radical critique of society from broad egalitarian premises" in which female emancipation is linked with the rise of a more equal (if not exactly "classless") society.[28] The epoch of true equality between the sexes, Wollstonecraft writes, must "wait, perhaps, till kings and nobles, enlightened by reason, and, preferring the real dignity of man to childish state, throw off their gaudy hereditary trappings" (*VRW*, 22), for the hierarchical system which oppresses women is the same system that engenders class oppression. Subjecting the traditional metonymic chain of authority – from God, to king, to father and husband – to a pervasive critique of all social relations predicated upon domination, Wollstonecraft attacks "tyrants of every denomination, from the weak king to the weak father of a family," comparing the specious "*divine right* of husbands" (and of parents) to the recently exploded "divine right of kings" (*VRW*, 5, 41, 157). Women's lack of political representation in England is likened to that of a "numerous class of hard working mechanics, who pay for the support of royalty when they can scarcely stop their children's mouths with bread"; the English system of representation is dismissed as a "convenient handle for despotism" (*VRW* 147). Wollstonecraft notes that the same arguments which writers like Rousseau advance against equal education for women are also made "against instructing the poor; for many are the forms that aristocracy assumes" (*VRW*, 62).

It is because social oppression is systemic, including forms of domination based on class hierarchies as well as on sexual difference, that private education alone can provide relatively little in the way of social change. For this reason, Wollstonecraft's proposal for educational reform entails a national rather than domestic scheme, and specifies bringing the several classes as well as the two sexes together within a single system of schools. The system of nationally supported day schools she proposes would be "absolutely free and open to all classes" in the elementary years (from five to nine years of age), with both sexes educated together as well. After this age, children intended for "domestic employments, or mechanical trades" would be separated from those destined for a "more extensive" academic education; the separation would be based on "superior abilities, or fortune" – a significant "or" – and boys and girls would continue to study together in each type of school (*VRW*, 167–68). Wollstonecraft's is one of the most radical educational proposals of the eighteenth century, although its segregation of older children into vocational and academic tracks reveals the limits to her vision of social change, limits which may be endemic to the progressive rationalist discourse in which she frames her ideas.[29] Wollstonecraft's program is virtually unique, however, in its recognition that educational reform will do little in the absence of a "truly equitable" social compact, that the "advantages of education and government" are not separable (*VRW*, 173, 167).

The decade and a half immediately following the publication of the *Rights of Woman* witnessed one of the most reactionary periods in British history, with the established interests feeling doubly threatened by the upheavals in France and by popular radicalism in England and Ireland, and with the middle classes rapidly positioning themselves into a defensive alliance with the aristocracy. As Jane West describes the contemporary political situation in her *Letters to a Young Lady* (1806), the "torrent of false theories and disorganizing principles" poured into England in the 1790s had gradually become "diffused among the lower orders"; "that 'mystery of iniquity'," she warns, "whose course is marked on the continent of Europe by subverted empires, and desolated realms, has on this island been at present busy in effecting those moral revolutions which are the precursors of political ones."[30] In place of Macaulay's and Wollstone-craft's assertions of women's "rights" – a now suspect term – and their radical program for equal education, writers like Reeve, Gisborne, More, and West developed a position on female education allowing for a certain measure of social reform while upholding traditional class and gender hierarchies, reasserting the separation of male and female spheres, re-emphasizing "negative" virtues (especially modesty), and advocating much greater attention to religious and moral discipline. Education and female manners had together become politically charged topics.

The new climate can be felt already in Reeve's *Plans of Education*, published the same year (1792) as Wollstonecraft's second *Vindication*. Reeve attacks the boarding schools for emphasizing "external accomplishments" over "moral duties" and "social virtues," particularly those "first principles of religion" that should be "early sown and strongly inculcated" (136, 42). Reeve's pupils will be taught a "habit of obedience" from childhood (192); girls will learn such knowledge as will "qualify them to govern and conduct a family" (144), and that "all their happiness, present and future," depends upon their chastity (174). Her educational system separates girls from boys and is based on class stratification ("the gradations of rank and fortune") and on restoring the "disciplinarian" character of English education undermined by the innovations of Rousseau and his followers (64, 40). Thomas Gisborne, in *An Enquiry into the Duties of the Female Sex* (1797), develops a similarly defensive educational agenda. He admonishes his women readers that the "distinctions of rank in society are instituted ... for the benefit of the whole" (86), would limit them to the "sphere of domestic life" (2), and warns that, while girls should learn more than "ornamental accomplishments" (76), the "more profound reaches of philosophy and learning" might unfit them for marriage (270).

Hannah More and Jane West, while largely sharing the conservative educational agenda set forth by Reeve and Gisborne, are much harsher than either of these writers (and indeed, than most previous conduct-book writers) on their own sex. Both attack Wollstonecraft directly: More as the corrupting author of *The Wrongs of Woman: or, Maria*, "a *woman*, a professed admirer and imitator of the German suicide Werter" (1 : 48), West for "affecting amazonian independence" and disseminating "democratic principles" in the second *Vindication* (50, 72).[31] More's *Strictures on the Modern System of*

Female Education (1799) shows particularly clearly how the celebration of women's maternal and pedagogical "power" ("a power wide in its extent, indefinite in its effect, and inestimable in its importance" [1 : 59]) can co-exist with a profound ambivalence regarding female desire and an educational program designed chiefly to contain it. Her treatise begins by addressing the "singular injustice" exercised toward women in giving them a "very defective Education" while demanding from them the "most undeviating purity of conduct" (ix), but the reforms she suggests are, as Poovey has noted, designed rather to support the "traditional hierarchy and values of patriarchal society" than to fundamentally alter women's social position.[32]

Like Macaulay or Wollstonecraft, More sees the issues of women's education, manners, and social role as inherently political: "The general state of civilized society depends ... on the prevailing sentiments and habits of women, and on the nature and degree of the estimation in which they are held" (2). But More is not about to endorse Wollstonecraft's feminist call for a "REVOLUTION in female manners" (192); rather, in the present crisis, women's duty is to play a counter-revolutionary role, to oppose a "bold and noble *unanimity* to the most tremendous confederacies against religion, and order, and governments, which the world ever saw" (1 : 4–6). Exhorting a patriotism "at once firm and feminine," More stresses that she is not calling for "female warriors" or "female politicians": "I hardly know which of the two is the most disgusting and unnatural character" (1 : 6). More instead asks women to work from within their proper sphere, to "raise the depressed tone of public morals," "awaken the drowsy spirit of religious principle," and guarantee the political conservatism and Christian orthodoxy of the "whole rising generation" (1 : 4, 60).

More's critique of contemporary female education is directed against the familiar "phrenzy of accomplishments" which she ties to a "revolution" in middle-class manners (1 : 69–70), but she proposes not to jettison but reconstruct the "superstructure of the accomplishments" on the "solid basis of Christian humility" (1 : 94). More also prescribes a return to the traditional negative virtues – "fortitude, temperance, meekness, faith, diligence, and self-denial" (1 : 166) – in an education designed for the domestic sphere, admonishing women to covet no "profession" but that of "daughters, wives, mothers, and mistresses of families" (1 : 107). Above all, women must study whatever "keeps back *self*" and keeps down the "violence of ungoverned passions and uncontrolled inclinations" (1 : 112, 2 : 105). Woman's fundamental role is for More, as it is within domestic ideology generally, that of "regulating her own desire," and her education is to be one in constraint, even humiliation.[33] "An early habitual restraint is peculiarly important to the future character and happiness of women ... They should when very young be enured to contradiction ... They should be led to distrust their own judgment; they should learn not to murmur at expostulation; but should be accustomed to expect and to endure opposition" (1 : 154–55).[34] As More's anti-feminist prescriptions make clear, her program for educational "reform" differs drastically from that of Wollstonecraft, although the two have recently been juxtaposed as twin expressions of "female domestic heroism."[35] To collapse their positions on female education together, however, is to do justice to the thought of neither, and to entirely lose sight of the politics of education in the Romantic era.

It is politics – and particularly the issue of political and civic equality between the sexes – that most obviously differentiates More's thought from that of Wollstonecraft and Macaulay. In place of Wollstonecraft's assertion of women's rights in the name of democratic principles, More equates "democracy" with "impiety" (1 : 22) and dismisses woman's "imaginary *rights*" as contrary to the "duties of her allotted station": "Is it not desireable to be the lawful possessors of a lesser domestic territory, rather than the turbulent usurpers of a wider foreign empire" (2 : 22–25). Woman's duties are "to regulate her own mind, and to be useful to others" (2 : 2); demanding rights will only make woman a Napoleon in petticoats, upsetting the divinely sanctioned order of things by unlawfully extending her allotted domain. West, sharing More's principles but writing for the middle classes (vi) rather than for "Women of Rank and Society," comes to much the same conclusion. In what sounds like a criticism but is actually a defense of women's political disenfranchisement, West writes that the "propriety of our seclusion from public affairs is necessarily interwoven with domestic sub-jection" (47); "If we wish our girls to be happy, we must try to make them docile, contented, prudent, and domestic" (418).

Liberal writers on education, such as Erasmus Darwin, Maria Edgeworth, and Sydney Smith, sought a middle ground between the backward-looking "reforms" of conservative moralists and the radical proposals of Macaulay and Wollstonecraft. Their compromise position involved advocating a series of curricular changes (such as adding the modern sciences to the list of subjects thought suitable for girls) without fundamentally challenging the separation of public and domestic spheres. Like the conservative writers, they sought to ameliorate women's position within a patriarchal society rather than address inequalities between the genders on political grounds. Unlike the conservatives, however, they based their educational reforms not on shoring up the existing order through training in orthodoxy and submission, but on appealing to the enlightened self-interest of educated, rational, middle-class women to embrace the apparent inequities of a system that ultimately worked for all. Their approach to female education parallels the Radical-Utilitarian program for educating the lower classes – through such institutions as the Society for the Diffusion of Useful Knowledge and the Mechanics' Institutes – in discovering their "true interests"; in both cases, social stability is increased rather than diminished by providing instruction for a subordinate group, whose perceived interests can be brought into line with the quest for greater middle-class hegemony through carefully limited political reform. Their commitment to progressive educational reform ran, as a result, deeper than that of their more conservative contemporaries; nevertheless, the question of women's education remained a politically charged one, forcing liberal writers to make greater concessions to tradition than they perhaps might have wished.

Some liberals were no less ambivalent about the genuine reform of female education than their more politically reactionary contemporaries. Anna Barbauld, for example, refused to head a women's college proposed by Elizabeth Montagu and other members of the "bluestocking" group, opining that girls were best instructed by "family intercourse," the teaching of "a father, a brother or friend"; her views have been criticized as being not only "retrograde" but also narrowly self-regarding, as Barbauld's own father was a famous classical tutor at the great Warrington Academy, an advantage few women could share.[36] Others attempted to reform the existing system without changing its basic design, as in Darwin's *Plan for the Conduct of Female Education in Boarding Schools* (1797). Darwin writes that female education should produce "internal strength and activity of mind" rather than "trivial accomplishments"; his curriculum includes both the traditional boarding-school subjects – English, French, Italian, simple arithmetic, history, drawing, and needlework

– and an "outline" of botany, chemistry, and other branches of "experimental philosophy."[37] The "useful cultivation of modern sciences," however, is aimed chiefly at making the girls better "companions" for their future husbands; Darwin also endorses the traditional emphasis on "CHASTITY" ("by which civilized society is held together"), the "retiring" virtues, and a ductile "female character" prepared to "take impressions" at the time of marriage (45, 54, 10).

Maria Edgeworth breaks more decisively with the conduct book tradition, particularly in her *Letters for Literary Ladies* (1795), although her reforms for women's education remain like Darwin's locked within the constraints of domestic ideology. Although the Edgeworths have been credited with advancing a notion of "female education ... in all essentials the same as men's," this is not precisely the case.[38] In *Practical Education*, girls are taught the same subjects as boys, but in a decidedly different manner; girls, for example, study the "principles of chemistry" only indirectly, as they "learn confectionary" (1: 34).[39] Moreover, the Edgeworths' agenda for women's education is an explicitly temporizing one: "We cannot help thinking that their happiness is of more consequence than their speculative rights; and we wish to educate women so that they may be happy in the situations in which they are most likely to be placed" (1: 212). Slated for a subordinate role within the "*domestick*" sphere (2: 427), girls are taught special lessons in regulating "temper" (1: 212), for "peculiar caution is necessary to manage female sensibility" (1: 380). As women, unlike men, "cannot always have recourse to what *ought to be*, they must adapt themselves to what is"; therefore, in keeping with the double standard for sexual morality which underpins domestic ideology, they must develop negative traits like "caution" (2: 393).

Maria Edgeworth seems, on the other hand, to undercut many of these same conduct book maxims by attributing them to the short-sighted "Gentleman" who writes his friend an ominous letter "upon the Birth of a Daughter" in *Letters for Literary Ladies*, in a fictional exchange based partly on correspondence between Richard Edgeworth and Thomas Day. (Day had urged that Maria be barred from a literary career).[40] Drawing both on Rousseau and Burke, the Day figure argues against a female literary education by citing woman's natural "inferiority" and "domestic" role (3–5), reaffirming "how much in society depends upon the honour of women" (15), and opposing the wisdom of "traditional maxims of experience" (or "prejudices") to the recent "metaphysical argument" that "as women are reasonable creatures, they should be governed only by reason" (20, 16). The "Friend" responds, however, not as a "*champion for women's rights*" but as one advocating their "happiness" within the status quo (45). Women cannot, by their very nature, wish to enter "public scenes of life": "They must become Amazons before they can effect this change; they must cease to be women before they can desire it" (52). Their embrace of domestic ideology will instead grow only tighter as they develop more "enlarged understandings" (55) and rationally discover how "common forms" and delicate "female manners" are inextricably connected with the "largest interests of society" (61–62). Women have commonly erred not from too much knowledge, but from too little wisdom: "they may have grown vain and presumptuous when they have learned but little, they will be sobered into good sense when they shall have learned more" (56). One could argue, of course, that Edgeworth distances herself from *both* the traditionalist and liberal positions by attributing them to male correspondents. But the arguments of the "Friend" are confirmed later in the book in the novelistic "Letters of Julia and Caroline," in which the rationally educated Caroline emerges as the champion of social "forms" (including the duty of Julia to remain with a brutish husband); the position they outline is the one Edgeworth will develop in later novels (particularly the story of the Delacours in *Belinda*) as well.

In her continuation of her father's *Memoirs*, Maria Edgeworth attributes to him a utilitarian argument for educating the lower classes essentially similar to the one she advances for women's education in the *Letters*: "He did not wish for the people any other education, but what might afford them a knowledge of their duty, what would make them virtuous and loyal, useful to themselves and to the state" (2: 138). A comparable position is developed at greater length by Sydney Smith, in an essay on "Female Education" written for the *Edinburgh Review* (1810). Like Wollstonecraft (from whom he tacitly borrows a great deal), Smith notes that the "same objection" has been made against educating women as against educating the lower classes – that they will forget their duties – and attacks prejudice in the name of gradual improvement: "Nothing is more common, or more stupid, than to take the actual for the possible – to believe that all which is, is all which can be."[41] Also like Wollstonecraft, Smith attacks the conduct book tradition by turning its own assumptions against it, although his language on the need for properly educated mothers takes on a more disciplinary cast: "If you educate women to attend to dignified and important subjects, you are multiplying, beyond measure, the chances of human improvement, by preparing and *medicating* those early impressions, which always come from the mother" (207). Smith's principal arguments, however, are utilitarian ones. As women are not educated to take part in an increasingly industrialized and literate society, "at present, half the talent in the universe runs to waste, and is totally unprofitable" (204). More importantly, properly educated women would not only be better equipped for a modern society, but would be more not less willing to accept a subordinate place within it. Since "all the salutary rules which are imposed on women" are "productive of the greatest happiness," they can only become more "sensible of this truth in proportion as their power of discovering truth in general is increased, and the habit of viewing questions with accuracy and comprehension established by education" (206). Women and the lower classes are equated within a broad social program for strengthening middle-class hegemony on the basis of the "greatest happiness"; education becomes central as the best means to bring the perceived interests of both dominated groups into line with those of the ascendant male bourgeoisie. If, as Nancy Armstrong argues, the "techniques of domestic regulation" first developed in the later eighteenth century for the containment of middle-class women were eventually extended "into the lives of those much lower down on the economic ladder," a process she calls the "feminization" of the lower classes, this connection was already explicit in the arguments for social control through education advanced by Edgeworth and Smith in the Romantic era.[42]

WELL-REGULATED MINDS: DEVELOPMENT IN THE DOMESTIC NOVEL

Writers on female behavior and education in the eighteenth and early nineteenth centuries were much concerned with the novel, a genre which had become widely identified with women as both its principal consumers (making up a notable segment of the new reading public) and producers. In an age when, as West writes, "*every young woman reads, and many* confine their knowledge to this species of misinformation" (319), it was widely felt that the novel had either to be banned altogether or refashioned into a vehicle for disseminating principle: More warns in *Strictures* that novel reading "has spread so wide, and descended so low, as to have become one of the most universal as well as one of the most pernicious sources of corruption among us" (1: 191). Whereas earlier writers of conduct books tend to counsel abstinence, warning their women readers against a genre which Gregory compares to "fatal poison" (117) and Fordyce characterizes as "unspeakably perverting and inflammatory" (*Sermons* 75), later writers like West similarly condemn the majority of novels but assert that, when properly written, the novel can on the contrary provide the "best introduction to the knowledge of life and manners" (320). The ambivalence of West and More (both of whom – like Wollstonecraft – wrote novels while condemning the genre as a whole) is anticipated by Chapone, for whom most novels "inflame" rather than curb the "passions of youth," although a select few instead join "excellent morality" with "the most lively pictures of the human mind" (148–49). With its corrupting tendencies checked, the novel could become an ideal species of reading for young women, who were trained in the modern languages rather than the classics, and whose peculiar task was to develop qualities of mind – sensibility, sympathy, modesty, prudence – which the novel could represent to them in its "most lively" fashion.[43]

The ambivalence toward the novel form that had developed by the end of the eighteenth century was not confined to conservatives but was shared by liberal and radical writers on female education as well. Darwin, for example, distinguishes between "amorous" novels, which should be "intirely [sic] interdicted," and a more recent "serious" tradition (mainly the "productions of ingenious ladies") which will instruct young women and rescue them from a debilitating "ignorance of mankind" (33–34). Barbauld similarly (if less censoriously) contrasts romance-like novels, which provide domestic entertainment but may give rise to unrealistic expectations, with those – a "very great proportion" of them written by women – which have been instrumental in "infusing principles and moral feelings" in their "youthful readers."[44] Maria Edgeworth warns against "immoderate novel reading" in *Practical Education* (1: 427) and regularly demonstrates the dangers of undirected reading in her stories for adolescents; Lady Augusta in Part Two of "Mademoiselle Panache," for example, is dropped by her worthy suitor when he discovers her reading not only a notoriously immoral French novel but the "*second* volume" at that.[45] Edgeworth herself, however, helped propagate the "serious" approach to women's fiction in her collections *Moral Tales* and *Tales of Fashionable Life* (1812), and in a series of domestic novels, at once instructive and decidedly "lively," running from *Belinda* (1801) to *Helen* (1834). In these works Edgeworth rescues the novel from the charges of corruption levied on it by writers on female manners and education precisely by bringing their central concerns – proper conduct, right and wrong methods of schooling, the growth of a sound moral and intellectual character – into the genre. As a writer of children's fiction featuring realistic portrayals of instruction and moral development within a domestic setting, and as an educational theorist of the "experimental" school, Edgeworth was uniquely fitted to bring the domestic novel and novel of education together. She could also find precedents in several "Jacobin" novelists of the 1790s: Elizabeth Inchbald, Mary Wollstonecraft, and Mary Hays.

In contrasting the fates of a fashionably educated mother and rationally (and religiously) educated daughter in *A Simple Story* (1791) – a novel greatly admired by Edgeworth – Inchbald showed how the domestic novel could, as she stresses in its concluding sentence, address the importance and character of "A PROPER EDUCATION."[46] The rigorously binary structure of *A Simple Story*, demonstrating the effects of two educational modes by embodying them in opposed characters, is obviously indebted to Day's *Sandford and Merton*, which itself marries the educational treatise to the "Kind and Unkind" folktale type; this basic pattern would be refined in such novels as Jane West's *Advantages of Education* and *A Gossip's Story*, Jane Austen's *Sense and Sensibility*, and Maria Edgeworth's *Helen*.[47] Wollstonecraft, who argued in the second *Vindication* that women were too prone to reading novels, and yet that novel reading was much preferable to a complete lack of mental culture ("leaving a blank still a blank" [*VRW*,184]), weds her pedagogical concerns to the sentimental novel in *Mary, A Fiction* (1788) and *The Wrongs of Woman: Or, Maria* (1798), both of which (like Hays's *Emma Courtney* [1796]) demonstrate how the female character is formed or malformed by education. In these works, conventional female education is condemned for rating the superficial over the substantial; Mary's fashionably educated mother, for example, has become a "mere machine" (1). In contrast, Mary's education is neglected, and she reads (much like Emma Courtney) "every book that came her way" without direction, learning to think on her own (4). To an extent, such neglect proves saving: it allows the heroine a certain liberty of mind, a freedom from stock prejudices and arbitrary social customs, which finds its extreme form in the *ingénu* hero of Inchbald's *Nature and Art* (1796), who owes his "natural simplicity" to having been brought up among "savages" on an island off the coast of Africa.[48]

At the same time, however, both Mary and Emma Courtney suffer from not having been granted the sound education which, as far as women are concerned, does not yet exist: Mary's undirected reading leaves her "too much the creature of impulse, and the slave of compassion" (7), while Emma, who at one point reads from ten to fourteen novels a week, too readily becomes the "dupe" of her imagination (1: 26, 84). Maria's "passion" for reading in *The Wrongs of Woman*, indulged by a fond uncle, leaves her with an "ideal picture of life" that she never quite manages to square with things as they are, rendering her unusually intolerant of social abuses but also prone to self-deception (128). If novel reading contributes to the unhappy fates of their heroines, however, these same works demonstrate how the novel can exercise didactic force through its unique capacity to delineate the formation of character and depict the struggle of reason and passion within the mind. Maria addresses her history to her absent daughter, scripting the vagaries of her own mental development as a form of "instruction" or "counsel" meant "rather to exercise than influence" her daughter's mind (124). Hays renders this program more explicit in Emma Courtney's address to her adopted son: "It is by tracing, by developing, the passions in the minds of others; tracing them, from the seeds by which they have been generated, through all their extended consequences, that we learn, the more effectually, to regulate and to subdue our own" (2: 1). In a novel which was widely considered immoral, Hays articulates the ethos which would underwrite the domestic novel's claim to constitute an instrument of self-regulation rather than a fount of "corruption."

Somewhat ironically, a number of the women writers who follow the lead of Inchbald, Wollstonecraft, and Hays in developing the courtship novel into the novel of female education establish their claim to sound morality in part by lampooning the figure of the free-thinking feminist. Even reformist liberals like Edgeworth and Amelia Opie distance themselves from the radical novel of the 1790s by producing such caricatures of the feminist thinker as Rachael Hodges in Edgeworth's "Angelina" (in *Moral Tales*) and Editha Mowbray in Opie's *Adeline Mowbray* (1804), false mother-figures whose radical arguments lead the naive heroines to court disaster through attempting to live outside of accepted social forms. Typically described as "masculine" or "amazonian" and often exhibited in male attire, the caricature feminist becomes a common feature of early nineteenth-century fiction: Lady Di Spanker in Edgeworth's "Mademoiselle Panache" (Part Two) and Harriot Freke in *Belinda*, Miss Sparkes in More's *Coelebs*, Bridgetina Botherim in Elizabeth Hamilton's anti-jacobin satire, *Memoirs of Modern Philosophers* (1800), and Elinor Joddrel in Fanny Burney's *The Wanderer* (1814) are well-known examples, and all are meant to evoke Wollstonecraft or Hays (or both). Claudia Johnson has argued that the portrayal of the "freakish feminist" allows the woman writer to establish her anti-radical credentials and then "advance reformist positions about women through the back door."[49] But smuggling reform in through the kitchen means limiting social change to what can be effected from within the domestic sphere, and to what can be advocated with the language of duty and indirect "influence"; the language of civil and political enfranchisement remains anathema to the early nineteenth-century domestic novel.

In place of the radical critique of society and pursuit of intellectual independence set forth in the novels of Wollstonecraft and Hays, the domestic novel of the Romantic era advances a cautiously diminished form of moral autonomy, representing an educational ideal designed to produce a "well-regulated mind" – a key phrase applied to the heroine in novels by West, More, Edgeworth, and Susan Ferrier.[50] At once rational and possessed of a refined sensibility, the domestic heroine learns, by regulating her expectations and desires, to conform to traditional conduct-book manners and embody the passive virtues; her capacity to help reform an increasingly commercialized, decadent, and fragmented society increases in direct proportion with her ability to restrain her own egotism. Barred from (and not desiring) participation in political and commercial life, she confines her reformist efforts to the domestic sphere, cautiously extended, however, to include such activities as caring for (and supervising) the local poor and educating not only her own children but those of her lower-class neighbors through setting up village schools. The infusion of the novel of female development with conduct book virtues – the domestication of the female *Bildungsroman* of the 1790s – can be seen most obviously in More's *Coelebs in Search of a Wife* and West's *The Advantages of Education*, works which are at once novel, conduct-book, and educational tract. Although these "novels" (particularly *Coelebs*) enjoyed a vogue, they were too openly didactic and too carelessly assembled to establish a tradition. Their principal elements were reworked in a more esthetically successful (and ultimately more influential) form, however, in the novels of Edgeworth, Ferrier, and Austen, the three writers singled out by Walter Scott for their convincing "portraits of real society" and their deft description of the characters' "thoughts and sentiments": "far superior to anything Man vain Man has produced of the like nature."[51] In opining that "the women do this better" Scott points up the enabling aspect of the woman novelist's relative confinement to a narrow, domestic canvas. Enjoined to study (in order to better regulate) their own minds, and encouraged to limit their narratives to the interaction of self and society within the "real" province of domestic life, women writers became particularly adept at representing intellectual and moral development, creating compelling psychological portraits well before the advent of the "psychological novel."

Edgeworth's fictional works have been criticized for portraying development too schematically, particularly for the "omniscient guardians" whose example and advice guarantee the heroine's proper maturation, but (however true of her stories for children and younger adolescents) this is not a fair criticism of *Belinda* or *Helen*, both of which significantly complicate the mother-daughter relationship.[52] *Belinda* (like *Helen*) is motherless; in order to properly negotiate her entrance into the world, she must choose between several maternal substitutes as well as weighing the claims of her various suitors. Although officially under the protection of her aunt, a worldly social climber, Belinda, "educated chiefly in the country," has earlier imbibed a taste for "domestic pleasures," particularly reading, and a disposition toward "prudence and integrity" in her conduct. "Her character, however, was yet to be developed by circumstances" (1); *Belinda* will show how the internally regulated female character develops through testing itself, with the right guidance, against the snares of the marriage market and the fashionable world. Distancing herself from her aunt, Belinda must choose among three potential female mentors, the aristocratic, brilliant, and dissipated Lady Delacour, the domestic and rational

Lady Anne Percival, and the caricature feminist Harriot Freke. Freke is dismissed out of hand (although she all but abducts Belinda in her search for a proselyte); Lady Delacour proves, however initially attractive, more an object lesson on the vanities of high society than a suitable model for Belinda to follow.

Belinda elects instead to emulate Lady Anne, who enjoys a companionate marriage with a well-educated country gentleman; the descriptions of their idyllic domestic life usually show them surrounded by (and continually finding opportunities to instruct) their group of pattern children, in scenes closely related to the family anecdotes scattered throughout *Practical Education*. Lady Delacour, in contrast, lives apart from her child and barely speaks with her husband; her lack of true maternal qualities is signified by an apparently cancerous breast, described in a passage highly reminiscent of Coleridge's *Christabel* (also a work about an *ingénue* dangerously attracted to a false mother-figure).[53] The opposition between Lady Anne and Lady Delacour is not so neat, however, as these contrasts suggest: the suitor (a West-Indian heir) whom the Percivals present to Belinda ultimately proves to be feckless, and she ends up choosing the fashionable Clarence Hervey, protégé and admirer of Lady Delacour.

Lady Delacour is the novel's brightest character, and critics tend to locate its center of interest in her story rather than in that of Belinda, in defiance of Edgeworth's title. Lady Delacour's narrative of her youthful adventures under the dubious wing of Harriot Freke provides some of the more engaging passages in the work, while her gradual refashioning (guided, in a significant role reversal, by Belinda) of her own life into one more resembling that of Lady Anne provides a good deal of the narrative drive.[54] Yet the title character is far more intriguing than is generally conceded. Edgeworth's characterization of Belinda borrows many of its features from eighteenth-century conduct literature: her modesty, her prudence, her decorous silences, even her marked tendency to blush, the most trustworthy sign, according to both Fordyce and Gregory, of a young woman's delicacy.[55] To this Edgeworth adds a greater stress on rationality and independent judgment, and gives Belinda a more extensive literary education as well. Edgeworth's characterization of Belinda does not, however, simply update the conduct book ideal – it also exposes one of its most problematic aspects in Belinda's difficulties in expressing, and even registering, her erotic desires. It is not that Belinda fails to experience such desires; rather, she has no means of representing them to herself or others. Her "cold tameness" (Edgeworth's own retrospective verdict) reflects more a failure of signification than a lack of sensibility.[56]

In Gregory's *Legacy*, young women are warned not to expect a love match; but if they do experience desire, they must never let their suitor know its full extent, "no not although you marry him" (87–88). More important, a truly modest woman will strive to keep any knowledge of her desire *even from herself*: "It is even long before a woman of delicacy dares avow to her own heart that she loves; and when all the subterfuges of ingenuity to conceal it from herself fail, she feels a violence done both to her pride and to her modesty" (67). Gregory enjoins upon his female reader a painfully divided consciousness, an impossible work of repression which will conceal her desires even from "her own heart" (leading one to wonder where indeed they arise or how they are sufficiently registered to inspire her "subterfuges"). This heroic task of repression and psychological splitting is what makes such Edgeworth heroines as Belinda, Caroline (in *Patronage*), and Helen interesting, particularly when read against the conduct book tradition; moreover, Edgeworth shows the cost of this self-division by negatively registering the psychic "violence" which asserts itself even within Gregory's prescriptive account. Belinda can only express her feelings for Clarence Hervey mutely: by blushing, by awkward gestures or silences, by ellipses, such as her sudden inability to pronounce his first name ("Cla – " [257]). This is not coquetry, but rather the effect of unremitting repression; hers is not, moreover, the "prudence of a cold and selfish, but of a modest and generous woman." Like the conduct-book heroine she resembles, Belinda hides her desire from others and herself in order to "guard her affections"; but the violence of her struggle to bring her passions "entirely under her command" leaves her both unable to judge the force of her feelings and deceived regarding their object (127). The more worldly (and lascivious) Lady Delacour must articulate Belinda's negative expressions of desire for her, as when Belinda declares her lack of feeling for Clarence: "It is a pity that your countenance, which is usually expressive enough, should not at this instant obey your wishes and express perfect felicity" (132). As Belinda continues to believe (wrongly) in her "conquest over herself" (232), Lady Delacour's intervention is required to bring the lovers together and close the narrative, and Delacour's ability to "name the heroine's secret desire" is closely related, as Kowaleski-Wallace suggests, to her having formerly inhabited the "dangerous reaches beyond the domestic sphere" inhabited by Harriot Freke.[57]

But if Belinda's reserve proves inadequate, Harriot Freke's quasi-feminist avowal of female desire is explicitly dismissed, in an important exchange between Freke, Belinda, and Mr. Percival, Lady Anne's husband (208–9). Using catch phrases from Wollstonecraft ("I'm a champion for the Rights of Woman"), Freke declares that "shame is the cause of all women's vices" and "*delicacy*" is an ideal invented by men to "enslave" women. Why, she asks, "when a woman likes a man, does she not go and tell him so honestly?" Neatly as this question applies to Belinda's own dilemma, its terms are so foreign to the social code she has internalized that she can reply only with the requisite blush. It is Mr. Percival, the rational patriarch, who takes up Freke's gauntlet, arguing from utilitarian premises for traditional sexual virtues. A woman's delicacy "conduces to [her] happiness," since articulating her desire would "disgust the object of her affection"; "Fortunately for society, the same conduct in ladies which best secures their happiness most increases ours." Freke has no answer to Percival's arguments; her lack of true femininity is definitively exposed later in the novel when she is caught – "in men's clothes" – in a man-trap (283). If Freke's open expression of desire is inadmissable, however, Belinda's inability to express desire (even to herself) has proved, in her own case, problematic; as a result, the status of desire in *Belinda* is left unresolved, a negative sign (like Belinda's ellipses) of the limits of domestic ideology. Reading *Belinda* from this perspective, one can interpret its heroine's silences as implying not coldness but rather as negatively registering the strength of her desire, much as Edgeworth read Inchbald's *Simple Story*: "By the force that is necessary to repress feeling, we judge of the intensity of the feeling; and you always contrive to give us by intelligible and simple signs the measure of this force."[58] Belinda's silences and ellipses signify the vacancy at the heart of domestic ideology, its failure to comprehend female desire.

In a novel concerned throughout with contemporary debates on female manners and education, it is telling that Edgeworth includes a sub-plot fictionalizing an infamous educational experiment of Thomas Day, his attempt, inspired by *Emile*, to form himself an ideal wife by personally educating two girls he purchased from foundling hospitals (Day eventually married an heiress).[59] In *Belinda*, Clarence

Hervey, fresh from admiring Rousseau's portrait of Sophie, undertakes the "romantic project of educating a wife for himself" (329). He is soon lucky enough to blunder into a beautiful, illiterate, unprotected young woman whose innocence has never been corrupted by a boarding school (333). Clarence renames her Virginia (after St. Pierre's Rousseauvian *Paul et Virginie*), establishes her in a lonely cottage, and teaches her to read and write; deprived of "social affections" and "real objects to occupy her senses and understanding," Virginia becomes an insatiable reader of romances and creates herself a visionary world (345). Meanwhile Clarence meets Belinda, compared to whom his "child of nature" comes to seem "insipid" (337, 344); through an awkward series of plot twists, Virginia finds a properly romantic object of her own and Clarence is at last free to declare his love for Belinda.

The embedded story of Virginia (however poorly integrated into the main plot) plays a complex thematic role in the novel: it contrasts a naive innocence based on ignorance of the world with an achieved innocence, like Belinda's, which has tested itself against the world; it allows Edgeworth to implicitly criticize the most infantilizing tendencies of the conduct-book tradition, showing how too strictly limiting a girl's education and social experience will produce a credulous and romantic, rather than stable and rational, woman; and it differentiates Edgeworth's experiential approach to education from one based on an untested "system" (338). It also implicitly exposes Rousseau's approach to female education in *Emile* – "Oh what lovable ignorance"; "She will not be her husband's teacher but his pupil" (410) – as a male fantasy of absolute control over woman through attempting to engineer her very subjectivity, through asserting (like Clarence) "his own power of developing her capacity" (341). In a more idealized form, however, the portrayal of a companionate marriage founded on the husband's education of his wife (or future wife) features in novels by several women authors in the Romantic period: Orlando and Monimia in Charlotte Smith's *The Old Manor House* (1794), Edmund and Maria in West's *Advantages of Education*, and Edmund and Fanny in Austen's *Mansfield Park* (1814).

Mansfield Park is, like *Belinda*, concerned explicitly with female education, manners, and development, and tacitly with the problematic status of desire in relation to domestic ideology.[60] A somewhat paradoxical measure of the novel's success in confronting this problem is that its main character, Fanny Price, has (like Belinda) often been found deficient, an "impossible" center for the narrative despite being its heroine. This apparent defect stems, as Johnson has argued, from Austen's recognition of the "intolerable costs" and "impossibility" of female modesty, her laying bare of the "confounding bind" in which women are placed by the contemporary code of propriety.[61] The plot is built up from the conjunction of two fairy tale plots, the "Kind and Unkind" daughter type, which Austen (after Smith and West) adapts to contrast competing educational modes, and the Cinderella story: Fanny is the poor cousin of two pampered beauties, her role in the household that of a virtual servant-"companion", and at the turn in her fortunes she figures as "Queen" of a ball.[62] Such adaptations of fairy tale plots in the "serious" domestic novel (anticipated by Richardson's *Pamela* [1740]) can be related to the appropriation of popular modes for didactic ends in the children's fiction of the period, particularly as the domestic novel was often aimed at adolescent girls and young women.[63] Indeed, a clear line between what would now be termed "adolescent fiction" and the novel intended for adults was not drawn before the 1880s, when writers like Henry James and George Moore would pointedly "renounce the effort to reconcile these two irreconcilable things – art and young girls."[64]

Austen sets up the opposition between rival educational modes at the beginning of the novel with Fanny's introduction (at age ten) into the Mansfield Park household. Her slightly older, superficially educated cousins, Maria and Julia, marvel at her ignorance; while they know the "difference between water-colours and crayons" and the "principal rivers in Russia," Fanny (as though the product of a charity school) can only "read, work, and write" (54–55). The sisters, however, prove entirely deficient in what Chapone calls the "improvement and regulation of the heart" (46), and Austen the "less common acquirements of self-knowledge, generosity, and humility" (55). Lacking either "affection or principle" (183), they fail to internalize their father's conventional notions of duty and religion, and Sir Thomas himself diagnoses the "direful mistake in his plan of education" at the novel's end: raising his daughters "without their understanding their first duties, or his being acquainted with their character and temper" (448). Habit, internalized authority ("principle"), and supervision, the three essential elements of the post-Lockean consensus, have all been neglected in favor of "elegance and accomplishments."[65] Fanny, for her part, is taken in hand by her cousin Edmund, who is being groomed for the Church at Eton and Oxford. With Edmund recommending books, encouraging her taste, and correcting her judgment (57), Fanny enjoys the sort of education guided by a superior "brother or friend" as recommended by Barbauld. Edmund eventually comes to reap the advantages, set forth by Rousseau, of educating his future wife himself, succeeding where Clarence Hervey fails: "Having formed her mind and gained her affections, he had a good chance of her thinking like him" (95).

For a good part of the novel the union of Fanny and Edmund is blocked by the latter's interest in their neighbor Mary Crawford, whose education has been both better and worse than that of Maria and Julia. Brought up in London, Mary is still more accomplished and elegant than the sisters, also more rational: Edmund groups Fanny and Mary together as the two "sensible women" who have spoiled him for "common female society" (351). But Mary too suffers from a lack of principle – diagnosed by Fanny as the "effect of education" (275) – and, deformed by the revolution in female manners which writers like West and More deplore, she does not even recognize the need for principles, failing, for example, to register the proper "modest loathings" when Maria commits adultery with Mary's brother, Henry (441). Mary's is ultimately exposed as a "mind led astray and bewildered, and without any suspicion of being so; dark, yet fancying itself light" (362).

Fanny, on the contrary, is partly forced by her subservient position in the household and partly guided by Edmund into becoming a "textbook Proper Lady," exemplifying what Gregory calls "that modest reserve, that retiring delicacy, which avoids the public eye, and is disconcerted even at the gaze of admiration" (26).[66] In addition to her profound modesty – which has inspired Austen critics with such epithets as "maddeningly inarticulate" – Fanny manifests the more narrowly religious qualities advocated by conservative writers like Gisborne, West, and More. Whereas Belinda and other Edgeworth heroines constitute rational variations on the conduct-book ideal, Fanny is a "Christian heroine";[67] as such she embodies the "self-denial and humility" which Sir Thomas comes to miss in his own daughters (448).

So passive and self-effacing is Fanny, in fact, that she brings out a problem which More had earlier foundered on in her characterization of Lucilla Stanley, the feminine ideal in *Coelebs*: "The perfectly proper young lady cannot be represented at all."[68] If the representation of a character who so purely embodies the "negative" virtues puts the novelist in an awkward situation, it is Fanny's dilemma in representing herself that most brings out the novel's uneasy relation to domestic ideology. Fanny's notorious inarticulateness is only intensified when it comes to expressing erotic wishes. Like Belinda, Fanny struggles to hide her amorous desires even from herself, entailing painful self-division: "Why did such an idea occur to her even enough to be reprobated and forbidden? It ought not to have touched on the confines of her imagination" (271). Her inability to express or even to acknowledge her love for Edmund both cramps her efforts to prevent his match with Mary Crawford and causes her to doubt her own motives in spurning Mary's equally charming and amoral brother. When she does act, she "acts by refusing" (refusing Henry, refusing to take part in *Lover's Vows*); her textbook passivity entails that she can triumph only by virtue of the other characters' mistakes.[69] The reader's frustration with Fanny attests to the novel's distance from the domestic ideology it superficially endorses. *Mansfield Park* will seem an "anti-jacobin novel" if Fanny's radically unsatisfying characterization is interpreted as a structural weakness, a "bitter parody of conservative fiction" if the same narrative problem is read as a sign of resistance.[70]

Developing the first of these positions, Marilyn Butler argues that Austen's portrayal of Fanny's "inner life" – her "first attempt at a sustained subjective piece of writing" – is at odds with the novel's conservative ideology: "Since Fanny is the representative of... orthodoxy, the individuality of her consciousness must to a large extent be denied."[71] Yet Fanny's subjectivity, her possession of a deeper inner life than most of the other characters, is just what marks her superiority – as Sir Thomas remarks of his daughters in retrospect, "something must have been wanting *within*" (448) – and the construction of her individualized consciousness is as much an ideological feature of the text as the debates on religion and the "improvement" of estates. Fanny's psychic depths provide the space in which the self is disciplined, the grounding of true principle, the refuge from (and alternative to) the materialism and frivolity of the social world, and a site for the outlands of erotic desire (beyond the "confines" of imagination) as well.

Somewhat unexpectedly, Austen adds a distinctly Romantic element to Fanny's character in establishing this inner world. In

scenes which contrast Fanny's sensibility to the other characters' lack
of subjective response, Fanny quotes Cowper's *Task* and Scott's *Lady
of the Lake* to Edmund, reminding us that her mind is formed largely
through reading (57). In the famous passage in which she registers
the "harmony" of a starry nightscape, Fanny's comment – "When I
look out on such a night as this, I feel as if there could be neither
wickedness or sorrow in the world; and there certainly would be less
of both if the sublimity of Nature were more attended to, and people
were carried more out of themselves by contemplating such a scene"
(139) – strongly recalls the pronouncements of both Wordsworth
and Coleridge that the developing child's most valuable experience is
to "forget" itself in reading or in contemplating nature. Also
evocative of the Lake poets is the emphasis on Fanny's intense love,
rooted in the "same first associations and habits" (244), for her
brother William; there is something distinctly incestuous in her love
for her cousin Edmund (which also depends on childhood associations) as well.[72] These references and thematic affinities begin to
suggest the complicity of the domestic novel with high Romantic
poetry in what Armstrong calls the "invention of depths in the self,"
the production, through certain kinds of literary experience, of a
modern "psychological" subject open to (and further carved out by)
new technologies of surveillance and self-discipline.[73]

The associations between the novel, domestic ideology, and
Romantic poetry which emerge faintly but distinctly from a reading
of Austen are rendered more overtly in Susan Ferrier's *Marriage*; a
novel that is closely related to *Mansfield Park* in many other respects
as well. *Marriage* is plotted along the same fairy tale lines as *Mansfield
Park*: the "Kind and Unkind" or "sisters" type, again adapted to
contrast opposing educational practices (here, making the contrast
more rigorous, the sisters are twins); and the Cinderella pattern,
traced by the neglected sister's rise from abasement to companionate
marriage (passively sitting out the inevitable "ball" along the way
[278]). Although perhaps less subtle than Austen's, Ferrier's adaptation of fairy tale material is more confident and self-conscious:
both "Cinderella" and "Diamonds and Toads" (Perrault's version
of "Kind and Unkind") are referred to explicitly in the course of the
novel (346, 483). Nor is the thematic opposition of rival educational
schemes as mechanistic as the use of twin sisters might suggest. A
third term, represented by a cousin educated with the "unkind"
sister but portrayed much more sympathetically, unsettles the text's

thematic dichotomies, suggesting that even slight changes in environment may so effect development as to counteract an entire educational system.

Although twins, Mary and Adelaide are raised by opposed maternal figures. Adelaide is the favorite of her mother Lady Juliana, herself educated solely for a "brilliant establishment" on a meretricious system with no provision for the "cultivation of her mind" or "correction of her temper" (6). She brings up Adelaide in Bath on a similarly fashionable plan, with two governesses (French and Italian) but without religion; at eighteen, Adelaide emerges "as heartless and ambitious as she was beautiful and accomplished," a more cynical version of her mother (194–96). Her fate is that of Maria in *Mansfield Park*: marriage to a wealthy "fool" followed by the "guilt and infamy" of an adulterous elopement (475). Her twin, Mary, rejected by her mother almost from the moment of birth, manages to live beyond infancy only because her aunt, Mrs. Douglas, decides to adopt her. Mrs. Douglas owes her superior character to a governess of "strong understanding and enlarged mind," who "early instilled into her a deep and strong sense of religion" (81); both rational and pious herself, she rejects "theories of education" altogether in favor of a combination of example and religious principles in raising Mary (163). Mary at eighteen lacks polish but has what proves to be essential: "principles of religion early and deeply engrafted into her soul" (167, 477). As a child, Mary learns Bible stories and has "all Watts' Hymns by heart" (465); taught early to tend the sick and instruct the lowly, she sometimes evokes the precocious children of Evangelical tracts, and the passage describing a child who dies while in her care recalls the exemplary deaths in Janeway's *Token* (165).

If Ferrier's critique of fashionable education follows More in rejecting secular alternatives like those of the Edgeworths, however, she is careful to oppose knee-jerk traditionalism as well, caricaturing it in the persons of Mary's maiden aunts, whose own "system of education" is based on Fordyce's *Sermons* and the occasional use of an iron collar (167–68, 188). Ferrier's rejection of "system" in favor of the role of example and environment closely follows Barbauld's essay "On Education," which (like the educational thought of Wordsworth and Coleridge) rejects excessive theorizing with the argument that the "education of circumstances – insensible education" plays an incomparably greater role in forming "the habit" than "that which is direct and apparent"; although Barbauld's essay places little specific emphasis on the experience of nature, her depictions of the child's experience of natural sublimity in *Hymns in Prose* have been considered a formative influence on Wordsworth's poetry of childhood.[74] Whereas Adelaide is raised in Bath, representing (as in Austen's novels) all that is artificial, Mary grows up in a lovingly described Scottish landscape, and her return to it (following a visit to Bath which proves a trial in more senses than one) inspires a Wordsworthian spot of time:

Rocks, woods, hills, and waters, all shone with a radiance that seemed of more than earthly beauty. "Oh! there are moments in life, keen, blissful, never to be forgotten!" and such was the moment to Mary when the carriage stopped, and she again heard the melody of that voice familiar from infancy – and looked on a face known with her being – and was pressed to that heart where glowed a parent's love! (511).

Mary's Romantic relation to nature lends her character – like that of Fanny Price – a deep and "mysterious" quality, which the superficially similar heroines of West and More lack as much as do the secular, rationalist heroines of Edgeworth's novels.[75]

Despite the pointed allusions to Fordyce (65, 188, 203), however, Mary is still, like Belinda and Fanny before her, a product of the conduct-book tradition, and is similarly unable to express erotic desire. Her "well-regulated mind" is explicitly formed for a companionate marriage and the ongoing "cultivation of the domestic virtues" (418). But when felicity presents itself in the shape of an eligible Scottish gentleman (later a hero of Waterloo), her excessive "delicacy" prevents her from responding to his "open manly" proposal (423). Her reticence toward Colonel Lennox arises superficially from his having been "solicited" for her by an overfond mother, beside whose death-bed the lovers finally, and wordlessly, come to terms. But Mary's difficulties ultimately stem from the kind of internal splitting, enjoined by the "impossible" dictates of propriety, which mark the characters of Belinda and Fanny as well. As she begins to "feel conscious that Colonel Lennox was not quite the object of indifference to her that he ought to be," she can only struggle to repress what she has barely allowed to grow conscious in the first place, becoming "more distant and reserved" than ever (381). It is her cousin, the "insupportably natural and sincere" Lady Emily (196), who must articulate her desire for her, playing a role similar to Lady Delacour's in *Belinda*; but this triangular scheme proves unstable as Lady Emily finds herself drawn to the same erotic object.

Lady Emily is a version of the brilliant, sensible, but insufficiently regulated female character which Edgeworth had explored in Lady Delacour and Austen in Mary Crawford: a study in the limitations of intelligence and wit without the grounding of principle. Although her "mind ... had undergone exactly the same process in its form-ation" as that of her cousin Adelaide, she manages to resist the "solecisms" of Lady Juliana and, as she tells Mary, had "got the better of" her Continental governesses (196, 306); her character is a walking testament to the subtleties of psychic development. Where Adelaide is beautiful and vacuous, Emily is beautiful and intelligent, with a generous (though undisciplined) heart and an independent (though unprincipled) mind. She protects Mary and shows her real affection while mocking her "Goody Two Shoes" manner (she condemns the Newbery books, as do Macaulay and Hunt, for their "canting and hypocrisy") and warns Mary that "patient Grizzels" like herself succeed only in "little books": "'tis a much wiser thing to resist tyranny than to submit to it" (276–77, 336). But Emily's "crude" (that is, secular and self-taught) ethical notions prove inadequate to guide her conduct or "operate as restraints upon a naturally high spirit, and impetuous temper" (196); lacking her cousin's "more fixed habits of reflection and self-examination," hers is a "noble mind ... running wild for want of early culture" (444) which Mary must help to redeem, becoming (like Belinda) her aristocratic sponsor's moral guardian.

Emily's moral regeneration is facilitated, however, by Romantic depths of her own. Although temporarily infatuated with Colonel Lennox, she has long considered herself in love with Edward Douglas, the twins' "boyish and unthinking" but handsome and good-humored brother (488). Guessing at Mary's (typically unspoken) doubt that minds of such unequal powers could unite in true marriage, Emily defends her choice with the language of "early attachments" and "habit" associated with Fanny, who similarly founds "wedded love" on "sisterly regard," in *Mansfield Park* (344, 349, 454). For Emily, even Edward's faults, because "familiar from infancy," carry the charm of "some snatch of an old nursery song" treasured, contrary to taste and reason, for its early associations. Enlisting Mary's favorite poet in her defense, Emily quotes one of the few passages of *The Prelude* published before 1850: "'Thus,' (as your favorite Wordsworth says) 'from my first dawn of childhood, didst thou intertwine for me the passions that build up a human soul'" (487). Ferrier's citation of Wordsworth's fragment (published in the 1815 *Poems* as "Influence of Natural Objects in Calling Forth and Strengthening the Imagination in Boyhood and Early Youth") suggests how, in its construction of a "deep" or "inner" self, the domestic novel drew increasingly on the strategies (and examples) of the first-generation Romantic poets, emphasizing childhood experience, primal associations, sibling love, an imagination formed by "early intercourse" with nature, and a moral consciousness established "early and deeply" (477) rather than through a later conversion experience (secular or religious).

The status of Wordsworth as Mary's "favorite" reading, like Fanny's allusions to Scott and Cowper in *Mansfield Park*, also underscores the growing role which imaginative literature, especially poetry, has begun to play in the education of the heart. Along with the many references to the literature of childhood – Watts and Janeway, fairy tales and bible stories, the Newbery books and nursery rhymes – the appeal to Wordsworth suggests not only that the domestic novel has learned from Romantic poetry to privilege childhood experience in the construction of an "inner" self, but also that such psychic depth is increasingly established through reference to a character's literary experience. In addition to her "deeply engrafted" principles, Ferrier's domestic heroine is marked by a history of sympathetic response to imaginative texts dating back to the nursery and culminating in Wordsworth. Whereas in *Belinda* the heroine's interiority is established almost wholly through the eliciting and repression of erotic wishes, in *Marriage* the workings of desire are supplemented by a history of reading and by the weight of childhood associations. Despite its diminished role, however, the problematic representation of desire remains important, in *Marriage* as in the domestic novel as a whole, both as a means for establishing the inner space requisite for deeply rooted self-discipline and, at the same time, for bringing both heroine and reader up against the contradictions inherent in an educational ideal founded on domestic ideology.

FROM *EMILE* TO *FRANKENSTEIN*: THE EDUCATION OF
MONSTERS

The Gothic novel, a form which developed alongside the domestic
novel and which was also particularly associated with women writers,
invites rather than silences the representation of erotic or aggressive
wishes. Within the "spectral arena of the Gothic castle," as Poovey
writes, women novelists of the Romantic era could "dramatize the
eruption of psychic material ordinarily controlled by the inhibitions
of bourgeois society."[76] What must always remain tacit in the post-
Jacobin domestic novel becomes overt in the lurid domain of the
Gothic, much to the chagrin of conservatives like More.[77] If its more
salient treatment of the problematic nature and expression of female
desire differentiates the "female Gothic" from the contemporary
domestic novel, however, its concern with questions of women's
education and moral development, which has largely gone unnoted,
provides an unexpected bridge between the two genres. In Radcliffe's
Romance of the Forest (1791), for example, the heroine finds herself in
the midst of a Rousseauvian educational idyll, nursed through a
mental and physical breakdown in Savoy by a benevolent pastor who
applies the "philosophy of nature" to the "gradual unfolding of [his
children's] infant minds"; the object lesson by which this Savoyard
vicar teaches his daughter the value of moderation reads like an
excerpt from *Emile* or *Sandford and Merton*.[78] In *The Mysteries of
Udolpho* (1794), Radcliffe carefully describes the "unfolding" of the
heroine's character under the tutelage of her father, St. Aubert;
Emily's education, including a "general view of the sciences,"
"every part of elegant literature," and the inculcation of "modesty,
simplicity, and correct manners," represents (despite the novel's
Renaissance setting) the most advanced eighteenth-century liberal
thinking, anticipating the educational programs of Darwin and the
Edgeworths.[79]

Such unexpected appearances of the rational pedagogue in the
haunted castle might seem merely to reflect the insistent presence of
education within Romantic culture, an accidental rather than
integral feature of the female Gothic. And yet, as Judith Wilt has
pointed out, the implicitly tyrannical relation of (male) teacher and
(female) student, the "exercise of power by the knowing over the
ignorant," is a "pure Gothic" convention and recognizable as such
even in the domestic novels of Austen, troubling such "charming

young man/naive young woman relationships" as those of Willough-
by and Marianne in *Sense and Sensibility* and Henry and Catherine in
Northanger Abbey.[80] The power/knowledge dynamic underlying the
relation of Emily St. Aubert and her father is structurally cognate
with that which facilitates Emily's exploitation by the villain
Montoni, who cruelly plays on this very resemblance, taking on the
voice of the father-instructor, when she balks at his designs: "Before
you undertake to regulate the morals of other persons, you should
learn and practise the virtues, which are indispensable to a woman
– sincerity, uniformity of conduct and obedience" (220). The same
inequality informs the pedagogical-romantic relations we have seen
in the domestic novel, marking not only doomed couplings like that
of Clarence Hervey and Virginia St. Pierre in *Belinda*, but successful
ones like that of Edmund and Fanny in *Mansfield Park* as well. The
thematization of pedagogy in the Gothic novel helps bring out
the element of social criticism implicit in its opposition of naive
(if well-regulated) heroines and knowing villains, who often –
like Montoni – assume a paternal position, suggesting that the
line between pedagogy and tyranny is an uncomfortably fine and
unstable one, particularly given the agenda for perpetuating male
domination built into most of the period's programs for female
education.

Mary Shelley's *Frankenstein* (1818) presents an especially complex
and elaborate version of the critique of female education which
Radcliffe brought into the Gothic, and which Austen comically
varies in *Northanger Abbey*. Shelley's concern with education – which
her father (Godwin) had described as inherently connected with
"despotism" and which her mother (Wollstonecraft) had shown as
central in establishing and maintaining male hegemony – emerges in
the opening pages of the novel's epistolary frame, in which Walton
laments his "neglected" studies and the limitations of a "self-
educated" intellect: "Now I am twenty-eight, and am in reality
more illiterate than many schoolboys of fifteen."[81] Walton's reliance
on a self-directed program of reading in place of a more regular and
directed course of studies allies him with most women of the period,
who could hope at best for a few years in a finishing school which
might (as Austen puts it in *Emma*) allow them to "scramble
themselves into a little education." His sense of inferiority to a
schoolboy also reflects a common female dilemma, what Swift, in his
"Letter to a Young Lady," had insisted that even the most "learned

Women" must endure, and the unflattering comparison had become commonplace in the discourse on female education of the period.[82] Anne Mellor has shown how Shelley's critique of a "sexual education" troubles the "cult of domesticity" informing such later novels as *Mathilda* (1819), *Lodore* (1835), and *Falkner* (1837), all of which feature "father-guardians" who mold the heroines along lines set out in Rousseau's *Emile*.[83] This critique is already present, however, in *Frankenstein*, which exposes the programmatic silences of domestic fiction by inflecting its discourse and conventions with a Gothic exposure of pedagogical tyranny and demonized female desire. Shelley's novel may be read as a "birth myth," but it does not stop there, taking up such "domestic" (and pedagogical) themes as the development and education of children as well.[84] More particularly, *Frankenstein* addresses the dilemma of the middle-class adolescent girl, caught between the equally unhappy alternatives of a haphazard self-education and a "sexual education" in passivity and self-containment.

Rousseau has been invoked in a number of recent critical discussions of *Frankenstein*. The monster is often compared to the "natural man" of Rousseau's *Second Discourse*, although such comparisons elide a crucial distinction between the two: man in Rousseau's imagined state of nature is essentially solitary, and barely recognizes other individuals as such, whereas Shelley's creature is instinctively social, and longing to join the De Lacey family almost from the moment he observes them (110).[85] More plausible (and more far-reaching in their implications) are the associations made between Victor Frankenstein and the autobiographical Rousseau of *The Confessions* and the *Reveries* who similarly abandons his children (earning Shelley's scorn in her essay on Rousseau for the *Cabinet Cyclopedia*); between the creature and Rousseau as self-styled victims who dwell upon their persecution by an unjust society; and between the often remarked relation of Victor and his creature as two halves of a divided self and the literal self-division of Rousseau in the *Dialogues* or *Rousseau Juge de Jean-Jacques*.[86] What has gone unnoticed, however, is that the narrative at the heart of *Frankenstein* – the creature's long speech describing his first sensations, his developing ideas of the natural and social worlds around him, and the "progress of [his] intellect" (127) – may well have been suggested by a passage in *Emile*, which Shelley had read in 1815 (a year before beginning *Frankenstein*):

Let us suppose that a child had at his birth the stature and the strength of a grown man, that he emerged, so to speak, fully armed from his mother's womb as did Pallas from the brain of Jupiter ... Not only would he perceive no object outside of himself, he would not even relate any object to the sense organ which made him perceive it ... all his sensations would come together in a single point ... he would have only a single idea, that is, of the *I* to which he would relate all his sensations; and this idea or, rather, this sentiment would be the only thing which he would have beyond what an ordinary baby has. (61)

Given life by a "creator" or god-figure without the mediation of woman, the monster is indeed a kind of Pallas Athena, and his "confused and indistinct" memories of his first moments are much as Rousseau describes them: "A strange multiplicity of sensations seized me, and I saw, felt, heard, and smelt, at the same time; and it was, indeed, a long time before I learned to distinguish between the operations of my various senses" (102).[87] If the scenario which Shelley develops in *Frankenstein* owes something to Rousseau's book on education, however, it is developed in a manner which suggests a critical engagement with *Emile* in the spirit of her mother's more overt attack.

In describing the education of a monster, Shelley challenges, through a program of critical hyperbole, the tradition of writing on female education and conduct associated especially (after Wollstonecraft) with *Emile*, in which women are at once sentimentalized and viewed, anxiously, as deformed or monstrous in comparison with an explicitly male norm. For Rousseau, woman's subordinate position in society is rooted both in her physical difference from man – her weakness, her capacity to bear children – and in certain moral differences which characterize her as well: her tendency to "unlimited desires" and to be "extreme in everything," which together make her life a "perpetual combat against herself" that can only be won with the aid of modesty and "habitual constraint" (359, 369–70). The notion that women are morally, as well as physically, deformed in comparison to men surfaces throughout British writing on female conduct and education as well, despite the growing emphasis on women's beneficial moral influence on their children, husbands, and the larger society around them informing these same works. For Gregory, women's "natural vivacity" and "unbridled imagination" will lead to dissipation if not carefully confined (12, 38); for Chapone, woman's volatile temper, if indulged, can lead to extreme fits of "*passion*" or anger – "an enraged woman is one of the most disgusting sights in nature" (92).[88] This tendency becomes much more marked in the reactionary writers who, like Gisborne, trace women's particular "failings and temptations" to the "native structure and dispositions" of the "female mind" (33). For More in *Strictures*, vanity is rooted in the "conformation of the human and especially the female heart" (1: 65), which is also uniquely susceptible to "irregular fancy," "ungoverned passion," and "uncontrolled inclinations" (1: 177, 2: 105). For West – developing the Biblical "weaker vessel" metaphor which even Fordyce had rejected as too degrading (*Sermons* 164) – woman "carries within her a rebellious crew of passions and affections, which are extremely apt to mutiny"; freighted with "irregular desires" and "unlawful cravings," woman is (stretching the metaphor further) a "slight felucca" which must be "taken in tow by some stouter vessel" if it is not to sink with the weight of its own iniquity (16–17, 49). If within this tradition woman is ideally a domestic angel like Elizabeth Lavenza – Victor Frankenstein's "more than sister" – she continually threatens to become a passionate, rebellious creature impelled by unlawful desires, like Frankenstein's monster, his more than child. The monster, as Poovey writes, is "doubly like" woman as construed by patriarchal ideology: formed as a subordinate vehicle for "someone else's desire," and yet exiled as the "deadly essence of passion itself."[89]

Other readers of *Frankenstein* who see the monster as, at least in part, a representation of nineteenth-century constructions of the feminine tend to emphasize one or the other of these polarities: either the creature's "initially ... feminine qualities," such as tractability, sympathy, and domesticity, which ally him to such female characters in the novel as Elizabeth and Agatha, or his monstrousness, his "very bodiliness," his deformed status as "a 'filthy' or obscene version of the human form divine."[90] But a good measure of Shelley's critique of the construction of femininity within the Rousseauvian tradition lies in her portrayal of how easily – perhaps how inevitably – the monster slides from one pole to the other, from a "creature of fine sensations" to a vessel of "evil passions" (146): what remains constant is its difference. A similar phenomenon can be seen in the case of Justine, a lower-class woman adopted by the Frankensteins and thus herself doubly other, who initially appears to those around her as docile and domestic but who, on being accused of William's murder, is immediately condemned as a "monster" (87) of criminal desires. This instability inheres in woman's status as "a creature of the second sex" defined in terms of her divergence from a masculine norm, who remains dangerously "other" – implicitly inhuman – even when viewed as a domestic angel.[91] Such an analysis is supported in the novel by the parallel descriptions of the monster as representing a "new species" (54) and of Elizabeth, the pattern domestic heroine, appearing "as of a different species" in her very "celestial" bearing (34). Here especially Shelley seems indebted to her mother's critique of the male conduct-book tradition, stemming from Rousseau, which considers "females rather as women than as human creatures"(*VRW*, 7). Moreover, by stressing as she does the role of education throughout the novel, Shelley evokes as well Wollstonecraft's view that "sexual" differences in character are aggravated, if not wholly produced, by male-instituted socializing practices which turn women into "artificial beings" (9), a cultural enterprise which finds its hyperbolic expression in Frankenstein's creation of a quasi-feminine monster from raw materials.

In developing the creature's account of his mental progress Shelley seems at first to follow Rousseau rather uncritically, both in portraying the creature's initial sensory confusion and in having him develop "ideas" before he has acquired language, drawing them from his gradually "distinct" sensations instead (104); as Rousseau had recommended in *Emile* (112), the creature's first ideas are based on "objects" rather than "words." But in depicting the creature's education proper, which he pursues in tandem with the "Arabian" Safie – whose very name evokes Rousseau's Sophie – Shelley's relation to *Emile* begins to take on a critical edge.[92] Safie, to begin with, is educated by her lover, Felix De Lacey, much as Sophie is educated by Emile (or Fanny by Edmund). This seems a happy enough arrangement, until one notices how the power relation implicit in the form of Safie's instruction (independent of its specific content) keeps her in a subordinate situation, helping to account for why a potential feminist (fleeing Turkish "bondage" for "higher powers of intellect, and an independence of spirit, forbidden to the female followers of Mahomet" [124]), nevertheless limits herself to a "strictly domestic motivation and role."[93] Moreover, Safie's status as an "Oriental" who refuses to be "immured within the walls of a haram" (124) itself suggests an implicit critique of the conduct book tradition which treats women, as Wollstonecraft had charged, "in the true style of

Mahometanism ... as a kind of subordinate beings, and not as part of the human species" (*VRW* 8). As both Macaulay and Wollstonecraft had acidly noted, Rousseau himself describes his approach to female education in terms of perpetuating a harem mentality: "I would want a young Englishwoman to cultivate pleasing talents that will entertain her future husband with as much care as a young Albanian cultivates them for the harem of Ispahan" (*Emile* 374).[94] Turning from this once infamous passage to the scene in which Safie "sat at the feet of the old man," playing "entrancingly beautiful" airs as her "voice flowed in a rich cadence," one must wonder just how far the harem has been left behind after all.

The creature's alienated relation to Felix and Safie's educational romance – he watches it unfold through a crack in the wall – enables him to profit from some of the lessons which are seemingly lost on Safie. As Felix reads from Volney's *Ruins*, a work closely associated with the ideology of the French Revolution in its most radical phase, the monster discovers the "strange system of human society": "the division of property, of immense wealth and squalid poverty; of rank, descent, and noble blood" (120). Other lessons are "impressed" upon him "even more deeply." "I heard of the difference of sexes; and the birth and growth of children; how the father doated on the smiles of the infant ... how all the life and cares of the mother were wrapped up in the precious charge" (121). Apprised of a class system based on the unequal division of property facilitated by inherited rank and wealth, and schooled in the equally "strange system" of sexual difference, particularly the unequal responsibility of men and women for children (a lesson painfully relevant to his own case), the monster is in a position to make the sort of connections between class and gender hierarchies, aristocratic and male domination, which Wollstonecraft develops in the *Rights of Woman*. But he has still to learn how deeply his own history is marked by the "strange" system of oppression in the name of difference.

Having shared vicariously in Safie's "sexual education," the creature struggles to educate himself. Now able to read, he fortuitously discovers a packet of books in the forest made up of *Paradise Lost*, Plutarch's *Lives*, and Goethe's *Werther* – all books which Mary Shelley had read or re-read in 1815 (along with *Emile* and the second *Vindication*) as part of her own ongoing program of self-education. The books at once puzzle and inspire him; he lacks the educational background which would make him a "competent" reader, and yet certain of his misreadings – such as taking Milton's epic as the "true history" of "an omnipotent God warring with his creatures" (129) – more accurately address his own situation than would a standard interpretation. His self-directed, arbitrary program of reading presents advantages and disadvantages similar to those of a Maria or Emma Courtney. More important, however, is his discovery of Victor Frankenstein's laboratory journal, his sole inheritance from his "father" along with the unspecified garment in which he finds it (130). The monster's reading of Victor's "papers," describing a man's creation of an artificial being, subtly evokes Wollstonecraft's reading, in the second *Vindication*, of Rousseau and other male writers on female conduct and education: "Every thing is related in them which bears reference to my accursed origin; the whole detail of that series of disgusting circumstances which produced it, is set in view." If this admittedly oblique parallel can be – at least provisionally – accepted, several further correspondences between Shelley's monstrous fiction and Wollstonecraft's analysis of woman's deformation by patriarchal ideology come into focus. Both the monster and woman within patriarchy crucially differ from man in point of strength, the monster's difference being produced wholly, woman's largely, by male intervention; ironically, the monster's greater strength entails (in Victor's view) his subordination no less than woman's relative weakness does for Rousseau, since the monster is potentially dangerous and must be contained. The monster's fate, as commentators often point out, is uniquely governed by his "physical appearance";[95] but perhaps not so uniquely. Throughout the conduct book tradition, as Wollstonecraft complains, women are taught to be concerned principally with such external factors as "*outward*" demeanor (19), "corporeal accomplishment" (23), and "dress," for which they have a supposedly "natural" instinct (28). Moreover, writers like Rousseau, Pennington, and Kames enjoin upon women an *appearance* of virtue (particularly sexual virtue) as or more important than moral behavior itself; David Marshall writes acutely of woman's consequent "theatricalized character" in *Emile*, her status as the object of the "regards and judgments of others."[96] By reading his creator's journal, the monster finds that his unequal and untenable position in human society is predicated on what a man has made of him. He responds with understandable rage at one who would turn in disgust and contempt from the deformity he himself has engineered.

The creature demands from his creator the only means to social equality which he can imagine; since his horrific appearance exiles him from human society, he will begin a monstrous society of his own with a "companion... of the same species" (and with the "same defects") which Victor is to create (144). The possibility of a female monster might seem to complicate any reading of the explicitly male creature as "feminine," and yet Victor's ultimate refusal to create a mate for him suggests a further link between the male monster and woman as constructed by domestic ideology: both are "forbidden to have their own desires."[97] What Victor professes to fear in the female monster, in fact, are qualities which would magnify those which already differentiate his creature from "man" – his emotionality, his physical difference, his unsublimated sexual desires – and inspire anxieties similar to those attached to woman within contemporary educational discourse. The monster's emotiveness might be aggravated in the female, rendering her "ten thousand times more malignant than her mate"; the monster's "deformity" might inspire still "greater abhorrence" when appearing in "the female form"; his proclivity to sexual desire (evident in his very request for a mate) would be aggravated in the female creature, prompting her to either "turn with disgust from him to the superior beauty of man," or propagate with him a "race of devils" (165). A female monster constitutes, in this sense, a kind of pleonasm within the cultural code which Shelley critically addresses in *Frankenstein*. At the same time, Victor's destruction of his half-finished female creature brings out the "dread of woman" which characterizes his relation to Elizabeth (the prospect of their wedding night strikes him as "dreadful, very dreadful" [194]) and which, in part, underlies his horror of the monster as well.[98]

Recalling his earlier banishment from the idyllic domesticity of the De Lacey household, the creature's "only link" to society is snapped by Victor's ultimate refusal to create him a mate, and again he responds with a vow to "spread havoc and destruction" among mankind (136), now concentrating his revenge on Victor and his family. *Frankenstein* becomes from this point a kind of anti-domestic fantasy, with one after another of Victor's relations and friends murdered, until creature and creator, locked in an isolating, specular relation, consummate their hatred on a remote and uninhabitable stretch of ice. Given the many connections suggested in the text between the monster and woman, what does one make of his apparently uncontrollable rage? It is possible to see the monster's uninhibited anger as an "outlet" for the "hatred not permissible for the nineteenth-century daughter," or as the projection of male fears of an "independent female will," or both.[99] One can even elicit a conservative reading from this aspect of the text; the monster's destructive rage, following the thwarting of his sexual desires, illustrates the dangers of an unregulated female mind.[100] To read *Frankenstein* in this way, however, is to underestimate the force of its Wollstonecraftian dimension, its exposure of the untenability of woman's position in a male-dominated society. Neither the domesticating process of a "sexual education" nor the independent rigors of self-education can, in the end, counteract woman's "otherness" within a male-defined society; the first leaves her too weak, a passive victim like Elizabeth or Justine, the second too independent, necessitating her exile and ultimately her destruction.

Frankenstein is not in any simple way a novel "about" education, any more than it is about, say, imperialism; nor can the monster's difference be reduced to a question of gender, any more than to a matter of social class.[101] Perhaps what makes the monster so famously compelling is that its "difference" is finally irreducible, marking (as Peter Brooks suggests) an "unappeasable lack."[102] But reading *Frankenstein* against the grain of eighteenth- and early nineteenth-century educational writings elicits a new range of meanings which, in turn, bring out unnoticed links between several of the groups the creature has been equated with: women, colonized peoples, and the nascent proletariat. All of these groups are, within the frankly hegemonic social discourses of Shelley's time, infantilized; all had become increasingly subject to programs of schooling or "civilization" designed to discipline them for an increasingly regulated and normatized world. (Again, the figures of Safie, attempting to evade the "infantile amusements" of the harem [124], and Justine, domesticated daughter of the "lower orders" [65], can be read as markers of such links within the text.)[103] All of these groups are seen as abnormal, or monstrous, within the dominant educational discourses of Shelley's age; *Frankenstein* suggests that, so long as these discourses are predicated on inequality, education will indeed remain, as Godwin had theorized and as Wollstonecraft had so powerfully demonstrated in relation to women, a form of tyranny.

CHAPTER 5

The pursuit of knowledge under difficulties

In her *Letters to a Young Lady*, after advice on dress, deportment, reading, and religious conformity, Jane West includes a brief section on writing tracts and stories for the "instruction of the lower orders" (433–35). For West, educating the poor through supporting Sunday Schools and handing out "cheap well principled tracts" (451) makes part of the middle-class woman's matriarchal cultural role – the section on the duty to "Servants and Inferiors" directly follows that "On the Duty of Mothers." While attesting to the considerable reformist energies of prominent women like West and Hannah More, this maternal approach to educating lower-class adults (along with their children) also bears witness to the pervasive infantilization of "inferiors" within the social discourses of the Romantic era. It is not surprising to find that the tradition of "popular" fiction written from above (as opposed to genuinely popular forms like chapbooks, street ballads, and murder sheets) is initially dominated by women writers also active in literary and educational ventures aimed at children: Trimmer, whose *Servant's Friend* (1786) and *Family Magazine* (1788–89) were among the earliest "improving" works aimed at "cottagers and servants"; More, who helped codify the genre with the *Cheap Repository Tracts*; and Sherwood, who described her novella *Susan Grey* (1802) as the first popular narrative to combine "correct writing" with a religious message (*Life* 206).

These works all adopt the simple and entertaining approach which West recommends to her female reader (454). They also proved (with the exception of *Susan Grey*, which found a place in the growing market for cheap religious works) singularly ineffective at reaching their audience.[1] However compelling their "providential" plots, however lively their colloquial but "correct" style (a conjunction reminiscent of Wordsworth's "purified" version of the "language of conversation in the middle and lower classes of society" [*WP* 1: 124,

116]), the tract-fiction of Trimmer, More, and their imitators looked backward to an increasingly outmoded ethos of order, rank, and subordination that had little to offer the new working-class reader.[2] Their wish to reinforce existing class distinctions and counter the "dissemination of the idea of universal liberty" (West 445) is generally all too apparent, despite the positive emphasis these texts share on limited self-improvement (keeping one's clothes neat and perhaps even putting something aside) and basic education. This last feature, in fact, only underscored the links with children's fiction: the detailed descriptions of the protagonist's career in a Charity or Sunday School that begin tracts like *The Servant's Friend* and More's *Hester Wilmot* could be taken verbatim from tales written for lower-class children. It became increasingly evident, as the nineteenth century progressed, that an appeal to the laborer's interest would succeed where recommendations of patience, deference, and child-like submission had failed. The Society for Promoting Christian Knowledge would give place to the Society for the Diffusion of Useful Knowledge.

This is not to say that the SPCK, or the nostalgic approach it exemplified, disappeared from the scene all at once. On the contrary, in response to a period of rick-burning, mob violence, and a resurgent radical press in the immediate post-war years 1816–19, the SPCK produced a new round of "counter-propaganda": More herself, at the age of 75, contributed a dozen new tracts.[3] But such openly reactionary attempts proved too crudely manipulative to counter the likes of Cobbett, with his ability to speak directly to the laborer's felt experience, needs, and political hopes. The early decades of the century also saw the decline of teaching institutions associated with the SPCK and its overtly paternalistic approach. The Charity School movement had been moribund since the late eighteenth century, and the Sunday Schools thrived most where they had slipped out of the control of their original sponsors and become locally controlled.[4] "Duty" and "submission' were no longer words to conjure with, although "habit" and "discipline" remained important terms in the educational lexicon of upper- and middle-class reformers.

By the 1820s a new discourse on the nature and social role of schooling and literacy had emerged, an outgrowth of the post-Lockean consensus but drawing more particularly on the educational proposals (and economic theories) of Adam Smith and Thomas Malthus. It took form in the writings of what might be seen as an *ad hoc* coalition for advancing educational and related reforms, bringing together the Utilitarian or Philosophical Radical group – most prominently Mill, Bentham, and their political ally Francis Place – with liberal Whigs like Henry Brougham and Francis Jeffrey (editor of the *Edinburgh Review*), as well as the SDUK and its chief publisher, Charles Knight.[5] Among this confederation it became axiomatic that literacy was to be managed rather than restrained, and that the "enlightened" interest of educated workers would prove a more sure path to social stability (and limited reform) than would the combination of passive literacy, Christian morals, and deferential behavior advanced by an earlier generation of educationalists. The monitorial system – particularly in its comparatively secular Lancasterian version – gained the temporary support of this set, as it directly and explicitly addressed the internalization of work habits, clock-time, and middle-class notions of orderly behavior and decency. But monitorial schools came to seem *too* crudely mechanistic, coming to dissatisfy not only Romantic supporters like Wordsworth and Coleridge, but also rational theorists like Robert Owen, whose early enthusiasm gave way to a critique of schools "conducted on the narrow principle of debasing man to a mere irrational military machine."[6] A more consensual and humanistic approach was demanded, and educational ventures like the Infant Schools, the Mechanics' Institutes, and the London University were developed accordingly.

New kinds of reading material also were called for in the 1820s and 1830s. The mass "Reading Public," as Coleridge had declared in the *Statesman's Manual*, was not going to disappear. What was wanted was a new sort of literature which would appeal to the self-improvement ethic rising steadily among the working classes, particularly the more highly skilled artisans and mechanics with their "autodidact culture."[7] An ill-defined but vigorous struggle ensued over who should control the provision of education and reading material for the lower classes: the state through a network of professionals and secular societies like the SDUK, as Brougham and the utilitarians argued; a "clerisy" rooted in the National Church, as Coleridge wished; or the workers themselves, through co-operative schools, reading groups, and an unstamped press. Complicating the picture was the rise, during the same period, of more purely commercial enterprises aimed at the burgeoning reading public, including the efforts of street publishers like James Catnach, experiments in popular journalism like John Limbird's *Mirror of Literature, Amusement and Instruction*, and cheap reprint editions of novels in serial "Library" formats.[8] Various readerships – "popular," radical, self-consciously middle-class – were defined and cultivated, and "literature" became a problematic and contested term.[9] So did "self-improvement" or "self-education," central to radical ideologies, but subject to appropriation by groups with reformist or even conservative agendas.

The contest over defining, supplying, and managing various readerships within the new reading public was now waged explicitly in terms of class. Discrimination among hierarchically arranged social groupings – the "lower orders," the "middling sort," the "upper ranks" – informs, as we have seen, British educational and other social discourses from at least the mid-eighteenth century.[10] What differentiates the terminology informing the writings of the 1820s and beyond is not the tripartite schema of lower, middle, and upper but rather the increasing use of "class," implying a view of social division as constructed, rather than terms like "rank" and "order" which imply that they are inherited and, like the "orders" of the animal kingdom, natural.[11] The instability inherent in this constructionist conception of social class helps account for an anxiety marking both reformist and conservative writing on education and literacy in this period, different in kind from the apprehension of a More or Trimmer that the lower orders might "forget" their (God-given) places. If the divisions by social class were produced, they were produced in part or even (as James Mill asserted) wholly by differences in education.[12] Certain radical writers, particularly those in the Owenite tradition, took the logical next step in arguing that changes in the provision and character of schooling and literacy could fundamentally alter the distribution of social power. However simplistically, education became seen as central not just to maintaining but to producing class distinctions, and (potentially) to remaking or even eliminating them.

E. P. Thompson has described in great detail the rise during this period not simply of a new terminology of class but of a working-class consciousness and (in reaction) a distinctively middle-class consciousness as well. I have drawn gratefully but with certain reservations on Thompson's monumental account in what follows. Although Thompson gives extraordinarily close attention to a variety of different expressions of working-class consciousness, he clearly finds some more genuine and forward-looking than others. But this is to assume, as Gareth Stedman Jones has argued, a class consciousness somehow prior to or independent of its articulation in these very discourses, which can then be judged against it. Consciousness, however, "cannot be related to experience except through the interposition of a particular language which organizes the under-standing of experience, and it is important to stress that more than one language is capable of articulating the same set of experiences."[13] What Jones calls languages of class, emphasizing their plurality, are nevertheless not arbitrarily developed and disseminated but remain subject to limitations, both extrinsic and intrinsic. A given political vocabulary will not take hold among large numbers of people if it does not enable them to comprehend, using its terms, "day to day problems of political and social experience."[14] This was something which the rhetoric crafted by Brougham and his allies for "popular" dissemination simply could not do, as the unstamped press never tired of pointing out. And yet, as will be seen, Brougham's liberal premises set intrinsic limitations on how popular his writing could become without losing its coherence. Owen's political and edu-cational writings did speak to the daily experience of working-class Britons in a way Brougham's could not; the son of an ironmonger, Owen had been working long hours from the age of ten and was largely self-educated as well as "self-made." But, despite the common ground of experience he shared with his working-class audience, Owen's discourse was intrinsically limited in its egalitarian appeal as well, not least by the intellectual and moral elitism which inhered within its progressive rationalist assumptions.

USEFUL KNOWLEDGE AND POPULAR TALES

Owen's writings and social experiments anticipated and helped shape the direction which educational discourse would take in the latter part of the Romantic era. His *New View of Society* (1813–16) advanced what have been called the most revolutionary educational proposals since Locke,[15] and Owen promoted them tirelessly, through public lectures, articles in journals and newspapers, and meetings with nearly anyone of importance he could interest in his schemes. His ideas gained still more notoriety – and a measure of authority as well – through the publicity surrounding Owen's model factory community at New Lanark, a practical illustration of Owen's principles literally at work. Although Owen departed signally from Brougham and his Utilitarian allies (then usually known as the "political economists") in his support for guaranteed employment and in his distaste for the spirit of competition, he agreed with them on the necessity of a national schools system and supported many of their educational initiatives.[16] Mill and Place, in turn, helped Owen compose the *New View*, and Bentham was a partner in the New Lanark concern.[17] More than any other single work, *A New View* marks the shift from a discourse on popular education stressing duty, order, and subordination, to that of the 1820s and 1830s, relying instead on terms like reason, motivation, diffusion, and above all interest.

Many aspects of Owen's thinking reflect his immersion in the rationalist tradition culminating in the Edgeworths' *Practical Education*: his associationism, his privileging of "things" over "artificial signs," his secularism (which caused Owen still more trouble than it did the Edgeworths). His teaching methods and curricula also follow familiar rationalist practice, including the division of pupils into discrete age-groups, an emphasis on science and other "practical" subjects, and the central role of the object lesson.[18] What makes Owen's educational proposals significantly new, however, is that he extends the language of self-motivation and rational assent previously reserved for middle- and upper-class children (and young women) to the "millions of... untrained labouring poor": "Train any population rationally, and they will be rational" (*New View* 21, 37). For Owen, the drilling in productive habits and unthinking obedience characteristic of the monitorial system, while preferable to no training at all, had to give place to a mass educational system based on rationalist notions of consent and autonomy. An appeal to motive, rather than to habit, grounds Owen's approach to popular education; the "clear and inseparable connection which exists between the interest and happiness of each individual and the interest and happiness of every individual" forms the "beginning and end of all instruction" (49). This marked a fundamentally new departure, as Owen noted in retrospect: "It was quite new to train the children of the working class to think and act rationally" (*Life* 1: 233).

Owen's approach to lower-class education was limited, however, by a strong dose of paternalism endemic to the tradition of bourgeois progressivism on which he drew so heavily for his basic terms, and his writings also manifest the class anxiety that marks both sides of the monitorial controversy. He characterizes the "working classes" as the "worst and most dangerous subjects in the empire," and promises the "privileged classes" that his proposed system will prevent "domestic revolution" (*New View* 14, 19). Addressing the working classes in 1819, Owen chastens them for feeling "anger" towards the dominant group and for desiring "violently to dispossess" them of their prerogatives, promising that once they understand their "real interests," they will lose all envy for the "fancied advantages" of the "higher classes."[19] As will Brougham and others in the Radical–Whig alliance, that is, Owen refashions his working-class audience's "interests" in a manner that reasserts their subordinate position in society. Commenting on Owen's "anti-democratic" character in retrospect, William Lovett characterized his one-time mentor as holding that laborers "must consent to be ruled by despots till we had acquired sufficient knowledge to govern ourselves."[20] It remains significant, however, that even at his most condescending, Owen assumes his auditors' eventual comprehension: "What has been said is sufficient for your minds to digest at one time. When you are prepared to receive more, it shall be given to you" (*New View*, 153). The consequences both for his system of factory discipline and for his pedagogy are remarkable. Coercion disappears almost entirely; self-motivation is encouraged wherever possible; drill and catechism are replaced by experiment and dialogue, with pupils of all ages encouraged to "ask any questions, or make any remarks" that occur to them during class time (*Outline* 38–39). More broadly, Owen identifies serious limitations in the "created opposition of interests" that drives a *laissez-faire* capitalist system, finding "true civilisation" impossible under such conditions (*Life* 1: 89); the schoolchildren at New Lanark are taught to compete in "friendly emulation" but also to value "*going forward with their companions*" over "*leaving them behind*" (*Outline*, 73). His son's account of the school ends by envisioning an era of more mutual (though still unequal) class relations, when workers will be seen not as "servile dependents" but as "enlightened assistants" (*Outline*, 75–76).

Owen's world-famous Institute for the Formation of Character at New Lanark provided a celebrated model of cradle-to-grave education (from an "infant school" to evening classes for adult workers) and a humanistic alternative to the monitorial method. But the characteristic educational enterprises of the 1820s and 1830s – such as the Infant Schools movement and the Mechanics' Institutes – while sharing Owen's predilection for informed consent over coercion, came to exacerbate the paternalism and class anxiety marking even Owen's approach. The Infant Schools, for example, while adopting Owen's innovatory "playgrounds," his use of natural objects in the schoolroom, and the singing and dancing he added to the curriculum, drew tellingly on the monitorial system as well, using drills to implant "habits of subordination" and transforming singing into a "moral engine" for exercising religious sentiment.[21] By 1830 Owen would dismiss the Infant School movement as a "mockery or caricature" of his own practice, yet its proponents' key argument – that working-class parents cannot properly raise their children, and must give them over to bourgeois professionals for their own good – is altogether in keeping with Owen's thought.[22]

The Mechanics' Institutes, despite a promising beginning, similarly degenerated into vehicles for disseminating middle-class ideology. The first such institutes were largely directed and financed by the "mechanics" (relatively skilled factory laborers) themselves, breaking with the bible reading and monitorial "rules of order" characteristic of the earlier Adult Schools movement, to concentrate instead on disseminating scientific and technical knowledge through lectures, readings, and discussions.[23] By the 1840s, however, the Mechanics' Institutes had become moribund, dominated by middle-class "sponsors," barred from addressing political issues, and catering mainly to clerks and small shopkeepers bent on acquiring a semblance of "culture."[24] Both the movement's promise and the seeds of its eventual failure can be seen in Brougham's *Practical Observations Upon the Education of the People* (1825), which ran through twenty editions in a year and rapidly made the Mechanics' Institutes a national issue.

Brougham had been the moving spirit behind the parliamentary Select Committee on Education which sat from 1816 to 1819, investigating the uneven spread of educational provisions and uncovering abuses among the endowed schools; in 1820 he proposed a parish schools bill similar to Whitbread's 1807 motion and just as unsuccessful.[25] Over the next two decades, Brougham shifted his attention to university reform and to the question of adult education, envisioning the Mechanics' Institutes and the SDUK (which he helped found) as means towards spreading scientific knowledge, increasing social stability, and gaining popular support for his liberal agenda. Throughout the *Practical Observations*, Brougham stresses self-determination – the "people themselves must be the great agents in accomplishing their own instruction" – and (like Owen) looks for the easing of class distinctions through the self-improvement of the lower classes.[26] He names the real difficulties in the way of self-education, "want of money, and want of time" (17), and heralds the small-scale and local endeavors arising throughout Britain to remedy at least the former want: book lending clubs and cheap serial editions, itinerant libraries, public lectures, reading and discussion groups, and experiments in popular journalism like the *Mirror of Literature* (priced at two pence) and the *Mechanics' Magazine* (three pence). Above all, Brougham calls for the spread of Mechanics' Institutes, which he traces back to George Birkbeck's lectures to artisans and factory workers in Glasgow beginning in 1800. There should be no "restriction upon politics" in the lectures and literature provided for them, and the "mechanics themselves" are to finance the institutes and hold the "principal share in the management" (15).

Yet even in *Practical Observations* Brougham backs away from these supposedly "fundamental" principles, which yield to the axiom of enlightened middle-class hegemony over the masses, constitutive of bourgeois "radicalism" as codified by Mill and Bentham. Workers may control and finance but not found their institutions; "patrons" must be solicited who, at the "beginning," will (naturally) exert a "powerful" influence in setting down "proper rules," selecting lecture topics, and choosing teachers. Political discussion, for example, will mean the exposition of "sounder views" for the "good of the working classes, as well as of their superiors." Imbibing the wisdom of Smith and Malthus, the "true principles and mutual relations of population and wages," workers will learn to see their interests as at one with the needs of capital (5). This program is worked out in greater detail in a set of lectures on political science edited by Brougham for use in the Institutes:

The necessity of some considerable degree of restraint to the well-being of society – the impossibility of the supreme power being left in the hands of the whole people – the fatal effects of disregarding the right of property, the great corner-stone of all civil society – the interest which all classes down to the humblest have in the protection afforded by the law to the accumulation of capital – the evils of resistance to established government unless in extreme and in very rare cases ... the almost uniform necessity of making all changes, even the most salutary, in any established institution, gradually and temperately – all these are the very first lessons which every political teacher must inculcate if he be fit for his office, and commonly honest.[27]

If such teachers are selected at the outset, the Mechanics' Institutes, despite their nominal control by workers, will clearly function to help establish the middle-class hegemony sought by Brougham and his Westminster allies. And yet even that nominal control proved too threatening a prospect given the climate of the times.[28]

However reformist their agendas, the educational initiatives of Brougham and the "political economists" must also be seen as reactionary. Brougham's advocacy of "sounder" political views in *Practical Observations* tacitly evokes the rival views they are meant to contest, the popular radicalism of the unstamped press, the "two-penny trash," the irreverent and "irresponsible" newspapers, tracts, and political weeklies of oppositional writers like Cobbett, Wooler, Carlile, and Hone. These writers had built a radical lower-class audience over the years 1816–20 by appealing directly to a newly literate working-class public, speaking to common experience in a vernacular inspired by Paine.[29] The threat of an unlicensed press, of the resurgence of 1790s radicalism, of free-wheeling political discussion in ale-houses and union benefit clubs, is everywhere present in the discourse of the 1820s and 1830s on popular education and mass literature. It was no longer a question, Brougham wrote, of "whether the people should be taught politics or not," for if not provided "sound doctrine" by "impartial men," they would instead "fall a prey to the more violent and interested class of politicians, to the incentives of agitators, and the nostrums of quacks."[30] "More knowledge," rather than less, was called for, as the *Westminster Review* (the organ of Bentham and Mill) concurred: "If Paine or Wolstone-croft [sic] have puzzled the parish clerk, let him study Paley, and Watson, and Grotius."[31] The same point was frequently made in the *Edinburgh Review* and in the *Quarterly Review of Education*, published by Knight for the SDUK, which warned that the only way to preserve an "inflammable" manufacturing populace from the dangerous seductions of "unsound" doctrines was to "instruct them in their real interests."[32]

Before joining forces with Brougham and the SDUK in 1828, Knight had been working on his own for some years in the "almost untrodden field of cheap and wholesome literature for the People."[33] In a newspaper article written in 1819, Knight had identified a "*new power*" at work among the masses – literacy and the "progress of knowledge" – and lamented that "seditious and infidel" journals were virtually left unchallenged in directing that power. "The work," he wrote, "must be taken out of their hands"; not through censorship and repression (still, as in the 1790s, the Tory prescriptions) but through competition (*Passages* 1: 234–37). Knight could appreciate, even envy, the appeal that radical journalists, particularly Cobbett, had for the new mass readership: "They state an argument with great clearness and precision; they divest knowledge of all its pedantic incumbrances; they make powerful appeals to the deepest passions of the human heart." Knight called for a "man of genius" to follow their lead, who would in addition cultivate reverence toward "national manners and institutions," tenderness toward "domestic associations," and a sense of the "high mysterious destiny of the human mind." It is a remarkable proposal: the "racy English" and direct appeal of Cobbett combined with the conservative wisdom of Burke's *Reflections*, and with a distinct touch of the Wordsworthian or egotistical sublime as well.[34]

This was not, however, the sort of literature that the SDUK eventually supplied. Instead, Brougham and Knight began in 1829 to issue a succession of scientific and technical treatises – the Library of Useful Knowledge – on subjects like *Hydraulics, Pneumatics*, and the *Polarisation of Light*, inspiring Peacock's brilliant satire on the "Steam Intellect Society" in *Crotchet Castle* (1831).[35] Not surprisingly, the series failed to build a wide audience, particularly among the working classes. The Library of Entertaining Knowledge, explicitly designed to lure the masses into reading, was devoted to topics which were hardly less dry than the "useful" ones, with volumes on *Insect Architecture, Egyptian Antiquities*, and *Vegetable Substances: Materials of Manufacture*. Both ventures were in part hamstrung by a narrow conception of utility – as though useful knowledge could reside only in compilations of well-ordered facts, in (as Coleridge sniffed) the "*plebification*" of "science and systematic knowledge" (*CCS*, 69). Brougham and Knight may also have been hampered, as the *Westminster Review* charged, by a failure of political nerve, choosing scientific topics as those least likely to cause anxiety or offense among their aristocratic sponsors and connections. But it was primarily information on political subjects which was needed to stem rick-burning and machine-breaking: "Hodge, with a firebrand in his hand, about to set the standing corn in a blaze, with the Committee for the Diffusion of Useful Knowledge presenting him with various of their treatises, say for example, their ill-digested papers on Heat, in hopes of thereby preventing him from his dreadful purpose, would form a very instructive, if somewhat ludicrous picture."[36]

The reviewer did not complain of what may strike us as another remarkable lack, particularly in the Library of Entertaining Knowledge: fiction. Although it had played an important role in the counter-revolutionary propaganda of the 1790s, and was playing an increasingly important one in the moral discipline of bourgeois children and young women, fiction was ignored or slighted in most of the educational and publishing ventures aimed at popular audiences at this time. There was no room for fiction in Owen's curriculum at New Lanark, in the lecture programs of the Mechanics' Institutes, or in the catalogue of the SDUK. Even Knight's *Penny Magazine*, begun in 1832 and by far the most successful of the SDUK's ventures, dispensed with the weekly tale that featured so centrally in its model, the *Mirror of Literature*. Fiction was not obviously "useful," it did not directly address a reader's immediate "interest" (not that hydraulics or insect architecture did either), it could prove dangerously irrational, as Knight's Lockean distaste for the "marvelous" implied.[37]

Given so inhospitable a climate, it is all the more striking that one seemingly indefatigable writer – Harriet Martineau – brought the "sounder" political and economic views called for by Brougham and others into fictional form toward the very end of the Romantic era in her twenty-five volume *Illustrations of Political Economy* (1832–34). Martineau did, however, have an important precedent in Maria Edgeworth's *Popular Tales* (1804), which, like Edgeworth's *Letters for Literary Ladies*, anticipates the emphasis on rational decision and perceived interest marking the discourse of Brougham and his allies.[38] *Popular Tales* was aimed not at one, but at several groups among the mass of readers excluded from "polite" circles: tales are variously addressed to the "situations" of farmers, shopkeepers, and clerks.[39] Only a few stories seem particularly aimed at the audience of artisans and skilled factory workers later targeted by the SDUK, of which "Lame Jervas" and "The Grateful Negro" are the most interesting.

Reviewing *Popular Tales* for the *Edinburgh Review*, Jeffrey praised Edgeworth's inculcation of "homely" virtues – "industry, perseverance, prudence, good humour" – appropriate to a "vulgar" readership: an attempt "somewhat superior in genius, as well as utility, to the laudable exertions of Mr Thomas Paine to bring disaffection and infidelity within the comprehension of the common people, or the charitable endeavours of Messrs Wirdsworth [sic] & Co. to accommodate them with an appropriate vein of poetry."[40] Edgeworth, that is, invents a fictional discourse which implicitly counters the popular radicalism of Paine, without vulgarizing a polite literary form in the manner of Wordsworth. Moreover, she renders attractive precisely those qualities that would enable a lower-class reader eager for self-improvement to make the most of his or her limited opportunities without expecting to rise too fast or too high (the lesson of "prudence," reiterated throughout the tales). In *Popular Tales*, any individual can succeed in life through hard work, self-denial, and patience. In order to become such an individual, however, the laborer in particular must cut himself off from other workers, aligning his interest not with theirs but with that of his employer, and yet never forgetting his humble beginnings and the "gratitude" owed to a benevolent patron. Edgeworth's is an ambivalent ideology at odds with itself, caught between the nostalgia of tract writers like Trimmer and More for an earlier era's vertical social hierarchies and bonds of patronage and obligation, and the ethos of self-improvement and rugged individualism which would come to mark the "popular" writing of the Victorian age.

"Lame Jervas," for example, is a story of self-help which looks back to Dick Whittington and forward to Samuel Smiles. Jervas, an orphan, begins life as a child laborer in a tin mine, educates himself, and eventually gains a fortune by taking advantage of Oriental barbarism (not, like Whittington, simply through luck, but rather through his mastery of European technology). In order to begin his rise, however, Jervas must first break with the other miners, by exposing a plot to embezzle a chance find of "Cornish diamonds." His fellow laborers attempt to murder Jervas in revenge, but he comes under the protection of the proprietor, hereafter his "kind monitor" (23), who sends him to London and has him taught to read and write. The narrative at this point becomes an educational romance, as Jervas pursues "useful information" through self-directed reading (26), works the popular lecture circuit with his model tin mine, and finally sails to India to assist none other than Dr. Bell at his famed Madras Orphan Asylum. From here, Jervas moves on to a native Sultanate, tutoring one of the princes in science, gaining applause and hefty rewards for demonstrating his scientific tools and tricks, modernizing the Sultan's tin mines, and finally re-organizing the diamond mines at Golconda. Putting his entire capital out to "compound interest" for a period of years (an act requiring both "patience" and "prudence"), Jervas ends his career in "ease and affluence," returning to Cornwall in order to astound his former companions, narrate his story, and acknowledge the "generosity" of his former master (41, 50).

Education had been thematized in earlier tales aimed at the lower classes, but Edgeworth's hero educates himself rather than attending a Charity or Sunday School in the tradition of the SPCK tracts. Jervas can be seen as a prototype of the self-educated technician and self-made inventor and entrepreneur who would constitute the ideal (if hardly the actual) reader of *The Mechanics' Magazine* and the Library of Useful Knowledge. The predominately colonial setting seems on one level to equate "Oriental" ignorance with the "brutal" manners of the worse sort of miner (10); rising above the latter, Jervas puts himself in a position to exploit the former. It may imply as well that imperial expansion would make opportunities for lower-class as well as more elite adventurers, a frequent theme in the popular journals of the 1830s.[41] But the tale's discursive center resides in its treatment of property, both the respect for another's property which begins Jervas's career, and the desire for "property of [his] own," which aligns Jervas with the more "sober and industrious" miners (10), and which might in turn inspire Edgeworth's reader to mend his or her ways in hopes of becoming a small capitalist.

Colonialism, property, and the shift from horizontal to vertical allegiance, from solidarity with fellow laborers to identification with the master's interest, also feature in "The Grateful Negro," set in Jamaica at the time of a slave rebellion. Comparisons between English laborers and West Indian slaves had become standard in the social and political discourse of the time, whether as a basis for criticizing the hypocrisy of reformers (charged with worrying over colonial slavery while ignoring the allegedly worse condition of the working classes at home), or in order to equate lower-class rebellion with the "savagery" of displaced Africans, as in Burke's comparison of the revolutionary masses in France with a "gang of Maroon slaves."[42] In "The Grateful Negro," the slaves are clearly of Burke's savage variety, plotting to cut their masters' throats, and poisoning their knives in a lurid obeah ritual.[43] The rebellion is betrayed, however, by Caesar, the titular "Grateful Negro," who has been saved by the model planter Edwards from being sold to Mexico and given a "provision-ground" to work on his own time (349). The paradox that slaves, being property themselves, can hold property, is crucial to Edgeworth's purpose here. It gives Caesar a basis (besides his gratitude) for identifying with his master; it also tells the reader that even a slave can become a small capitalist through "industry" and perseverance (347). Caesar's betrayal of the slave revolt is all the more remarkable given his double bond to the chief conspirator, Hector: they are of the same tribe, and were brought from Africa on the same ship, the "strongest ties" thought to exist among slaves (350). That he sides with Edwards nevertheless attests not only to Caesar's gratitude – a nostalgic, quasi-feudal gesture – but also to how thoroughly his perceived interest has been aligned with that of the proprietor.

One might have expected an anti-slavery tale in a professedly "popular" collection, but Edgeworth does not provide one. Rather, her attitude toward slavery parallels her liberal attitude toward the plight of the British laborer. The benevolent Edwards treats his slaves kindly, and professes to oppose slavery; nevertheless, "he was convinced, by the arguments of those who have the best means of obtaining information, that the sudden emancipation of the negroes would rather increase than diminish their miseries." His plantation management style anticipates the program of selective reforms called for by Brougham, the Utilitarian group, and other allies of the upper middle class, professional interest cultivated by the Edgeworths: "He adopted those plans for the amelioration of the slaves which appeared to him the most likely to succeed without producing any violent agitation or revolution" (346). This opposition between gradual amelioration and revolution signals the tale's implicit agenda as a reformist allegory for British laborers which associates "violent agitation" with African savagery and superstition. Edgeworth cites as her source on obeah the work of Bryan Edwards, who had made the same connection explicit in his *Historical Survey* (1797) of Saint Domingue, contrasting the "progressive improvement in the situation of the lower ranks in England" with the spectacle of class warfare in France, and the sudden emancipation schemes of "detestable incendiaries" with the "slow and gradual" phasing out of the slave system. "A perseverance in the same benevolent system, progressively leading the objects of it to civilization and mental improvement, preparatory to greater indulgence, is all that humanity can require; for it is all that prudence can indicate."[44] This last statement sums up both Edwards' view of the slavery question and his approach to the "amelioration" of the British laborer; it could also be taken as the moral to "The Grateful Negro" or to *Popular Tales* as a whole, which throughout advocates individual "prudence" over concerted action, and which seeks to advance the work of "civilization and mental improvement" even while preaching its necessity.

There are a number of continuities between Edgeworth's pioneering collection and Martineau's *Illustrations* (reissued later in the century under the same title, *Popular Tales*). Martineau also favors colonial settings, celebrates the virtues of industry and capital accumulation, and programmatically advocates individual initiative over collective working-class action.[45] But where Edgeworth's *Popular Tales* was, as Jeffrey remarked, an "experiment" in adapting various styles to a variety of lower-class groups (330), the twenty-five volumes of Martineau's *Illustrations* constitute an elaborate, thorough, and painstakingly developed exposition of the teachings of the "political economists" for an undifferentiated mass audience.[46] In the world of these tales, in part grittily realistic, in part absurdly utopian, each member of society enters into rational discussion with nearly everyone else, either coming to see his or her interest as aligned with the free movement of capital or failing to get the point and, as a result, jeopardizing the workings of an otherwise infallible system. The enlightened proprietor of Edgeworth's imagination does not entirely disappear from Martineau's moral economy, but his role is greatly diminished, and his claim on his subordinates resides not in an archaic relation of benevolence and grateful dependency but instead in his mastery of political science.

In *The Rioters* (1827), for example, Martineau's prototype for the *Illustrations*, the narrator, a "commercial traveller" who arrives at Manchester at a time of machine-breaking, takes a poor laborer and his family under his protection. He does so, however, only because a "starving man" cannot listen to reason; once his protégé has been fed, he resorts to rational dialogue ("I think I can show you how the poor cut their own throats by destroying their masters' property, if the masters take it ever so tamely").[47] Martineau's dialogues are not catechistic, for she leaves a great deal of room for objections, counterexamples, and blunt questions. But the work is nevertheless pseudo-dialogic, as there is only one legitimate and coherent ideology in her tales, and the reader always knows which speakers to trust, which to discount. The authority of her enlightened characters (who can belong to any class and either gender) is reinforced in each tale by a concluding summary, which lists the economic principles exposed in the tale in tabular form, and encourages the reader to fit each tale into the larger system of which it makes a part.[48]

Martineau's approach to fiction is much more ambivalent than that of Edgeworth, reflecting perhaps the distaste for imaginative literature of her utilitarian mentors. In the preface to *Life in the Wilds* (1832), the first volume of *Illustrations*, Martineau disclaims any attempt to write the sort of didactic tales that (like More's or Edgeworth's) "pretend to be stories, and turn out to be catechisms," fiction of the "*trap* kind."[49] She justifies her fictional format on the basis that "explanations of the principles which regulate society" can be made both clear and interesting through "pictures of what those principles are actually doing in communities" (x) – a rather tortuous use of "actually." The imagined community of *Life in the Wilds* is in fact decidedly ideal, a representation of "Labour uncombined with Capital, and proceeding through many stages to a perfect Union with Capital" (xiv). The setting for this ideal community, however, is made to appear "actual," by placing it in a colonial context, a "small British settlement in the north of the European territories of South Africa" (27), overrun by "savages" so thorough in their depredations that they manage to carry off every tool, cord, knife, and needle in the infant colony.

True to her preface, Martineau regularly punctures the fictionality of the tale by including incredible dialogues, as when the settlement's leaders decide to rebuild the community as an economic experiment: "I should like our people to remain in this settlement... that we might observe how fast they will advance from the primitive state to which we are reduced to that in which their countrymen are, in England." "They will advance rapidly ... because they know how to apply their labour" (59–60). The situation that gives rise to the tale, however, is not only highly fictional, but a notorious fiction at that: a *robinsonnade* as dreamed by Bentham. Not content to "live like savages" (98) – for the break with savage society is the starting point for all political economy – the *de facto* castaways discover the "division of labour," the use of "machinery," and the wisdom of a *laissez-faire* or "'letting alone' course of policy." "Governments should protect the natural liberty of industry by removing all obstacles, – all bounties and prohibitions, – all devices by which one set of people tries to obtain unfair advantages over another set" (126, 176, 147). Free from government intrusion, possessed of European know-how (and yet developing much of their primitive technology through careful imitation of the "natives"), the colonists build a functioning labor economy, wedded at last to Capital when a shipment of tools arrives from Cape Town.

Martineau's tales all follow a similar design: contrived situations within realistic settings, impossible dialogues between otherwise naturalistic characters, a sprinkling of exciting or affecting incidents, and telling, carefully researched details (like the various skills imitated from the "savages" in *Life in the Wilds*). There is also, occasionally, a small space for resistance to the principles so remorselessly illustrated in tale after tale. Although we learn in *Life in the Wilds* that "Nature appears to be inexhaustible" (144), a curmudgeonly solitary in the next tale, *The Hill and the Valley*, is allowed to demure at the erection of an iron-works in his Welsh exile. "The birds will be driven from yonder wood, the fishes will be poisoned in the streams, and where my eye had rested with pleasure on the purple heath, I shall see brick walls and a column of smoke" (2: 29). The capitalist's reply ("when you see some hundreds of human beings thriving, where there are now only woodcocks and trout, you will be reconciled to the change") seems for once unconvincing, particularly when the works shut down (thanks to an ill-advised bout of machine-breaking) and the landscape is left both idle and irremediably scarred. In the same tale a mysterious laborer, fallen from the privileged classes into beggary and successfully lifting himself back up through unremitting labor and parsimony, is admonished for *too* thoroughly embodying the principles outlined in the tale's "Summary," and virtually dehumanizing himself in the process: "Leave off accumulating money before it is too late" (2: 210). But neither Martineau's quasi-Romantic appreciation of nature, nor her faintly Christian sense of the limitations of material wealth, does much to undermine the tale's didactic purpose – demonstrating (again) that working-class agitation will hurt the workers themselves more than their employers, that the individual worker can best withstand the fluctuations of a market economy by saving and becoming a "capitalist" (44), that the "interests of the two classes of producers, laborers and capitalists, are the same; the prosperity of both depending on the accumulation of CAPITAL" (216).[50]

Martineau's *Illustrations* made her a celebrated author, and provided a safe, "useful" alternative to novels for patrons to bestow on the libraries of Mechanics' Institutes.[51] Her real accomplishment, however, may be seen in retrospect as a negative one: demonstrating exhaustively how *not* to produce popular fiction. On the one hand, her tales have almost none of the immediate appeal of the street literature of the time, which in its unabashed fascination with crime, sex, and the habits of royalty tapped a popular vein which has yet to give out.[52] On the other, Martineau overvalues system and rationality, and undervalues the imaginative appeal and sense of human potentiality which Knight had presciently called for in 1819. Where Martineau failed to reach the growing body of "serious" lower-class readers bent on self-improvement, series like the *Penny Poets* and *Cassell's Library of English Literature* would succeed, appealing not to readers' narrowly defined economic interests, but rather to their desire for imaginative encounter with a transfigured, transcendent image of human nature. Criticizing "ordinary popular literature" in *Culture and Anarchy*, Matthew Arnold would dismiss attempts like Martineau's to "indoctrinate the masses" with the ideology of a "profession and party"; real culture "works differently," seeking to "make the best that has been thought and known in the world current everywhere," inviting readers of all classes to participate in a classless, ideal society of the mind.[53]

Arnold's position may, of course, be criticized in turn as an "ideology against ideology," a discursive ploy he inherits (along with the notion of imaginative literature as the prime vehicle of the "*social idea*") from Wordsworth and Coleridge.[54] But Arnold must be credited for refusing to infantilize the common reader, for admonishing those who "give the masses, as they call them, an intellectual food" specially "prepared and adapted" (475). Several Romantic-era writers, including Knight, had begun warning against addressing a popular audience in the "language of the nursery," and Jeffrey had taken exception to the "childish" character of Edgeworth's plots in his review of *Popular Tales*.[55] But neither Edgeworth nor Martineau, who could write of producing popular histories "as plain as Red Ridinghood" for an audience of "poor people, children, etc.," were innocent of this tendency.[56] In the era of the first Reform Bill, when middle-class reformers claimed the franchise for themselves, but would effectively hold political representation "in trust" for their working-class allies, the infantilization of the lower-class subject had serious political repercussions.[57] It also had significant literary repercussions, particularly in relation to autobiography and to the marketing and reception of lower-class poets.

SELF-EDUCATION AND SELF-REPRESENTATION

A spate of recently published memoirs and autobiographies by (among others) a soldier, a silversmith, a ship's boy, and a condemned criminal prompted an indignant attack in the *Quarterly Review* for 1827. "Cabin-boys and drummers are busy with their commentaries *de bello Gallico*... and, thanks to the 'march of intellect,' we are already rich in the autobiography of pickpockets"; every "driveller" now pens his memorabilia like so many Rousseaus. But if the spread of writing among the lower orders gives rise to "this garbage of Confessions," the still wider spread of reading fosters an undiscriminating, vulgar audience to consume them. "It seems as if the ear of the grand impersonation, the Reading Public, had [sic] become as filthily prurient as that of an eaves-dropping lackey."[58]

The class slurs spattered throughout the article are motivated by more than patrician outrage or the recoil of a finicky, anti-Jacobin palate. Reviewed among the lower-class memoirs is, significantly, a biography of the *déclassé* Major Cartwright, "by birth a gentleman" but by choice a supporter of "radical reform, annual parliaments, and universal suffrage" (154). The inclusion of Cartwright, with the requisite condemnation of his "impracticable" cause, helps reveal what is really at stake in the *Quarterly*'s attack on "Autobiography." As the growth of a Reading Public had encouraged "mean and base" writers to claim the "attention and the sympathy of mankind" (164), the spread of literacy and with it the capacity for informed participation in political debate had weakened one of the readiest arguments against the "absurd" demand for "universal" (male) suffrage. Burke had already linked the self-representation of the English with the specter of "popular representation" in the *Reflections*; now the widening capacity of individual English citizens to represent themselves in prose helped force the issue of political representation, kept at the forefront of debate by Cobbett and other radical journalists in the post-Waterloo period and coming to a crisis with the Reform agitation of 1831–32.[59]

Although the booklist in the *Quarterly* featured examples of two emergent genres within autobiographical writing – the common soldier's or sailor's memoirs (inspired by the Napoleonic Wars) and the "reminiscences of low life" which fed a market carved out by the *Newgate Calendar* – it was a third category, the "autobiography of self-improvement," which most profoundly addressed the contemporary politics of literacy and representation.[60] Although the development of this genre broadly overlaps with the emergence of working-class autobiography, narratives of struggle from "obscurity" to a certain level of mental culture and economic independence were also produced by sons of the lower middle classes, like Francis Place and Charles Knight, who were both denied classical educations, apprenticed in their early teens, and left, in Knight's words, to make the most of "desultory reading" and "self-instruction" (1 : 55, 125).[61] What remains constant is the lack of extended formal schooling, the pursuit of "really useful knowledge" despite a severe shortage of time, funds, and direction, and the embattled sense of beating the odds through sheer energy and self-discipline. It is a distinctly male genre, not because women had greater access to formal education (they had still less), but because women, when they wrote autobiographies at all, did not frame their lives in such agonistic terms.[62] The "life and struggles" genre demonstrated that a shrewd political sensibility and a credible public voice could be attained by individuals from the lowest reaches of society under the most unlikely conditions. Even when couched in the soothing tones of moderate liberalism, the narrative of self-improvement held radical implications.

It is appropriate that the radical tailor Thomas Hardy, in the course of the first "working-man's autobiography," should recall his friend "Gustavus Vassa, the African" writing his own memoirs (the "prototype" of the slave narrative) as Hardy's guest in 1792.[63] The autobiographies of self-educated British writers share a number of features with the nineteenth-century slave narrative, despite the obvious differences in the range of experience represented and the distinct linguistic and cultural barriers confronted by displaced Africans and by native Europeans, however bleak their upbringings. For both groups, the difficulties in becoming literate and assuming a public voice claim a central role, one evinced in the common subtitle, "Written by Himself," that figures on the title pages of Equiano, Hardy, and the lives of many other former slaves and self-taught Britons alike. Marking a critical phase in the subject's youth, a principal goal of his struggle, and the means through which his life will find public expression, the quest for literacy informs the autobiography's rhetorical structure as well as shaping its content.[64] Whereas in the autobiography of self-improvement, however, literacy serves primarily to ground the author's claim to equal participation in social and political life – his cultural as well as electoral enfranchisement – in the slave narrative literacy also functions to demonstrate the author's very claim to humanity in the face of racist definitions of black Africans and their descendants as sub-human.[65] Along with the representation, often quite dramatic, of a hard-won education, one also finds in both autobiographical genres contradictory feelings of separation from those left behind (sometimes verging on a sense of election) and of continuing solidarity with them based on shared experience, suffering, and aspirations. Many authors in both groups present themselves explicitly as working for the freedom and self-determination of their unrepresented fellows. Where Equiano and Frederick Douglass highlight their eventual involvement in the British and American Abolition movements, most of the self-taught writers considered below recount (though in some cases apologetically) their association with such radical reform groups as the London Corresponding Society, the Hampden Clubs, the Owenite co-operative movement, and the National Union of the Working Classes.[66]

The difficulty for the self-taught writer of attaining not merely adequate literary skills but a confident public voice leaves its mark on the openings of many of these works. For William Hutton, even assuming the "simple letter *I*" can inspire narrative diffidence in a writer who has "usher[ed] himself into life" (iv) and remains unnerved by his independence of traditional cultural supports. Hardy abjures the "great *I*" altogether and writes in the third person (35), evincing not only, as Reginia Gagnier suggests, a resistance to the "egotism" she associates with bourgeois individualism, but also his dilemma in positioning himself as a writing subject in a discursive world more accustomed to objectifying his class.[67] In the preface to his *Autobiography of an Artisan*, Christopher Thomson imagines the educated reader's stock response: "The artisan! what does he want with literature? – what has he to do with mind?" (5). But the autobiographer's lack of the rhetorical skills traditionally taught through study of the classical languages can also function to underscore the veracity of one (as Hardy puts it) "untutored in any language but that of truth" (73). Beginnings are frequently complicated as well by the author's forced break with what Thomas Cooper calls the "good old-established practice ... of commencing with the venerable theme of ancestry" (3), but this too can help establish a tone of candor and plain dealing. Thomson, who begins by confessing his "diffidence" and acknowledging his "humble birth," establishes a more confident voice in disposing of the expected description of his family's genealogical tree: "we never had one" (v–vi, 26). The blunt confession of "poor but honest" origins was in fact a well-established rhetorical move by the early nineteenth century, played out brilliantly and unforgettably by Cobbett in the opening pages of his apologia, *The Life and Adventures of Peter Porcupine* (1796).[68]

The extensive treatment of education in nearly all of these works also proves both a source of embarrassment or regret and a manifestation of the author's self-discipline, autonomy, and strength of will. Although Cobbett assailed the identification of illiteracy – the inability to "make upon paper certain marks with a pen" – with ignorance, the self-taught autobiographer is typically so invested in his own hard-won pursuit of knowledge that he overvalues the more "regular" education withheld from him.[69] Thomas Cooper, who attended a dame school, a Sunday School, a monitorial school, and a private day school, nevertheless considered himself "almost entirely" self-educated, and regretted the professional or classical education that would have opened to him a career "in which mind is needed" (43, 17). Nor is Cooper's claim disingenuous, given the generally poor quality of instruction, the short amount of time usually spent in school, and the haphazard quality of an education that might at any moment be interrupted by a drop in family income, the illness or relocation of a master, or the gleaning season. Cooper's dame, "Old Gatty," taught basic reading and the Madras school offered only a "monotonous" two-year program in Bible-reading, writing, and the "first four rules of arithmetic." At the day school he seems to have spent most of his time either assisting younger pupils or reading books lent by his more prosperous schoolfellows; at the age of fifteen, he was working long hours as a shoemaker (14, 32).

Although a few self-taught writers praise institutions like the Sunday Schools – Samuel Bamford credits them with training up the local working-class leaderships of the radical reform movement (2, Part 1: 8) – their accounts give on the whole a still more dismal picture than that sketched by Cooper. Thomas Carter's mother kept a dame school though he describes her as too uneducated to "teach others" (37), Thomson's dame confined her instruction to the "A,B,C, and goblin lore" (35–37), and William Lovett went through "all the dame-schools of the town" before his great-grandmother finally taught him to write (3). None of the various day schools attended by this group of writers taught anything beyond reading, writing, and simple arithmetic, and though some masters are described as benevolent and sensible, others are "savage," "harsh," or "often more than half-intoxicated."[70] One rarely finds the generalized contempt for "provided" education advanced in Cobbett's *Register* or Hetherington's *Poor Man's Guardian* among self-taught autobiographers, who support in various ways the spread of more and better educational institutions, but they have scant praise for the schools they themselves attended.[71]

If formal schooling was limited, haphazard, and foreshortened by full-time labor beginning at any age from seven to fifteen, the means and opportunities for instructing oneself were scarcely better. The most common complaint made is simply the absence of available, cheap books. Nearly all of these writers welcome the recent changes in the book market and appreciate – again in contrast to the radical press – the efforts of "diffusers" like Chambers, Knight, and Brougham, whatever their motives. Some, like Place, grew up in homes without a single book besides the Bible; at twenty Timothy Claxton had only *seen* a single book, "borrowed for a short time," on "any subject connected with the arts and sciences" (25). William Hone read through Bailey's *Dictionary* when he could find nothing else to read. A book's loan or chance discovery or rare purchase (often made by "cheating the stomach") frequently marks an epoch in the self-taught writer's life, particularly in adolescence. An encounter, at the age of eleven, with Swift's *Tale of a Tub* marked a "sort of new birth of intellect" for Cobbett (140), and Cooper felt "a new sense" emerge within himself after the few hours' loan of Byron's *Manfred* at age twelve. Hone at eleven made and sold cardboard boxes and toys until he could afford *The Trial of John Lilburne*, which he had painstakingly hunted down after discovering a stray sheet of it in a cheesemonger's shop (40). Place made kites and scavenged scrap iron to buy books and, like Carter, would read standing at London book stalls (the poor man's library) until shooed away.

The leisure for reading books was often as hard won as the stray pence for purchasing them. Owen, who began at age ten working from eight in the morning to six or seven at night in a linen draper's, would rise in the summer as early as three to read in a nearby park, returning there to read until dark (1 : 14). As a child, Carter taught himself to read while knitting, and as an apprentice working fourteen-hour days or longer he would read while eating (a common practice) and walking (25, 74). Apprenticed to a shoemaker at the age of fourteen, James Lackington made a habit of reading in "*Cloacina's Temple,*" and as a journeyman cut his sleep to three hours to have more reading time (62). But self-tuition was not always so lonely or furtive. A neighbor, a friendly co-worker, or a fellow lodger might lend and discuss a book, go over the difficult parts in a "cyphering book," or teach the elements of grammar, rarely learned in school. (It was to help supply this lack that Cobbett published his popular *Grammar of the English Language* in 1816.)[72] Young men formed reading and discussion groups, pooled their funds to join circulating libraries, read aloud to one another during working hours and in pubs or coffee-houses. The radical press has itself been called one of the period's most flexible and widespread educational forms, and many of the autobiographers considered here express their debt to journals like the *Register*, the *Black Dwarf*, and *The Poor Man's Guardian*, often read and talked over in groups.[73] The political organization often functioned as a mutual improvement society as well. Place's depiction of the London Corresponding Society (founded by Hardy and numbering Hone and Holcroft among its members) includes joint book subscriptions, Sunday evening reading and discussion sessions, and debating meetings. "It induced men to read books, instead of wasting their time in public houses, it taught them to respect themselves, and to desire to educate their children. It elevated them in their own opinions" and "opened to them views which they had never before taken" (131, 198).

Such co-operative educational ventures, however, tended to be provisional and short-lived, and the dominant figure in these accounts of self-tuition remains that of the "solitary and obscure young man" who figures as both hero and idealized reader of Knight's narrative (125). Indeed, the life of "self-denial and earnest mental toil" required for the task tends to isolate the autobiographer from his fellow laborers more often than it joins him to them (Cooper, 45).[74] At times, the sense of estrangement takes a harsh or self-righteous form. "I despised my companions," writes Holcroft of his term as a stable boy, "for the grossness of their ideas, and the total absence of every pursuit, in which the mind appeared to have any share" (70). This sense of detachment is compounded by programs of study which necessarily involve introspection under crowded working conditions. Carrying out his almost maniacal program of self-tuition in his mother's home shop, Cooper would scandalize their friends and neighbors not only by his habit of reciting Latin declensions or *Paradise Lost* while cobbling, but by insisting on speaking "grammatically" and "with propriety" instead of in dialect. "Who was I, that I should sit on the cobbler's stall, and 'talk fine!'" (56). The strain of unremitting study, sleeplessness, and isolation mounted until Cooper's almost inevitable mental and physical collapse. And yet a key impetus for his ambitious and lonely endeavor had been his earlier membership in a mutual improvement group, "intellectual friends" who met to study together and practice "refined" English (56–57).

The tension marking Cooper's narrative between communality and alienation, autonomy and collaboration, is one of the most pervasive and compelling features of the autobiography of self-improvement. The self-taught writer remains acutely conscious that in representing himself, he represents his class, an awareness informing even the titles of Claxton's *Memoir of a Mechanic*, Thomson's *Autobiography of an Artisan*, and Carter's *Memoirs of a Working Man*. Those who, like Owen and Hutton, have left their lower-class origins behind them still affirm rather than downplay their roots, in part to show how far they have "risen" and in part to demonstrate that merit is independent of birth and that a youth spent in laboring does not prevent the growth of a rich intellectual life. Knight's middle-class background (his father sold books) does not keep him from depicting his as a "*Working Life*" and claiming to speak for "self-teachers" whose opportunities are earned rather than inherited (1: 55). In their different ways – bracketing for the moment the differences – these writers seek to justify not only their own right to participate fully in public discourse, but also the potential right of any man (not necessarily any woman) to do the like. Since they know, however, that the perception of a "mean beginning" will predispose certain readers to doubt the value of their experience and the validity of their discourse (Lackington, 282), they attempt to establish credibility by emphasizing their own pursuit of knowledge, mastery of linguistic skills, and personal qualities of "industry, perseverance, and economy" (Claxton 6), distancing themselves in the process from the origins they set out to affirm.

It would be imprecise, however, to conclude that the self-taught writer necessarily "betrays" his origin in adapting the terms of an elitist discourse.[75] Nor should one too readily assume that because the qualities of individual effort, orderliness, and self-restraint were among those being pushed by middle-class reformers, their exemplary illustration in these autobiographies can be reduced to a simple matter of "embourgeoisment."[76] As Thomas Walter Laqueur has argued in his important study of the Sunday School movement, working-class communities had their own reasons to create a "culture of discipline, self-respect and improvement within which to wage the battle for social justice and political equality."[77] The autobiography of self-improvement functions both to promote and to assert the existence and value of such a culture, presenting education not as an end in itself but as a means toward social amelioration and political enfranchisement.[78] In certain of its themes, however, and in its narrative trajectory such a represented life – the "history of an individual, struggling, unsupported, up a mountain of difficulties" (Hutton iv) – approaches the *laissez-faire* fables of an Edgeworth or Martineau nearly enough that we may suspect it of coming up against the same discursive limits as well. When Lovett writes that laborers "undervalue *mental and moral effort* for raising their class," or that a "drunken, and dissipated, and an immoral people, will never attain to political or social greatness," he seems less to be speaking for the "*unrepresented*" than lecturing them on behalf of the SDUK, as though middle-class anxieties regarding the undisciplined masses have indeed entered his writing along with the bourgeois conventions for narrating a life (iv, 127, 119).

The autobiography of self-improvement nevertheless diverges in important ways from the middle-class social and fictive discourses from which it borrowed so heavily. A key difference between the liberal rhetoric of Edgeworth and Brougham and most of the narratives of "rising" discussed here – including those by Knight and Place – concerns a greater emphasis in the autobiographies on mutuality and co-operation, even if these values remain in a tense relation with the individualism endemic to self-representation in this era. (Place remarks that "no man ever wrote about himself without being an egotist" [7].) Owen, who tends to see himself as a "chosen spirit," nevertheless distinguishes himself from the "political economists" by his faith in "unity and co-operation" (129); Lovett, though he comes to abjure his youthful belief in "community of property" (inspired by Owen) on the grounds of "*individualism,*" still calls for a system of "*Co-operation in the Production of Wealth*" (45). Thomson, one of the most interesting autobiographers in this regard, suggests throughout his narrative that the dichotomies between self-improvement and solidarity, self-discipline and concerted action characteristic of liberal discourse are false ones, even if his efforts to bridge them seem strained. "Until education shall teach a majority of the toiling artisans of England to become calm, sober, thinking, and self-dependent men, uniting themselves into a deliberative league for the emancipation of labour, they will continue to be at the mercy of the mammon-lovers, who thrive by their ignorance and division." Individual autonomy, in a somewhat paradoxical fashion, functions to *overcome* rather than to facilitate "division" among workers, and fosters rather than displaces combined action; "universal brotherhood" will in turn "concrete their independence" (169). Lackington and Hutton, writing earlier, seem more one-sidedly individualistic, and yet neither can be written off as a Bounderby: both detail the assistance and encouragement they received in their early studies from others in similarly desperate circumstances, and Lackington links his good fortune as a bookseller to the growth of a self-improvement culture and with it a "general desire for READING" among the lower orders (232). Even when he most nearly approaches mere self-advertisement, that is, the self-taught autobiographer can envision his life as exemplary of a "great improvement" among the lower classes generally (Lovett 32).

Each writer manages the dialectic between self-determination and mutuality, personal "rise" and general improvement, in a distinct manner, and the specific differences can prove as revealing as the shared impulse behind them. Both Place and Bamford, for example, set their individual quests for useful knowledge, economic security, and political reform against a backdrop of large-scale social transformation, but one is guided by a qualified rationalist progressivism, the other by an uneasy blend of political reportage, Romantic nostalgia, and domestic ideology. Place began his "Self written Biography" in 1823 after repeated urging by Bentham and Mill, who seem to have expected the sort of "amusing and instructive" narrative Edgeworth had supplied in "Lame Jervas" (6). And, to an extent, this is what Place produces: the "useful" example of "how from very inauspicious beginnings, by a little honesty, a little practical good sense, a due portion of self respect, and continued exertion a great deal of what is most desirable may be accomplished" (12). Place claims at the outset to have "risen ... *solely*, by [his] own exertions," saving the intellectual influence of chance teachers and books (12); among the former is a schoolmaster who "was not learned in any thing" yet taught his pupils to "observe to think and to reason," to become "honest independent, patient and intrepid," imparting above all the lesson of "perseverance under unfavourable circumstances" (44).

But a proto-Victorian, self-help ideology is only one of several discursive strands woven through his narrative. A second is his ongoing demonstration, through contrasting the social practices of his childhood and youth with those of the present, that the "manners of the people" have progressed along with industry and commerce (15, 82). This project is inseparable from Place's conviction that only popular education can lead to a "wholly representative government," that the advantages of political representation must be understood before they can be desired (144). Place's self-education functions synechdocically to convey a widespread progress in manners and political knowledge, which remain linked in his account; his point is to show that the lower classes are both more politically sophisticated and socially responsible than opponents of reform would allow. And the portrayal of his "vulgar" youth risks fulfilling the expectations of critics like the "exclusive" writer on autobiography for the *Quarterly Review*, cited in Place's introduction, in the hope of demonstrating through contrast that such class prejudice is at least dated (51, 10).

Personal experience yields political lessons throughout the *Autobiography*, for example in Place's ambivalent portrait of his father, whom he clearly admires but decisively rejects. Variously a baker, publican, and keeper of a "spunging house," Place's muscular, rather charismatic father exemplifies a lower-class, urban male culture of "Drinking, Whoring, Gaming, Fishing and Fighting" (20). He beats his sons mercilessly, is "barbarous" toward his wife, and comes to epitomize the "dissolute" lower-class manners of the bad old days (24). But Place also shows how his father's casual brutality is implicated in and representative of a much wider culture of patriarchal authority: "In his opinion coercion was the only way to eradicate faults, and by its terror to prevent their recurrence.

These were common notions, and were carried into practice not only by the heads of families and the teachers of youth generally, but by the government itself and every man in authority under it" (62). "Gross and brutal" lower-class manners are further made cognate with the "indiscriminating, sanguinary and cruel" statutes of an arbitrary political system. Having himself, moreover, profited from a patently corrupt legal system as a bailiff "spunging" off debtors, Place's father gives paternalism a bad name.

Place, of course, endorses paternalism of a different, more consensual sort in his embrace of the political and educational agenda associated with Brougham and the SDUK; indeed, Place helped shape this agenda. But if Place's "educational quietism" fits neatly with the liberal vision of gradual reform led by the middle classes, his narrative occasionally erupts into powerful evocations and condemnations of class prejudice, which starkly distinguish his discourse from that of his utilitarian mentors.[79] Place never forgets that, however influential as a behind-the-scenes politician, he will always remain a "*tailoring creature*" in the eyes of some of the well-born, and would risk being "patronized" by others if he returned their advances (247). More trenchantly, Place shows through describing his own difficulties how class "hatred," rooted in resentment for having to pay wages at all, works systematically to suppress the efforts of journeymen, laborers, and servants to become independent, to attain dignity, even to educate themselves (127–28). Place describes a time when "to be able to read and to indulge in reading" could easily cost a journeyman his chance of employment; and as a small tradesman, Place lost at least one "valuable" customer when he chanced to discover Place's extensive library (222). Place accepted "indignity, and insolence," "tyranny and injustice" as among the costs of doing business; it was a choice between "doing this and being a beggar" (216). Though Place begins his autobiography by listing the personal qualities which facilitate his success, in the course of it he argues that such qualities are widespread among the lower classes, are steadily becoming more so, and are rarely sufficient in the absence of good luck to overcome the many obstacles which have been set against efforts at self-help. Education and self-discipline are necessary forerunners of political reform, but they will only go so far toward bettering the condition of the working classes in the absence of the political enfranchisement they herald.

Bamford, who published his autobiography in two installments (*Passages in the Life of a Radical* [1839–41] and *Early Days* [1848–49]), shares Place's sense of a "great change" having taken place in the "tastes and habits of the working classes" (1: 132) and his condemnation of "class-ism," a term Bamford seems to have coined (2, Part 2: 90). His narrative of a "self-taught" weaver-become-writer "struggling to rise" (2, Part 2: 232–34) similarly sets one man's education and working life against the popular movement for political reform in the early nineteenth century, but in Bamford the gap between individual experience and collective action becomes more pronounced, and his efforts to bridge it take a markedly different ideological form. The long section on the vanished "pastimes and diversions" of his childhood and youth in *Early Days* is allegedly included to help the reader measure the advance of "Civilization" among the "labouring classes" (1: 132). But whereas Place describes the cruel and dangerous (and exhilarating) custom of running bullocks to their deaths in London streets, episodes of what would now be called gang warfare with other boys, and the practice, among his father's set, of selling a niece or a mistress's daughter for ready cash, Bamford retails mainly the quaint and sentimental, Christmas caroling, rush-bearing, the finer points of exchanging valentines. Of course, as a supporter of middle-class reform movements, Place might be expected to give a bleak account of the days before Progress, and Bamford could be seen as countering ethnographic-style portrayals of working-class life in the manufacturing districts with images of simple joys and innocent rituals maintained in the face of harsh economic adversity. But there is in fact a great deal more gusto in Place's disapproving but energetic accounts of street life than in Bamford's bland urban pastorals, which seem calculated to appeal to the market for sentimental traditionalism staked out by Lamb and the young Dickens. Bamford's idealized portrayal of his childhood also comes to support his self-portrait as a responsible family man whose "steadfastness" and domestic sensibility militate against his radical reputation. In his description of the machine-breaking riots of 1812, the Middleton community becomes a "mob" led by "amazons," from which Bamford, the responsible family man, holds aloof (1: 304).

The conflict between the political and the domestic is more blatant in *Passages in the Life of a Radical*, taking narrative form as a series of digressions in which Bamford reproves his younger self along with the irresponsible Chartists of the present. Rather than holding collective action at arms' length as in *Early Days*, in *Passages* Bamford gives a series of stirring first-hand accounts of the reform agitation of 1816–21, including a classic eye-witness report of the Peterloo massacre. If Bamford's political education in *Early Days* is limited to experiencing economic hardship and devouring Cobbett's *Register*, *Passages* gives a rich sense of the era's working-class political culture as well, the "weekly readings and discussions" of the Hampden clubs (2, Part 1: 8), the speeches at village meetings and at mass demonstrations, the writing and presentation of petitions and addresses, the composition of political poems and songs. But in Bamford's "retrospections" the ethos of self-improvement comes to displace political action seemingly altogether. No "redemption for the masses could exist," Bamford writes in hindsight, "save one that should arise from their own virtue and knowledge" (2, Part 1: 154), from within the "hearts" and "households" of the people. Adapting the domestic ideology developed by Edgeworth and others in relation to middle-class women, Bamford writes that the "industrious and poor man" best serves England by "giving it children," by correcting the "irregularities on his own hearth," and by the "cultivation of good feeling in the hearts, and of good sense in the heads of those around him" (2, Part 1: 112). The working-class father takes on the role and duties which domestic ideology assigns to the middle-class mother, forming and regulating the subjectivities of children while disciplining himself as well, learning (as More would have women do) to "endure," "subdue himself," and "obey." Bamford's debt to domestic ideology becomes patent as he assumes a maternal voice: "Mildly and persuasively as a mother entreating, would reason lead us to self-examination, self-control, and self-amendment, as the basis for all public reform."

In Bamford, education also becomes a feminized alternative to political reform: "The masses should be elevated; instruction becoming the hand-maid of God's grace" (2, Part 1: 279). Bamford represents an extreme case among self-taught autobiographers, however, many of whom ground an ideology of education in their personal experience of self-tuition and self-discipline *without* abjuring politics or reinscribing the public sphere within the domestic. Thomson envisions education as facilitating rather than superseding a working-class political movement, calling on his fellow artisans to create their own schools and curricula in place of hegemonic institutions meant to fill churches and "keep a perfect surveillance over the poor": "The great labour class shall put their shoulders to the wheel of improvement, calling no longer to those 'in authority above us' to help them out of the mud of debasement" (19). Owen, however paternalistic, similarly articulates the need for new institutions and a new pedagogy if schooling is indeed to lay the groundwork for radical social reform (1: 113).

A materialist sense of how education is bound up in institutions and practices emerges casually as well throughout these narratives. Most of the autobiographers, to begin with, seek to extend the benefits of education to others in difficult circumstances by becoming directly involved in disseminating knowledge, as both an outgrowth of their dedication to self-culture and an expression of fellow-feeling. Cobbett and Knight, of course, in their quite different ways, helped transform the writing and distribution of "cheap" periodical literature, and Hone produced a genuinely popular tract literature of his own.[80] Owen did as much as anyone to humanize education in the early nineteenth century, and Lackington revolutionized the book trade by selling rather than destroying remainders, turning over vast numbers of second-hand books through introducing a cash-only sales policy, and regularly issuing public sales catalogs. Others worked to broaden the diffusion of knowledge on a smaller scale. Hone, Hutton, Bamford, and Lovett all ran bookshops and/or circulating libraries, as did Cobbett; Claxton invented and manufactured scientific instruments for use in popular lectures and in schoolrooms. Carter, Thomson, Lovett, and Cooper all tried their hands at schoolteaching, "one of the few comfortable trades," as Thomson remarks, which "require no previous training" (207). Claxton, Cooper, and Lovett assisted at the formation of Mechanics' Institutes. Claxton returned to his home town of Bungay to establish a Lyceum, and Thomson founded an Artisans' Library and an Association of Self-Help once he settled in Edwinstowe. Many besides Cobbett and Knight worked at selling, publishing, or writing for journals.

Finally, the writing of an autobiography can itself be seen as a work of mutual assistance, whether its designated addressee is a "solitary and obscure" youth as in Knight or the "great labour class" itself as in Thomson. The self-taught writer, that is, not only represents his community to a middle-class reading public but also represents that community to itself. He at once affirms the value of his group's experience by portraying it in a literary form and, by example, legitimizes the voices of other potential writers (and speakers, and thinkers) from the same group. What Gagnier states of the "political" autobiographers in this era (e.g., Hardy, Bamford, and Lovett), that they "assume the authority to write their own working-class history in order to ensure the subjecthood of working-class writers in the future" (160), can be extended to the self-taught autobiographer generally, though (as Gagnier's inclusion of Bamford suggests) this act is hardly unproblematic. But the mere recording of the considerable material difficulties and arbitrary social barriers confronted in the struggle for "bread, freedom, and knowledge," as well as the acknowledgement of assistance given and received along the way, ensures that none of these texts simply reflects a transcendent "self-help" creed, even when its author seems to endorse such a reading.

The case is quite different in the narrative of self-improvement as appropriated for (and idealized by) bourgeois ideology.[81] G. L. Craik's *The Pursuit of Knowledge under Difficulties*, published in 1830 by the SDUK, redefines "difficulties" as nearly anything from abject destitution to the distractions of royalty, abstracting the rise of self-education as a cultural phenomenon from its base in the social conditions of the early nineteenth century and presenting it instead as a universal phenomenon occurring throughout history and across the "civilized" globe. What happens when self-representation becomes exemplary biography can be seen in Craik's sketch of Holcroft, innocently paired with William Gifford (editor of the *Quarterly Review*) in a chapter on literary tailors. Holcroft's sense of alienation from his fellow grooms is highlighted, but his activities as a member of radical associations are dismissed as "certain political opinions which he was supposed to hold." Craik describes his work's purpose as (contrary to its title) one that negates the very existence of "difficulties" when met by "self-denial": "in the pursuit of any description of knowledge, no difficulties, arising from external circumstances, can eventually resist a steady determination to excel; so that a man's success or failure ... depends, in fact, more upon himself, than upon any circumstances in which he may be placed." Craik specifies "knowledge" (rather than more tangible goals) because he wishes the reader to remember that, "with regard to the great mass of the population, any counsel or exhortation, which would attempt to raise them above the rank in which they have been born and reared, must, from the nature of things, be totally inoperative."[82] Trimmer or More would not have said it much differently.

One of the few entertaining titles in the Library of Entertaining Knowledge, the *Pursuit* was almost immediately copied in America and by the new mass audience journals, and swiftly established a new sub-genre of biography that would find its apotheosis in Samuel Smiles' *Self-Help* (1859).[83] In Smiles the political subtext of Craik's transcendental approach to self-improvement becomes overt: "Whatever is done *for* men or classes, to a certain extent takes away the stimulus and necessity of doing for themselves"; "reforms can only be effected by means of individual action, economy, and self-denial, by better habits, rather than by greater rights."[84] In place of political knowledge, then, Smiles supplies brief lives of exemplary self-made men with whom the reader can imaginatively identify. Still better than Craik, Smiles understands that the lower classes will come to align their own interests with those of a *laissez-faire* system not through a simplified or fictionalized course in political economy, but through wishful identification with the few who have spectacularly benefitted under such a system. Brougham seems to intuit this development when he concludes *Practical Observations* by urging his reader to save up three-pence, buy Benjamin Franklin's *Life*, and read at least the first page. The same strategy remains at work today, save that inventors and industrialists rising through hard work and discipline have been joined and in part supplanted in the public mind by "stars" in sports and entertainment and, recently, by lottery winners. The narrative of self-improvement, once freed from any real connection to social experience, can shrink to the instantaneous and seemingly magical effect of a single "hit," inspired or just lucky.

UNEDUCATED POETS

Paradoxically, the Romantic cult of auto-didacticism found its most celebrated expression in relation to what Southey called the "uneducated" poet. The life of the working-class or "peasant" poet, which in outline closely resembles the autobiography of self-improvement, found expression in a variety of formats: from extended first-person narratives like James Hogg's *Memoir of the Author's Life* (1807) to the sketches written by a patron or publisher and included with a first collection of poems to build interest and sympathy, such as Capel Lofft's preface to Robert Bloomfield's *Farmer's Boy* (1800). Southey's *Lives of the Uneducated Poets* (1831) was itself originally published as an extended preface to the *Attempts in Verse* of a servant, John Jones, whom Southey had taken under his wing. The plebeian poet's life was generally seen as equal in significance to his or her work, constituting an exemplary self-help narrative in itself and an implicit apology for the poetry's lack of polish or sophistication. Particularly when written by a patron, a publisher, or to the specifications of either, it also served to place the poet's production safely within an increasingly archaic framework of upper-class benevolence and lower-class deference. Whereas the autobiography of the self-taught writer could constitute a threat to the dominant group's hegemonic control of literary discourse, the "uneducated" poet represented instead the last vestige of the system of literary patronage otherwise outmoded by an increasingly market-oriented publishing system.[85]

Even in the case of the plebeian poet, however, patronage had become in the Romantic era less a matter of personal relations (however unequal) than a quasi-public institution.[86] Rather than answering to a single patron or clique, the poet owed his or her fealty to an ever-widening circle of well-wishers. If the initial "discovery" of the prodigy was made by a local bookseller, pastor, or literary figure, a better-connected benefactor might well be required to negotiate with publishers; a group of subscribers (perhaps headed by a titled aristocrat) would be solicited to subsidize printing costs; and, finally, reviewers might appeal to the book-buying public in the name of charity as well as curiosity. The subscription system (like the Charity and Sunday Schools) meant that the middle classes could play at patronage as well as their aristocratic betters. Any book purchaser, moreover, might feel entitled to write the poet a letter of advice (with or without an enclosed bank-note) or drop by his or her home uninvited to witness "native" genius in its own habitat. One "dandified gentleman" who descended on John Clare had no qualms about "begging" a walking stick and asking pointed questions about Clare's courtship of his wife.[87]

The work of the plebeian poet was contained or accommodated in various ways under the system of patronage, subscription, and "benevolent" consumption. The preface generally served to undermine the poet's discursive authority, underscoring his or her lack of formal education, grammatical skills, and the grounding in classical literature deemed essential to full participation in literary culture, in the very process of making a pitch for "untutored genius." A typically condescending "Advertisement" for a first book of poems printed in 1783 is brief enough to quote in full:

The following Sketches were the production of untutored youth, commenced in his twelfth, and occasionally resumed by the author till his twentieth year; since which time, his talents having been wholly directed to the attainment of excellence in his profession, he has been deprived of the leisure requisite to such a revisal of these sheets, as might have rendered them less unfit to meet the public eye.

Conscious of the irregularities and defects to be found in almost every page, his friends have still believed that they possessed a poetic originality, which merited some respite from oblivion. These their opinions remain, however, to be now reproved or confirmed by a less partial public. (846)

The artisan-poet in question, William Blake, took to printing his own works after this initial appearance courtesy of "friends." But Blake's was a unique strategy and one that relegated his works to virtual obscurity during his own lifetime.

Another youthful prodigy, Thomas Dermody, paid more dearly for poetic independence. The son of yet another alcoholic schoolmaster, Dermody was taken up by a series of patrons after he ran away from home at the age of ten. One patron, Robert Owenson (father of the novelist Lady Morgan) would introduce Dermody in "rags" so that his auditors would be all the more startled by his learning and poetic skill. Another, a Rev. Austin, attempted to complete Dermody's education while getting up a sizeable subscription for his first book of poems, produced when he was only fourteen. When it got out that Dermody had written a satire on his latest protector, however, the printed copies were destroyed and the 150 pounds returned to the subscribers. Dermody continued to write poetry, find patrons, and lose favor; within three years he was destitute and dying in London.[88] Bloomfield, an agricultural laborer and shoemaker before turning poet, also died impoverished despite his huge initial success with *The Farmer's Boy*, falling victim both to changing fashion and to suspicions regarding his political loyalties. Accused of having "imbibed both Deistical and Republican principles," Bloomfield had to reassure his friends by denouncing Cobbett and Henry Hunt as power-mongers and universal suffrage as an "impracticable piece of nonsense."[89] The patronage system functioned to guarantee political quiescence as well as personal "gratitude," and lapses (or perceived lapses) in either could end a poet's career.

The emphasis on youth in the public debuts of Blake, Dermody (the "Irish Chatterton"), and Bloomfield (the "Farmer's Boy") suggests how a foreshortened formal education and youthfulness could work together at once to underwrite claims for the poet's "naive" genius and to further contain the poet's work through a complex gesture of infantilization. (The same combination could, of course, also help to discredit a non-classically educated poet seen as threatening the dominant group through *not* going the "prodigy" route, as Keats found when denounced in *Blackwood's* as an "uneducated and flimsy stripling.")[90] The Romantic vogue for naive genius was steeped to begin with in primitivism, and the "uneducated" poet was given a lineage in the minstrels of Percy's *Reliques*, Homer and the "Oriental" poets of the Old Testament as reinterpreted by Lowth and Blair, and invented bards like MacPherson's "Ossian" and Beattie's Minstrel. Particularly in the case of peasant writers, this matrix could be drawn on in constructing the poet as a sort of living antique, his culture the remnant of a more pristine (and childlike) era.

Robert Burns presents a particularly intriguing case of the peasant poet, as reviewers were initially unsure whether to portray him as naive (the "Heaven-taught ploughman") or sophisticated, given his obvious mastery of linguistic skills, his canniness in manipulating his own literary and social image, and (not least) his ambiguous class status as a tenant farmer.[91] Both Robert Heron, Burns's first biographer, and James Currie, his first editor, explain his cultural sophistication by reference to the Scottish parochial schools system, which (at least in the Lowlands) resulted in a much more democratic spread of book learning than in England; yet Heron also compares Burns to Omai, the Tahitian "noble savage" brought to London by Captain Cook, and Currie describes Burns as a "bard of nature" whose simplicity or "nakedness" might not have survived a classical education.[92] Jeffrey, writing in the *Edinburgh Review*, is still more obviously ambivalent, insisting at the outset that Burns was neither "uneducated or illiterate," yet proceeding to contrast the genuine simplicity of this "self-taught and illiterate poet" with the "babyish" affectations of the Lake school.[93] Though he clearly finds the gesture of grouping Burns with such "poetical prodigies" as Dermody and Stephen Duck inadequate, even reductive, he also suggests that a "regular education" represses the "vigour and originality" of poetic genius, which thrives in "comparatively rude and unlettered" historical eras and, in modern times, among the "recluse and uninstructed" (249–51). The "rustic and illiterate" poet is a throwback to the golden age, for the "present time is to him what the rude times of old were to the vigorous writers which adorned them" (251–52). Jeffrey's estimate of Burns remains profoundly, and instructively, divided throughout. He claims Burns as evidence of an "enlightened" lower-class culture, yet he cannot resist the image of an inspired, illiterate bard reincarnating a more primitive culture in all its rude vigor. A liberal faith in progress through institutions is undercut by a nostalgic theory of cultural decline which finds a counterpart, though Jeffrey would be hard-pressed to admit it, in Wordsworth's theory of poetic diction produced in defense of *Lyrical Ballads*. In fact, Wordsworth's implicit equation between the pristine language of the "earliest Poets of all nations" and that spoken among the "lower ranks of society" finds unexpected echoes in the contemporary reception of plebeian poets (*WP* 1: 160, 116). Southey, for example, considers that once English became "fully formed" in the Elizabethan era, the "mother tongue" of the peasantry became "antiquated"; the peasant poet relies on a pre-modern dialect at once immature and archaic – pristine and decrepit – in comparison with the dominant "language of composition."[94] Taylor, defending Clare's "provincialisms," describes his dialect terms as including some of the "oldest" words in the language: "many of them are extant in the works of our earliest authors; and a still greater number float on the popular voice, preserved only by tradition."[95] The peasant's "traditional" culture is viewed as effectively archaic not only in its oral character and relative lack of civilized sophistication but in the very language, outdated and quaint, that sustains it.

If the lower-class poet was celebrated as an original genius, he or she was by the same token considered primitive and childlike, and therefore all the more in want of ongoing patronage and supervision. At a time when education had come increasingly to define stages of maturity, the "uneducated poet" was by definition aligned with the child; the "rustic" poet in particular was relegated to a quasi-primitive stage of human culture. Blake and Burns stand out for having evaded, in their different ways, the full burden of such a position, and to this day neither is included in studies of peasant or laboring-class verse.[96] But those who remained more or less locked into the contemporary construction of the plebeian poet could find ways of eluding its limitations from within. The careers of Ann Yearsley and John Clare, to cite two signal examples, both attest to the ingenuity of lower-class poetic expression in this era as much as to the constraints of the role each was required to play.

Yearsley's unhappy relationship with Hannah More has recently gained notoriety as a "parable" for feminist literary theory, manifesting as it does how unequal class relations can preempt an apparently natural alliance between women writers.[97] More cultivated the "Milkwoman of Bristol" less as a sister author than as a naive prodigy and educational project, and her sponsorship of Yearsley was, like her management of Sunday Schools, qualified by anxieties regarding class mobility and the desire to manage and contain lower-class subjectivity. In the open letter to Elizabeth Montagu with which she introduced Yearsley's work to the public, More specifies that their joint patronage should neither place Yearsley in a "state of independence" nor "indispose her for the laborious employments of her humble condition."[98] More represents Yearsley as an "untutored" genius whose "wild wood notes," if they ally her to Shakespeare, also define her talent as a freak of nature. Yearsley's ignorance is stressed throughout: she has read almost nothing, has not learned a "single rule of Grammar" and has not so much as "*seen* a Dictionary" (viii). Her style, like the "primitive" and "Oriental" poetry then in vogue, abounds in imagery and metaphor and suffers from redundancy and obscurity (vii–viii). More's Christian sensibility, interestingly, allows her to see Yearsley's lack of a classical education as an advantage: rather than drinking at the Helicon of "Pagan Poesy," she draws on the "true fountain of divine Inspiration" (vi–vii).[99] But Yearsley's necessary reliance on the Bible as a stylistic model also helps underscore the "Oriental" character of her verse, marking her yet again as "wild" or primitive in relation to the dominant literary culture with which More and Montagu have aligned themselves.

In the volume More helped her publish, *Poems, on Several Occasions* (1785), Yearsley initially represents herself in her patron's terms, and in her self-abasement and gratitude for "enlightenment" she at times evokes missionary tracts like *The Black Prince* and *The Negro Servant*.[100] In the opening poem of her first collection, "Night," addressed to "Stella" (More), Yearsley characterizes her own mind as "Uncouth, unciviliz'd, and rudely rough," a "Chaos" which Stella may "illumine." In her eulogy on Montagu, Yearsley identifies herself with Edwin, the "rude" hero of Beattie's *The Minstrel*, and Montagu with the classically educated "Sage" who instructs him; Yearsley's mind is a den of "native darkness" into which the "dawn of light" symbolizing More and Montagu has begun to gleam ("On Mrs. Montagu"). In another poem to "Stella," Yearsley further develops the conceit of More as a "heavenly" mind, and (twice) characterizes herself as "savage." This last figure returned to haunt Yearsley when she eventually broke with More over her desire, after all, to attain a measure of independence and gain financial control over her book's receipts. In an open letter to her subscribers which supplements (and functions to counteract) the original preface by More, Yearsley writes that in their final interview More "imperiously" called her a "savage"; Yearsley replies that "she descended in calling me a savage, nor would she have had the temerity to do it, had I not given myself that name!"[101]

Yearsley's new willingness here to struggle for control of an unequal discursive situation – to talk back – is manifest throughout her second collection, *Poems, on Various Subjects* (1787), although she continued to depend on patronage. (Her new protector, the Earl of Bristol, seems to have practiced an earlier, more aristocratic form of patronage free of the bourgeois fear of lower-class mobility and obsession with discipline which haunted her relations with More.)[102] This collection opens with an address not to "Stella" but to "Sensibility," source and emblem of Yearsley's poetic powers prior to, and independent of the learned culture represented by More:

> Does Education give the transport keen,
> Or swell your vaunted grief? No, Nature feels
> Most poignant, undefended; hails with me
> The Pow'rs of Sensibility untaught.[103]

In contrast to an epistle in her first collection thanking Robert Raikes for putting the "poor unletter'd tribe" of street children to Sunday School, Yearsley includes an elegy on Chatterton, remembered not as a boy-genius but as a fellow victim of false patronage. In place of epistles celebrating (and further developing) deferential relations with influential Blue-Stockings, in the 1787 collection Yearsley forges a horizontal literary alliance with an "Unlettered Poet", equally "estrang'd" from "classic" knowledge but free, like Yearsley, to express an unfettered Promethean energy:

Dauntless Thought
I eager seiz'd, no formal Rule e'er aw'd;
No Precedent controul'd; no Custom fix'd
My independent spirit; on the wing
She still shall guideless soar, nor shall the Fool,
Wounding her pow'rs, e'er bring her to the ground.

"Thank God I never was sent to school," Blake wrote in the same spirit, "To be Flogd into following the Style of a Fool" (510). Although her 1785 collection is not without its subtleties and its moments of resistance, in it Yearsley's dominant image for herself is the uncouth savage pleading for enlightenment. Fired by "independence," two years later she entirely reconstructs that self-image along lines reminiscent not of "popular" tracts but of Burns and Blake, who also attempted to turn a limited formal education to poetic advantage.

John Clare, introduced to the reading public by his publisher, John Taylor, in the preface to *Poems Descriptive of Rural Life and Scenery* (1820), was similarly constructed as a "Child of Nature" whose "native powers" outweigh an ignorance of grammar and a deficient vocabulary. Taylor also worries, as did Yearsley's patroness, that Clare might be "injured by prosperity" should the public prove *too* generous and remove him "suddenly" from his natural sphere.[104] An obliging early reviewer concurred, recommending a "situation of honourable industry" which would raise Clare above absolute want but not remove the "necessity of daily exertion," such that poetry would remain not his "occupation" but his "solace."[105] The young prodigy must neither leave off his rural labors – or his constructed identity as "peasant poet" would be forfeit – nor dare to compete with formally educated writers by making poetry his profession. Clare's "Sketches" of his life, written for Taylor in 1821, serve more to confirm than to contradict the representations of his early "friends," though the higher level of detail alone in Clare's self-representation works against the stock image of the "rude unlettered" minstrel advanced by patrons and contemporary reviewers. Clare presents himself here as a frail but "stubborn stomachful" laborer, whose hard-won literacy contrasts with the cultural backwardness endemic among the "labouring classes," who "remain as blind in such matters as the Slaves in Africa" (3, 15). His reading of *Paradise Lost*, Thomson's *Seasons*, and little else besides the Bible contrasts with the "wretched" broadside ballads sung by his illiterate father, though he treasures the fairy tales and other "Sixpenny Romances" which he childishly believed constituted the "chief learning and literature of the country" (5). Clare's credulity also helps account for his unquestioning political orthodoxy and "terror" of the very "words 'revolution and reform'" so much in fashion with "infidels," for he once read a "small pamphlet on the Murder of the french King" which early "cured" him from thinking well of radicalism (26).

The "Sketches" can hardly be taken at face value. To begin with, Clare – like Bloomfield – was required to reassure his patrons regarding his political quiescence, particularly when his verses broached criticism of the status quo. One of his principal "friends," Lord Radstock, sent a simple message through an intermediary when detecting "'*Radical* and *ungrateful* sentiments" in a few lines from Clare's first collection: "he must give me unquestionable *proofs*, of being that man I would have him to be – he *must expunge!*"[106] But the autobiographical fragments and other memoranda which Clare continued to jot down after completing his "Sketch" for Taylor tell other stories, including a quite different estimate of "popular" tracts: "I had a tract thrust into my hand tother day by a neighbour containing the dreadful end of an atheist ... this is one of the white lies that are suffered to be hawked about the country to meet the superstitions of the unwary – & though it may make the weak shake their heads & believe it – other will despise the cant."[107] Clare's fragments suggest a keen sense of the precarious discursive position he was made to occupy as an "unlettered" writer, his public identity as naive genius not much more subtle a fabrication than the representations of lower-class sensibility and dialogue retailed in conservative tracts. He resents not only the "pretending scholars" who judge it impossible for Clare to have written his own poems but the "gossiping gentry" who descend on Clare's village to make sure the poet really is a "laboring rustic" – and still prove disappointed by his "vulgar" manners (112, 118).

In his autobiographical poem, *The Village Minstrel* (1821), Clare again plays up the image of the "rhyming peasant" but inflects it in ways which distance it from the idealized picture popularized by Beattie.[108] Clare gives his minstrel the clownish name "Lubin," makes him one of "nature's children" (25), and places him in an atmosphere of village games and pastimes and traditional culture that Clare himself eventually faulted as overly generalized.[109] He begins, however, in an unusual revision of the Promethean conceit, by contrasting the "learned" poet's borrowed Classical authority ("And sunbeams snatch to light the muse's fire") with the rustic who sings "what nature and what truth inspires," working the stock opposition of the "artless" and the artificial to his own purposes. His avowed realist esthetic also licenses Clare to highlight the peasant's bleak economic and social condition, particularly under the rigors of the modern agricultural system, which has encouraged a village economy of local "tyrants" and "parish-slaves" (97). Clare echoes Crabbe in displacing the "mock song" of traditional pastoral verse with a poetry cognizant of rural pain and hardship (26). But he also took issue with the bleakness of Crabbe's allegedly "real picture of the poor," which lacks the generosity and fellow-feeling of Bloom-field's vision: "Crabbe writes about the peasantry as much like the Magistrate as the Poet. He is determined to show you their worst side; and, as to their simple pleasures and pastoral feelings, he knows little or nothing about them compared to the other, who not only lived amongst them, but felt and shared the pastoral pleasures with the peasantry of whom he sung" (*JCL*, 302). Clare's depictions of village sports, however, are neither quaint nor prettified; his villagers chase larded pigs with "monstrous" glee, his wrestlers "thrust and kick with hard revengeful toe" (84–85).[110] Indeed, Clare's cel-ebration of traditional tales and ballads contrasts markedly with the sentimental tribute of Wordsworth in representing them not as quasi-natural products of the soil, but as a means for local communities to preserve their collective memories over time:

> And thousands such the village keeps alive:
> Beings that people superstitious earth,
> That e'er in rural manners will survive
> As long as wild rusticity has birth
> To spread their wonders round the cottage-hearth.   (10)

For Clare, folklore is still largely oral and communal, and though his evocations of it may be partly tailored to a sentimental vogue for the "traditionary," his own relation to popular culture is much more direct.[111]

Yearsley and Clare attempted to wrest control of their own literary images from a network of patrons, publishers, and "charitable" readers; each produced complex, sophisticated poetic and auto-biographical works predicated on this very set of tensions. In

Southey's reading of "uneducated poets," however, literary sophistication can only mean poetic decline, an "almost inevitable" process instanced by the careers of Stephen Duck and James Woodhouse: "they began by expressing their own thoughts and feelings, in their own language; all which, owing to their stations in life, had a certain charm of freshness as well as truth; but that attraction passes away when they begin to form their style upon some approved model" (118–19). The "charm" of lower-class poetry depends, like the new culture of childhood, on its artlessness. Southey's analysis serves to bracket off the lower-class poet in a separate and decidedly inferior literary realm. By labelling these poets "uneducated" rather than "self-educated," Southey implies that, by definition, their works gain their facility from native wit rather than self-culture and their interest from novelty and reportage rather than from art. Clare himself, after reading extracts from the *Lives* in the *Quarterly Review*, took exception to Southey's low estimation of working-class poets, his "sneering" remarks on the progress of popular knowledge, his classification of poets by reference to their "humble situation in life," and his failure to recognize that education "aids very little in bringing forth that which is poetry," concluding that the review "exceeds all the twaddle I ever met with" (*JCL*, 538).

Just as his style should not rise above a certain level, Southey's uneducated poet may properly be "raised from poverty" (121) but too much independence can prove fatal. Duck, who becomes a parish priest, goes mad and drowns himself; Yearsley, who uses the funds wrested from More to open a circulating library, fails to prosper and allegedly dies insane as well. Woodhouse, on the other hand, more safely enjoys the lasting patronage of a "generous friend" (120). Southey is less troubled by the spectacle of lower-class mobility than More, and can make exceptions for poets he regards as especially talented: Henry Kirke White, the butcher's son sent to Cambridge by his patrons and whose *Remains* Southey edited, or Bloomfield, too "worthy" a poet to be grouped among the uneducated (163). And yet John Jones earns Southey's protection precisely because he demonstrates the Laureate's belief that a properly guided and limited education will render the lower-classes more contented with their stations and less supportive of organized reform (12). Jones's "innocent" pursuit of poetry suggests the "beneficial direction" which might be given to the "March of Intellect" – code for the efforts of the Brougham set – by "those who are not for beating it to the tune of *ça ira*" (165, 167).

The two major journals which noticed Southey's *Lives* responded in overtly politicized terms. The *Edinburgh Review* took issue, as had Clare, with Southey's "sarcastic" allusions to popular education; the reviewer, T. H. Lister, interpreted the volume as a veiled attack on the spread of "*useful*" knowledge among the poor. Apparently for Southey, "it is better either to keep them ignorant, or to give them just so much information as will encourage a development of the imaginative or poetical part of their natures, without awakening them, more than can be helped, to any exercise of their reasoning powers."[112] In its support of Brougham and the SDUK the *Edinburgh Review* endorsed a utilitarian view of education much too uncritically, but this analysis is a remarkably canny one, and could apply equally to the Lake poets' "defense" of fairy tales and religious education at the expense of rationalist pedagogy and enterprises like the Mechanics' Institutes and the London University. Lister also takes a stand against the last vestiges of literary patronage, dismissing Southey's selection of poets as a group of "*literary mendicants*" whose verse could not have survived the rigors of the marketplace unaided. Southey would revive the "humble servility" of the patronage system in reaction to the increasingly "independent" spirit of the present age. That the marketplace is structurally biassed against the working-class writer, or that cultural institutions like the *Edinburgh Review* itself calculate literary value according to interested standards, does not occur to Lister, who appeals to "experience" in concluding that "persons in humble life and of defective education" do not make good poets.[113]

John Gibson Lockhart's long notice in the *Quarterly Review* took, not surprisingly, the opposite stance, praising Southey's act of critical condescension for the "moral lesson" it provided in how literary pursuits could facilitate working-class contentment. Unlike the lower-class autobiographers excoriated by the same journal a few years earlier, the plebeian "imitators" of the "great poets who have ennobled our language" remain at a safe second remove from the dominant idiom and attest to a wholesome taste for imaginative literature among the "humbler classes of society." The new reading public will never be contented with the crude, painfully dull volumes of "*Useful Knowledge*" vended by the self-appointed schoolmasters of the day. The most "serviceable" – and the most acceptable –

literature for working people "will ever be that which tends to elevate and humanize the heart, through its appeals to the imagination."[114] Lockhart's remarks not only locate (again) the weakest aspect of the SDUK program – its narrowly instrumental view of knowledge – but also stake out a new locus for the ideological struggles over education and mass literacy. Although often raised in connection with political fears, and cynically exploited to screen the demand for child labor, questions of religious orthodoxy had fueled much of the debate on public education throughout the Romantic era and contributed to the downfall of one legislative effort after another. The stalemate between supporters of the established church, religious dissenters, and secularizers would not be officially resolved until 1870. Imaginative literature, however, had already begun to emerge as an alternative to religious doctrine for the work of sublimating or "humanizing" the heart. It was a work that Romantic writing was prepared to take up.

CHAPTER 6

Epilogue: Romanticism and the idea of literature

In its 1825 attack on Brougham and the SDUK, *Blackwood's* had staked out the ideological ground on which Southey would promote and the *Quarterly Review* defend the provision of imaginative literature for the "humbler classes." Arguing that laborers are already possessed of a good deal of useful knowledge, not to be confused with book learning, the reviewer for *Blackwood's* finds instead "moral education" wanting among the working classes, a study which should precede useful or merely "professional" knowledge and which Brougham's proposals sadly lack.[1] He particularly recommends the reading of novels, valued for their ability to "implant good feelings" while beguiling the reader with "fascinating" narratives. Much as the novel had been rehabilitated as a moral form appropriate for young middle-class women, it is now singled out for another group innocent of Classical learning and lacking in direct "knowledge of the principles... habits, and character of good society." The reviewer means to endorse only, of course, those "good novels" – chosen by the "better classes" who must wield vigilant control over their dissemination – designed to make readers "intelligent, well-principled, moral, and respectable" (548, 550–51). The rival program of the "Fox and Bentham schools" is calculated to "dissolve the bonds between the poor and the rich" and will render working men "slaves of the worst kind of faction" (549); the remedy is sought in the best kind of fiction.

By the end of the Romantic era, literature – previously considered "everything that is printed in a book" – was becoming redefined in terms of certain kinds of fictive or imaginative writing, specifically those which seemed to speak, through "affections of pleasure and sympathy," to the "general and common interest of man" (*DQW* 11: 53–54). It is now commonplace to set the emergence of literature in its modern sense – what De Quincey calls the "literature of *power*"

– within the "basic assumptions" of Romanticism.[2] These would include the heightened prestige of the imagination, such values as originality, spontaneity, and sympathy, the autonomy (and social detachment) of the artist, and the transcendence or universality of the esthetic vision and the "creative" writing which gives it form. Less often remarked, though, is how this seemingly rarefied and ideal conception of literature was forged, over many decades of educational experimentation and debate, within institutions and discourses aimed at the disciplining of socially subordinate populations.[3] Indeed, when the development of Literature from the "margins of power and status" is noted, it is generally only with one or another marginal group in mind. Some historians of the "rise of English," for example, emphasize the early teaching of rhetoric and *belle-lettres* in the Dissenting Academies and at the Scottish universities in the later eighteenth century; others concentrate on the first professorship in English literature and history at the London University, founded in 1828 by Brougham and his Utilitarian allies for the education of such disenfranchised middle-class groups as Catholics, Jews, and Protestant Dissenters.[4] Nancy Armstrong traces the central role of the "British classics" in the modern educational curriculum to the development of a canon of vernacular imaginative works in Romantic-era conduct books aimed at young women, whereas Guari Viswanathan locates the development of "English literature as a subject of study" in colonial India during the early nineteenth century.[5] All of these accounts are valuable, but none of them on its own proves adequate to accommodate the dense historical matrix within which the modern study of English literature was gradually constituted. What each loses by its partiality is a sense of the relatedness of the multiple projects for educating, civilizing, or humanizing variously subordinated groups within the compass of late eighteenth- and early nineteenth-century British society: children, women, laborers, and colonized peoples of the expanding empire.

It would be both oversimplifying and naive, however, to consider these projects, and the institutions and pedagogies which they gave rise to, as homologous in their methods and aims.[6] Rather, what links these diverse enterprises is a common acceptance of literacy as the field within which to manage subjected groups and a convergence, from quite different starting points, toward a select (but neither common nor fixed) canon of fictional works, which would perform

their educative function as humanely and with as little overt
didacticism as possible. Fairy tales and other "innocent" works for
children, novels for women and the "humbler classes," reprints of
English "classics" for lower-class readers and Bengali clerks: all of
these became valued as forms which promoted personal discipline
and social harmony not through prescriptive maxims or coded
appeals to narrowly defined "interests," but through awakening a
common, essential human selfhood, conveying a sense of an ideal
mental community to which all readers might belong. Literature
could best, perhaps could alone perform this function because – as
Coleridge claimed of poetry broadly defined to take in "high"
fictional forms generally – it brought the "whole soul of man into
activity," fusing the particular and the general, the individual and
the representative, the local and the universal through the "synthetic
and magical" power of imagination (*CBL* 2: 15–16). The poet, for
Wordsworth, has become the "rock of defense for human nature,"
bearing "relationship and love" with him literally "everywhere."
"In spite of difference of soil and climate, of language and manners,
of laws and customs, in spite of things silently gone out of mind and
things violently destroyed, the Poet binds together by passion and
knowledge the vast empire of human society, as it is spread over the
whole earth, and over all time" (*WP* 1: 141).

In Book IX of *The Excursion*, as the culmination of the Wanderer's
call for a national system of parochial schools, Wordsworth envisions
British cultural forms binding together a more worldly empire: the
"universal" spread of English "civil arts" begins with the humbler
but necessary work of "unambitious schools" bringing a common
culture first to England's own children (9.386–95). *The Prelude* also
concludes with a pedagogical imperative, this one directed not to
British legislators but to Wordsworth himself and to Coleridge as
fellow laborers in the epic task of humanizing society through poetry.
"What we have loved / Others will love, and we will teach them
how" (1850 XIV.448–49).[7] The function of poetry, for Wordsworth,
is not didactic yet is fundamentally pedagogical. "Every great Poet
is a Teacher," he wrote to Sir George Beaumont in 1808: "I wish
either to be considered as a Teacher, or as nothing" (*WLM* 1: 195).
Didactic poetry could not, in fact, perform the educative function
which Wordsworth wished his own writing to exemplify. Rather than
conveying or embodying one sort of doctrine or another, poetry
rightly performs its work of "educing" through the very process of its

reception, bringing the reader's imagination into responsive activity and thus stimulating, fostering, and refining it.[8] But much as English culture's imperial reach is enabled only by the prior work of "unambitious schools," the humanizing reception of Wordsworth's own verse depends on its dissemination through texts, anthologies, reading groups, and schools. As an index to how Romantic writing itself became central to the modern institution of literature which it helped effect, I want to look briefly at some of the channels through which Wordsworth's poetry passed on its way to becoming canonical: a set of paths that, once more, converge from the margins toward the center.

It may be surprising to learn, for example, that half a century before Wordsworth had been endorsed as an English "classic" by Matthew Arnold, a large selection of his poetry had been edited "Chiefly for the Use of Schools and Young Persons" by a schoolmaster named Joseph Hine in 1831.[9] This publication marked the first time that Wordsworth, who was almost obsessively concerned with the packaging and distribution of his works, authorized anyone else to select and oversee an edition of his poems. Wordsworth's qualms over editorial control gave way not simply to Hine's enthusiasm and dedication as a pedagogue (Wordsworth had visited Hine's school in Brixton and good-naturedly assisted the boys in explicating the "Westminster Bridge" sonnet), but to the promise of seeing his poems circulated, as Hine wrote, among "every private family, and every school in this and other countries where the English language, in its simplicity, force, purity, and elegance, is culti-vated."[10] The poet's confidence seems to have been justified: by the time Arnold would claim to rescue Wordsworth's reputation through his own judicious selection, Wordsworth had become one of the two poets (the other is Shakespeare) most widely and fully represented in British school anthologies.[11] The "simplicity" and deep sympathy with "all parts of God's creation" that in Hine's judgment rendered Wordsworth's poetry so eminently appropriate for young people made it seem ideal reading for self-educated adults as well. In 1832 Charles Knight introduced the lower-class readers of *The Penny Magazine* to poetry with a reprinting of Wordsworth's "To a Daisy," noting that "such images every body may enjoy, and may gradually learn to associate the commonest appearances of nature with a high moral feeling" (1 [1832]: 15). Knight published four more lyrics by Wordsworth in the inaugural

volume, along with poems by Cowper, Burns, Coleridge, Byron, and
Southey.

In 1826 Felicia Hemans, in her address "To the Author of the
Excursion and the Lyrical Ballads" in the *Literary Magazine*, had lent
her growing cultural authority to an endorsement of Wordsworth's
verse for domestic consumption by children and women especially:

> Or by some hearth where happy faces meet,
> When night hath hush'd the woods with all their birds,
> There, from some gentle voice, that lay were sweet
> As antique music, link'd with household words;
> While in pleased murmurs woman's lip might move,
> And the raised eye of childhood shine in love.

Hemans was particularly well-regarded in America, and her tribute
to Wordsworth may have had its effect on Eliza Farrar, who included
Wordsworth (along with Cowper, Campbell, Burns, and Southey)
among the "great poets" with whom young women should "become
intimately acquainted" in her chapter on "Mental Culture" in *The
Young Lady's Friend*, published a decade later in Boston.[12] The next
year (1837) saw the publication of a Boston edition of Wordsworth's
poems in a first printing of 20,000 copies, prompting him to remark
that an "Author in the English Language is becoming a great Power
for good or evil – if he writes with spirit."[13] By the 1850s Wordsworth
was being taught in mission schools in India, in an anthology that
also included selected poems by Southey, Campbell, and James
Montgomery.[14] In 1861, still two decades prior to Arnold's selected
edition, Wordsworth was made widely available to middle-class
English readers through Francis Palgrave's hugely successful *Golden
Treasury of the Best Songs and Lyrical Poems in the English Language*;
Wordsworth's poetry so dominated its fourth and last section (the
nineteenth century) that Palgrave dubbed it the "Book" of Wordsworth. In the preface Palgrave reasserts the vision in *The Excursion* of
an English imperial culture by claiming his volume will be read
"wherever the Poets of England are honoured, wherever the
dominant language of the world is spoken."[15]

The "rise" of Wordsworth's reputation is more often gauged
through examining a series of influential comments by prominent
cultural figures like Coleridge, Jeffrey, Hazlitt, J. S. Mill, Arnold,
and Pater, perhaps with reference to the publication of collected
editions and other monumental events (such as Wordsworth's
assumption of the Laureateship upon Southey's death in 1843). By

sketching out a quite different pattern of reception, I want not only to suggest an alternative way of thinking about poetic reputation. I also mean to underscore that the early dissemination of Wordsworth's poetry remained strikingly true to his own sense of how an English poet becomes a "great Power": less by means of influential reviews, Oxford lectures, and authoritative prefaces than through massive printings, publication in popular magazines and anthologies, circulation among the colonial and post-colonial English-speaking nations, and diligent study by children and young women in schools and private homes. Wordsworth was as acutely aware as anyone of how a society which increasingly relied on literacy and print for its cohesion and reproduction offered unprecedented opportunities to the author who wrote with "spirit"; and how, moreover, those opportunities had been vastly expanded through the now global reach of the English language. The poet's role was now to help hold an extended, fragmenting, increasingly far-flung social group together through creating a "common 'human' discourse" that could cut across class, age, profession, gender, geo-political and ideological lines, acknowledging the force of those divisions even in the act of disavowing them, while attempting to disarm their force through the greater power of his own creative and sympathetic imagination.[16]

By the time of Arnold and J. S. Mill, the "Romantic" idea of literature was becoming ascendant, valued precisely for the broadly social function envisioned for it not only by Wordsworth, Coleridge, and others destined for canonical status, but also by Romantic-era writers, editors, and anthologists more directly concerned with emergent reading publics – Hemans, Knight, Lockhart, Hine, and many whose names have been forgotten. It is significant that both Arnold and Mill themselves, in the course of helping establish a primary role for literary studies in middle-class education, kept lower-class readerships very much in view. In his preface to an anthology of English verse later reprinted as "The Study of Poetry," Arnold ends by noting the burgeoning "multitudes of a common sort of readers" and with them a mass book industry, warning, however, that only "good literature" will answer to the "instinct of self-preservation in humanity." As literature seizes the leading role in "forming" and "sustaining" its growing public, that is, its dissemination across class lines will become necessary for the very survival of modern society.[17] Mill, whose education (supervised by James Mill and Bentham) had been the rationalist dream of a "nursery of genius" come true, famously broke with his Utilitarian upbringing to acknowledge the power, and necessity, of the "internal culture of the individual," a "cultivation of the feelings" by means of the "imaginative arts," which could heal class-division as well as self-division. It was the reading of Wordsworth's poems that both "taught" Mill this lesson and that best illustrated it: "They seemed to be the very culture of the feelings, which I was in quest of. In them I seemed to draw from a source of inward joy, of sympathetic and imaginative pleasure, which could be shared in by all human beings."[18]

It is because Literature was constituted as a socializing and socially unifying force, positioned beyond politics (and for that very reason considered politically efficacious) that debates on the literary canon, on how literary works should be studied and taught, and on the value and function of "great books" so readily become as heated and as conspicuously ideological as they have in recent years. But one should not conclude from this that the reading and teaching of canonical literary works will necessarily serve the hegemonic interests of a dominant group or that, even in cases where literary works are clearly being asked to perform such a function, they will do so readily and predictably. As every teacher of literature well knows, the uses to which a fictional work may be put by a given reader (or group of readers) cannot be determined in advance or controlled with any great rigor.[19] They remain open to oppositional as well as to hegemonic readings, and one cannot in any case always be certain which is which. When Edmund Gosse in *Father and Son* attests to how the "romantic classics" – Campbell, Burns, Keats, Byron – helped him overcome a cloistered religious upbringing as devoid of fiction and "sympathetic imagination" as Mill's utilitarian one had been, a critical reader might view him as having simply replaced one set of scriptures with another, equally apolitical (but more socially "distinctive") one.[20] Yet a Christian fundamentalist in sympathy with Gosse's parents – or, alternatively, the disenchanted child of parents like them – might feel that Gosse's reading of imaginative works had proved subversive indeed.

In any case, we may note that the works of the same Romantic poets who impressed Gosse for their esthetic and imaginative qualities had frequently been reprinted in the newspapers and anthologies of the Chartist agitators, who saw in them subversive elements of a more directly political tenor. *The Chartist Circular* from 1839 to 1841, for example, carried a series on "The Politics of Poets" in which Burns, Shelley, Byron, Campbell, and Coleridge all merit praise for signally embodying libertarian ideals in their verse; Wordsworth in particular is acclaimed for the "deeply, essentially, entirely Radical" tendency of his poems and their power to "cheer the heart of the oppressed" and admonish their oppressors.[21] If canonical Romantic poetry has been seen as escapist, disciplinary, and promoting illusory transcendence, it has also been regarded as democratic, empowering, and revolutionary.[22]

Nevertheless, it remains clear that Wordsworth and Coleridge (among other writers who have retrospectively come to define British "Romanticism") not only imagined a hegemonic function for literature, but also helped make it possible, through their esthetic theory and poetic practice, for literature to seem capable of performing such a function. Both poets can be seen as motivated in this regard by a deep-lying anxiety regarding the undirected (or misdirected) spread of written material among multitudes of relatively untrained readers. As early as the "Preface" to *Lyrical Ballads*, Wordsworth decries the "rapid communication of intelligence" (an apparent reference to the growing circulation of newspapers) among urban masses, as well as the "frantic novels" and "idle and extravagant" verse narratives they consume to the neglect of Shakespeare and Milton. Casually adapting a standard figure of contemporary social discourse, that conflating an uneducated domestic populace with the "uncivilized" peoples coming under British dominion, Wordsworth characterizes the result of this promiscuous reading as a "state of almost savage torpor," as though a badly managed literacy will render the urban mob more rather than less primitive (*WP* 1: 128). A little learning is a degenerative as well as dangerous thing. This anxiety resurfaces, as we have seen, throughout Wordsworth's career, in his distaste for the wrong sort of chapbook and tract, in his prescriptions for children's reading, in his support for a national education system marked by discipline and religious orthodoxy, and in his suspicions regarding such institutions as the British and Foreign Schools Society, the Mechanics' Institutes, and the London University.

Coleridge shares almost identical attitudes regarding the dangers of mass literacy ("books are in every hovel") and the various institutions developed to foster, direct, or contain it, as is particularly evident in the two *Lay Sermons* and in his later polemic *On the*

Constitution of Church and State (1829). For Coleridge, only a "clerisy" or "philosophic class" can be properly trusted with the great work of superintending universal education, an education grounded in the Bible and carried out under the aegis of the Established Church (*CLS* 170, 174).[23] By the "clerisy," an intentionally ambiguous term, Coleridge means at once the "learned of all denominations" (the "sages and professors of... all the so called liberal arts and sciences... as well as the Theological") and an institutionalized "permanent learned class" rooted in the Established clergy, which would retain its traditional control over Oxford and Cambridge (the "fountain heads of the humanities") and over parish schools (*CCS* 46, 50). Against this "national clerisy or church" Coleridge opposes the familiar list of suspects: "tract societies" (that is, the SDUK), dissenting "conventicles," Lancasterian schools, "mechanics institutions," and "lecture-bazaars under the absurd name of universities," all tending toward a "despotism of maxims" and an "anarchism of minds" (*CCS* 69, 67). The popular teaching of the clerisy will not, however, consist in the dissemination of particular doctrines but rather in the "essential" moral cultivation that for Wordsworth is the peculiar province of literature: the "harmonious development of those qualities and faculties that characterise our *humanity*," which distinguish us from the "barbarian, the savage, the animal" (*CCS* 42–43, 74). It is envisioned as an education which, precisely because it addresses the "abiding essential interest of the individual" rather than any given political or narrowly religious agenda, will transform a potentially brutish, savage, anarchic populace into "obedient, free, useful, organizable subjects, citizens, and patriots" (*CCS* 45, 54). Training in the proper interpretation of literary and other densely symbolic texts (above all, the Bible) exemplifies such an education, though literature in its post-Romantic sense is not, for Coleridge, at its center. Yet in the "modern humanist academy," with its emphasis on textual interpretation and its "ethos of reading," Coleridge's clerisy finds its nearest realization.[24]

Assessing the role of Romanticism within the recent history of alternative education, Edgar Friedenberg, a canny and somewhat chastened veteran of the American "free school" movement of the 1960s and 1970s, locates in the Romantic "exaltation of the individual" a crucial and enduring heritage. "It is the source of our most fundamental opposition to schooling, and our vigilant opposition to the processes by which schooling systematically alienates pupils from their own experience, and represses, ignores, or re-interprets that experience in terms compatible with conventional social demands." He notes, however, as an important corollary to this enabling precedent, a certain blindness among Romantic critics of education to the manner in which an uncritical individualism has "served to shield the very institutions they attacked." In too simply dichotomizing the individual and the social, they obscure how "individuality itself, awareness of oneself as an individual, is a social construct and a much more imposing construction in societies like our own than in many others," ignoring the extent to which possibilities for autonomous human development are socially defined and delimited in advance, and masking the social inequities (particularly those based on gender) which are built into the specific version of individuality they champion and enshrine.[25]

Friedenberg's is a thoughtful and engagingly ambivalent estimate from which to begin a revaluation of the ongoing Romantic contribution to educational thinking and practice. The celebration and defense of the individual, the peculiar, and the excessive which we rightly associate with canonical Romantic writing has indeed played an urgent, perhaps indispensable role for a long line of irreverent, libertarian assessments of mass education, from *Hard Times* to *Growing Up Absurd*. This tendency within Romanticism contrasts sharply with an undeniable predilection among "progressive" rationalist educators and theorists for mechanisms of social control and for micro-managing the pupil's subjectivity according to normative schemas, as well as a profound unwillingness to leave children unsupervised and at large in the absence of internalized monitory checks and disciplined habits. Even in its most anti-authoritarian manifestations, as in Godwin's *Enquirer* or Owen's New Lanark experiment, a certain and perhaps inevitable elitism and corresponding paternalism inheres within the enlightenment rationalist tradition, which has great difficulty imagining self-determination prior to self-improvement guided by an intellectual vanguard.

That the emancipatory and egalitarian tendencies within Romanticism, which still remain vital, have long been available and valued is evident not only in the importance of Romanticism for a long tradition of critics of institutionalized education, but in the uses which political groups like the Chartists found for Romantic literature as well. There are two serious qualifications to any favorable assessment of the Romantic contribution to prospects for genuinely democratic educational practices, however, in addition to the willed isolation from the social realm which renders Romantic transcendence as problematic as it is powerful. First, one must keep in mind how much the Romantics in fact held in concert with the rationalist educators to whom they are conventionally opposed. Writers in both traditions relied on a progressive model of individual development which could readily lend itself both to regulative programs of "mental improvement" and to an elitism as evident in Coleridge's "clerisy" as in the paternalism of the Edgeworths or Owen or Brougham. Those we retrospectively label Romantic or rationalist, equally helped to promote the "discipline of love" to apparently soften while subtly augmenting pedagogical and parental authority – however disingenuously – and to reconfigure childhood as an "innocent" stage of life, in the interests of at once protecting the child and confining its possibilities.

Second, we may recall how starkly the limitations of the Romantic approach to education become evident in their support – and here one thinks especially of the Lake poets – of various forms of censorship, their sponsorship of the repressive and anti-intellectual Madras system, their reliance on colonialist educational metaphors, their distaste for working-class educational ventures unless rigorously controlled by established interests, their resistance to an equal education for girls.[26] The Romantic "exaltation of the individual" may have signally provided inspiration to a succession of educational skeptics and reformers, but it has readily given way, even in the careers and writings of the Romantic authors most closely associated with the "defense" of children's imaginative freedom, to the very sorts of disciplinarian and elitist practices that critics of modern institutionalized education find most obnoxious. This is one pressing reason for placing canonical Romantic representations of and pronouncements on education within the broader social and historical context from which they are too often abstracted. More generally, if we are to comprehend such issues as compulsory education, universal literacy, the primary socializing function of schooling, even the status of childhood as a period devoted to study and play rather than apprenticeship and labor, we need to recognize through recovering their histories that none of these developments is a "natural" one, and to be reminded – as so much Romantic-era discourse makes evident – that their widespread acceptance initially owed more to the pursuit of social discipline, ideological conformity, and state security than to the democratic and humanistic impulses with which they have since become associated.

Finally, considering the historical context and textual record more fully also yields a number of alternative legacies, which may prove no less valuable to prospects for more humane educational institutions and methods than the Romantic faith in the child's uniqueness and unconstrained imaginative life. A crucial aspect of this larger inheritance, one already well in the process of being reclaimed and reassessed, is the critique of masculinist pedagogies and the demand for educational parity articulated by such Romantic-era feminists as Macaulay, Wollstonecraft, and Hays. A less familiar resource may be located in the attempts of Owen, William Thompson, and others in the early socialist tradition to create self-determined, community-based schools promoting a critical sense of inquiry rather than unquestioned conformity to community ideals in their pupils. The arguments developed by Paine, Priestley, and other English radicals for autonomous schools, supported by the state but independent of state control, might prove worth reconsidering in light of recent calls for the decentralization and large-scale privatization of public schooling, which have tended to provoke shudders rather than constructive debate among proponents of democratic educational reform.

At a time when various manifestations of irrationality – racial bigotry and xenophobia, nationalistic and ethnic chauvinism, religious fanaticism, domestic violence of epidemic proportions – threaten our shared future so palpably, we may wish to look again (however warily) at certain aspects of educational thought in the Enlightenment tradition, such as the discouragement of credulity and superstition in favor of reasoned, critical judgment that so provoked the Wordsworth circle. More could be made in particular of Godwin's cogent articulation of the value of self-motivated learning, his forceful arguments against censorship (which has continued to plague mass education), and his case for maximizing the child's freedom from punishment and coercion without idealizing childhood or wilfully forgetting that children eventually become adults. Much greater attention could be paid as well to the neglected autobiographical records of self-educated workers and activists, in which self-assertion and a communal ethos are characteristically represented as mutually reinforcing rather than opposed impulses.

The "educational legacy" which has recently been sought in the works of the canonical Romantics represents only a fraction of what is available for revaluation from a half century during which so much of what we now take for granted about literacy and education took form.[27] I hope to have established here, in addition to new directions for further critical study, a larger sense of the era's richness and diversity in examples, provocations, and possibilities for reimagining educational change.

Notes

I. CHILDHOOD, EDUCATION, AND POWER

1 Elizabeth Gaskell, *The Works of Mrs. Gaskell*, ed. A. W. Ward, 8 vols. (1906; rpt. New York: AMS Press, 1972), 5: 39, 19. Hereafter cited in the text.

2 See, e.g., Marilyn Butler, *Romantics, Rebels and Reactionaries: English Literature and Its Background 1760–1830* (Oxford University Press, 1981), 1–10, 178–87; James K. Chandler, "Representative Men, Spirits of the Age, and Other Romantic Types," in *Romantic Revolutions: Criticism and Theory*, ed. Kenneth R. Johnston, Gilbert Chaitin, Karen Hanson, and Herbert Marks (Bloomington: Indiana University Press, 1990), 104–32; and David Perkins, *Is Literary History Possible?* (Baltimore: Johns Hopkins University Press, 1992), 85–119.

3 Jerome J. McGann, *The Romantic Ideology: A Critical Investigation* (University of Chicago Press, 1983), 19.

4 Robert Southey, *The Doctor, &c.*, ed. John Wood Warter (London: Longman, 1848), 37.

5 David V. Erdman, *Blake: Prophet Against Empire*, 3rd edn. (Princeton University Press, 1977), 129.

6 William Cobbett, *Rural Rides*, ed. George Woodcock (Harmondsworth: Penguin, 1967), 262, 41.

7 *Don Juan* is cited (by canto and stanza) following volume 5 of *The Complete Poetical Works*, ed. Jerome J. McGann, 7 vols. (Oxford: Clarendon Press, 1980–93).

8 Stuart Curran, *Shelley's Annus Mirabilis: The Maturing of an Epic Vision* (San Marino: Huntington Library, 1975), 25–26.

9 Judith Plotz, "The Perpetual Messiah: Romanticism, Childhood, and the Paradoxes of Human Development," *Regulated Children/Liberated Children: Education in Psychohistorical Perspective*, ed. Barbara Finkelstein (New York: Psychohistory Press, 1979), 66.

10 See Robert Pattison, *The Child Figure in English Literature* (Athens: University of Georgia Press, 1978), 43.

11 William Godwin, *Enquiry Concerning Political Justice and Its Influence on*

Modern Morals and Happiness, ed. Isaac Kramnick (Harmondsworth: Penguin, 1976), 111. Hereafter cited in the text.

12 Mary Wollstonecraft, *Mary* and *The Wrongs of Women*, ed. Gary Kelly (Oxford University Press, 1976), 4.

13 Mitzi Myers, "The Dilemmas of Gender as Double-Voiced Narrative; Or, Maria Edgeworth Mothers the Bildungsroman," *The Idea of the Novel in the Eighteenth Century*, ed. Robert W. Uphaus (East Lansing: Colleagues Press, 1988), 71.

14 Peter Coveney, *The Image of Childhood* (Harmondsworth: Penguin, 1967), 106.

15 Ibid., 33.

16 Phillipe Ariès, *Centuries of Childhood: A Social History of Family Life*, trans. Robert Baldick (New York: Vintage, 1962). For qualifications of Ariès's thesis, see *The History of Childhood*, ed. Lloyd de Mause (New York: Psychohistory Press, 1974); Lawrence Stone, *The Family, Sex and Marriage in England 1500–1800*, abridged edn. (New York: Harper, 1979); Simon Schama, *The Embarrassment of Riches: An Interpretation of Dutch Culture in the Golden Age* (New York: Knopf, 1987), 481–561. For a dissent from the notion that an extended, distinct period of childhood is a relatively modern and socially constructed phenomenon, see Linda A. Pollock, *Forgotten Children: Parent-Child Relations from 1500–1900* (Cambridge University Press, 1983). Shulamith Shahar, in *Childhood in the Middle Ages* (London: Routledge, 1990), takes issue with Ariès's portrait of medieval childhood and, like Pollock, stresses the "biologically determined" elements of childhood without, however, dismissing its "culturally constructed" aspects (1).

17 J. H. Plumb, "The New World of Children in Eighteenth-Century England," *Past and Present* 67 (1975): 64–93.

18 Ariès, *Centuries*, 412; Stone, *Family*, 424; Ivy Pinchbeck and Margaret Hewitt, *Children in English Society*, 2 vols. (London: Routledge and Kegan Paul, 1969–73), 1: 297.

19 The importance of Rousseau, who is oddly marginalized in Ariès's account, is stressed in such studies of childhood as J. H. Van den Berg, *The Changing Nature of Man: Introduction to a Historical Psychology (Metabolica)* (New York: Norton, 1961), 26; George Boas, *The Cult of Childhood* (London: The Warburg Institute, 1966), 31; David Grylls, *Guardians and Angels: Parents and Children in Nineteenth-Century Literature* (London: Faber and Faber, 1978), 18. See also Neil Postman, *The Disappearance of Childhood* (New York: Delacorte Press, 1982), 57–59.

20 Pattison, *Child Figure*, 20; M. J. Tucker, "The Child as Beginning and End: Fifteenth and Sixteenth Century English Childhood," in de Mause, *History of Childhood*, 229–30.

21 Leah Sinanoglou Marcus, *Childhood and Cultural Despair: A Theme and Variations in Seventeenth-Century Literature* (University of Pittsburgh Press, 1978), 3.

22 A. Charles Babenroth, *English Childhood: Wordsworth's Treatment of Childhood in Light of English Poetry from Prior to Crabbe* (New York: Columbia University Press, 1922), 12.

23 Stone, *Family*, 254–55.

24 Pattison, *Child Figure*, 49.

25 I borrow the term "ethnographic" from Patrick Brantliger, who uses it to characterize the British tradition of "patronizing" descriptions of lower-class subjects in both literary and sociological texts, in *Crusoe's Footprints: Cultural Studies in Britain and America* (New York: Routledge, 1990), 45.

26 John Locke, *The Educational Writings of John Locke: A Critical Edition with Introduction and Notes*, ed. James L. Axtell (Cambridge University Press, 1968), 325. Hereafter cited in the text.

27 John Earle, *Microcosmography*, ed. Alfred S. West (Cambridge University Press, 1951), 1.

28 Mary Hays, *Memoirs of Emma Courtney*, ed. Gina Luria, 2 vols. (New York: Garland, 1974), 1: 4–5. Hereafter cited in the text.

29 See Lucy Newlyn, *Coleridge, Wordsworth, and the Language of Allusion* (Oxford: Clarendon Press, 1986), 142.

30 Basil Willey, *The Eighteenth Century Background* (London: Chatto and Windus, 1940), 149.

31 Jean-Jacques Rousseau, *Emile or Education*, trans. Allan Bloom (New York: Basic Books, 1979), 38, 92; hereafter cited in the text.

32 See Boas, *Cult of Childhood*.

33 Robert Bage, *Hermsprong; or, Man as He Is Not*, ed. Peter Faulkner (Oxford University Press, 1985), 170.

34 John Wesley, *The Works of the Rev'd John Wesley*, 10 vols. (New York: J. and J. Harper, 1827), 10: 151–52, 6: 172–73. For a survey of Methodist and Evangelical attitudes toward childhood in this period, see Paul Sangster, *Pity My Simplicity: The Evangelical Revival and the Religious Education of Children 1738–1800* (London: Epworth Press, 1963), 24–39.

35 Hannah More, *Strictures on the Modern System of Female Education*, 6th edn., 2 vols. in one (London: Cadell and Davies, 1799), 1: 64.

36 Isaac Watts, *Divine Songs*, ed. Bennett A. Brockman (New York: Garland, 1978), Songs XIII and XVI (19–20, 23–24).

37 Thomas Walter Laqueur, *Religion and Respectability: Sunday Schools and Working Class Culture 1780–1850* (New Haven: Yale University Press, 1976), 12; my examples of the Wesleys' hymns are taken from Laqueur's account, 11–14.

38 Gray is quoted from *The Poems of Thomas Gray, William Collins, Oliver Goldsmith*, ed. Roger Lonsdale (London: Longman, 1969). For the sentimental tradition in eighteenth-century verse and its relation to Wordsworth, see Babenroth, *English Childhood*.

39 Friedrich von Schiller, *On Naive and Sentimental Poetry and On the Sublime: Two Essays*, trans. Julius A. Elias (New York: Ungar, 1966), 87.

40 My text for Baillie is *The Dramatic and Poetical Works of Joanna Baillie*, 2nd edn. (London: Longman, 1853); for Barbauld, *The Works of Anna Laetitia Barbauld. With a Memoir*, ed. Lucy Aikin, 2 vols. (London: Longman, 1825), hereafter cited in the text.

41 See Babenroth, *English Childhood*, 97–161.

42 Zohar Shavit, *Poetics of Children's Literature* (Athens: University of Georgia Press, 1986), 26.

43 See Pinchbeck and Hewitt, *Children in English Society*, 2: 351–413; esp. 351–53, 391–92, 394–406.

44 For surveys of the childhood theme in Wordsworth's poetry, see: Babenroth, *English Childhood*, 299–396; Mary Moorman, "Wordsworth and His Children," *Bicentenary Wordsworth Studies in Memory of John Alban Finch* (Ithaca: Cornell University Press, 1970), 111–41; and Willard Spiegelman, *Wordsworth's Heroes* (Berkeley: University of California Press, 1985), 50–82.

45 See U. C. Knoepflmacher, "Mutations of the Wordsworthian Child of Nature," *Nature and the Victorian Imagination*, ed. Knoepflmacher and G. B. Tennyson (Berkeley: University of California Press, 1977), 391–425.

46 On the prevalence of death in Wordsworth's poetry of childhood, see Spiegelman's fine account in *Wordsworth's Heroes* (esp. 56–68).

47 Knoepflmacher, "Mutations," 415.

48 Barbara Garlitz, "The Immortality Ode: Its Cultural Progeny," *Studies in English Literature* 6 (1966): 647.

49 Coveney, *Image*, 33; Pattison, *Child Figure*, 65.

50 See the "dialectical" reading of Blake's *Songs* brilliantly developed by Tilottama Rajan in *The Supplement of Reading: Figures of Understanding in Romantic Theory and Practice* (Ithaca: Cornell University Press, 1990), 222–28; Rajan, however, goes on to call this reading into question (228–34).

51 Pattison, *Child Figure*, 67.

52 In his poems on poor and working children, Blake seeks to avoid the distancing and condescension of the ethnographic style by means of an ongoing critique of it: "Pity would be no more, / If we did not make somebody Poor" ("The Human Abstract").

53 Thomas De Quincey, "Suspiria de Profundus," in *Confessions of an English Opium Eater and Other Writings*, ed. Grevel Lindop (Oxford University Press, 1985), 92. Hereafter cited in the text.

54 Letter to Dorothy Wordsworth 13–15 June 1812, in John E. Jordan, *De Quincey to Wordsworth: A Biography of a Relationship* (Berkeley: University of California Press, 1962), 265. Cf. the prurient transcendentalizing of Thomas Campbell's poems on young girls, especially "On Getting Home the Portrait of a Female Child, Six Years Old" and "Lines on My New Child-Sweetheart."

55 E. Michael Thron, "The Significance of Catherine Wordsworth's Death to Thomas De Quincey and William Wordsworth," *Studies in English Literature* 28 (1988): 561–62.

56 Clifford Geertz, "Ideology as a Cultural System," *The Interpretation of Cultures: Selected Essays* (New York: Basic Books, 1973), 218–19.

57 David McClellan, *Ideology* (Minneapolis: University of Minnesota Press, 1986), 2–3. Cf. Terry Eagleton, *Ideology: An Introduction* (London: Verso, 1991), 106–7.

58 For the *ideologues*, education, and the French Revolution, see James K. Chandler, *Wordsworth's Second Nature: A Study of the Poetry and Politics* (University of Chicago Press, 1984), 99–104, 218. See also Emmet Kennedy, *A Philosophe in the Age of Revolution: Destutt de Tracy and the Origins of "Ideology"* (Philadelphia: American Philosophical Society, 1978), esp. 38–97; and R. R. Palmer, *The Improvement of Humanity: Education and the French Revolution* (Princeton University Press, 1985).

59 Antonio Gramsci, *Selections from the Prison Notebooks*, trans. Quintin Hoare and Geoffrey Nowell Smith (New York: International, 1971), 12; Louis Althusser, "Ideology and Ideological State Apparatuses (Notes towards an Investigation)," *Lenin and Philosophy*, trans. Ben Brewster (New York: Monthly Review Press, 1971), 127 (hereafter cited in the text).

60 Pierre Bourdieu, "Cultural Reproduction and Social Reproduction," *Power and Ideology in Education*, ed. Jerome Karabel and A. H. Halsey (New York: Oxford University Press, 1977), 87–88. See also Bourdieu and Jean-Claude Passeron, *Reproduction in Education, Society and Culture*, trans. Richard Nice (London: SAGE, 1977).

61 See Bourdieu, "Cultural Reproduction," Bourdieu and Passeron, *Reproduction*, esp. 71–106, and Bourdieu, *Distinction: A Social Critique of the Judgement of Taste* (Cambridge: Harvard University Press, 1984), esp. 63–168.

62 Henry A. Giroux, *Theory and Resistance in Education: A Pedagogy for the Opposition* (London: Heinemann, 1983), 148.

63 Giroux, *Theory and Resistance*, 86. See also Peter McLaren, "On Ideology and Education: Critical Pedagogy and the Politics of Empowerment," *Social Text* 19/20 (1988): 153–85.

64 Raymond Williams, *Marxism and Literature* (Oxford University Press, 1977), 109.

65 Ibid., 93.

66 McLaren, "On Ideology and Education," 174.

67 Williams, "Base and Superstructure in Marxist Cultural Theory," *Problems in Materialism and Culture: Selected Essays* (London: Verso, 1980), 38–39.

68 Chantal Mouffe, "Hegemony and Ideology in Gramsci," *Gramsci and Marxist Theory*, ed. Mouffe (London: Routledge and Kegan Paul, 1979), 171; Mouffe, "Hegemony and New Political Subjects: Toward a New Concept of Democracy," *Marxism and the Interpretation of Culture*, ed. Cary Nelson and Lawrence Grossberg (Urbana: University of Illinois Press, 1988), 89–90.

69 Cf. Cathy Urwin, "Power Relations and the Emergence of Language,"

in Julian Henriques et al., *Changing the Subject: Psychology, Social Regulation and Subjectivity* (London: Methuen, 1984), 265.

70 Mouffe, "Hegemony and Ideology," 186; Valerie Walkerdine, "On the Regulation of Speaking and Silence: Subjectivity, Class, and Gender in Contemporary Schooling," *Language, Gender and Childhood*, ed. Carolyn Steedman, Cathy Urwin, and Valerie Walkerdine (London: Routledge and Kegan Paul, 1985), 238 (hereafter cited in the text).

71 Frederic Jameson, *The Political Unconscious: Narrative as a Socially Symbolic Act* (Ithaca: Cornell University Press, 1981), 152–53, 64.

72 Walkerdine, "Developmental Psychology and the Child-Centred Pedagogy: The Insertion of Piaget into Early Education," in Henriques et al., *Changing the Subject*, 165, 155. I follow Walkerdine and her co-authors in supplementing reproduction theories of education such as Althusser's with the work of Foucault, which attends more closely to the "specific historical circumstances" under which disciplinary institutions and technologies have been produced, does not need to posit a "monolithic" state power to account for their collaboration, and allows for a range of ideological motivations (including liberal and radical ones) behind the rise of "techniques of social regulation" (107–8, 165). I also share their awareness of the limitations of Foucault's work, particularly what Edward W. Said has called its "curiously passive" view of "how and why power is gained, used, and held onto," its lack of interest in the "ascertainable changes stemming from who holds power and who dominates whom" (*The World, the Text, and the Critic* [Cambridge: Harvard University Press, 1983], 221).

73 It should be noted, however, that a number of historians locate the last two decades of the eighteenth century in England as the beginning of a period of profound and accelerated social change, brought on by the "dual revolution," industrial (at first primarily in England) and political (at first primarily in France). See (to name only a few salient examples) E. J. Hobsbawm, *The Age of Revolution 1789–1848* (New York: New American Library, 1962), esp. 22–73; Asa Briggs, *The Making of Modern England 1783–1867: The Age of Improvement* (1959; New York: Harper and Row, 1965); J. H. Plumb, *England in the Eighteenth Century* (1950; Baltimore: Penguin, 1963), esp. 143–62; Roy Porter, *English Society in the Eighteenth Century* (Harmondsworth: Penguin, 1982), esp. 329–67; E. P. Thompson, *The Making of the English Working Class* (1963; New York: Vintage, 1966); Harold Perkin, *The Origin of Modern English Society 1780–1880* (London: Routledge and Kegan Paul, 1969); Leonore Davidoff and Catherine Hall, *Family Fortunes: Men and Women of the English Middle Class, 1780–1850* (University of Chicago Press, 1987).

74 Jameson, *Political Unconscious*, 96; Williams, *Marxism and Literature*, 114.

75 Walkerdine, "Developmental Psychology," 165.

76 These positions are represented by, respectively, Geoffrey Summerfield, *Fantasy and Reason: Children's Literature in the Eighteenth Century* (Athens:

University of Georgia Press, 1984), and Mitzi Myers, "Impeccable Governesses, Rational Dames, and Moral Mothers: Mary Wollstone-craft and the Female Tradition in Georgian Children's Books," *Children's Literature* 14 (1986): 31–59.

77 Ariel Dorfman, *The Empire's Old Clothes: What the Lone Ranger, Babar, and Other Innocent Heroes Do to Our Minds* (New York: Pantheon, 1983), 85.

78 Terry Eagleton, *Criticism and Ideology: A Study in Marxist Literary Theory* (1976; rpt. London: Verso, 1978), 56–58.

79 V. N. Volosinov, "Discourse in Life and Discourse in Art (Concerning Sociological Poetics," *Freudianism: A Critical Sketch*, trans. I. R. Titunik, ed. Titunik and Neal H. Bruss (Bloomington: Indiana University Press, 1987), 105.

80 Mikhail Bakhtin, *Problems of Dostoevsky's Poetics*, ed. and trans. Caryl Emerson (Minneapolis: University of Minnesota Press, 1984), 181, 202.

81 Mouffe, "Hegemony and New Political Subjects," 90.

82 Williams, "Base and Superstructure," 45.

83 Williams, *Marxism and Literature*, 134.

84 Coleridge, *The Friend*, 2 vols., ed. Barbara E. Rooke (Princeton University Press, 1969) 2: 73.

85 See Alan Richardson, "Wordsworth at the Crossroads: 'Spots of Time' in the 'Two-Part Prelude,'" *The Wordsworth Circle* 19 (1988): 15–20, and the previous psychoanalytic studies of *The Prelude* cited therein.

86 Laurence Goldstein, *Ruins and Empire: The Evolution of a Theme in Augustan and Romantic Literature* (University of Pittsburgh Press, 1977), 187.

87 Ronald Paulson, *Representations of Revolution (1789–1820)* (New Haven: Yale University Press, 1983), 77–78, 89.

88 Ibid., 101.

89 More, *Strictures* 1: 146–47.

90 Hannah More, *Coelebs in Search of a Wife* (New York: Derby and Jackson, 1857), 215–16. Hereafter cited in the text.

91 Graves's lyric can be found in *The New Oxford Book of Eighteenth Century Verse*, ed. Roger Lonsdale (Oxford University Press, 1984), 791–92. Although it is unclear whether Graves or More knew of it, the radical Thomas Spence had in fact published a pamphlet entitled *The Rights of Infants* in 1797; it is concerned, however, not with swaddling or parental despotism, but with arguing for a redistribution of land rents on the basis of natural rights. *Pig's Meat: The Selected Writings of Thomas Spence, Radical and Pioneer Land Reformer*, ed. G. I. Gallop (Nottingham: Spokesman, 1982), 114–126.

92 Chandler, *Wordsworth's Second Nature*, 216.

93 Ibid., 109–12; on the "monster birth" as evocative of the French Revolution and, in turn, the "dissociated" character of Enlightenment thought, cf. Paulson, *Representations*, 256.

94 See, e.g., William Walsh, *The Use of Imagination: Educational Thought and*

the *Literary Mind* (London: Chatto and Windus, 1959), 30–51; and Thomas McFarland, *Originality and Imagination* (Baltimore: Johns Hopkins University Press), 1985, 60–89.

95 James Janeway, *A Token for Children*, ed. Robert Miner (New York: Garland, 1977), introductory notice "To all Parents, School-masters and School-Mistresses" [unpaginated]; hereafter cited (by Part and page number) in the text.

96 In Charles Lamb's poem "Dialogue Between a Mother and Child," the child scolds his mother (who plans to remarry) in tones reminiscent of Janeway: "O Lady, lay your costly robes aside, / No longer may you glory in your pride."

97 C. Kegan Paul, *William Godwin: His Friends and Contemporaries*, 2 vols. (Boston: Roberts Brothers, 1876) 1: 7–8.

98 Laqueur, *Religion and Respectability*, 15, 10.

99 Cf. Marjorie Levinson, *Wordsworth's Great Period Poems: Four Essays* (Cambridge University Press, 1986), 96–7. Paul Magnuson notes that the "supernatural" treatment of childhood is minimal in the sections of the "Immortality" ode composed in 1802, becoming much more evident in 1804; see *Coleridge and Wordsworth: A Lyrical Dialogue* (Princeton University Press, 1988), 279–80.

100 Marcus, *Childhood and Cultural Despair*, 246.

2. SCHOOL TIME

1 For discussions of the educational writings of Locke and Rousseau within the context of their political theories, see Henry J. Parkinson, *Since Socrates: Studies in the History of Educational Thought* (New York: Longman, 1980), 111–145; and Frances Ferguson, "Reading Morals: Locke and Rousseau on Education and Inequality," *Representations* 6 (1984): 66–84.

2 Raymond Williams, *The Long Revolution: An Analysis of the Democratic, Industrial, and Cultural Changes Transforming Our Society* (New York: Columbia University Press, 1961), 158.

3 Frederic Jameson, "The Realist Floor-Plan," in *On Signs*, ed. Marshall Blonsky (Baltimore: Johns Hopkins University Press, 1985), 373–74.

4 Plumb, *England*, 119; Richard D. Altick, *The English Common Reader: A Social History of the Mass Reading Public, 1800–1900* (University of Chicago Press, 1957), 70, 74–5; Briggs, *Making of Modern England*, 174. Raymond Williams gives a much higher figure ("as many as one and a half million") for the inexpensive edition of Paine's tract (*Long Revolution*, 163).

5 Lawrence Stone, "Literacy and Education in England 1640–1900," *Past and Present* 42 (1969): 109–112; R. S. Schofield, "Dimensions of Illiteracy, 1750–1850," *Explorations in Economic History* 10 (1972): 437–54. See also Thomas W. Laqueur, "Toward a Cultural Ecology of Literacy in England, 1600–1850," *Literacy in Historical Perspective*, ed.

Daniel P. Resnick (Washington: Library of Congress, 1983), 43–57; and Harvey J. Graff, *The Legacies of Literacy: Continuities and Contradictions in Western Culture and Society* (Bloomington: Indiana University Press, 1987), 230–48, 313–40.

6 Richard S. Tompson, *Classics or Charity? The Dilemma of the Eighteenth Century Grammar School* (University of Manchester Press, 1971), 1–2; M. G. Jones, *The Charity School Movement: A Study of Eighteenth Century Puritanism in Action* (1938; Hamden: Archon, 1964), 27; see also Chris Cook and John Stevenson, *British Historical Facts 1760–1830* (London: MacMillan, 1980), 194. W. O. B. Allen and Edmund McClure give a considerably larger figure (7,125) for the number of Sunday Schools in 1803: see *Two Hundred Years: The History of the Society for Promoting Christian Knowledge 1698–1898* (1898; New York: Burt Franklin, 1970), 181.

7 See John William Adamson, *A Short History of Education* (Cambridge University Press, 1922), 261; and H. C. Barnard, *A History of English Education From 1760*, 2nd edn. (University of London Press, 1961), 66.

8 Adamson, *Short History*, 265. The number of educational institutions had grown considerably earlier in the period as well; in addition to the Sunday School movement (which began in earnest in the 1780s), the rival monitorial systems (Bell's and Lancaster's), which together accounted for 1,520 schools and 200,000 students, had been established in the first decade of the nineteenth century. See Barnard, *History of English Education*, 66.

9 Altick, *English Common Reader*, 39; Laqueur, *Religion and Respectability*, 193.

10 Thomas Love Peacock, *Nightmare Abbey; Crotchet Castle*, ed. Raymond Wright (Harmondsworth: Penguin, 1969), 103.

11 Cobbett, *Rural Rides*, 75, 42.

12 Thompson, *Making*, 375.

13 E. P. Thompson characterizes the "real structure of power in England as the Industrial Revolution advanced" as the "complex interpenetration of aristocratic privilege and commercial and industrial wealth" (*Making*, 763). Eagleton (citing Gramsci) describes the middle class as economically determinant and the aristocracy as politically dominant in nineteenth-century Britain – the "economically determinant middle class largely 'delegated' its political power to the aristocracy," and the "resultant ruling ideology' should be considered a "hybrid of elements drawn from the experience of *both* classes" (*Ideology*, 123).

14 This is the principal argument of Laqueur's study, *Religion and Respectability*.

15 Aries, *Centuries of Childhood*, 313.

16 Stone, *Family, Sex and Marriage*, 276–77.

17 M. M. Sherwood, *The Life of Mrs Sherwood (Chiefly Autobiographical)*, ed. Sophia Kelly (London: Darton, 1857), 36–37.

18 Stone, *Family*, 279.

19 See G. H. Bantock, *Studies in the History of Educational Theory*, 2 vols. (London: Allen and Unwin, 1980), 1: 245–46.
20 Parkinson, *Since Socrates*, 137.
21 Elizabeth Gaskell, writing of the early nineteenth-century educations of the Brontës and of her own aunt, notes that the "ideas of Rousseau and Mr Day on education had filtered down through many classes, and spread themselves widely out." *The Life of Charlotte Brontë*, ed. Alan Shelston (Harmondsworth: Penguin, 1975), 87.
22 Thomas Day, *The History of Sandford and Merton*, ed. Isaac Kramnick, 3 vols. (New York: Garland, 1977) 3: 89. Hereafter cited in the text. But note that the tutor, Mr. Barlow, assures Mr. Merton early on that he considers "a difference of conditions and an inequality of fortune" necessary "in the present state of things" (1: 23).
23 Parkinson, *Since Socrates*, 126, 145; Joel Morkan, "Structure and Meaning in *The Prelude*, Book v," *PMLA* 87 (1972): 250.
24 Maria and Richard Lovell Edgeworth, *Essays on Practical Education*, 3rd edn., 2 vols. (London: J. Johnson, 1811), 1: 11. Hereafter cited parenthetically within the text.
25 David V. Erdman, "Coleridge, Wordsworth, and the Wedgwood Fund," *Bulletin of the New York Public Library* 60 (1956): 489–91.
26 Joseph Priestley, *Miscellaneous Observations Relating to Education* (1796; Millwood: Kraus Reprint, 1977), 12.
27 Thomas Wedgwood, letter to William Godwin, 31 July 1797; included by Erdman in "Coleridge, Wordsworth, and the Wedgwood Fund": 430–33. Erdman argues that "Wordsworth's answer was, ultimately, the whole detailed statement of *The Prelude*" (495).
28 *Practical Education* (London: J. Johnson, 1798), 125. Hereafter cited in the text as "1798"; all other citations are to the third edition of 1811, which fundamentally agrees with the second edition of 1801.
29 Henry Homes, Lord Kames, *Loose Hints Upon Education, Chiefly Concerning the Culture of the Heart*, 2nd edn. (Edinburgh: John Bell, 1782), 157; Catherine Macaulay, *Letters on Education, With Observations on Religious and Metaphysical Subjects*, ed. Gina Luria (New York: Garland, 1974), 72. See also Mitzi Myers, "'Servants as They are Now Educated': Women Writers and Georgian Pedagogy," *Essays in Literature* 16 (1989): 51–69.
30 See Marilyn Butler, *Maria Edgeworth*, 32–35.
31 Edmund Burke, *A Philosophical Enquiry into the Origin of Our Ideas of the Sublime and Beautiful*, ed. James T. Boulton (1958; University of Notre Dame Press, 1968), 63.
32 Burke, *Enquiry*, 62.
33 See R. L. Edgeworth, *Poetry Explained for the Use of Young People* (London: J. Johnson, 1802), and R. L. and Maria Edgeworth, *Readings on Poetry*, 2nd edn. (London: R. Hunter, 1816). In this the Edgeworths were again following Rousseau, who gives a detailed (and ingenious) analysis of La Fontaine's verse fable "Le Corbeau et le renard" in *Emile* (112–15).

34 William Hazlitt, *The Round Table*; *Characters of Shakespear's Plays*, ed. Catherine Macdonald Maclean (London: Dent, 1969), 5–6.

35 See Butler, *Maria Edgeworth*, 169.

36 Priestley, *Miscellaneous Observations*, 47–8; Macaulay, *Letters*, 89–91. Macaulay, however, would "totally exclude" the Bible from early education.

37 Summerfield, *Fantasy and Reason*, 200; William Scolfield, *Bible Stories: Memorable Acts of the Ancient Patriarchs, Judges, and Kings: Extracted from their Original Historians for the Use of Children* (New York: Collins, 1804), 2. William St Clair has recently attributed this work to William Godwin on persuasive grounds, although *Bible Stories* continues to strike me as very out of character with Godwin's writing about and for children. St Clair points out that the attribution (assuming it is correct) casts an ironic light on Summerfield's contrast between the "imaginative wisdom of Scolfield and the conventional stupidity of Godwin." William St Clair, *The Godwins and the Shelleys: A Biography of a Family* (Baltimore: Johns Hopkins University Press, 1989), 279–80, 545.

38 Wordsworth calls education "everything that *draws* out the human being, of which *tuition*, the teaching of the schools especially, however important, is comparatively an insignificant part" (*WLL* 2: 19). Cf. Wordsworth's "Speech at the Laying of the Foundation Stone of the New School in the Village at Bowness, Windermere, 1836" (*WP* 3: 295). De Quincey similarly writes that "Whatsoever *educes* or developes – *educates*," and defines "education" as "not the poor machinery that moves by spelling books and grammars, but that mighty system of central forces hidden in the deep bosom of human life, which by passion, by strife, by temptation, by the energies of resistance, works for ever upon children" (*Confessions*, 147).

39 Karen Clarke, "Public and Private Children: Infant Education in the 1820s and 1830s," in Steedman et al., *Language, Gender and Childhood*, 78. For a compelling account of the move in eighteenth-century educational theory from coercive to non-coercive modes of authority, in the context of similar developments in political theory, see Jay Fliegelman, *Prodigals and Pilgrims: The American Revolution against Patriarchal Authority* (Cambridge University Press, 1982), 9–35.

40 In this Wordsworth and rationalist writers could draw on a common source in Comenius; see Alan G. Hill, "Wordsworth, Comenius, and the Meaning of Education," *RES* (n.s.) 26 (1975): 301–12.

41 M. S. letter (1780–1) quoted in Butler, *Maria Edgeworth*, 65.

42 As Stone points out, the conception of education as a "stage process adapted to the growing capacities and self-development of the child" goes back to Locke (*Family*, 256). Cf. Michel Foucault's remarks on "descending" individualization in *Discipline and Punish: The Birth of the Prison*, trans. Alan Sheridan (1977; New York: Vintage, 1979), 193.

43 Review of R. L. and Maria Edgeworth, *Memoirs of Richard Lovell*

Edgeworth, Esq., *Quarterly Review* 23 (1820): 541–42; attributed to Croker in Butler, *Maria Edgeworth*, 410–12.

44 Clifford Siskin, *The Historicity of Romantic Discourse* (New York: Oxford University Press, 1988), 3. Compare Foucault in *Discipline and Punish*: "And if from the early Middle Ages to the present the 'adventure' is an account of individuality, the passage from the epic to the novel, from the noble deed to the secret singularity, from long exiles to the internal search for childhood, from combats to phantasies, it is also inscribed in the formation of a disciplinary society" (193).

45 Review of Maria Edgeworth's *Tales of Fashionable Life*, *Quarterly Review* 2 (1809): 147.

46 See Marilyn Butler, *Romantics, Rebels and Reactionaries*, 33. For Beddoes and the younger Wedgwoods as links between the Birmingham Lunar Society and the Bristol literary circle of the 1790s (which included Southey as well as Coleridge), see Butler, *Maria Edgeworth*, 142, 442. On the relation between child study and Maria Edgeworth's development of the English *Bildungsroman*, see also Myers, "The Dilemmas of Gender as Double-Voiced Narrative": 67–96.

47 Stephen J. Greenblatt, "Improvisation and Power" in *Literature and Society*, ed. Edward W. Said (Baltimore: Johns Hopkins University Press, 1986), 64–5.

48 Foucault, *Discipline and Punish*, 165.

49 Lawson and Silver, *Social History of Education*, 176; Barnard, *History of English Education*, 20; Charles Edward Mallet, *A History of the University of Oxford*, 3 vols. (London: Methuen, 1927) 3: 163–66.

50 Stone, "Literacy and Education": 89.

51 Claude Lévi-Strauss, *Tristes Tropiques*, trans. John and Doreen Weightman (New York: Washington Square Press, 1977), 337.

52 Stone, "Literacy": 71.

53 Altick, *English Common Reader*, 67–77.

54 Stone, "Literacy": 86.

55 Sarah Trimmer, *The Guardian of Education* 1 (1802): 2–4, 245.

56 Trimmer, *The Sunday-School Catechist: Consisting of Familiar Lectures with Questions, For the Use of Visitors and Teachers* (London: Longman, 1788), 2, 4. Hereafter cited in the text.

57 Allen and McClure, *Two Hundred Years*, 135; Jones, *Charity School*, 5.

58 *An Account of the Society for Promoting Christian Knowledge*, appended to Thomas Lewis, *A Sermon Preached in the Cathedral Church of St. Paul, London: On Thursday, May 21, 1801* (London: Rivington, 1801), 96.

59 Raikes's letter on Sunday Schools to the *Gentleman's Magazine* 54 (1784), rpt. in J. M. Goldstrom (ed.), *Education: Elementary Education 1780–1900* (New York: Barnes and Noble, 1972), 17. Raikes did not discourage the teaching of writing in the Sunday Schools, but others such as Hannah More ("I allow of no writing") and the Wesleyan Methodists did: see Stone, "Literacy": 89 and Jones, *Charity School*, 159–60.

60 Sydney Smith, rev. of Sarah Trimmer's *A Comparative View of the New Plan of Education as Promulgated by Mr. Joseph Lancaster*, Edinburgh Review 9 (1805); rpt. in Goldstrom, *Education*, 42.

61 John Barrell, *English Literature in History 1730–80: An Equal, Wide Survey* (New York: St. Martin's Press, 1983), 141; Zachary Leader, *Reading Blake's Songs* (Boston: Routledge and Kegan Paul, 1981), 35; Ruth K. MacDonald, *Literature for Children in England and America from 1646 to 1774* (Troy: Whitston, 1982), 66.

62 Anna Laetitia Barbauld, *Hymns in Prose for Children*, ed. Miriam Kramnick (New York: Garland, 1977), 13–14.

63 Heather Glen, *Vision and Disenchantment: Blake's Songs and Wordsworth's Lyrical Ballads* (Cambridge University Press, 1983), 55; Olivia Smith, *The Politics of Language 1791–1819* (Oxford: Clarendon Press, 1984), 35. See also Susan Pedersen, "Hannah More Meets Simple Simon: Tracts, Chapbooks, and Popular Culture in Late Eighteenth-Century England," *Journal of British Studies* 25 (1986): 84–113.

64 M. M. Bakhtin, *Problems of Dostoevsky's Poetics*, ed. and trans. Caryl Emerson (Minneapolis: University of Minnesota Press, 1984), 160.

65 Isaac Watts, *Catechisms* (London: E. Matthews, 1730), 16.

66 Roger Ingpen and Walter E. Peck, *The Complete Works of Percy Bysshe Shelley*, 10 vols. (London: Benn and New York: Scribner, 1927), 3: 159.

67 My text in this section for the first edition of *Lyrical Ballads* is *Lyrical Ballads 1798*, ed. W. J. B. Owen, 2nd edn. (Oxford University Press, 1969).

68 See Jacques Donzelot, *The Policing of Families*, trans. Robert Hurley (New York: Pantheon, 1979).

69 Trimmer, *Sunday-School Catechist*, xxi, 41. Watts (who draws heavily on Locke) had declared in *Catechisms* that "Words written on the Memory without Ideas or Sense in the Mind, will never incline a Child to his Duty, nor save his Soul" (17). Hannah More's fictional Sunday School teacher, Mrs. Crew, is praised for having "so managed, that *saying the Catechism* was not merely an act of the memory, but of the understanding" in "The History of Hester Wilmot; Or, The Second Part of the Sunday School," *Cheap Repository Tracts; Entertaining, Moral, and Religious*, 3 vols. (London: Rivington, 1798) 1: 351.

70 Trimmer, *Sunday-School Catechist*, 41.

71 Cf. De Quincey: "The religion becomes nonsense, and the child becomes a hypocrite. The religion is transfigured into cant, and the innocent child into a dissembling liar" (*Confessions*, 113).

72 Don H. Bialostosky, *Making Tales: The Poetics of Wordsworth's Narrative Experiments* (Chicago University Press, 1984), 107.

73 I quote from Fenn's *Cobwebs to Catch Flies* as excerpted in *From Instruction to Delight: An Anthology of Children's Literature to 1850*, ed. Patricia Demers and Gordon Moyle (Toronto: Oxford University Press, 1982), 135–36.

74 Bakhtin, *Problems*, 110.

75 For the adult catechizer's willingness to repeat himself, cf. Hannah More's "History of Hester Wilmot" in the *Cheap Repository Tracts*: "No one, Madam, can know till they try, that after they have asked a poor untaught child the same question nineteen times, they must not lose their temper, but go on and ask it the twentieth." More et al., *Cheap Repository Tracts* 1 : 352.

76 Bakhtin, *Problems*, 126.

77 Mary Jacobus, *Tradition and Experiment in Wordsworth's Lyrical Ballads (1798)* (Oxford: Clarendon Press, 1976), 102–3; Glen, *Vision*, 43.

78 I. F. note, quoted in Owen, *Lyrical Ballads*, 137.

79 E. D. Hirsch, Jr., *Innocence and Experience: An Introduction to Blake* (New Haven: Yale University Press, 1964), 177; Leader, *Reading*, 88; Harold Bloom, *The Visionary Company: A Reading of English Romantic Poetry*, rev. edn. (Ithaca: Cornell University Press, 1971), 35–39.

80 John Cotton, *Milk for Babes, Drawn Out of the Breast of Both Testaments*, in Demers and Moyles, *From Instruction to Delight*, 24.

81 Watts, *Catechisms*, 79.

82 Watts, 98; cf. Cotton, "I was conceived in sinne, and born in iniquity" (24).

83 Trimmer, *The Teacher's Assistant: Consisting of Lectures in the Catechetical Form: Being Part of a Plan of Appropriate Instruction for the Children of the Poor*, 7th edn. (London: Rivington, 1812), 3, 4, 18. *The Teacher's Assistant* was designed for use in the Charity Schools and was distributed by the SPCK.

84 Trimmer, *The Oeconomy of Charity; or, an Address to the Ladies Concerning Sunday Schools* (London: Longman, 1787), 2, 7, 26.

85 Leader, *Reading*, 32; Glen, *Vision*, 8–9.

86 Martha Winburn England, "Wesley's Hymns for Children and Blake's Songs," in *Hymns Unbidden: Donne, Herbert, Blake, Emily Dickinson and the Hymnographers*, ed. England and John Sparrow (New York Public Library, 1966), 53.

87 Bloom, 35; England, 54.

88 Shavit, *Poetics*, 63; U. C. Knoepflmacher, "The Balancing of Child and Adult: An Approach to Victorian Fantasies for Children," *Nineteenth-Century Fiction* 37 (1983): 500.

89 Glen, *Vision*, 25.

90 Bakhtin, *Problems*, 193.

91 Erdman, *Blake*, 126–27.

92 John Brenkman, *Culture and Domination* (Ithaca: Cornell University Press, 1987), 117.

93 Ibid., 231.

94 See Morris Marples, *Romantics at School* (London: Faber and Faber, 1967), 76–111.

95 Pollack, *Forgotten Children*, 249; Kelley, *Life of Mrs. Sherwood*, 22, 38.

96 Emily W. Sunstein, *Mary Shelley: Romance and Reality* (Boston: Little, Brown, 1989), 26.

97 *Memoirs of Thomas Holcroft*, ed. (and continued by) William Hazlitt (Oxford University Press, 1926), 5, 59–60.

98 William Shenstone, "The School-Mistress" (1737), in Lonsdale, *New Oxford Book of Eighteenth Century Verse*, 305–7; Crabbe, *Poetical Works*, 205.

99 Marples, *Romantics*, 18, 49, 80.

100 Richard Johnson, "Notes on the Schooling of the English Working Class 1780–1850," *Schooling and Capitalism: A Sociological Reader*, ed. Roger Dale, Geoff Elsand, and Madelaine MacDonald (London: Routledge and Kegan Paul, 1976), 44. See also Thomas W. Laqueur, "Working-Class Demand and the Growth of English Elementary Education, 1750–1850," *Schooling and Society: Studies in the History of Education*, ed. Lawrence Stone (Baltimore: Johns Hopkins University Press, 1976), 192–205, and Clarke, "Public and Private Children."

101 See Victor E. Neuburg, *Popular Education in Eighteenth Century England* (London: Woburn Press, 1971), 50–51.

102 See Brian Simon, *Studies in the History of Education 1780–1870* (London: Lawrence and Wishart, 1960), 17–125.

103 Rosemary O'Day, *Education and Society 1500–1800: The Social Foundations of Education in Early Modern Britain* (London: Longman, 1982), 214–15.

104 Simon, *Studies*, 69.

105 Barnard, *History of English Education*, 16.

106 Marples, *Romantics*, 21; see also Mary Moorman, *Wordsworth, A Biography: The Early Years 1770–1803* (Oxford: Clarendon Press, 1957), 28. Richard S. Tompson argues throughout *Classics or Charity?* that grammar schools as a whole did not decay during the eighteenth century, but rather diversified and adapted to the changing market, coming to emphasize classics less and elementary instruction more (see esp. 71–72).

107 See O'Day, *Education and Society*, 245.

108 Adamson, *English Education*, 54–55, 63.

109 Simon, *Studies*, 99.

110 *The Life and Correspondence of the Late Robert Southey*, ed. Charles Cuthbert Southey, 2nd edn., 6 vols. (London: Longman, 1849) 1: 80, 149.

111 *The Autobiography of Leigh Hunt*, ed. Edmund Blunden (Oxford University Press, 1928), 108; Barnard, *History of English Education*, 17; *Boswell's Life of Johnson*, ed. R. W. Chapman (London: Oxford University Press, 1953), 662.

112 Edgeworth, *Memoirs*, 20.

113 Barnard, *History of English Education*, 18; Adamson, *Short History*, 220.

114 Sydney Smith, "Public Education," *Edinburgh Review* (1810); rpt. *The Works of the Rev. Sydney Smith*, 2nd edn. (London: Longmans, 1869), 213.

115 Bernard Mandeville, *The Fable of the Bees: Or, Private Vices, Publick Benefits*, ed. F. B. Kaye, 2 vols. (Oxford: Clarendon Press, 1924), 1: 268. Hereafter cited in the text.

116 Mandeville, however, does not abjure religious indoctrination alto-

gether, but explicitly recommends that children be required to attend church on Sundays, where they can be instructed "by Preaching or Catechizing" (1: 307).

117 Isaac Watts, *An Essay Towards the Encouragement of Charity Schools, Particularly* THOSE *which are Supported by* PROTESTANT DISSENTERS, for teaching the Children of the POOR to read and work (London: John Clark and Richard Hett, 1728), 14.

118 John Locke, "Report to the Board of Trade," excerpted in *Some Thoughts Concerning Education*, ed. R. H. Quick, 2nd edn. (Cambridge University Press, 1892), 189–91.

119 See Briggs, *Making of Modern England*, 61, and Porter, *English Society*, 344.

120 Clara Reeve, *Plans of Education; With Remarks on the Systems of Other Writers*, ed. Gina Luria (New York: Garland, 1974), 86.

121 Rev. Joseph Berington, *An Essay on the Depravity of the Nation, With a View to the Promotion of Sunday Schools, &c. Of Which a More Extended Plan is Proposed* (Birmingham: Myles Swinney, 1788), 22–24.

122 Palmer, *Improvement of Humanity*, 84, 139–42.

123 Adamson, *Short History*, 213–14.

124 Palmer, *Improvement of Humanity*, 82.

125 Adamson, *Short History*, 216.

126 John Brown, *Thoughts on Civil Liberty, On Licentiousness, and Faction*, 2nd edn. (London: Davies and Reymers, 1765), 26–27.

127 Joseph Priestley, *An Essay on the First Principles of Government*, 2nd edn. (London: J. Johnson, 1771), 90–105.

128 Thomas Paine, *Rights of Man*, ed. Eric Foner (Harmondsworth: Penguin, 1985), 245.

129 Adam Smith, *An Inquiry into the Nature and Causes of the Wealth of Nations*, 2 vols, ed. R. H. Campbell, A. S. Skinner, and W. B. Todd (1979; Indianapolis: Liberty Classics, 1981), 2: 782.

130 Thomas Robert Malthus, *An Essay on the Principle of Population*, ed. T. H. Hollingsworth, 2 vols. (London: Dent, 1973), 2: 211.

131 T. C. Hansard, *The Parliamentary Debates from the Year 1803 to the Present Time*, 41 vols. (London: Hansard, 1812–20), 9: 795, 798. Hereafter cited in the text.

132 [Robert Southey], "Inquiry into the Poor Laws, &c.," *Quarterly Review* 8 (1812): 353.

133 Wordsworth, *Poems* 2: 967.

134 Joseph Lancaster, *Improvements in Education, As It Relates to the Industrious Classes of the Community*, 3rd edn. "with Additions" (New York: Collins and Perkins, 1807), 7. Hereafter cited in the text.

135 Andrew Bell, *An Analysis of the Experiment in Education, Made at Egmore, Near Madras*, 3rd edn. (London: Cadell and Davies, 1807), 6. Hereafter cited in the text.

136 Foucault, *Discipline and Punish*, 165.

137 Bell, *The Madras School, or Elements of Tuition* (London: J. Murray, 1808), 3.
138 Sydney Smith, "Trimmer and Lancaster," *Works*, 87.
139 See, for example, E. P. Thompson's discussion of Andrew Ure's *Philosophy of Manufactures* (1835) in *Making*, 359–62.
140 Jeremy Bentham, *Chrestomathia*, ed. M. J. Smith and W. H. Burston (Oxford: Clarendon Press, 1983), 104. On "Panopticism" see Foucault, *Discipline and Punish*, 195–228.
141 Lancaster, *The British System of Education* (Georgetown: Joseph Milligan and William Cooper, 1812), 84.
142 Johnson, "Notes": 48.
143 R. A. Foakes, "'Thriving Prisoners': Coleridge, Wordsworth, and the Child at School," *Studies in Romanticism* 28 (1989): 204; see also Carl Woodring, *Politics in English Romantic Poetry* (Cambridge: Harvard University Press, 1970), 136–37. More critical is David Simpson, *Wordsworth's Historical Imagination: The Poetry of Displacement* (New York: Methuen, 1987), 196–200.
144 [Robert Southey], "*Bell* and *Lancaster's* Systems of Education," *Quarterly Review* 6 (1811): 289, 303. This article was later expanded into a pamphlet on *The Origin, Nature, and Object of the New System of Education* (1812).
145 Southey, "Inquiry into the Poor Laws," 319; hereafter cited in the text. For the article's context see Geoffrey Carnall, *Robert Southey and His Age: The Development of a Conservative Mind* (Oxford: Clarendon Press, 1960), 120–70.
146 Woodring, *Politics*, 131; Barnard, *History of English Education*, 56.
147 Southey, "*Bell* and *Lancaster's* Systems," 293; [Henry Brougham], "Education of the Poor," *Edinburgh Review* 17 (1810): 63.
148 Foakes, "'Thriving Prisoners,'" 197; Trimmer, *A Comparative View of the New Plan of Education Promulgated by Mr. Joseph Lancaster*, excerpted in Kaestle, *Joseph Lancaster*, 107.
149 Cf. Mandeville: "in a free Nation where Slaves are not allow'd of, the surest Wealth consists in a Multitude of laborious Poor" (*Fable* 1: 282).
150 William Lisle Bowles, *The Church and Parochial School. A Sermon, Preached at Bremhill, for the Benefit of the National Schools; August 31st, 1823* (Calne: Baily, [1823]), 14.
151 James Mill, *Schools for All in Preference to Schools for Churchmen Only*, in *James Mill on Education*, ed. W. H. Burston (Cambridge University Press, 1969), 135.
152 Johnson, "Notes": 47.
153 Coleridge, *Logic*, ed. J. R. de Jackson (Princeton University Press, 1981), 8.
154 Thomas Holcroft, *The Adventures of Hugh Trevor*, ed. Seamus Deane (Oxford University Press, 1978), 8–9. Hereafter cited in the text.
155 Godwin's distance from other educational theorists in the rationalist

tradition may well reflect a movement in his thinking, by the time he came to write *The Enquirer*, toward a more sceptical and empirical position. See Mark Philp, *Godwin's Political Justice* (Ithaca: Cornell University Press, 1986), esp. 202–13.

3. CHILDREN'S LITERATURE AND THE WORK OF CULTURE

1 For the early history of children's books in England see MacDonald, *Literature for Children*, F. J. Harvey Darton, *Children's Books in England: Five Centuries of Social Life*, 3rd edn. (Cambridge University Press, 1982); M. F. Thwaite, *From Primer to Pleasure: An Introduction to the History of Children's Books in England, from the Invention of Printing to 1900* (London: The Library Association, 1966); and Mary V. Jackson, *Engines of Instruction, Mischief, and Magic: Children's Literature in England from Its Beginnings to 1839* (Lincoln: University of Nebraska Press, 1989).

2 J. H. Plumb, "The First Flourishing of Children's Books," in The Pierpont Morgan Library, *Early Children's Books and Their Illustration* (Boston: David R. Godine, 1975), xvii–xxx.

3 Samuel F. Pickering, *John Locke and Children's Books in Eighteenth-Century England* (Knoxville: University of Tennessee Press, 1981).

4 Jackson, *Engines*, 71–99.

5 Oliver Goldsmith, *Collected Works of Oliver Goldsmith*, ed. Arthur Friedman, 5 vols. (Oxford: Clarendon Press, 1966) 1: 461.

6 Jackson, *Engines*, 5, 83.

7 Southey, *Life*, 37; Edgeworth, *Memoirs*, 22.

8 Leigh Hunt, *Autobiography*, 70–72.

9 Newbery, *The Twelfth-Day Gift*, quoted in Jackson, *Engines*, 104.

10 Isaac Kramnick, "Children's Literature and Bourgeois Ideology: Observations on Culture and Industrial Capitalism in the Later Eighteenth Century," *Studies in Eighteenth-Century Culture* 12 (1983): 13, 23, 32. Kramnick's "progressive" approach to early children's literature is extended and importantly qualified by Mitzi Myers, whose work is discussed in the introduction to chapter 4, below.

11 Hunt, *Autobiography*, 71; Jackson, *Engines*, 129–48, 169–74.

12 See Ronald Paulsen, "*The History of Little Goody Two-Shoes* as a Children's Book," *Literary Theory and Criticism*, ed. Joseph P. Strelka, 2 vols. (Bern: Peter Lang, 1984), 2: 1075–76.

13 MacDonald, *Literature for Children*, 1; Jackson, *Engines*, 16.

14 Jackson, *Engines*, 245.

15 John Aubrey, *Three Prose Works: Miscellanies, Remaines of Gentilisme, Observations*, ed. John Buchanan-Brown (Carbondale: Southern Illinois University Press, 1972), 50, 290.

16 Stith Thompson, *The Folktale* (1946; Berkeley: University of California Press, 1977), 19; Pickering, *John Locke*, 40; Muhsin Jassim Ali, *Scheherazade in England: A Study of Nineteenth-Century English Criticism of the Arabian Nights* (Washington: Three Continents Press, 1981), 11.

17 Pickering, *John Locke*, 40–69; see also Sylvia W. Patterson, *Rousseau's Emile and Early Children's Literature* (Metuchen: Scarecrow Press, 1971).

18 Maria Edgeworth, *The Parent's Assistant*, ed. Christina Edgeworth Colvin (New York: Garland, 1976), xi. Hereafter cited in the text.

19 Kelley, *Life of Mrs Sherwood*, 37, 39; M. M. Sherwood, *The Governess, or The Little Female Academy* (Wellington: F. Houston and Sons, 1820), iv.

20 Darton, *Children's Books*, vii, 214–18.

21 Pickering, *John Locke*, 69.

22 Percy Muir, *English Children's Books 1600–1900* (London: Batsford, 1954), 82.

23 See, e.g., Michael C. Kotzin, *Dickens and the Fairy Tale* (Bowling Green: Popular Press, 1972), 12–14.

24 Summerfield, *Fantasy and Reason*, xvii, 200.

25 Altick, *English Common Reader*, 67–77.

26 John Newbery, *A Little Pretty Pocket-Book*, ed. M. F. Thwaite (London: Oxford University Press, 1966); Darton, *Children's Books*, 141. Cf. Pickering, *John Locke*, 47.

27 Rousseau, "La Reine Fantasque," *Oeuvres Completes*, 4 vols. (Paris: Galimard, 1959–69), 1179–92; Samuel Johnson, "The Fountains: A Fairy Tale," *Children's Literature* 6 (1977): 42–53.

28 Maria Edgeworth, *Early Lessons*, 10 parts in 5 vols. (London: J. Johnson, 1801), Part III, 27.

29 See Vladimir Propp, *Morphology of the Folktale*, trans. Laurence Scott and Louis A. Wagner, 2nd edn. (Austin: University of Texas Press, 1968), 39–43; Iona and Peter Opie, *The Classic Fairy Tales* (New York: Oxford University Press, 1974), 126–32.

30 Gillian Avery, *Childhood's Pattern: A Study of the Heroes and Heroines of Children's Fiction 1770–1950* (London: Hodder and Stoughton, 1975), 17; *The History of Little Goody Two-Shoes* (London: J. Newbery, 1765), 56; Pickering, *John Locke*, 49.

31 Thwaite, *Primer*, 37; see also Brian Alderson, "Scheherazade in the Nursery," in *The Arabian Nights in English Literature*, ed. Peter L. Caracciolo (New York: St. Martin's, 1988), 81–94.

32 Avery, *Childhood's Pattern*, 43–44.

33 Opie, *Classic Fairy Tales*, 211–26.

34 John M. Ellis, *One Fairy Story Too Many: The Brothers Grimm and Their Tales* (Chicago University Press, 1983); Maria Tatar, *The Hard Facts of the Grimms' Fairy Tales* (Princeton University Press, 1987), 3–38.

35 Summerfield, *Fantasy and Reason*, xvi; Jack Zipes, *Breaking the Magic Spell: Radical Theories of Folk and Fairy Tales* (Austin: University of Texas Press, 1979), 29.

36 Edgar Taylor, *Grimms' Fairy Tales*, 2 vols. (London: Scolar Press, 1977) 1: xi.

37 Translations of the Basile and Grimm versions can be found in Alan Dundes, *Cinderella: A Folklore Casebook* (New York: Garland, 1982), 3–13, 22–29.

38 Mitzi Myers, "Impeccable Governesses, Rational Dames, and Moral Mothers: Mary Wollstonecraft and the Female Tradition in Georgian Children's Books," *Children's Literature* 14 (1986): 31.

39 Darton, *Children's Books*, 129.

40 See "Edward Baldwin, Esq." [William Godwin], *Fables, Ancient and Modern, Adapted For the Use of Children* (Philadelphia: Johnson and Warner, 1811).

41 Victor E. Neuburg, *Popular Literature: A History and Guide* (London: Penguin, 1977), 102–11.

42 Smith, *Politics of Language*, ix.

43 [T. J. Mathias], *The Pursuits of Literature. A Satirical Poem. In Four Dialogues. With Notes*, 5th edn. (London: T. Becket, 1798), 194.

44 Altick, *English Common Reader*, 70–75.

45 Stone, "Literacy and Education": 89, 71.

46 Stone, "Literacy," 86.

47 Smith, *Politics*, 89.

48 Hazlitt, "What Is the People," *Works* 7: 273; cf. Hazlitt's scathing review of *The Statesman's Manual* for *The Examiner* (29 December 1816), *Works* 7: 124–26.

49 Charlotte Yonge, "Children's Literature of the Last Century," *MacMillan's Magazine* 20 (1869): 229; Altick, *English Common Reader*, 100; Smith, *Politics*, 68.

50 Smith, *Politics*, 91; Altick, *English Common Reader*, 75–76; Neuberg, *Popular Literature*, 256.

51 Smith, *Politics*, 72.

52 Pickering, *John Locke*, 129.

53 Review of Thomas Bowdler, *The Family Shakespeare*, *Christian Observer* 7 (1808): 328.

54 "The Literature of the Nursery," *The London Magazine* 2 (1820): 480–81.

55 Mark Parker trenchantly examines the Burkean conservatism of the *London Magazine* under the editorship of John Scott (to whom he attributes "Literature of the Nursery") in "Ideology and Editing: The Political Context of the Elia Essay," *Studies in Romanticism* 30 (1991): 473–94.

56 Chandler, *Wordsworth's Second Nature*, 66–67.

57 Ibid., 144.

58 For a recent critique of this figure and the broader tendency it represents, see Mary Jacobus, "'Behold the Parent Hen': Romantic Pedagogy and Sexual Difference," *Romanticism, Writing, and Sexual Difference* (Oxford: Clarendon Press, 1989), 237–66.

59 W. H. Auden, "Afterward" to George MacDonald, *The Golden Key* (New York: Farrar, Straus, and Giroux, 1967), 83.

60 I argue these points at greater length and with specific reference to recent literary and folkloristic work on fairy tales in an earlier version of this section, "Wordsworth, Fairy Tales, and the Politics of Children's

Reading," *Romanticism and Children's Literature in Nineteenth-Century England*, ed. James Holt McGavran, Jr. (Athens: University of Georgia Press, 1991), esp. 45–48.

61 See Alan Dundes, "Texture, Text, and Context," *Interpreting Folklore*, ed. Dundes (Bloomington: Indiana University Press, 1980), 20–32. For trenchant examples of how the significance of tales (oral or written) changes with the purpose of the teller, see Robert Darnton, "Peasants Tell Tales: The Meaning of Mother Goose," *The Great Cat Massacre and Other Episodes in French Cultural History* (New York: Vintage, 1984), 9–72; and Ruth Bottigheimer, "Silenced Women in the Grimms' Tales: The 'Fit' Between Fairy Tales and Society in Their Historical Context," *Fairy Tales and Society: Illusion, Allusion,and Paradigm*, ed. Bottigheimer (Philadelphia: University of Pennsylvania Press, 1986).

62 David Reisman, with Nathan Glazer and Reuel Denney, *The Lonely Crowd: A Study of the Changing American Character*, abridged edn. (New York: Doubleday, 1953), 112.

63 Ibid., 119.

64 Rudolf Schenda, "Telling Tales – Spreading Tales: Change in the Communicative Forms of a Popular Genre," in Bottigheimer, *Fairy Tales*, 78–79.

65 For the latter, utopian view see esp. Jack Zipes, *Fairy Tales and the Art of Subversion: The Classical Genre for Children and the Process of Civilization* (New York: Wildman, 1983).

66 Godwin, letter to William Cole, 2 March 1802, in Kegan Paul, *William Godwin*, 1: 119–20. Wordsworth demurred at Godwin's suggestion that he versify "Beauty and the Beast": "I confess there is to me something disgusting in the notion of a human Being consenting to *Mate* with a Beast, however amiable his qualities of heart" (*WLM* 1: 468).

67 Butler, *Maria Edgeworth*, 156.

68 See Barbauld, *Hymns in Prose*, 60–61; Maria Edgeworth, "The Grateful Negro," *Tales and Novels*, 10 vols. (London: Routledge, 1893), 2: 399–419; Wollstonecraft, *Original Stories*, 20–21, 112–14; Trimmer, *Guardian* 1 (1802): 431.

69 Butler, *Maria Edgeworth*, 62.

70 Earle, *Microsmographie*, 1; John Bunyan, *A Book for Boys and Girls*, ed. Barry Adams (New York: Garland, 1978), 74–75.

71 Sir Roger L'Estrange, *Fables, of Aesop And other Eminent Mythologists: With Morals and Reflections* (London: T. Sawbridge, 1692), [preface unpaginated].

72 [John Parsons], *The First Book for English Schools; or The Rational Schoolmaster's First Assistant* (Nottingham: Rivington, n.d. [c. 1780]), i. Hereafter cited in the text.

73 Spiegelman notes that Wordsworth uses the term "character," in poems like "Character of the Happy Warrior," with "a full awareness of its Greek original, 'to scratch' or 'etch.' A character is indelible, engraved" (*Wordsworth's Heroes*, 3.) Cf. Parsons' ambiguous statement that the

"mind is at first, a meer blank, on which may be inscribed, what *characters* you please" (*First Book* i; my italics).

74 Ian Hunter argues that not only didactic texts, but literary texts of many kinds can be made to perform such functions within an educative setting, facilitating the modern alliance of "literature" and schooling: "Both popular and serious literature provided the school with points of identification already saturated with the new normativities of the social sphere. As such, they gradually outstripped the other arts subjects in the moral economy of the school, functioning either as a point of identification channelling the degraded inner life of the child into the school, or as a repository of exemplary figures and tactics through which the teacher might mould his life," *Culture and Government: The Emergence of Literary Education* (London: MacMillan, 1988), 119.

75 Edgeworth, *Memoirs* 2: 188.

76 Trimmer's *The Charity School Spelling Book*, Part i (in both the boys' and girls' versions) and Part ii can be found in vol. 12 of *Religious Tracts, Dispersed by the Society for Promoting Christian Knowledge*, 12 vols. (London: Rivington, 1800).

77 Richard Edgeworth, "Address to Mothers" in vol. 3 of Maria Edgeworth, *Early Lessons*, 6th edn., 4 vols. (London: R. Hunter, 1829) 3: xxiii–iv.

78 Summerfield, *Fantasy and Reason*, 128. Rousseau dismisses the imaginary object lesson quite explicitly in *Emile*: "Now, you can be certain that he will not in his life forget this day's lesson; whereas if I had only made him suppose all this in his room, my speech would have been forgotten the very next day. One must speak as much as one can by deeds and say only what one does not know how to do" (181–82).

79 [Ellenor Fenn], *Fables of Monosyllables By Mrs. Teachwell; To Which Are Added Morals in Dialogue Between a Mother and Children*, 2 vols. in one ([1783]; rpt. New York: Johnson Reprint Corp., 1970) 2: x.

80 Barbauld, *Lessons for Children*, 4 parts in 1 vol. (Boston: O. Everett, 1823) 3: 4.

81 Maria and Richard Lovell Edgeworth, *A Rational Primer* (London: J. Johnson, 1799), 69.

82 [John Aikin and Anna Laetitia Barbauld], *Evenings at Home; Or, The Juvenile Budget Opened*, 2nd edn., 6 vols. in two (London: J. Johnson, 1794–96) 1: 1–3.

83 Eliza Fenwick, *Visits to the Juvenile Library*, ed. Claire Tomalin (New York: Garland, 1977), 11, 23–24, 72.

84 Sarah Fielding, *The Governess or, Little Female Academy*, ed. Mary Cadogan (London: Pandora, 1987), xiii. Hereafter cited in the text.

85 Mary Wollstonecraft, *Original Stories, From Real Life; With Conversations, Calculated to Regulate the Affections, and Form the Mind to Truth and Goodness*, ed. Miriam Brody Kramnick (New York: Garland, 1977), xi. Hereafter cited in the text.

86 Stone, "Literacy": 76.

87 Watts, *Catechisms*, v.
88 Trimmer, *An Easy Introduction to the Knowledge of Nature, and Reading the Holy Scriptures* (London: Longman and Rees, 1799), vi, 142.
89 [M. M. Sherwood], *The Works of Mrs. Sherwood*, 16 vols. (New York: Harper & Brothers, 1834–46), 2: 16, 23, 26.
90 Sangster writes that such journals were commonly kept by children of Evangelicals and Methodists, and that Wesley "especially encouraged children" to keep "diaries of their spiritual condition," which functioned as a "form of self-examination" (*Pity My Simplicity*, 69, 146). Wesley published one such diary (in 1768) to "animate those who are in the morning of life, to a due improvement of their time": see *An Extract of Miss Mary Gilbert's Journal*, ed. John Wesley, 4th edn. (London: J. Paramore, 1787), v.
91 Ellenor Fenn, *The Fairy Spectator*, in Jonathan Cott (ed.), *Masterworks of Children's Literature*, 8 vols. (New York: Stonehill, 1983–86); vol. 3, *The Middle Period*, ed. Robert Bator, 410–12.
92 Sherwood, *Works* 13: 129.
93 In adding a third term to the usual fantastic/didactic dyad, Mary Jackson has, in *Engines of Instruction, Mischief, and Magic*, provided the first historical account which gives adequate attention to satire and humor in children's books; but in failing to distinguish between satire and the more innocuous humor of what she calls the "pappillonade" (209), Jackson leaves "mischief" insufficiently examined.
94 *Coleridge's Miscellaneous Criticism*, ed. Thomas Middleton Raysor (Cambridge: Harvard University Press, 1936), 405.
95 Nicholas Tucker, *The Child and the Book: A Psychological and Literary Exploration* (Cambridge University Press, 1981), 76; Humphrey Carpenter, *Secret Gardens: A Study of the Golden Age of Children's Literature* (Boston: Houghton-Mifflin, 1985), 4.
96 Craig Howes, "Rhetorics of Attack: Bakhtin and the Aesthetics of Satire," *Genre* 19 (1986): 217.
97 See Grylls, *Guardians and Angels*, 28–38, and Laqueur, *Religion and Respectability*, 9–18.
98 Jacqueline Rose, *The Case of Peter Pan or The Impossibility of Children's Fiction* (London: MacMillan, 1984), 2, 43–44.
99 Rosamond Bayne-Powell, *The English Child in the Eighteenth Century* (New York: Dutton, 1939), 229.
100 Tatar, *Hard Facts*, 222; Darton, *Children's Books*, 81. Grimm's formula remained central to the great Victorian defenses of the traditional fairy tale: Dickens, in "Frauds on the Fairies" (1853), demands that fairy tales be "preserved in their simplicity, and purity, and innocent extravagance," while Ruskin, in his essay on "Fairy Stories" prefixed to a 1868 reissue of Taylor's Grimm, explicitly connects the "simplicity" of the traditional tales to the "unquestioning innocence" of the child reader. Both essays can be found in Lance Salway (ed.), *A Peculiar*

Gift: Nineteenth Century Writings on Books for Children (Harmondsworth: Kestrel, 1976), 111, 128.

101 Rose, *Case of Peter Pan*, 50.

102 Isaac Watts, *The Improvement of the Mind; Or, A Supplement to the Art of Logic. To Which Is Added, A Discourse on the Education of Children and Youth*, 2 parts in 1 vol. (London: Edwards and Knibb, 1821), 282.

103 Paulson, "*History of Little Goody Two-Shoes*" 2: 1080.

104 Jackson, 131.

105 Mary Ann Kilner, *The Adventures of a Pincushion Designed Chiefly for the Use of Young Ladies*, in Cott and Bator, *Masterworks of Children's Literature* 8: 184–85. Cf. Ruskin's dismissal of satire in "Fairy Stories": "Children should laugh but not mock; and when they laugh, it should not be at the weaknesses and faults of others." Salway, *Peculiar Gift*, 127–28.

106 Margaret R. Higgonet, "Narrative Fractures and Fragments," *Children's Literature* 15 (1987): 47; C. W. Sullivan III, "Narrative Expectations: The Folklore Connection," *Children's Literature Association Quarterly* 15 (1990): 54; Perry Nodelman, "Interpretation and the Apparent Sameness of Children's Novels," *Studies in the Literary Imagination* 18 (1985): 5; Tucker, *Child*, 18.

107 Peter Hunt, "Necessary Misreadings: Directions in Narrative Theory for Children's Literature," *Studies in the Literary Imagination* 18 (1985): 112.

108 Aidan Chambers, "The Reader in the Book," *The Signal Approach to Children's Books*, ed. Nancy Chambers (Metuchen: Scarecrow Press, 1981), 253–54.

109 Rose, *Case of Peter Pan*, 2.

110 For the relatively late censorship of nursery rhymes, see Tucker, *Child*, 194–7 and MacDonald, *Literature for Children*, 117.

111 William Scolfield, *Bible Stories: Memorable Acts of the Ancient Patriarchs, Judges, and Kings: Extracted from their Original Historians for the Use of Children* (New York: Collins, 1804), 2–4. As noted in chapter 2, "Scolfield" has been identified, on indirect evidence, as a pseudonym for William Godwin: see William St Clair, "William Godwin as Children's Bookseller," in *Children and Their Books: A Celebration of the Work of Iona and Peter Opie*, ed. Gillian Avery and Julia Briggs (Oxford: Clarendon Press, 1989), 168–70, and St Clair, *The Godwins and the Shelleys*, 279–80, 545. As St Clair remarks, it seems "astonishing" that Godwin should have produced a children's book on this subject (282).

112 J. B. B. Clarke, *An Account of the Infancy, Religious and Literary Life of Adam Clarke*, 2 vols. (London: T. S. Clarke, 1833) 1: 45.

113 Review of *The Christian Teacher*, by Rev. T. Harper, *Eclectic Review* 2 (1806): 840.

114 Pedersen, "Hannah More Meets Simple Simon": 104, 107. "Ribald crudity" is Gillian Avery's phrase for the chapbooks in *Childhood's Pattern*, 18.

115 Pedersen, "Hannah More" 87; Sangster, *Pity My Simplicity*, 67 (quoting Trimmer's subtitle).

116 See Marjorie Moon, *John Harris's Books for Youth 1801–1803: A Checklist*, rev. ed. (Winchester: St. Paul's Bibliographies, 1987), esp. 1–8; and Justin G. Schiller, *Nursery Rhymes and Chapbooks 1805–1814* (New York: Garland, 1978), esp. vii–xxiii.

117 See, e.g., Jackson, *Engines*, 209–13. *Pug's Visit, The Butterfly's Ball, The Peacock "At Home"*, and the "Old Mother Hubbard" books are all reprinted in Schiller, *Nursery Rhymes*.

118 For the exchange between Godwin and Lamb see *LW* 3: 479–80.

119 Jean Marsden, "Shakespeare for Girls: Mary Lamb and *Tales from Shakespeare*," *Children's Literature* 17 (1989): 47, 52.

120 Lamb's *King & Queen of Hearts* is also reprinted in Schiller, *Nursery Rhymes*. For the comic book, see Tucker, *Child*, 134–37.

121 See Alan Richardson, "Nineteenth-Century Children's Satire and the Ambivalent Reader," *Children's Literature Association Quarterly* 15 (1990): 124–25. I have borrowed from an earlier section of this essay (122–24) above.

122 See Glen, *Vision and Disenchantment*; Stewart Crehen, *Blake in Context* (Atlantic Highlands: Humanities Press, 1984); Edward Larrissy, *William Blake*, Rereading Literature Series (Oxford: Basil Blackwell, 1985); Michael Ferber, *The Social Vision of William Blake* (Princeton University Press, 1985).

123 S. Foster Damon, *William Blake: His Philosophy and Symbols* (1924; rpt. Gloucester: Peter Smith, 1958), 269.

124 Ngugi Wa Thiong'o, *Writers in Politics: Essays* (London: Heinemann, 1981), 14, 19–20.

125 Cf. Leader, *Reading Blake's Songs*, 109.

126 For "The Little Black Boy" as an unproblematic text in the anti-slavery tradition see Wylie Sypher's standard account, *Guinea's Captive Kings: British Anti-Slavery Literature of the XVIIIth Century* (Chapel Hill: University of North Carolina Press, 1942), 157; Eva Beatrice Dykes, *The Negro in English Romantic Thought: A Study in Sympathy for the Oppressed* (Washington: Associated Publishers, 1942), 19; and Erdman, *Blake*, 132. The "dramatic" character of "The Little Black Boy" (primarily concerned with portraying "a particular state of mind" and "the limitations of childish innocence") is noted by Hazard Adams in *William Blake: A Reading of the Shorter Poems* (Seattle: University of Washington Press, 1963), 263–66; the "more universal meaning" (that "all children are lambs and the Lamb") by Robert F. Gleckner in *The Piper and the Bard: A Study of William Blake* (Detroit: Wayne State University Press, 1959), 106–8; "Christian paradox" is from Hirsch, *Innocence and Experience*, 180, and "Christian dualism" from Bloom, *Visionary Company*, 40.

127 For recent studies of Blake's relation to the children's book industry and the children's hymn tradition see Leader, *Reading Blake's Songs*, 1–37;

Glen, *Vision and Disenchantment*, 8–32; and Summerfield, *Fantasy and Reason*, 208–40.

128 Trimmer, *Guardian* 1 (1802): 245; for Day, Aikin, Barbauld, and Edgeworth see Sypher, *Guinea's Captive Kings*; for the Taylors and Legh Richmond, see below. *The Black Prince* and *The Sorrows of Yamba* can be found in Hannah More et al., *Cheap Repository Tracts; Entertaining, Moral, and Religious: Consisting of a Great Variety of Separate Performances, Written in a Neat, Yet Simple Style, and Eminently Calculated for the Amusement and Instruction of Both Sexes*, 3 vols. (Boston: E. Lincoln, 1803), 1: 173–87 and 374–80.

129 Rose, *The Case of Peter Pan*, 50.

130 Dorfman, *Empire's Old Clothes*, 8.

131 For *Sandford and Merton* see Rose, *Peter Pan*, 51–54; for the *Robinsonnade*, see Darton, *Children's Books in England*, 106–19.

132 Watts, "An Essay ... Charity Schools," 12; Goldstrom, *Education*, 17.

133 For the Society for Promoting Christian Knowledge, see Jones, *The Charity School Movement* and W. K. Lowther Clarke, *A History of the SPCK* (London: Society for Promoting Christian Knowledge, 1959).

134 Religious Tract Society, *The Story of the Religious Tract Society* (London: RTS, 1898).

135 Frank J. Klingberg, *Anglican Humanitarianism in Colonial New York* (Philadelphia: The Church Historical Society, 1950), 5.

136 See Sypher, *Guinea's Captive Kings*, 10, 19.

137 See Dorothy Hammond and Alta Jablow, *The Africa That Never Was: Four Centuries of British Writing About Africa* (New York: Twayne, 1970), 28 and Patrick Brantliger, "Victorians and Africans: The Genealogy of the Myth of the Dark Continent" in "*Race,*" *Writing, and Difference*, ed. Henry Louis Gates, Jr. (University of Chicago Press, 1986), 185–222.

138 James Montgomery, *The West Indies*, lines 47, 51–52 in *The Poetical Works of James Montgomery. Collected by Himself* (London: Longman, 1850).

139 Hannah More, *Slavery, A Poem* (London: T. Cadell, 1788).

140 More, *Cheap Repository Tracts* 1: 177, 185–86.

141 Legh Richmond, *The Negro Servant*, in *Twelve Witnesses to the Happy Effects of Experimental Religion, in Life and Death* (Boston: N. Willis, 1814), 10–12.

142 Abdul R. JanMohamed, "The Economy of Manichean Allegory: The Function of Racial Difference in Colonialist Literature," in Gates, "*Race,*" *Writing, and Difference*, 78–106.

143 For the plates see Blake, *Songs of Innocence and of Experience*, ed. Sir Geoffrey Keynes (New York: Orion Press, 1967), plates 9 and 10.

144 Quoted in Sypher, *Guinea's Captive Kings*, 52 and in David Dabydeen, "Eighteenth-century English literature on commerce and slavery," *The Black Presence in English Literature*, ed. Dabydeen (Manchester University Press, 1985), 29.

145 Ashton Nichols, "Silencing the Other: The Discourse of Domination in

Nineteenth-Century Exploration Narratives," *Nineteenth-Century Studies* 3 (1989): 1–22.

146 Dorfman, *Empire's Old Clothes*, 85, 36.

147 See Katherine George, "The Civilized West Looks at Primitive Africa: 1400–1800. A Study in Ethnocentrism," *Isis* 49 (1958): 62–72 and Richard M. Kain, "The Problem of Civilization in English Abolition Literature, 1772–1808," *Philological Quarterly* 15 (1936): 103–25; JanMohamed, "Economy," 81.

148 Johannes Fabian, *Time and the Other: How Anthropology Makes Its Object* (New York: Columbia University Press, 1983), 31, 143.

149 Charles H. Lyons, *To Wash an Aethiop White: British Ideas About Black African Educability 1530–1960* (New York: Teachers College Press, 1975), 52. See also Philip D. Curtin, *The Image of Africa: British Ideas and Action, 1780–1850* (Madison: University of Wisconsin Press, 1964), 28–57 and David Brion Davis, *The Problem of Slavery in Western Culture* (Ithaca: Cornell University Press, 1966), 446–82.

150 Sypher, *Guinea's Captive Kings*, 9.

151 Thomas Day, *The Dying Negro, A Poetical Epistle* (London: W. Flexney, 1773), 7. For sun-worship and the conventional "noble" African, see Sypher, *Guinea's Captive Kings*, 120, 130.

152 Glen, *Vision and Disenchantment*, 31.

153 V. N. Volosinov, *Freudianism: A Critical Sketch*, trans. I. R. Titunik, ed. Titunik and Neal H. Bruss (Bloomington: Indiana University Press, 1987), 113.

154 Hirsch, *Innocence and Experience*, 180.

155 The Society for the Propagation of the Gospel managed a plantation, the Codrington estate, with an eye to the conversion of its three hundred slaves: see Klingberg, *Anglican Humanitarianism*, 11–48. Other missionary efforts in the colonial British West Indies are described in George Eaton Simpson, *Black Religions in the New World* (New York: Columbia University Press, 1978), 26–45. For an account of the black community in eighteenth-century England see James Walvin, *Black and White: The Negro and English Society 1555–1945* (London: Penguin, 1973), 46–79. In *England, Slaves and Freedom, 1776–1838* (Jackson: University Press of Mississippi, 1986), Walvin notes that some African children were brought directly from Africa to England "for education and conversion" in the late 1780s (54).

156 Frantz Fanon, *Black Skin, White Masks*, trans. Charles Lam Markmann (New York: Grove Press, 1967), 45.

157 See Crehen, *Blake in Context*, 99.

158 For Blake's uncompromising anti-imperialism and his critical attitude towards the anti-slavery movement, see Erdman, *Blake*, 226–42.

159 Eugene D. Genovese, *Roll, Jordan, Roll: The World the Slaves Made* (1974; rpt. New York: Vintage, 1976), 168–82; Frederic Jameson, *Political Unconscious*, 86.

160 Erdman, *Blake*, 239.

161 Harold Pagliaro, *Selfhood and Redemption in Blake's Songs* (University Park: Pennsylvania State University Press, 1987), 10.
162 Genovese, *Roll, Jordan, Roll*, 148, 266, 165.
163 Contrast the more conventional pictorial representation of a "simple Christian child" with "skin of whitest lustre" instructing a "tawny Ethiop" as described in Charles Lamb's poem "The Young Catechist."
164 Leader, *Reading*, 32. For the children's book as an "ambivalent" text, addressing two implied readers (child and adult), see Knoepflmacher, "The Balancing of Child and Adult," and Shavit, *Poetics*, 63–71.
165 Ann and Jane Taylor, *Original Poems for Infant Minds and Rhymes for the Nursery*, ed. Christina Duff Stewart (New York; Garland, 1976), 72–73.
166 Smith, *Politics of Language*, 35.

4. WOMEN, EDUCATION, AND THE NOVEL

1 Beth Kowaleski-Wallace defines "domestic ideology" in terms of a larger shift from "old style patriarchy," with an emphasis on "paternal prerogative, hierarchy and the exercise of force" to "new-style patriarchy with its appeal to reason, co-operation between the sexes and the non-coercive exercise of authority," operating no longer according to fear but to the "more psychologically compelling themes of guilt and obligation" in "Home Economics: Domestic Ideology in Maria Edgeworth's *Belinda*," *The Eighteenth-Century* 29 (1988): 242–62. For parallel developments in educational theory, see chapter 2, above. For domestic ideology, see also Mary Poovey, *The Proper Lady and the Woman Writer: Ideology and Style in the Works of Mary Wollstonecraft, Mary Shelley, and Jane Austen* (University of Chicago Press, 1984), esp. 3–47.
2 Mitzi Myers, "Impeccable Governesses, Rational Dames," 33–34. See also Myers, "Hannah More's Tracts for the Times: Social Fiction and Female Ideology," *Fetter'd or Free: British Women Novelists, 1670–1815*, ed. Mary Anne Scholfield and Cecelia Macheski (Athens: Ohio University Press, 1986), 264–84.
3 Myers, "Hannah More's Tracts," 265; for the "monstrous regiment," see Muir, *English Children's Books*, 82.
4 Kramnick, "Children's Literature," 30; Myers, "Impeccable Governesses," 34, 48.
5 Myers, "Hannah More's Tracts," 264, 269.
6 Myers, "Impeccable Governesses," 36; letters from Edgeworth to Barbauld (30 August 1804) and Barbauld to Edgeworth (4 September 1804) in Anna Letitia Le Breton, *Memoir of Mrs. Barbauld, Including Letters and Notices of Her Family and Friends* (London: George Bell, 1874), 84, 86–87.
7 Cf. Donna Landry's critique of Myers's position in *The Muses of Resistance: Laboring-class Women's Poetry in Britain, 1739–1796* (Cambridge University Press, 1990), 259–60.

8 Maria Edgeworth, *Belinda*, ed. Eva Figes (London: Pandora, 1986), 204–13. Wollstonecraft had approvingly cited Barbauld's "Song V" in support of her argument on the transiency of "beauty's empire" in the *Rights of Woman* (56), and Barbauld's "Rights of Woman" may be seen as a distancing manoeuvre in response.

9 Noelle Bisseret, *Education, Class, Language and Ideology* (London: Routledge and Kegan Paul, 1979), 47. See also Catherine Hall, "Private persons versus public someones: class, gender and politics in England, 1780–1850," in Steedman et al, *Language, Gender and Childhood*, 10–33; Nancy Armstrong, *Desire and Domestic Fiction: A Political History of the Novel* (New York: Oxford University Press, 1987), 59–95; and Davidoff and Hall, *Family Fortunes*. As Davidoff and Hall argue, the private/public split within middle-class discourse is artificial or "ideological" because it occludes the economic contribution and value of women's (unpaid) domestic labor, the economic role of women as consumers, and the dependence of the "apparently autonomous individual man" on the women who serviced and supported him: "Public was not really public and private not really private despite the potent imagery of 'separate spheres'" (33).

10 Terry Eagleton, *The Rape of Clarissa: Writing, Sexuality and Class Struggle in Samuel Richardson* (Minneapolis: University of Minnesota Press, 1982), 13, 15; see also Alan Richardson, "Romanticism and the Colonization of the Feminine," in *Romanticism and Feminism*, ed. Anne K. Mellor (Indianapolis: University of Indiana Press, 1988), 13–25.

11 Poovey, *Proper Lady*, 18.

12 Walkerdine, "On the regulation of speaking," 205–9.

13 Kowaleski-Wallace, "Home Economics": 244; Myers, "Servants": 52, "Sensibility," 121.

14 Marilyn Butler, *Jane Austen and the War of Ideas*, rev. edn. (Oxford: Clarendon Press, 1987), 54–55; Gary Kelly, "Jane Austen and the English Novel of the 1790s," in Schofield and Macheski, *Fetter'd or Free*, 298; Claudia Johnson, *Jane Austen: Women, Politics, and the Novel* (University of Chicago Press, 1988), 19.

15 Kowaleski-Wallace, "Home Economics": 293; Jane Austen, *Sense and Sensibility*, ed. Tony Tanner (Harmondsworth: Penguin, 1969), 192.

16 For the continuities, see Butler, *Jane Austen*, xxxiv and Myers, "Reform or Ruin: 'A Revolution in Female Manners'," *Studies in Eighteenth-Century Culture* 11 (1982): 199–216; see also Dorothy Gardiner, *English Girlhood at School: A Study of Women's Education Through Twelve Centuries* (London: Oxford University Press, 1929), 440.

17 The best account of women's education during this period is still Gardiner, *English Girlhood*, 300–485; see also Mary Cathcart Borer, *Willingly to School: A History of Women's Education* (Guildford and London: Lutterworth Press, 1975), 124–246, and Barry Turner, *Equality for Some: The Story of Girls' Education* (London: Ward Lock Educational, 1974), 28–53. As Turner points out, even the more rudimentary forms of

education aimed at lower class children, such as the charity schools, had a "distinctly feminine" girls' curriculum, with less arithmetic and more sewing (29–30); cf. Gardiner (300–32).

18 R. M. James, "On the Reception of Mary Wollstonecraft's *A Vindication of the Rights of Woman*," *Journal of the History of Ideas* 39 (1978): 293–302.

19 James Fordyce, *Sermons for Young Women* (Boston: Thomas Hall, 1796), 15, 19, 23. Hereafter cited in the text.

20 John Gregory, *A Father's Legacy to His Daughters*, ed. Gina Luria (New York: Garland, 1974), 6–7, 26.

21 Hester Chapone, *Letters on the Improvement of the Mind. Addressed to a Lady* (London: John Sharpe, 1822), 55, 66–67, 89, 104.

22 Thomas Gisborne, *An Enquiry into the Duties of the Female Sex*, ed. Gina Luria (New York: Garland, 1974), 12–13 (hereafter cited in the text); William Wilberforce, *A Practical View of the Prevailing Religious System of Professed Christians*, quoted in Beth Kowaleski-Wallace, "Hannah and Her Sister: Women and Evangelicalism in Early Nineteenth-Century England," *Nineteenth-Century Contexts* 12 (1988): 48.

23 Kowaleski-Wallace, "Hannah and Her Sister": 45, 33.

24 James Fordyce, *The Character and Conduct of the Female Sex, And the Advantages to Be Derived by Young Men from the Society of Virtuous Women* (London: Cadell, 1776), 8, 86.

25 On the infantilization of women in this period compare Davidoff and Hall: "Women, like children, represented the innocence of the natural world which active masculinity must support, protect – and oversee." *Family Fortunes*, 28.

26 Catherine Macaulay, *Observations on the Reflections of the Right Hon. Edmund Burke, on the Revolution in France, in a Letter to the Right Hon. the Earl of Stanhope* (London: C. Dilly, 1790), 78.

27 This is not to say, however, that the *Rights of Woman* is without ambivalence on the subject of female desire: see Poovey's discussion of Wollstonecraft's "defensive denial of female sexuality" in *The Proper Lady*, 74–81.

28 Elissa S. Guralnick, "Radical Politics in Mary Wollstonecraft's *A Vindication of the Rights of Woman*," *Studies in Burke and His Time* 18 (1977): 155–66.

29 For discussions of the limitations of Wollstonecraft's social critique see Landry, *Muses of Resistance*, 254–80, and Timothy J. Reiss, "Revolution in Bounds: Wollstonecraft, Women, and Reason," in *Gender and Theory: Dialogues in Feminist Criticism* (London: Basil Blackwell, 1989), 11–50.

30 Jane West, *Letters to a Young Lady, In Which the Duties and Characters of Women Are Considered, Chiefly with a Reference to Prevailing Opinions* (Troy: O. Penniman and New York: I. Riley, 1806), 10–11.

31 In a letter to Horace Walpole in 1793, More had registered her refusal, though "much pestered," to read Wollstonecraft's *Rights of Woman*, noting that "there is something fantastic and absurd in the very title." "To be unstable and capricious, I really think, is but too characteristic

of our sex; and there is perhaps no animal so much indebted to subordination for its good behaviour as woman" (*MLC* 1:427).

32 Poovey, *Proper Lady*, 9.

33 Armstrong, *Desire*, 81.

34 More's phrasing here recalls a passage from Burke's *Reflections* (appropriately) dismissing "natural rights" arguments. "Government is a contrivance of human wisdom to provide for human *wants* ... Among these wants is to be reckoned the want, out of civil society, of a sufficient restraint upon their passions. Society requires not only that the passions of individuals should be subjected, but that even in the mass and body as well as in the individuals, the inclinations of men should be frequently thwarted, their will controlled, and their passions brought into subjection." Edmund Burke, *Reflections on the Revolution in France* (Garden City: New York, 1973), 72–73. More's revision, however, makes a political necessity into a pedagogical program, and inflicts upon women the burden which for Burke is to be endured by the "mass and body" of society.

35 Myers, "Reform or Ruin," 204.

36 Barbauld, *Works* 1: xviii; Gardiner, *English Girlhood*, 336.

37 Erasmus Darwin, *A Plan for the Conduct of Female Education in Boarding Schools* (New York: Johnson Reprint Corporation, 1968), 11–12, 40–42. (Hereafter cited in the text.)

38 Butler, *Jane Austen*, 127.

39 Similarly in the first volume of *Early Lessons* ("Harry and Lucy," Part One), Lucy receives "useful lessons" through visiting her mother's dairy, while Harry is taken by his father to a blacksmith's and a brickyard.

40 See Butler, *Maria Edgeworth*, 149 and Maria Edgeworth, *Letters for Literary Ladies*, ed. Gina Luria (New York: Garland, 1974), 5–9 (hereafter cited in the text).

41 Sydney Smith, "Female Education," *Works*, 197–98; cf. Wollstonecraft: "Rousseau exerts himself to prove that all *was* right originally: a crowd of authors that all *is* now right: and I, that all will *be* right" (*VRW*, 15).

42 Armstrong, *Desire*, 93.

43 See ibid., 96–160.

44 Anna Laetitia Barbauld, "On the Origin and Progress of Novel-Writing," *The British Novelists; With an Essay, and Prefaces, Biographical and Critical*, 2nd edn., 50 vols. (London: Rivington, 1820) 1: 45–46, 56.

45 Maria Edgeworth, "Mademoiselle Panache," Part Two, in *Tales and Novels*, 10 vols. (London: Routledge and Sons, 1893) 1: 396–97.

46 Elizabeth Inchbald, *A Simple Story*, ed. Jeanette Winterson (London: Pandora, 1987), 294. For Inchbald's treatment of education in this work and its importance for Maria Edgeworth, see Gary Kelly, *The English Jacobin Novel 1780–1805* (Oxford: Clarendon Press, 1976), 64–93.

47 Cf. Patricia Meyer Spacks, "Sisters," in Schofield and Macheski, *Fetter'd or Free?*, 136–51.

48 Elizabeth Inchbald, *A Simple Story and Nature and Art*, 3 vols. (London: De la Rue, 1880), 3: 398, 428.

49 Johnson, *Jane Austen*, 19–20.

50 [Jane West], *A Gossip's Story, And a Legendary Tale*, 2 vols. (London: Longman, 1798), 1: 18; More, *Coelebs*, 110; Maria Edgeworth, *Patronage*, ed. Eva Figes (London: Pandora, 1986), 348; Susan Ferrier, *Marriage*, ed. Rosemary Ashton (Harmondsworth: Penguin, 1986), 299, 418 (hereafter cited in the text).

51 *The Journal of Sir Walter Scott*, ed. W. E. K. Anderson (Oxford: Clarendon Press, 1972), 121 (28 March 1826).

52 J. M. S. Tompkins, *The Popular Novel in England 1770–1800* (1932; rpt. Lincoln: University of Nebraska Press, 1961), 180.

53 Kowaleski-Wallace, "Home Economics": 250–51.

54 See, for example, Butler, *Maria Edgeworth*, 311; Kowaleski-Wallace, 242–43; Gary Kelly, *English Fiction of the Romantic Period 1789–1830* (London: Longman, 1989), 79.

55 See Fordyce, *Sermons*, 48; Gregory, *A Father's Legacy*, 26 ("When a girl ceases to blush, she has lost the most powerful charm of beauty"). Isabella, the young heroine of Edgeworth's "The Good French Governess" in *Moral Tales*, cites this passage in defense of her own habit of blushing (1: 339). Fordyce's *Sermons*, incidentally, may have helped inspire *Belinda* with its contrasting portraits of a domestic mother, "surrounded by a circle of youth innocently gay," and a "decayed beauty," an opposition that anticipates in many of its details that of Lady Anne and Lady Delacour (154–55).

56 Quoted in Kowaleski-Wallace, "Home Economics": 242.

57 Ibid.: 260.

58 Letter to Elizabeth Inchbald, 14 January 1820, quoted in Kelly, *Jacobin Novel*, 78.

59 Edgeworth, *Memoirs* 1: 94–95.

60 *Mansfield Park* and *Belinda* have been compared on these grounds by both Butler (*Jane Austen*, 219–22) and Kelly (*English Fiction*, 80); see also D. D. Devlin, *Jane Austen and Education* (London: MacMillan, 1975), esp. 76–126.

61 Butler, *Jane Austen*, 248; Johnson, *Jane Austen*, 103, 109.

62 Jane Austen, *Mansfield Park*, ed. Tony Tanner (Harmondsworth: Penguin, 1966), 273, 276. Hereafter cited in the text.

63 Tompkins, *Popular Novel*, 34.

64 George Moore, *Literature at Nurse or Circulating Morals* (1885), quoted in Felicity A. Hughes, "Children's Literature: Theory and Practice," *ELH* 45 (1978): 547.

65 The Lockean aspects of Austen's fictional treatment of education are brought out well by Devlin throughout *Jane Austen and Education*, although he ignores the disciplinary aspect of Locke's educational thought.

66 Poovey, *Proper Lady*, 217.
67 Butler, *Jane Austen*, 230, 221–22.
68 Johnson, *Jane Austen*, 19.
69 Kelly, *English Fiction*, 129; cf. Poovey, *Proper Lady*, 223.
70 Butler, *Jane Austen*, 219; Johnson, *Jane Austen*, 96.
71 Butler, *Jane Austen*, 246–48.
72 For the incestuous nature of Fanny's love for Edmund, see Johnson, *Jane Austen*, 117; for the sibling relation as represented in Romantic poetry, see Alan Richardson, "The Dangers of Sympathy: Sibling Incest in English Romantic Poetry," *SEL* 25 (1985): 737–54.
73 Armstrong, *Desire and Domestic Fiction*, 76. Cf. Jonathan Arac on Wordsworth's construction in *The Prelude* of a psychologized "deep, inward self" in *Critical Genealogies: Historical Situations for Postmodern Literary Studies* (New York: Columbia University Press, 1987), 55. Clifford Siskin argues for an "intergeneric" reading of Austen's novels and Wordsworth's poetry on the grounds of their common construction of a "psychologized subject" or "self made continuously deeper by interpretive revision," what he also terms a "self-disciplinary" subject (*Historicity* 126, 153). Both Armstrong and Siskin are principally interested in the politics of the "deep" self, the implication of new disciplinary technologies in structures of social domination; Arac also stresses that the disciplines emerging in the Romantic era, including new forms of self-discipline, can also be seen as "productive" or "empowering" (126).
74 Barbauld, *Works* 2: 307. For Barbauld and Wordsworth, see Pall M. Zall, "Wordsworth's 'Ode' and Mrs. Barbauld's *Hymns*," *The Wordsworth Circle* 1 (1970): 177–79.
75 "Mysterious" is the quality Tompkins finds missing in Edgeworth's excessively schematic portrayals of psychological development in her novels and "nursery stories" alike, which neglect the "operations of nature and solitude" depicted by Wollstonecraft in *Mary, A Fiction* (*Popular Novel*, 180).
76 Mary Poovey, "Ideology and *The Mysteries of Udolpho*," *Criticism* 21 (1979): 321.
77 See More's animadversions against the Gothic novel in *Strictures* 1: 39–40.
78 Ann Radcliffe, *The Romance of the Forest*, ed. Chloe Chard (Oxford University Press, 1986), 245–53.
79 Ann Radcliffe, *The Mysteries of Udolpho: A Romance* (London: Oxford, 1970), 5–6, 24.
80 Judith Wilt, *Ghosts of the Gothic: Austen, Eliot, and Lawrence* (Princeton University Press, 1980), 138–39.
81 Mary Shelley, *Frankenstein, Or The Modern Prometheus*, ed. M. K. Joseph (Oxford University Press, 1969), 16, 19. Hereafter cited in the text.
82 Austen, *Emma*, ed. Ronald Blythe (Harmondsworth: Penguin, 1966),

52; Jonathan Swift, "A Letter to a Young Lady, On Her Marriage," *Irish Tracts 1720–1723 and Sermons*, ed. Louis Landa (Oxford: Basil Blackwell, 1948), 92; cf. More, *Strictures* 1: 188.

83 Anne K. Mellor, *Mary Shelley: Her Life Her Fiction Her Monsters* (New York: Methuen, 1988), 184, 212.

84 Ellen Moers, "Female Gothic," in *The Endurance of Frankenstein: Essays on Mary Shelley's Novel*, ed. George Levine and U. C. Knoepflmacher (Berkeley: University of California Press, 1979), 72.

85 For the creature as Rousseau's "natural man," see Paul Cantor, *Creature and Creator: Myth-making and English Romanticism* (Cambridge University Press, 1984), 120–22; Mellor, *Mary Shelley*, 47; David Marshall, *The Surprising Effects of Sympathy: Marivaux, Diderot, Rousseau, and Mary Shelley* (University of Chicago Press, 1988), 183; James O'Rourke, "'Nothing More Unnatural': Mary Shelley's Revision of Rousseau," *ELH* 56 (1989): 549. Rousseau, however, explicitly rejects an "instinct of sociability" in the preface to the *Second Discourse*, and emphasizes the solitary character of human beings in the state of nature (who do not even form couples, let alone families) throughout: Jean-Jacques Rousseau, *The First and Second Discourses*, ed. Roger D. Masters, trans. Masters and Judith R. Masters (New York: St. Martin's Press, 1964), 95, 137.

86 Marshall, *Sympathy*, 178–227 (esp. 187–93); O'Rourke, "'Nothing More Unnatural'": 543–69 (esp. 545–46, 559).

87 There are also some important differences between Rousseau's sketch and the creature's narrative: Rousseau imagines the man/child as an "imbecile, an automaton, an immobile and almost insensible statue" who would learn to stand, if he attempted it at all, with the greatest difficulty and would not connect hunger with food (61–2), while Shelley's monster gains motor control almost at once and instinctively slakes his hunger with berries.

88 Cf. the Edgeworths on a woman's "disgusting" passion in *Practical Education*, 1: 212.

89 Poovey, *Proper Lady*, 128.

90 U. C. Knoepflmacher, "Thoughts on the Aggression of Daughters," in Levine and Knoepflmacher, *Endurance*, 106; Margaret Homans, *Bearing the Word: Language and Female Experience in Nineteenth-Century Women's Writing* (University of Chicago Press, 1986), 106; Sandra M. Gilbert and Susan Gubar, *The Madwoman in the Attic: The Woman Writer and the Nineteenth-Century Literary Imagination* (New Haven: Yale University Press, 1979), 240.

91 Gilbert and Gubar, *Madwoman*, 235.

92 For the parallel between Safie and Sophie see Peter Dale Scott, "Vital Artifice: Mary, Percy, and the Psychological Integrity of *Frankenstein*," in Levine and Knoepflmacher, *Endurance*, 174.

93 See Mellor, *Mary Shelley*, 118, 209.

94 See Macaulay, *Letters*, 213 and Wollstonecraft, *Rights of Woman*, 86.

Mary Hays cites the same passage in a letter to the *Monthly Magazine* dated 2 March 1797, rpt. in Moira Ferguson, *First Feminists: British Women Writers 1578–1799* (Bloomington: Indiana University Press, 1985), 417. As Landry points out, the "Oriental" topos in British feminist writing (which also comes up in the work of conservative reformers like More) must be read in terms of its implication in colonialist discourse as well (*Muses of Resistance*, 267–68).

95 See Mellor, *Mary Shelley*, 128; cf. Cantor, *Creature*, 125, O'Rourke, "'Nothing More Unnatural'": 552.

96 Marshall, *Surprising Effects*, 140.

97 Homans, *Bearing*, 106.

98 See Karen Horney, "The Dread of Woman," in *Feminine Psychology*, ed. Harold Kelman (New York: Norton, 1967), 133–46; equally relevant to a reading of *Frankenstein* is Horney's essay in the same collection on "The Flight from Womanhood," which links both men's "depreciation" of femininity and their greater "impulse to creative work" to an intense "envy of pregnancy, childbirth, and motherhood" (60–61).

99 Knoepflmacher, "Thoughts," 95; Mellor, *Mary Shelley*, 119.

100 See Poovey, *Proper Lady*, 123.

101 See Gayatri Chakravorty Spivak, "Three Women's Texts and a Critique of Imperialism," in *"Race," Writing and Difference*, ed. Henry Louis Gates, Jr. (University of Chicago Press, 1986), 273–78; Franco Moretti, *Signs Taken for Wonders: Essays in the Sociology of Literary Forms*, tr. Susan Fischer, David Forgacs, and David Miller (London: Verso, 1983), 85–90.

102 Peter Brooks, "'Godlike Science/Unhallowed Arts': Language, Nature, and Monstrosity," in Levine and Knoepflmacher, *Endurance*, 213.

103 For the colonial subject as infantilized in British educational discourse see, for example, Gauri Viswanathan, *Masks of Conquest: Literary Study and British Rule in India* (New York: Columbia University Press, 1989), 79, 84; Viswanathan notes as well the "comparability of the English working classes to the Indian colonial subject" within this discourse (71). See also Mellor, who cites an intriguing allusion to *Frankenstein* made by George Canning in the course of an 1824 speech on the dangers of freeing the African slaves in the West Indies (*Mary Shelley*, 113).

5. THE PURSUIT OF KNOWLEDGE UNDER DIFFICULTIES

1 See Neuburg, *Popular Literature*, 259; and R. K. Webb, *The British Working Class Reader 1790–1848: Literacy and Social Tension* (London, 1955; rpt. New York: Augustus M. Kelley, 1971), 27–28.

2 For a helpful overview of More's tract fiction, discussing her "providential plots" and the central role of "submission" in her tales, see

Catherine Gallagher, *The Industrial Reformation of English Fiction; Social Discourse and Narrative Form 1832–1867* (University of Chicago Press, 1985), 37–40. For an influential argument that by the 1790s "paternalist" social relations had been greatly eroded and were becoming replaced by a free labor economy, see E. P. Thompson, "Patrician Society, Plebeian Culture," *Journal of Social History* 7 (1974): 382–405.

3 Webb, *Working Class Reader*, 56–58.

4 See Laqueur, *Religion and Respectability*.

5 This alliance is discussed in Harold Silver, *The Concept of Popular Education: A Study of Ideas and Social Movements in the Early Nineteenth Century* (London: MacGibbon and Kee, 1965), 217.

6 Robert Owen, *A New View of Society and Other Writings*, ed. John Butt (London: Dent 1972), 81. Hereafter cited in the text.

7 E. P. Thompson, *Making*, 734.

8 See Neuburg, *Popular Literature* and Altick, *English Common Reader*.

9 The creation of various reading "publics" during this period is discussed by E. P. Thompson in *Making* (719) and, at much greater length, by Jon Klancher in *The Making of English Reading Audiences, 1790–1832* (Madison: University of Wisconsin Press, 1987). Neither mentions the large religious audience which accounted for the unprecedented circulation figures of *The Methodist Magazine* and *The Evangelical Magazine* in the early part of the century and the popularity of works like Sherwood's *Susan Grey* and Legh Richmond's *Dairyman's Daughter*: see Altick, *English Common Reader*, 392, and Laqueur, *Religion and Respectability*, 15.

10 See P. J. Corfield, "Class by Name and Number in Eighteenth-Century Britain," *History* 72 (1987): 38–61.

11 Raymond Williams, *Keywords: A Vocabulary of Culture and Society* (New York: Oxford University Press, 1976), 52. See also Asa Briggs, "The Language of 'Class' in Early Nineteenth-Century England," *Essays in Labour History*, ed. Briggs and John Saville (London: MacMillan, 1960), 43–73.

12 In his article on "Education" for the *Encyclopaedia Britannica* (1818), Mill states that "all the difference which exists, or can ever be made to exist, between one *class* of men, and another, is wholly owing to education" (*James Mill on Education*, 52).

13 Gareth Stedman Jones, *Languages of Class: Studies in English Working Class History 1832–1982* (Cambridge University Press, 1983), 101–2; see also 21–22.

14 Jones, *Languages of Class*, 96. Cf. Pierre Bourdieu, who argues that "because the relation of experience to expression, that is, to consciousness, is relatively undetermined, the same experiences may recognize their images in very different discourses," and yet that this "flexibility is not unlimited, and it would be wrong to credit political language with the power of arbitrarily bringing into being what it designates" (*Distinction*, 461).

15 Silver, *Concept of Popular Education*, 97–98.
16 These differences are discussed by Owen in *The Life of Robert Owen. Written By Himself*, 2 vols. (London, 1857; rpt. New York: Augustus M. Kelley, 1967) 1: 103, 127–29. Hereafter cited in the text.
17 Simon, *Studies*, 193; see also Owen, *Life* 1: 89.
18 The methods and curriculum of the New Lanark school are detailed by Owen's son, Robert Dale Owen, in *An Outline of the System of Education at New Lanark* (Glasgow: Wardlaw and Cunninghame, 1824); for the suspicion toward "artificial signs" see 34–35 (where "Miss Edgeworth's little works" are recommended). Hereafter cited in the text.
19 "An Address to the Working Classes," *New View*, 149, 152.
20 William Lovett, *The Life and Struggles of William Lovett, in His Pursuit of Bread, Knowledge, and Freedom* (1876; rpt. New York: Garland, 1984), 48.
21 For a compelling analysis of the Infant Schools movement, see Clarke, "Public and Private Children."
22 Silver, *Concept*, 147; for characteristic statements by Owen on the desirability of separating working-class children from their families, see *New View*, 41, 99 and *Life*, 1: 83–84.
23 For a contemporary account of the Adult Schools, see Thomas Pole, *A History of the Origin and Progress of Adult Schools* (1816; rpt. New York: Augustus M. Kelley, 1969).
24 J. F. C. Harrison, *Living and Learning 1790–1960: A Study in the History of the English Adult Education Movement* (London: Routledge and Kegan Paul, 1961), 57–89.
25 Robert Stewart, *Henry Brougham 1778–1868: His Public Career* (London: Bodley Head, 1986). The 1820 education bill failed in part because of opposition from Dissenters, who felt Brougham had conceded too much to Establishment interests, and in part because the latter considered the proposal too secular; but the most pressing reason, as Simon argues, was that no compulsory system of popular education could be established "when the new factory system was insistently demanding child labour" (*Studies*, 152).
26 Henry Brougham, *Practical Observations Upon the Education of the People, Addressed to the Working Classes and Their Employers*, 15th edn. (1825; rpt. Didsbury: E. J. Morton, 1971) 1, 4. Hereafter cited in the text.
27 Henry Brougham, "Discourse of the Objects, Pleasures, and Advantages of Political Science," *Works of Henry Lord Brougham*, 11 vols. (Edinburgh: Adam and Charles Black, 1872–73) 7: 397–98.
28 Thompson describes how control of the London Institute passed from its working class members to its middle-class sponsors within a few years of its founding, and notes a similar pattern in the provincial Mechanics' Institutes (*Making*, 744–45).
29 See Thompson, *Making*, 746–78; Klancher, *Making*, 98–134; Webb, *British Working Class Reader*, 45–59.
30 Brougham, *Works* 7: 407–8.

31 Review of Henry Brougham, *The Objects, Advantages, and Pleasures of Science, Westminster Review* 7 (1827): 274.

32 "Reasons for Establishing a Public System of Elementary Instruction in England," *Quarterly Review of Education* 1 (1831): 214. Cf. (as typical) "The New Plan of Education for England," *Edinburgh Review* 34 (1820): 214–54. By the mid 1820s even the Tory journals, the *Quarterly Review* and *Blackwood's*, had taken a similar stance, supporting the extension of popular education (if only because of its inevitability), but insisting it not be controlled by Brougham and his allies. See "Brougham on the Education of the People," *Blackwood's Edinburgh Magazine* 17 (1825): 534–51, and "Mechanics' Institutes and Infant Schools," *Quarterly Review* 32 (1825): 410–28.

33 Charles Knight, *Passages of a Working Life During Half a Century: With a Prelude of Early Reminiscences*, 3 vols. (1864–65; rpt. Shannon: Irish University Press, 1971) 1: 227. Hereafter cited parenthetically within the text.

34 For Knight's high valuation of Wordsworth's poetry, see *Passages* 1: 206.

35 One character, Dr. Folliot, nearly has his house burned down when his cook falls asleep over a sixpenny tract on hydrostatics "published by the Steam Intellect Society, and written by a learned friend" [Brougham]. Fortunately the footman is nearby to put out the flame; when asked to account for the latter's presence in the cook's room, Folliot supposes "he was going to study hydrostatics, and he found himself under the necessity of practicing hydraulics." Thomas Love Peacock, *Nightmare Abbey, Crotchet Castle*, ed. Raymond Wright (Harmondsworth: Penguin, 1969), 133–36.

36 Review of the SDUK, "Reports and Prospectus [1830]," *Westminster Review* 14 (1831): 376.

37 See Knight's (unpaginated) preface to *The Penny Magazine* 1 (1832).

38 Both Brougham and James Mill, for their part, publicly endorsed Edgeworth's fiction for children, Brougham in his *Discourse on the Objects, Advantages, and Pleasures of Science (Works* 7: 363), Mill in his 1818 article on "Education" for the *Encyclopaedia Britannica* (Burston, *James Mill on Education*, 98).

39 R. L. Edgeworth, preface to Maria Edgeworth, *Popular Tales* (Boston: Samuel H. Parker, 1823), iv. Hereafter cited in the text.

40 Francis Jeffrey, rev. of Maria Edgeworth, *Popular Tales, Edinburgh Review* 4 (1804): 330.

41 See, e.g., the series on "Emigration" in the first volume of *Chamber's Edinburgh Journal* (1832).

42 Edmund Burke, *Reflections on the Revolution in France* (Garden City: Doubleday, 1961), 48. For the discursive links between West Indian slaves and British laborers, see Gallagher, *Industrial Reformation*, 3–35 and Peter Hulme, *Colonial Encounters: Europe and the Native Caribbean, 1492–1797* (London: Methuen, 1986), 265.

43 For the contemporary significance of obeah (with reference to "The Grateful Negro"), see Alan Richardson, "Romantic Voodoo: Obeah and British Culture, 1797–1807," *Studies in Romanticism* 32 (1993): 3–28.

44 Bryan Edwards, *An Historical Survey of the French Colony in the Island of St. Domingo* (London: John Stockdale, 1797), xix, 193–94.

45 Martineau's dim view of collective working-class action is particularly evident in vol. 5 of the series, *A Manchester Strike* (1833).

46 Jeffrey, rev. of *Popular Tales*: 330. Martineau went on to produce ten tales in four volumes on *Poor Laws and Paupers Illustrated* (1833–34) for the SDUK and a five-tale *Illustrations of Taxation* (1834) as well.

47 Harriet Martineau, *The Rioters: A Tale*, 2nd edn. (London: Houston and Stoneman, 1842), 17, 30.

48 This structure is replicated in that of the series as a whole, which ends with an expository volume entitled *The Moral of Many Fables*.

49 Harriet Martineau, *Illustrations of Political Economy*, 25 vols. (Boston: L. C. Bowles, 1832–35) 1: xi. Hereafter cited in the text.

50 The rather facile advice, tendered by both Edgeworth and Martineau, that laborers, through industry and economy, become small capitalists in order to protect themselves from the vagaries of a market economy (rather than turning to measures like rioting, strikes, or political action) was a commonplace of the political economists. It was expressed perhaps most famously by Knight in his pamphlet *The Results of Machinery* (published in 1831 by the SDUK): "When there is too much labour in the market, and wages are too low, do not combine to raise the wages … We say to you, get something else; acquire something to fall back upon. When there is a glut of labour go at once out of the market; become yourselves capitalists" (quoted in Webb, *British Working Class Reader*, 119). Not surprisingly, such advice was widely scorned by working-class writers and lecturers: "A greater insult," William Pare remarked, "could not have been offered to the working classes of this great empire" (Silver, *Concept* 224).

51 Webb, *British Working Class Reader*, 146; Altick, *English Common Reader*, 197.

52 Neuburg, *Popular Literature*, 142; cf. Webb, *British Working Class Reader*, 160.

53 Matthew Arnold, *Culture and Anarchy*, ed. J. Dover Wilson (Cambridge University Press, 1935), 69–70.

54 See Chandler, *Wordsworth's Second Nature*, 216; and Klancher, *Making*, 135–70.

55 Knight, *Passages* 1: 236, 241, 243; Jeffrey, rev. of *Popular Tales*: 331. Cf. the hostile review of the SDUK "Reports and Prospectus" in the *Westminster Review* (cited above): "It is a fatal error in a popular teacher to believe ignorant men possessed of the same feeling, and requiring the same inducements, as children" (380).

56 Webb, *British Working Class Reader*, 96. William Chambers, describing

his new weekly to the public, similarly writes that it is aimed particularly at serving the "interests of the Young, and of the Poor; two classes towards whose improvement the greatest men of the present age have been proud to direct their efforts," *Chamber's Edinburgh Journal* 1 (1832): 104.

57 Simon, *Studies*, 126–28.

58 "Autobiography," *Quarterly Review* 35 (1827): 149, 164.

59 On Burke see James Chandler, "Poetical Liberties: Burke's France and the 'Adequate Representation' of the English," *The Transformation of Political Culture 1789–1848*, ed. Francois Furet and Mona Ozouf (Oxford: Pergamon Press, 1989), 45–58; on the relation in the period between popular literacy and suffrage see Smith, *Politics of Language*, and Barrell, *English Literature*, 110–75.

60 See John Burnett, David Vincent, and David Mayall, *The Autobiography of the Working Class*, 3 vols. (New York: New York University Press, 1984–89) 1: xvi.

61 Speaking specifically of Place and Thomas Hardy, E. P. Thompson notes that the "line between the journeymen and the small masters was often crossed," and that the "line between the artisan of independent status … and the small shopkeeper or tradesman was even fainter" (*Making*, 20).

62 On the paucity of autobiographies by nineteenth-century women, see Burnett, et al., *Autobiography*, xviii; their bibliography includes only a handful of autobiographies by working-class women born before 1815, and several of these are in the form of conversion narratives. Donna Landry points out that "labouring-class" women poets of the era are less likely to produce extended autobiographical introductions or supplements to their works than their male counterparts (*Muses of Resistance*, 14).

63 Thomas Hardy, *Memoirs of Thomas Hardy*, in *Testaments of Radicalism: Memoirs of Working Class Politicians 1790–1885*, ed. David Vincent (London: Europa, 1977), 3, 45. Although *The Interesting Narrative of the Life of Olaudah Equiano, or Gustavus Vassa, the African* had been first published in 1789, several "enlarged" editions were issued, including a fifth edition in 1792.

64 See Robert B. Stepto, "Distrust of the Reader in Afro-American Narratives," *Reconstructing American Literary History*, ed. Sacvan Bercovitch (Cambridge: Harvard University Press, 1986), 301.

65 See Henry Louis Gates, Jr., *Figures in Black: Words, Signs, and the "Racial" Self* (New York: Oxford University Press, 1987), 11–14, 27, 104–8.

66 In this section I have drawn principally on the following autobiographical works (hereafter cited in the text) in addition to those by Holcroft, Owen, Knight, Hardy, and Lovett cited above. William Hutton, *The Life of William Hutton, F.A.S.S.*, 2nd edn. (London: Baldwin, Cradock, and Joy, 1817); James Lackington, *Memoirs of the First Forty-*

Five Years of the Life of James Lackington, 7th edn. (London: Lackington, 1810); Francis Place, *The Autobiography of Francis Place*, ed. Mary Thrale (Cambridge University Press, 1972); William Hone, "Memoirs from Childhood," in Frederick William Hackwood, *William Hone: His Life and Times* (London: Unwin, 1912), 22–63; Samuel Bamford, *The Autobiography of Samuel Bamford*, ed. W. H. Chaloner, 2 vols. (New York: Augustus M. Kelley, 1967); Timothy Claxton, *Memoirs of a Mechanic* (Boston: Light, 1839); Thomas Carter, *Memoirs of a Working Man* (London: Knight, 1845); Christopher Thomson, *The Autobiography of an Artisan* (London: Chapman, 1847); Thomas Cooper, *The Life of Thomas Cooper* (London: Houghton and Stoddard, 1875).

67 Reginia Gagnier, *Subjectivities: A History of Self-Representation in Britain, 1832–1920* (New York: Oxford University Press, 1991) 142, 42.

68 William Cobbett, *Life and Adventures of Peter Porcupine*, ed. G. D. H. Cole (1927; rpt. Port Washington: Kennikat Press, 1970), 17–19.

69 William Cobbett, *Advice to Young Men*, ed. George Spater (Oxford University Press, 1980), 42.

70 See, e.g., Place (40), Hutton (79), and Carter (53). Thomson, who attended a somewhat better evening school offering navigation and other "useful" subjects, considers himself among the "few" artisans to have profited from the new "educational institutions for the masses" (61, vi).

71 On the "running critique of all forms of 'provided' education" in the radical press, see Richard Johnson's valuable essay, "'Really Useful Knowledge': Radical Education and Working-Class Culture, 1790–1848," in *Working-Class Culture: Studies in History and Theory*, ed. John Clarke, Chas Critcher, and Richard Johnson (London: Hutchinson, 1979), 76–79.

72 For sales figures, see Olivia Smith, who remarks that Cobbett saw the "act of learning grammar by one of his readers as an act of class warfare" (*Politics*, 1, 231).

73 See Johnson, "Really Useful Knowledge," 80.

74 For a helpful discussion of this aspect of the autobiography of self-improvement see David Vincent, *Bread, Knowledge, and Freedom: A Study of Nineteenth-Century Working Class Autobiography* (London: Europa, 1981), 177–95.

75 Cf. ibid., 37.

76 Gagnier suggests instead that although many working-class autobiographers "self-consciously distinguished themselves from others in order to establish themselves as subjects" they nevertheless persisted in "questioning the rightness of individualism or social distinction generally" (*Subjectivities*, 143–44). I have drawn significantly on Gagnier's work in my thinking on these issues, although I have not always found that the distinctions and categories she constructs adequately reflect the complexities of the works she discusses.

77 Laqueur, *Religion and Respectability*, 241. Of course, one could counter

Laqueur's point by arguing that middle-class values could not become hegemonic *unless* they were perceived as beneficial by sufficient numbers of workers, and that emphasizing their appropriation of these values might screen the extent to which their adoption was compelled by economic forces. The strength of Laqueur's analysis, however, is to leave more space for working-class agency – "small-scale, personal struggles for education, decency, and self-improvement" (iv) – than a rigidly economistic analysis would allow.

78 See Vincent, *Bread, Freedom, and Knowledge*, 195.

79 Thompson, *Making*, 172; elsewhere Thompson rather viciously describes Place as "sitting [in his memoirs] to James Mill for his own portrait, as the White Man's Trusty Nigger" (155).

80 According to Knight, the *Plain Englishman* failed in large part because the "pamphlet-buyers rushed to Hone" (1: 246).

81 See Altick, *English Common Reader*, 242–43.

82 [G. L. Craik], *The Pursuit of Knowledge Under Difficulties*, rev. by Francis Wayland, 2 vols. (Boston: March, Capen, Lyon, and Webb, 1840) 1: 330–32, 2: 159, 1: 57–58.

83 See B. B. Edwards, *Biography of Self-Taught Men* (Boston: Perkins and Marvin, 1832); and the series on "The Efforts of Genius" in the first volume of *Chambers' Journal* (1832).

84 Samuel Smiles, *Self-Help: With Illustrations of Conduct and Perseverance*, ed. Asa Briggs (London: John Murray, 1969), 35–36. Briggs notes in his introduction that Smiles had been inspired as a boy by reading Craik's *Pursuit* (8).

85 See Rayner Unwin, *The Rural Muse: Studies in the Peasant Poetry of England* (London: Allen and Unwin, 1954), 34; Martha Vicinus, *The Industrial Muse: A Study of Nineteenth Century British Working-Class Literature* (London: Croom Helm, 1974), 6, 168; Nigel Cross, *The Common Writer: Life in Nineteenth-Century Grub Street* (Cambridge University Press, 1985), 6.

86 H. Gustav Klaus, *The Literature of Labour: Two Hundred Years of Working-Class Writing* (New York: St. Martin's, 1985), 8–9.

87 John Clare, *John Clare's Autobiographical Writings*, ed. Eric Robinson (Oxford University Press, 1983), 119. Hereafter cited in the text.

88 Dermody's career is summarized in Cross, *Common Writer*, 47–50.

89 Unwin, *Rural Muse*, 105.

90 J. G. Lockhart, "Cockney School of Poetry" no. 3, *Blackwood's* 3 (1818): 520.

91 Henry MacKenzie, "Surprising Effects of Original Genius, exemplified in the Poetical Productions of Robert Burns, an Ayrshire Ploughman," *The Lounger* 97 (9 December 1786), rpt. in *Robert Burns: The Critical Heritage*, ed. Donald A. Low (London: Routledge and Kegan Paul, 1974), 70. The early reception of Burns's poetry is interestingly discussed by Carol McGuirk in *Robert Burns and the Sentimental Era* (Athens: University of Georgia Press, 1985), 59–100.

92 Robert Heron, *A Memoir of the Life of the Late Robert Burns* (1797), rpt. in Hans Hecht, *Robert Burns: The Man and His Work*, 2nd edn. (London: Hodge, 1950), 260–61, 269; Robert Burns, *The Works of Robert Burns, With an Account of His Life, and Criticism of His Writings to which are prefaced Some Observations on the Character and Condition of the Scottish Peasantry*, ed. James Currie, rev. edn., 2 vols. in 1 (Philadelphia: Crissy and Markley, 1851) 2: 1–9, 71, 88.

93 Francis Jeffrey, rev. of *Reliques of Robert Burns*, ed. R. H. Cromek, *Edinburgh Review* 26 (1809): 249, 276. Hereafter cited parenthetically within the text.

94 Robert Southey, *The Lives and Works of the Uneducated Poets*, ed. J. S. Childers (London: Humphrey Milford, 1925), 13. Hereafter cited in the text.

95 John Taylor, "Introduction" to John Clare, *Poems Descriptive of Rural Life and Scenery*, rpt. in *Clare: The Critical Heritage*, ed. Mark Storey (London: Routledge and Kegan Paul, 1973), 48.

96 That Burns and Blake do not figure in studies of "plebeian" or "peasant poets" may also suggest that these remain, at least in part, evaluative categories, as they clearly were when first adumbrated by Southey: Bloomfield is not included with the *Uneducated Poets*, for example, because his verse is "worthy of preservation separately, and in general collections" (163).

97 See Landry, *Muses of Resistance*, 16–22.

98 Ann Yearsley, *Poems, on Several Occasions* (London: Cadell, 1785), xi. Hereafter cited in the text.

99 Blake, speaking on his own account, would more trenchantly oppose the "Stolen and Perverted Writings of Homer & Ovid" to the "Sublime of the Bible" in his preface to *Milton* (95).

100 For More's conflation of lower-class "ignorance" and the mental "darkness" of the colonial subject, see the discussion of Blake's "The Little Black Boy" in chapter 3, above.

101 Quoted in Landry, *Muses of Resistance*, 152. I have found Landry's reading of Yearsley (120–85) immensely helpful; see also Moira Ferguson, "Resistance and Power in the Writings of Ann Yearsley," *The Eighteenth Century* 27 (1986): 247–68.

102 See Landry, *Muses of Resistance*, 155–56.

103 Ann Yearsley, *Poems, On Various Subjects* (London: Robinson, 1787).

104 Storey, *Critical Heritage*, 50, 47, 53.

105 Rev. of *Poems Descriptive* in *The Eclectic Review* (1820), rpt. in Storey, *Critical Heritage*, 91. For useful analyses of the contemporary reception of Clare see Johanna Clare, *John Clare and the Bounds of Circumstance* (Kingston: McGill-Queens University Press, 1987), 70–73 and Juliet Sychrava, *Schiller to Derrida: Idealism in Aesthetics* (Cambridge University Press, 1989), 80–82.

106 Letter to Clare from Eliza Emmerson, 11 May 1820, in Storey, *Critical Heritage*, 61.

107 Quoted in George Deacon, *John Clare and the Folk Tradition* (London: Sinclair Browne, 1983), 33. Johanna Clare provides an informed overview of Clare's political views in *John Clare*, 12–24.

108 My text for *The Village Minstrel* (cited by stanza) is John Clare, *Selected Poems*, ed. J. W. Tibble and Anne Tibble (London: Dent, 1965).

109 In his autobiographical fragments Clare noted: "The reason why I dislike it is that it does not describe the feelings of a rhyming peasant strongly or localy enough" (106).

110 In her reading of *The Village Minstrel* Johanna Clare notes the "Dionysian" character of Clare's depiction of rural sports and his "image of a people who lose themselves in recreation in order to recreate themselves as a community" (*John Clare*, 99).

111 Cf. Johanna Clare, *John Clare*, 104–6 and Deacon, *John Clare*, 10.

112 T. H. Lister, rev. of *Attempts in Verse, by John Jones, an old Servant; with Some Account of the Writer, Written by Himself; and an Introductory Essay on the Lives and Works of the Uneducated Poets*, ed. Robert Southey, *Edinburgh Review* 54 (1831): 74.

113 Lister, rev. of *Attempts*: 79, 81. Writing in the *Edinburgh Review* a year later, Carlyle would develop a quite different position, discounting the fact that the "Corn-Law" poet, Ebenezer Elliott, lacked a formal education, suggesting that schooling, in its contemporary form, could prove more disadvantageous than not, and rejecting the category of "uneducated poets" as misguided. See "Corn-Law Rhymes" in Thomas Carlyle, *Works*, ed. Henry Duff Traill, 30 vols. (1896–1901; rpt. New York: AMS Press, 1969) 28: 136–66.

114 J. G. Lockhart, rev. of Jones, *Attempts*, *Quarterly Review* 44 (1831): 53, 57.

6. EPILOGUE: ROMANTICISM AND THE IDEA OF LITERATURE

1 "Brougham on the Education of the People," *Blackwood's* 17 (1825): 543 (hereafter cited in the text).

2 Williams, *Keywords*, 153. Cf. Terry Eagleton, *Literary Theory: An Introduction* (Minneapolis: University of Minnesota Press, 1983), 17–22; Arac, *Critical Genealogies*, 47–49; Siskin, *Historicity*, 67–93.

3 For two notable recent critical discussions, however, see Klancher, *Making*, 135–71 and Gary Kelly, "The Limits of Genre and the Institution of Literature: Romanticism between Fact and Fiction," in Johnston, *Romantic Revolutions*, 158–75.

4 Brian Doyle, *English and Englishness* (London: Routledge, 1989), 11. See also D. J. Palmer, *The Rise of English Studies: An Account of the Study of English Language and Literature from its Origins to the Making of the Oxford English School* (London: Oxford University Press, 1965), Franklin E. Court, *Institutionalizing English Literature: The Culture and Politics of Literary Study, 1750–1900* (Stanford University Press, 1992), and Hunter, *Culture*

and Government. Chris Baldick, in *The Social Mission of English Criticism 1848–1932* (Oxford: Clarendon Press, 1983), shows an exemplary awareness of the multiple contexts in which English studies developed in remarking how, in the later nineteenth century, the Arnoldian "social project" of literary education was developed primarily in relation to the "teaching of workers, school-children, women, and Indians" (82), but he has little to say of the earlier history which makes these connections seem inevitable.

5 Armstrong, *Desire*, 103; Viswanathan, *Masks of Conquest*, 2–3.

6 See Viswanathan, *Masks of Conquest*, 6–7.

7 The parallel is discussed by Clifford Siskin, "Wordsworth's Prescriptions: Romanticism and Professional Power," in *The Romantics and Us: Essays in Literature and Culture*, ed. Gene W. Ruoff (New Brunswick: Rutgers University Press, 1990), 316–17.

8 See Palmer, *Rise of English*, 41 and Klancher, *Making*, 146.

9 Matthew Arnold, "Wordsworth," *English Literature and Irish Politics*, ed. R. H. Super (Ann Arbor: University of Michigan Press, 1973), 42.

10 Stephen Gill, *William Wordsworth: A Life* (Oxford University Press, 1989), 349; Joseph Hine, ed., *Selections from the Poems of William Wordsworth, Esq. Chiefly for the Use of Schools and Young Persons* (London: Edward Moxon, 1831), vi.

11 Ian Michael, *The Teaching of English: From the Sixteenth Century to 1870* (Cambridge University Press, 1987), 236.

12 Eliza Farrar, *The Young Lady's Friend* (Boston: American Stationer's Company, 1836), 429.

13 Quoted in Gill, *William Wordsworth*, 382.

14 Viswanathan, *Masks of Conquest*, 54.

15 Quoted in Anne Janowitz, *England's Ruins: Poetic Purpose and the National Landscape* (Oxford: Basil Blackwell, 1990), 18; see also Christopher Clausen, *The Place of Poetry: Two Centuries of an Art in Crisis* (Lexington: University Press of Kentucky, 1981), 65–82.

16 Klancher, *Making*, 140; see also Arac, *Critical Genealogies*, 34–49.

17 Arnold, "The Study of Poetry" (originally published as the general introduction to T. H. Ward's *The English Poets* [1880]), *English Literature*, 163, 188.

18 John Stuart Mill, *Autobiography*, ed. Jack Stillinger (Boston: Houghton Mifflin, 1969), 86–87, 38, 89.

19 Doyle writes that although longstanding and widespread attempts to "regulate fiction making and consumption" may "indeed tend towards the achievement of monopoly control," even such wholesale appropriations will "never be total, since even politically-harmonized fictional forms are subject to symbolic fragmentation by virtue of their basis in potentially disordered fantasies" (*English*, 9). In an important response to recent critiques of Romanticism, Don Bialostosky argues that one cannot reliably determine "when poets will be the retailers of common-

places and when they will be the instruments of liberation," nor "when readers will be the standardizers and regularizers of poetic novelties and when they will be the stone-throwing shatterers of old, fixed images," "Wordsworth, New Literary Histories, and the Constitution of Literature," in Johnston, *Romantic Revolutions*, 419. See also David Bromwich, *Politics by Other Means: Higher Education and Group Thinking* (New Haven: Yale University Press, 1992), 225–29.

20 Edmund Gosse, *Father and Son: A Study of Two Temperaments* (New York: Norton, 1963), 189, 58.

21 See Bouthaina Shaaban, "The Romantics in the Chartist Press," *Keats-Shelley Journal* 38 (1989): 26–29.

22 For influential critiques of Romanticism see Christopher Caudwell, *Illusion and Reality: A Study of the Sources of Poetry* (New York: International, 1937), 88–98, Siskin, *Historicity*, and McGann, *Romantic Ideology*. The positive characterizations are found in Bromwich, *Politics*, 219, Bialostosky, "Wordsworth," 415–21, and Terry Eagleton, *The Function of Criticism: From the Spectator to Post-Structuralism* (London: Verso, 1984), 41. For Eagleton, however, the "revolutionary force" of Romantic literature, its "production of a powerful yet decentred human subjectivity which cannot be formalized within the protocols of a rational exchange," is offset by its social alienation and "guilt-stricken self-isolation"; cf. the "ambivalent" views of Romanticism of both Raymond Williams and Frederic Jameson discussed in chapter one, above.

23 For relevant discussions of Coleridge's "clerisy," see Klancher, *Making*, 150–70 and Charles DePaolo, "Coleridge and the Idea of a University," *Romanticism Past and Present* 8 (1984): 17–34.

24 See Klancher, *Making*, 5, 136, 164–70.

25 Edgar Z. Friedenberg, "Romanticism and Alternatives in Schooling," in *The Educational Legacy of Romanticism*, ed. John Willinsky (Waterloo: Wilfrid Laurier University Press, 1990), 176–79.

26 On this last point, see Wordsworth's letter on the Madras school for girls at Ambleside (*WLL* 1: 685–86) and Coleridge's dismissal of Wollstonecraft and his remarks on man's intellectual superiority (*CLL* 1: 594–95). In an earlier letter, however, Wordsworth outlines a (for the time) quite substantial education for the daughter of an unknown but assuredly middle-class seeker of advice which contrasts markedly with his pronouncement on the Ambleside school for lower-class girls (*WLM* 1: 284–88).

27 Willinsky, *Educational Legacy of Romanticism*.

Index

Printed in the United Kingdom
by Lightning Source UK Ltd.
132817UK00001B/307-315/A